MW01012990

From Texas to the East

From Texas to the East

A STRATEGIC HISTORY
OF TEXAS EASTERN CORPORATION

Christopher J. Castaneda and Joseph A. Pratt

Texas A&M University Press
College Station

LIBRARY OF CONGRESS CATALOGING-IN-PUBLICATION DATA

Castaneda, Christopher James, 1959–
    From Texas to the East : a strategic history of Texas Eastern
  Corporation / Christopher J. Castaneda and Joseph A. Pratt. —
  1st ed.
        p.   cm.
    Includes index.
    ISBN 0-89096-551-X
    1. Texas Eastern Corporation — History.   2. Natural gas
  pipelines — United States — History.   3. Gas industry — United
  States — History — 20th century.   I. Pratt, Joseph A.   II. Title.
  HD9581.U53T4935   1993
  388.5′6′0973 — dc20   93-3073
                                                                           CIP

Contents

Illustrations

Maps

Tables and Charts

Preface

As we sought to complete our work on the history of the Texas Eastern Corporation in the spring of 1989, history happened to us. A hostile takeover bid sent shockwaves throughout the company, calling into question the continued existence of Texas Eastern and, of course, the status of all projects underway. Thus, as we continued to research past events, we also became inside observers of history in the making. When the dust from the takeover battle had settled, Texas Eastern had been acquired by a friendly "white knight," Panhandle Eastern Corporation. While breathing a sigh of relief at having escaped the grasp of an unfriendly suitor, Texas Eastern's executives now faced the unpleasant tasks of selling off various subsidiaries and preparing for the absorption of their company into another concern. Although the heart of the company, its gas pipeline system, would remain within the newly merged organization, Texas Eastern as a corporate entity faced a premature death at the tender age of forty-two.[1]

Having lived inside the company for several years, we shared with its employees a sense of disappointment—and even something akin to grief. In the months between the announcement of the intent to merge with Panhandle Eastern and the actual combination of the two companies, long-time employees of Texas Eastern voiced many concerns. All agreed that the world of natural gas had come to a strange turn when a company so large and strong could become vulnerable to a takeover. Some of the old-timers wondered aloud if George Brown and other prominent founders were turning over in their graves. And many focused on the more immediate question raised by a merger: What would happen to their jobs and their pensions?

We shared condolences with our friends from Texas Eastern at the wake, but by the time of the funeral we could not suppress an embarrassed smile. One of the most difficult choices remaining for us in early 1989 had been choosing a cutoff point at which to end our history. Now events had presented an obvious choice. By bringing the history on up to 1989, we could have a luxury seldom available to organizational historians: a logical ending. Texas Eastern's dramatic demise offered a good narrative counterpoint to its equally dramatic birth in 1947, when the company's founders had acquired its original two pipelines in a controversial and much publicized bidding process for war surplus properties built by the U.S. government during World War II.

We entered the project well aware of both the potential pitfalls and opportunities of sponsored corporate history. Both authors previously had worked on a similar project at the Houston-based law firm of Baker & Botts.[2] Pratt had published books or articles based on research projects sponsored by Consolidated Edison of New York and Texas Commerce Banks (of Houston).[3] More than once his fellow academic historians had chided him, not too gently, for selling his soul to the corporate devil. Their concerns reflected the real difficulties of retaining the status of independent scholar while working in organizations accustomed to hiring academics as consultants on directed research and accustomed to placing a high value on good public relations. At its best, sponsored organizational history retains an uneasy balance between the needs of the organization and the duties of the professional scholar.

Yet we also knew from experience the great benefit of sponsored research: access to records and people not readily available to historians. As a major gas transmission company, Texas Eastern had been deeply involved in significant events which shaped the evolution of an important, yet little studied, industry. It was also a significant force in the regional economy of Houston. Its history offered a window through which to view eras of change in the natural gas industry and its "capital," Houston.

Potential misunderstandings between us and Texas Eastern were minimized by the fact that we shared a common goal: the publication of a professionally researched history. A series of discussions with representatives of the company gradually coalesced into a formal contract. Our earlier experience at Baker & Botts gave us an excellent model for an agreement, and we ultimately adopted a modified version of that contract. The Business History Group, a historical consulting firm with Louis Galambos, of Johns Hopkins University, Robert Lewis, of AT & T, and Pratt as principals, took part in these negotiations and became the primary vehicle for managing the project. The process of negotiating a contract proved useful to all parties, since it forced us all to take a hard look at the nature of the project and the relationship of the firm and the historians. The clarity of language required in a contract forced a close consideration of the hard issues raised when outsiders are entrusted with an organization's past. The final moment of decision symbolized by the signing of a contract provided a sense of assurance that everyone knew what we were getting into and that we all felt comfortable enough with each other to make a long-term commitment to work together—while nonetheless retaining the distance required to write a professional history.

The broad outlines of the contract assured our independent status within the company. We asked for and received full access to corporate records and personnel, with the use of this material constrained only by our agreement not to publish proprietary information such as documents relevant to ongoing legal disputes. We asked for and received final editorial control of the manuscript, with a stipulation that Texas Eastern could review all drafts and make recommendations for our consideration. If such recommendations proved unacceptable to us, the company retained the right to insert footnotes explaining their views. We asked for and received "final disposition of the manuscript," that is, the right to publish the resulting book where we thought best. This was important to us, since the contract stipulated that the goal of the project was a "university press–quality book." We felt that the choice of a university press would establish a buffer between us and the company; the knowledge that the final manuscript would face the scrutiny of professional historians in a pre-publication review process would restrain any impulse toward a "public relations" approach. To avoid possible confusion about the focus of the book, we included in the contract a tentative chapter outline.

Acceptance of the provisions of this contract by Texas Eastern was facilitated by the fact that several top executives had read with approval Pratt's earlier history (with Walter Buenger) of Texas Commerce Banks. But the company's agreement to grant outsiders control of a corporate history still required a leap of faith. Our agreement to complete the work reflected a sense that under the terms of the contract we could produce a book worthy of several years of our professional lives.

During those years we were very well treated by the company, which never flinched from fulfilling the terms of the contract. Texas Eastern provided generous financial assistance to allow Castaneda to work full-time on the project for two years and Pratt to buy release time from teaching at the University of Houston for approximately one year. The company also covered research expenses to complete an ambitious oral history project, travel to archives, edit the manuscript, and manage the project. We worked out of an office provided by the company, complete with computers and secretarial assistance. In short, this book resulted from a well-funded and, we believe, well-designed corporate history project. From our perspective, shortcomings of the book perceived by the reader are not the result of problems inherent in an agreement to write a sponsored organizational history; rather, they result from our own limitations in taking advantage of an excellent opportunity to produce a useful history. By the same token, any faults of interpretation or omission are the responsibilities of the authors.

One related opportunity proved fruitful. In our original contract we included a provision that we could use the archives generated by the Texas Eastern history for other academic projects. Castaneda subsequently put these records to good use in writing a dissertation about the cross-country natural gas industry in the years immediately after World War II. Drawing also on a variety of other records, he took a broad, industry-wide view of events in these pivotal years. His book, *Regulated Enterprise: Natural Gas Pipelines and Northeastern Markets, 1938–1954*, was published in the winter of 1993 by Ohio State University Press.[4]

As is often the case in corporate history, the records available to us proved at once limited and overwhelming. Particularly disappointing was the lack of long runs of executive correspondence from the formative years of the company. Yet some fifty thousand boxes of historical materials of assorted quality housed in the company's off-site storage facilities yielded considerable raw material for our work. A well-maintained cataloguing system allowed the authors to ascertain fairly quickly which of those boxes would be useful for the study. In addition, valuable records on particular issues were uncovered by employees during the project. The authors also used the usual assortment of minutes, annual reports, and various company publications as well as secondary sources and articles from newspapers and from technical and trade journals. In addition, the authors interviewed a wide variety of current and former company officials who took the time, often during more than one interview, to share their experiences. Because Texas Eastern required regulatory approval for most major decisions involving its gas pipelines, the records of the Federal Power Commission (FPC) and its successor, the Federal Energy Regulatory Commission (FERC), proved quite useful.

Several Texas Eastern officials were instrumental in making the project possible and allowing it to continue during the uncertain period of the company's acquisition. Chief among these persons was Dennis R. Hendrix, Texas Eastern's chief executive officer. Hendrix joined Texas Eastern in 1985, only a few years before our project began. He previously had been CEO of Texas Gas Transmission Company, where he had also instituted a history project. Hendrix assured the company's cooperation, made himself available for interviews, and commented on several drafts of the manuscript. Two other Texas Eastern officials also played important roles in launching and maintaining the history project. Henry H. King, vice chairman of the company, and Fred Wichlep, vice president for public affairs, both went beyond the call of duty in facilitating our work.

At Panhandle Eastern, James W. Hart, Jr., assured us that Texas Eastern's records would remain open to us after the merger. Jan Huber served as our new contact person. Tom Overton and Tony Turbeville led us to photographs, Shari Stafford helped prepare the tables, and the Panhandle Eastern Design and Graphic Department produced the maps. All the photographs included in the book are courtesy of Panhandle Eastern.

Numerous other individuals assisted the project in a variety of ways. John O. King, professor of history at the University of Houston, conducted extensive research on the early history of the company and on the New England episode in particular. His early assistance helped give the project momentum. Louis Marchiafava, oral historian and director of the Houston Metropolitan Research Center, helped conduct several interviews while training Castaneda in oral history. Louis Galambos, of Johns Hopkins University and the Business History Group, edited several versions of the manuscript. Diane Nesrsta typed and retyped the entire manuscript on numerous occasions, and she also transcribed many of the oral history interviews. Others, including David Munday, of the corporate secretary's office, Bob Kirtner, corporate librarian, and Trey Mecom, of stockholder relations, provided useful insights and directions for research.

While completing this project, we were both affiliated with the University of Houston, Pratt as Cullen Professor of History and Business and Castaneda as a graduate student and then as Director of the Oral History of the Houston Economy. Few universities could provide the sort of freedom, support, and collegiality that we have found at the University of Houston.

Joseph A. Pratt
Christopher J. Castaneda

From Texas to the East

Introduction

A quiet revolution altered the energy mix of the United States after World War II. While international attention remained focused on the issue of oil imports by the industrial nations, natural gas emerged as the fuel of choice for many American consumers. From the late 1940s through the 1960s natural gas was the fastest growing domestic energy source. This relatively inexpensive and clean-burning fuel made steady and at times spectacular inroads into markets previously served by coal and petroleum.[1]

At the center of the dynamic American gas industry were the large transmission companies that built and operated cross-country pipeline systems. The loosening of technological and economic constraints on gas pipeline expansion produced a creative moment in the industry after World War II, when thousands of miles of new gas pipelines crisscrossed the nation.[2] Of special importance in this era were several Houston-based companies that surged forward to connect the large supplies of natural gas readily available in southwestern fields with the vast demand for energy in markets in the Northeast. These companies provided a vital link missing before World War II; their pipeline systems gave gas producers in the Southwest access for the first time to the large utility companies that distributed energy in the urban and industrial centers along the East Coast. Because of the giant investments required to construct long distance pipelines, their owners grew into forces to be reckoned with on the national economic stage. The size of these firms made them particularly significant in the Houston-area economy, where they quickly took a place among the largest companies based in the region.

Texas Eastern Transmission Corporation was one of the first pipeline companies to reach from Texas to the East. From its creation in 1947 until its acquisition by Panhandle Eastern Corporation in 1989, the company remained a major competitor in an industry that helped shape the nation's energy outlook. Texas Eastern's history thus provides a window through which to observe the sharp swings and great uncertainties marking the nation's energy history in the years after World War II. During this time, the company's leaders joined others in the industry in adapting to often sweeping economic and political changes, from the pipeline boom in the 1940s and 1950s, to the widespread diversification of transmission companies in the 1960s, to the gas shortages and energy crises of the 1970s, to the deregulation of gas prices and the tidal wave of mergers and acquisitions of the 1980s. Our history of a single company examines such broad changes as they were perceived and acted upon at the corporate level.

Such a focus offers both advantages and disadvantages to the historian. For issues of aggregate supply and demand, the most obvious analytical focus is at the industry level.[3] Studies of gas transmission companies as a group, of all segments of the gas industry, or even of the energy industries as a whole yield broad generalizations of particular usefulness in understanding long-term trends in energy production and use and in public policies affecting energy.[4] Such studies put to good use the views of industry leaders, prominent regulators, and national political leaders to recreate the broad context of economic and political factors shaping energy issues. Yet they often slight one critical viewpoint, that of the managers responsible for guiding the fortunes of the individual energy companies. This neglect has been especially evident in the historical literature on natural gas, which includes very few studies of specific firms.[5]

At the microeconomic or corporate level, decision-makers must evaluate the imperfect information available and then define a strategy appropriate to the company's strengths and weakenesses. Subsequently, managers must adapt this strategy to changing conditions. The cumulative impact of the choices of individual managers shape the evolution of firms, of industries, and ultimately of the economy as a whole. Our history of Texas Eastern focuses on the strategic choices which shaped the company's evolution. We have attempted to place the company's managers back into the world as they saw it, to reconstruct their options, and to evaluate the choices they made.

This requires the recreation of the competitive and regulatory contexts in which choices were made. In search of such contexts, we have included material on the history of the company's primary competitors and of the evolving regulatory system within which the firm operated. Throughout, we have sought to show the reader how executives organized the company, "read" the various opportunities available to it, and devised and implemented their firm's strategies.

In essence, our book is an extended historical study of strategy in a regulated industry. The central concern of most managers and management professors in studying strategy has been competitive forces: the capacities of rival companies, the ease of entry for new competitors, the bargaining power of suppliers and of buyers of a company's products, and the threat of the development of substitute products by other companies in related industries. One of the leading scholars notes that "the goal of competitive strategy for a business unit in an industry is to find a position in the industry where the company can best defend itself against these competitive forces or can influence them in its favor."[6]

In its gas transmission business Texas Eastern faced a quite limited set of direct competitors, most notably two other Houston-based companies,

Tennessee Gas Transmission Company and Transcontinental Gas Pipe Line Corporation.[7] Entry into major markets was strictly limited by regulation. Suppliers of natural gas had limited bargaining power, because they were subject to price regulation, and they had relatively few options in shipping gas long distances. The primary customers for Texas Eastern's product, the major utility companies, likewise had limited bargaining power, although they did prove effective in aggressively using state utility commissions to pursue lower prices. Competitive pressures from companies with "substitutable products," notably the coal companies and their allies in the railroad industry, presented recurring and at times frustrating political challenges to the growth of natural gas markets. But Texas Eastern and other natural gas companies had the ultimate competitive tool to use in beating back these challenges: They had a cheaper, better product. At least until the deregulation of gas in the 1980s began to open the industry to new competitive pressures, Texas Eastern faced fewer competitive pressures in its core business than did less-regulated firms in other industries.

From its creation through the purchase of war surplus properties from the U.S. government to its more recent efforts to adapt to the phased deregulation of natural gas prices, Texas Eastern's choices were shaped by public policies. Its managers invested much effort in what might best be called "political entrepreneurship," including lobbying for various laws and defending the company's political interests against those of competitors within the natural gas industry and in other competing industries, most notably coal. Of necessity, managers became adept at "regulatory management," including efforts to shape regulatory rules and adapt to the prevailing policies of the Federal Power Commission and of various state utility commissions. Charting strategy in this regulated environment required the company's executives to master the political intricacies of an often confrontational regulatory system.[8]

The key federal agency regulating the natural gas industry has been the Federal Power Commission (FPC) and its successor, the Federal Energy Regulatory Commission (FERC).[9] Created in 1920, the FPC was given powers over the gas industry in 1938. Initially, its primary function was to regulate the entry of gas transmission companies into new markets. After the Supreme Court's decision in the *Phillips* case in 1954, which gave the FPC authority over gas production sold into interstate commerce, the commission spent more and more of its energies on the difficult task of managing an often controversial system of gas price regulation. Then in the 1970s and 1980s the commission's powers were sharply altered by the phased deregulation of newly discovered gas, which unleashed a wave of far-reaching changes in gas regulations. Throughout its history, Texas Eastern had to take account of the demands of regulators, whose decisions defined the rules within which the company formulated strategy for its gas transmission business.

Within its regulatory and competitive contexts, the company learned to recognize and respond to failure as well as to success. No vital business can expect to experience only success. Choice carries risk. The attempt to expand or innovate assures that a business will encounter sobering failures. One good measure of effective management is the extent to which unsuccessful endeavors are identified quickly and their costs contained. From the company's formative years, its management had a strong predisposition to operate on a grand scale, undertaking ambitious projects which often involved great risks. Our account of this firm's strategic history describes and analyzes those episodes when the company's reach exceeded its grasp.

Just beneath the surface of our account are questions about the company's ultimate failure, its inability in the late 1980s to maintain its separate corporate existence. We do not yet have the historical perspective needed to judge whether this ending should be considered a failure or a success. Although Texas Eastern disappeared as an internationally diversified corporate entity, its managers had created an enterprise that was sought after and ultimately puchased for an excellent price. Many of the key programs and employees of Texas Eastern flourished within their new companies. In a capitalist system there is a market for companies as well as for products and services. But whatever the ultimate verdict of history on these recent developments, they provided in this instance a clear-cut, decisive ending for our strategic history. That ending called for analysis. Why did this particular company find itself vulnerable to takeover at this particular time? We think that our historical approach to the strategy of Texas Eastern provides useful insights into the merger process and into the dilemmas confronting this company and many others in the present tumultuous era in our industrial history.[10]

Historical perspective is the primary contribution of our study of the rise of this natural gas transmission company. As historians, we quite naturally favor a long view grounded in archival research; we feel that it provides a useful addition to those management studies which stress short-term performance. The most interesting questions raised by our strategic history are those generated by transition periods, phases of rapid and often bewildering change in either the competitive or regulatory environments, when the company's managers had to recognize and adapt to fundamental changes in markets and technology. To plan effectively, they had to anticipate periods of regulatory discontinuity, when the rules of the game changed and they could no longer simply pursue business as usual. If the full implications of changes in regulation were ignored, the costs could be unacceptably high.

Lurking behind our discussions of these developments is the ultimate historian's question: How much leeway did strategists within an individual company have in understanding and managing the broad forces of change? To what extent did such planners actually control their own destinies in periods of rapid and far-reaching change such as occurred in the energy-related sectors of the economy since the early 1970s? In short, what were the limits of strategy?

6

Answers to such questions cannot be conclusive. Quarterly profitability can be measured and compared with some exactness; adaptation to long-term competitive and regulatory change is more difficult to measure, more open to different interpretations of success and failure. We looked for and found both. Do not expect in this history to find corporate executives bounding from great triumph to great triumph without the hint of a misstep. Nor will you find a muckraking account of evil corporate executives bent on cheating the poor and raping the environment. Rather, we depict executives as people doing their best to juggle a variety of demands, including the desire to make a profit, the need to comply with regulatory rules, and the human desire to do work worthy of one's vital energies.

We have divided our account of Texas Eastern's history into three parts: the entrepreneurial era, from 1941 to 1954; the lure of diversification, 1954 to 1971; and the limits to strategy, 1971 to 1989. A measure of continuity characterized the first two eras, allowing executives to chart strategy within a more or less constant competitive-regulatory framework. During the third era, however, dramatic economic and regulatory changes confronted managers at Texas Eastern, severely limiting their capacity to define and implement a coherent long-term strategy.

During the years from 1941 to 1954, the company's founders mounted determined initiatives that enabled them to overcome difficult challenges. The mobilization for World War II required a sort of "public" entrepreneurship, as business and government cooperated to build the new equipment and infrastructure required by modern warfare. Included was the construction of the Big Inch and the Little Big Inch pipelines which would later become the backbone of Texas Eastern's business (see map I.1)[11] The end of the war set the stage for a different sort of entrepreneurship, as Texas Eastern's founders, led by George Brown, of the Houston-based construction firm Brown & Root, seized the opportunity presented by demobilization to acquire the Inch lines in a highly publicized bidding process. The founders then faced the more traditional entrepreneurial tasks of organizing a new company to convert the Inch Lines to carry natural gas to the vast markets of the northeastern United States.

From a strategic perspective, the overriding priority of this era was easily defined: Get there first. Texas Eastern's basic goal was to become a major supplier of southwestern gas to the Northeast. These were exciting times, with pipelines to be built, gas supplies to be acquired, and new markets to be penetrated. Optimism mixed with aggressive competitiveness to give the company a sense of purpose and enthusiasm. One lasting legacy for Texas Eastern was a certain swagger in its step, a confidence instilled by its founders and heightened by the shared experience of success. The corporate culture long reflected the sense of entrepreneurship and adventure acquired in these formative years. Texas Eastern, the culture proclaimed, was a major league company, capable of doing big things in a big way. This attitude

MAP I.1. War Emergency Pipelines, Inc.

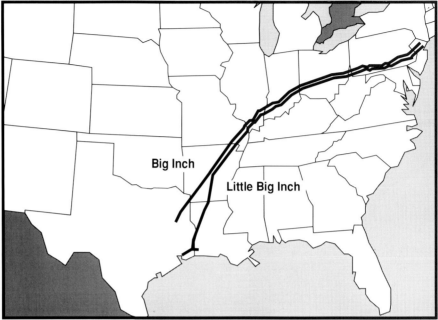

reflected the heady experience of building a new company in a booming industry.

By the early 1950s, however, the need for orderly expansion had begun to replace the race for new markets. Texas Eastern entered a new period in its history, one marked by an intensified search for supplies of natural gas and by diversification into other businesses. Changing regulatory policy shaped both of these choices. Before 1954 the FPC had focused on managing the construction of pipelines into expanding markets, but after the *Phillips* decision of that year the commission became more and more involved in the regulation of gas prices at the wellhead. In the long term, low prices for gas fixed by the FPC initially encouraged the rapid expansion of the natural gas industry, which benefitted Texas Eastern in the short term. But in the long term such policies created disincentives for suppliers to develop new sources of natural gas for sale in interstate markets.[12] This was a major concern for an interstate transmission company such as Texas Eastern, and the company explored several novel legal avenues to augment gas supplies. The firm was successful enough in the 1950s and 1960s to achieve dramatic system growth. The sustained expansion of the transmission business included the purchase in 1967 of Transwestern Pipeline Company, whose pipeline connections to the booming market for natural gas in southern California made Texas Eastern the first gas transmission company serving both coasts.

Texas Eastern's prosperous transmission business gave it the resources with which to diversify; frustrations with regulations gave it a strong incentive to look for opportunities in unregulated industries. After the company first entered oil- and gas-related businesses, its leaders coined the phrase "pipe-liners of energy" to give focus to the company's strategy of diversification. From the early 1950s forward Texas Eastern became in reality at least two different companies: the regulated natural gas transmission company, and the cluster of subsidiaries active in other related pursuits not subject to rate regulation by the FPC. This division shaped a dual strategy: On the one hand, management sought expansion of the rate base in natural gas transmission whenever possible; on the other, it pursued diversification into related activities when promising opportunities presented themselves.

The company's diversification encompassed a variety of ventures in both domestic and foreign markets. Some of these were closely tied to natural gas transmission; others were not. Included were oil and gas exploration, oil refining, the transportation of petroleum products, the sale of liquefied petroleum gas (LPG), and real estate development. Two particularly significant initiatives went forward in the late 1960s, when Texas Eastern became an early entrant into North Sea oil and gas exploration and production while also announcing plans for Houston Center, a massive downtown development.

The benefits of diversification were quite evident in the profits which poured in from oil and gas production in the North Sea. The costs were less obvious. Organizational tensions inevitably arose, as those responsible for the core industry of natural gas transmission felt understandable resentments toward their counterparts in the more glamorous, but generally less profitable, diversified businesses developed by Texas Eastern. The corporate culture came to embody two distinct strains: the attitudes engendered by managing in a strictly regulated industry, and those developed in more competitive industries such as oil exploration and real estate. A final cost of diversification was the time, energy, and resources spent in exploring for new opportunities, many of which ultimately did not materialize.

In the early 1970s diversification took new paths as gas shortages forced all transmission companies to scamper for new supplies. In 1973 the Arab oil embargo hurled the United States into a full-fledged energy crisis, leaving few energy companies unscathed and marking a new era in energy history and in the history of Texas Eastern. In subsequent years the company struggled to adapt to a dizzying sequence of challenges, which severely limited its capacity to plan for the future. Both the supply and the price of gas and oil fluctuated wildly in these years, frustrating efforts to sustain strategic choices. Supply shortages and government promotional policies pushed the major transmission companies into risky initiatives in developing supplemental sources of gas such as liquefied natural gas (LNG), coal gasification, and arctic gas. At the same time, deregulation radically altered the traditional regulatory system. But the process of change left much uncertainty concerning the ultimate outcome of regulatory reform. All of these developments complicated the task of managing Texas Eastern. Now the firm's managers and staff planners had few fixed points to use as they tried to chart the company's future.

In the 1970s and 1980s Texas Eastern generally described itself as "an international diversified energy company." For much of this period high oil prices produced extraordinary revenues from the company's production of oil and gas in the North Sea, and Texas Eastern enjoyed a buoyant period of oil-driven diversification. The company did not move far outside of its traditional strongholds in gas and oil. This did not present serious difficulties as long as energy prices stayed high, but the collapse of oil prices in the mid-1980s undermined the company's short-term prosperity. In this challenging period the company — along with many others in the energy industries — was forced to reevaluate its long-standing commitment to diversification. Its efforts to "refocus on the core" brought fundamental adjustments, including the divestment of several subsidiaries.

These hard choices came in the 1980s at a time of far-reaching changes in the natural gas industry, as a sweeping merger-and-acquisitions wave steadily reduced the number of competitors in the industry. As it sought to adapt to the new conditions of the 1980s, Texas Eastern's valuable and easily divested North Sea interests made it an especially attractive acquisition. The company's efforts to adapt to new conditions in its industry ended abruptly in 1989 after a heated takeover battle resulted in its purchase by Panhandle Eastern Corporation.

The new owner helped finance its purchase by selling off holdings, including North Sea production, Houston real estate, the petroleum products pipeline, the refinery, and the LPG business. These properties were purchased by specialists who valued them as potentially profitable additions to existing businesses. After these sales, Panhandle Eastern retained only Texas Eastern's gas transmission system, which became part of one of the largest gas pipeline systems in the nation. In this sense, the breakup of the diversified holdings of Texas Eastern represented a return to the company's roots in gas transmission. It is thus fitting that our history of Texas Eastern begins with the building of its first pipelines, the Big Inch and the Little Big Inch.

Part One

THE ENTREPRENEURIAL ERA

1941–54

Chapter 1

THE INCH LINES

Texas Eastern displayed its origins in its corporate logo, a circle within a larger circle representing the Little Big Inch and the Big Inch pipelines. Well before the firm's creation, these lines had played a vital role in the waging of World War II. When it purchased the Inch Lines in 1947, TE acquired more than a set of cross-country pipelines. The newly created company bought a piece of history, a symbol of the nation's successful response to the demands of total war. It also acquired the experience of many of those who joined the company after working on the pipelines during the war and the cooperative spirit engendered by the all-out push to build these vital supply lines in a national emergency.

These events should remind us that World War II was a watershed in the nation's economic development. Government direction of vital sectors such as natural gas encouraged technical changes while channeling millions of investment dollars into these war-related industries. Wartime prosperity pulled the economy out of the Great Depression and loosened the purse strings on private as well as public investment. And even as the nation moved forward toward victory, the founders of Texas Eastern joined others in jockeying for competitive position in the coming postwar economy. The events of the war years accelerated the pace of change in the cross-country shipment of natural gas and eased the way for the birth of Texas Eastern.

The war transformed many vital industries and set the stage for sustained expansion in the late 1940s and 1950s. Wartime cooperation between business and government hastened the flow of men and supplies to the fronts, blurring traditional American distinctions between "private" and "public." Government investment bolstered critical manufacturing industries. By war's end, the government owned an estimated 20 to 25 percent of the nation's industrial capacity. Few questioned the propriety of this public investment during the war. The spirit of self-sacrifice in pursuit of a common good generally prevailed. Whatever was necessary to win the war would be done. Once victorious, the nation could grapple with the problem of returning to a peacetime economy. Of course, many industries would never quite be the same after the experience of the long mobilization, which accelerated many prewar economic trends while deflecting the paths of others.[1]

The war effort made heavy demands on the oil and gas industries, since the abundance of these products was one key advantage of the Allied powers. Petroleum products — from 100 octane aviation fuel, to gasoline for mechanized warfare, to synthetic rubber — contributed greatly to the defeat of the oil-starved Axis nations. Building the infrastructure needed to keep these materials moving to the fronts was a top priority of war planners, who targeted money, men, and materials for the construction of pipelines, oil tankers, and state-of-the-art petroleum refineries. As domestic oil fueled the Allied war effort, natural gas, coal, and conservation took up some of the slack in energy supply within the United States.[2] Few operations in any of the major energy industries remained untouched by mobilization, and many private energy companies felt the impact of war long after the end of hostilities. In the case of the pipeline construction industry, World War II hastened the coming of cross-country shipments of oil and natural gas.

Before World War II the development of vast new supplies of natural gas had spurred a wave of new pipeline construction. The Appalachian fields of West Virginia and Pennsylvania had been the focus of U.S. gas production before the 1920s, but in that decade a series of spectacular discoveries in Texas, Oklahoma, and Louisiana shifted the center of supply sharply toward the Southwest. Many cities near these surging new fields quickly converted to natural gas, but they did not come close to absorbing the new supplies. The construction of longer pipelines quickly went forward to link western supply with eastern demand. After advances in pipe rolling and welding made longer lines technically feasible, a flurry of construction between 1925 and 1931 (see map 1.1) left lines as large as twenty-four inches in diameter extending from nine hundred to eleven hundred miles from the fields in the Texas Panhandle and southern Oklahoma to Chicago, Indianapolis, and Minneapolis.[3] Although the depression of the 1930s slowed further developments, the gas pipeline boom before the Great Depression paved the way for the rapid changes required by the war effort.

Pearl Harbor altered the peacetime patterns of business development, placing control of vital sectors of the economy in government hands. The nation closed ranks, submerging many of the tensions of the New Deal era, at least for the duration. Patterns of economic development, as well as patterns of political and regulatory conflict, did not, of course, entirely disappear. They endured. But they became secondary to the larger purpose of winning the war. No one who has read through the various hearings on mobilization held during and after the war could doubt that many businessmen had one nervous eye cocked on the postwar competitive implications of the industrial policies required by war. But most businessmen and government officials involved in mobilization focused most of their energies on the successful prosecution of the war. In this sense, the national strategy of victory against aggression overrode considerations of corporate strategy.

14

MAP 1.1 Pipeline Construction of the Late 1920s

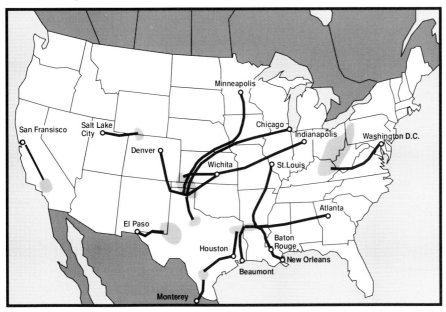

Source: Adapted from Arlon R. Tussing and Connie C. Barlow, *The Natural Gas Industry: Evolution, Structure, and Economics* (Cambridge: Ballinger Publishing Company, 1984), 38.

For the natural gas industry, this meant contributing increasing supplies of domestic fuel through newly constructed pipelines to free petroleum for use at the fronts, and it also meant producing the feedstocks needed to create such vital commodities as 100 octane aviation fuel and synthetic rubber. Although these tasks were not as highly publicized as the petroleum industry's push to build the Inch Lines, they nonetheless contributed to winning the war. These efforts also brought to the fore two men who would later play pivotal roles in creating Texas Eastern. E. Holley Poe and Everette DeGolyer were prominent industry leaders during the war, and their experiences laid the foundation for the organization of Texas Eastern and its quest for the Inch Lines.

Poe's career before, during, and after the war gave him a unique perspective on the potential impact of the Inch Lines on postwar patterns of supply and demand in the natural gas industry. Born and raised in Oklahoma, Poe worked first in the newspaper industry and then with oil and utility companies. In the mid-1930s he became secretary of the natural gas department of the American Gas Association (AGA), which was then the industry's sole national trade association. After a brief stay in the AGA's Dallas office, Poe moved to New York City, where he took charge of both the manufactured gas and natural gas sections of the AGA. This work gave Poe extensive contacts among gas suppliers, consumers, and distributors throughout the nation. His work gave him a good perspective on the evolution of prewar gas markets while also marking him as a leading spokesman for his industry.

15

With the outbreak of war, his standing within the industry made him an obvious choice to head the Natural Gas and Natural Gasoline Division of the Petroleum Administration for War (PAW), the government agency responsible for all wartime petroleum and natural gas operations. His tenure in this important office lasted from June of 1942 through October of 1943, when he was called to work on other war-related matters for the Department of Interior. His service during the critical early phase of the war effort won for him high praise from his superiors at the PAW, who called Poe "a tower of strength in Washington."[4]

During his stay with the AGA in Dallas, Poe had met Everette DeGolyer, of the geological consulting firm of DeGolyer and MacNaughton. By the late 1930s DeGolyer was already a famous name in the petroleum industry. His pioneering work in petroleum geology had contributed to the discovery of vast oil reserves in Mexico in the early twentieth century and had carried him to the position of president and chairman of the board of Amerada Petroleum Corporation. After retiring from Amerada in 1932, he organized a consulting firm that specialized in reports on potential and proven oil reserves. His firm of DeGolyer and MacNaughton quickly built a reputation as the leading geophysical consulting firm in the world.[5] In 1941 DeGolyer became the assistant deputy petroleum administrator for war, one of the highest officials in the oil mobilization agency. He remained in that position through 1943, when he was put in charge of successive U.S. government missions to study the petroleum reserves of Mexico and the Middle East. DeGolyer and Poe, who discovered during their wartime service that they shared a scientific approach to the study of conditions in the oil and gas industries, became close personal friends.

The two colleagues also came to share an interest in one of the glamour projects of the PAW, the construction and operation of the Big Inch and Little Big Inch pipelines. During the war the Inch Lines captured widespread attention. Indeed, for a time the entire nation followed the progress of the lines as they made their way halfway across the continent. Whereas newspapers carried maps of the various battle fronts in Europe, trade journals regularly provided updates on the progress of the pipelines. Such attention was well deserved, since the Inch Lines were desperately needed to fuel the war effort. Prewar patterns of oil transportation had been disrupted by German submarines. The nation, as well as petroleum industry leaders, understood the connection between the battlefront news from Europe and the news of the struggle at home to link southwestern oil regions with northeastern factories and ports.

For decades before the war, ocean-going tankers had transported most crude oil and oil products shipped from Texas and Louisiana to the Northeast. Fairly extensive oil pipeline systems existed in the midwestern and northeastern states, but none of these reached from the Southwest to the major eastern cities. These shipments moved almost exclusively in oil tankers, which on the eve of the war transported 95 percent of all petroleum deliveries from the Gulf Coast to the East. Only 2 percent was transported by pipelines. The tankers carried approximately 1.5 million barrels of oil a day, and even before the nation entered the war, the reliance on oil tankers had become a serious concern.[6] Beginning in early 1941 President Roosevelt ordered approximately fifty American tankers to be removed from the Atlantic route and transferred to Britain for its wartime use. In April of 1942, four months after Pearl Harbor, the president again diverted a substantial number of tankers, this time for service in the South Pacific. By then Britain had already borrowed more than eighty tankers (although some were subsequently returned). As a result, the U.S. tanker system was stretched thin by the demands of wartime traffic. All who understood the vital role of oil in modern warfare had to be concerned about the national oil transportation system's vulnerability to submarine attacks.

Well before the outbreak of war prominent government officials and industry leaders had warned of a coming crisis in oil transportation. They failed, however, to get a forceful public response to what was still only a potential problem. Secretary of the Interior Harold L. Ickes would be responsible for maintaining the nation's petroleum supply and transportation network if the United States were drawn into the war. Observing the European fighting in the late 1930s, Ickes recognized that America's petroleum transportation system was likely to be vulnerable if war ensued.[7] He decided that an overland petroleum pipeline would solve the problem. On July 20, 1940, Ickes told President Franklin D. Roosevelt that "the building of a crude-oil pipeline from Texas to the east might not be *economically sound;* but that in the event of an emergency it might be absolutely necessary."[8] Although he received little encouragement from others in government, Ickes pursued the idea of constructing an overland pipeline network to replace the vulnerable tanker transportation system. Some oil companies active in oil tanker construction initially opposed him, but events overseas soon convinced the entire industry of the value of developing overland oil transportation.[9]

There was nevertheless an obvious barrier to cooperative planning to meet this crisis: an ongoing investigation of the oil industry for possible violations of the antitrust laws. Thurman Arnold's Justice Department was pursuing the investigation with vigor. Oil executives had ample reason to be wary; they were still smarting from a bitter confrontation with antitrust officials in the late 1930s. Ickes and others pressured the Justice Department to settle its antimonopoly cases so that the companies involved could cooperate in developing a wartime petroleum strategy.[10] But many oil men were skeptical of these early efforts to organize a consortium of private companies to help plan a new pipeline. They feared that such cooperation might spark another round of antitrust prosecutions.

While Ickes pressured the government to prepare for war, the industry forged ahead with its own plan for dealing with the potential crisis. In May of 1941 Standard Oil Company (New Jersey) President William S. Farish telegraphed several executives from other major American oil companies about the necessity for a long distance oil pipeline. At his invitation, representatives of seven oil companies met for two days at his offices, concluding with a recommendation for the construction of a twenty-four-inch crude oil pipeline with the capacity to carry 250,000 barrels per day from the Southwest to the Northeast.[11] The next day, representatives of a subcommittee of the Petroleum Industry War Council (PIWC) — a voluntary group of concerned oil men — began conducting aerial surveys of possible pipeline routes and working on preliminary engineering plans.[12] At about the same time, the major national oil trade association, the American Petroleum Institute (API), called for oil conservation and increased shipments of oil to the Northeast.

As oil men and their voluntary organizations went ahead with plans for a privately owned and constructed overland pipeline, Harold Ickes sought to consolidate his authority over the industry. A chaotic welter of agencies had sprung up to regulate different aspects of the oil industry and its mobilization, and Ickes lobbied Roosevelt for a single federal agency to supervise war time petroleum industry operations. Roosevelt finally agreed, and on May 28, 1941, he appointed Ickes to the newly created position of Petroleum Coordinator for National Defense (renamed the Petroleum Administration for War in December of 1942); unofficially, Ickes was known as the oil "czar."[13] He now had sufficient clout to take charge of planning for war mobilization in the industry.

Ickes's organization grew into the PAW. Along with its predecessor, the Office of Petroleum Coordinator (OPC) for National Defense, the PAW was a cooperative effort between government and business to manage the flow of oil and gas for the war effort. It included a separate Natural Gas and Gasoline Division. To coordinate activities throughout the nation, there were five district offices, each including representatives of each of the functional divisions. Staffing for most of these offices came from specialists on leave from oil and gas companies. The organization chart also shows a line from the administrator to the "national industry committees." In the case of oil, this meant the Petroleum Industry War Council (PIWC), whose organization paralleled that of the PAW, complete with PIWC district committees. Under the direction of the prewar head of the American Petroleum Institute, William R. Boyd, Jr., the PIWC assisted the government in mobilizing the oil and gas industries. Industry representatives initially suspected the motives of Secretary of Interior Ickes, who became the PAW's administrator. But Ickes' appointment of the widely respected Ralph K. Davis, of Standard Oil of California, as deputy administrator soothed these fears, opening the way for close and ultimately successful cooperation between business and government.

During June of 1941 Davies held two meetings to explore ways of relieving transportation shortages on the Atlantic seaboard. The participants also discussed the advantages and disadvantages of pipelines versus tankers for oil transportation. These discussions and other meetings continued into the summer of 1941, when Secretary Ickes appointed industry committees to assist in planning strategy for the petroleum industry. At that time transportation-related planning became the primary responsibility of a transportation committee under the direction of W. Alton Jones, whose career with Cities Service included long experience in the construction and operation of oil and gas pipelines.

By this time a consensus had developed within the oil industry on the need to build a new cross-country pipeline. Secretary Ickes strongly supported this view, but not all government agencies agreed that the expansion of the nation's oil transportation system was a top priority for war planners. The Supply Priorities and Allocation Board (SPAB), a federal agency created to evaluate all wartime requests for steel, had authority to allocate scarce materials for large construction projects. SPAB rejected the initial application for materials for a new cross-country pipeline, giving it a lower priority than other competing projects. Undeterred, the original seven petroleum companies, joined now by four other firms, submitted a second application in July of 1941. SPAB again turned down the application. Neither Ickes nor the petroleum companies could convince SPAB that severe domestic shortages of petroleum existed or were imminent in the United States without the pipelines.[14]

Other potential problems for the cross-country line had surfaced during the planning phases of two smaller privately owned transmission companies, Southeastern Pipe Line and Plantation Pipe Line. The Plantation project had encountered significant opposition in Georgia from railroad companies seeking to protect their own markets in petroleum transportation by blocking the construction of pipelines. A long struggle ended with the state government refusing to grant the pipeline the right of eminent domain to obtain needed rights-of-way. Representative William Cole, of Maryland, responded by introducing a bill in the U.S. Congress to give the president the power to assign the right of eminent domain to an interstate petroleum pipeline deemed in the interest of national defense. With the support of President Roosevelt, Congress passed this bill in July of 1941, clearing the way for the completion of both the Plantation Pipe Line and the Southeastern line. The Cole Act also assured that the proposed twenty-four-inch Texas-to-New Jersey pipeline would receive the right of eminent domain, when and if deemed vital to national security.[15]

The consortium of private companies planning for the Inch Line relentlessly pushed forward, hoping that sooner or later this day would arrive. On September 1, 1941, members of the consortium completed an aerial survey and preliminary design for the proposed National Defense Pipeline. A few days later these companies organized the National Defense Pipelines, Incorporated to build and finance a twenty-four-inch pipeline from the Southwest to the Northeast. This agreement provided that the effort to build the line would continue until December 5, at which time the agreement could be renewed if significant progress had been made. The creation of this new corporate structure provided a basis for still another priority application, which SPAB again rejected. Without approval for steel, the pipeline could not be built, and National Defense Pipelines was immobilized. When the original agreement expired on December 5, it seemed unlikely that the long line would ever be built.

Two days later the Japanese bombing for Pearl Harbor jolted the project back to life. Ickes and the PIWC pressed again for a large-diameter, Southwest-to-Northeast pipeline, but even after Pearl Harbor and the United States's entry into the war, SPAB at first gave only mild support to the proposal. Many of the tankers borrowed by Britain were being returned, and the severe domestic oil shortages predicted by Ickes had not yet materialized. The existing tanker transportation system, while clearly vulnerable to attack, had not yet come under siege. SPAB still considered that the massive amounts of steel necessary to construct the proposed pipeline were more important for other construction projects.

In early 1942, however, attacks against American oil tankers began in earnest. During February a German submarine sank the first American tanker off the Atlantic Coast. By the end of the month a total of twelve had gone down. March held even greater horrors, as the subs sank an average of three tankers per day.[16] The oil supply in the Northeast began to dwindle noticeably as fewer and fewer tankers got through the sea lanes in the Atlantic. From a prewar level of 1.5 million barrels of oil per day, tanker shipments had plummeted to 70,000 barrels per day by May of 1943. Increased oil shipments by barge and rail made up part of the loss, but these forms of transportation could not keep pace with the surging demand for oil. This dramatic submarine assault on the tankers gave new impetus to Ickes's pipeline plan.

In response to the sinkings and shortages on the East Coast, W. Alton Jones, chairman of the Transportation Committee of the PAW for District 1 (which included the Atlantic seaboard), requested a meeting with representatives from the transportation committees of other districts. At the meeting they formed a Temporary Joint Pipe Line Subcommittee, which called an industry-wide meeting at the Mayo Hotel, in Tulsa, Oklahoma, from March twenty-third to twenty-sixth. Engineers and executives from sixty-seven companies attended the conference and devised what became the basic American wartime pipeline strategy.

Extracting a ten-point "Tulsa Plan" from the recommendations of the conference, the subcommittee issued its final report in April of 1942. This plan focused on developing the nation's petroleum transportation system and reconditioning existing pipelines. The ninth point called for the construction of a twenty-four-inch, three-hundred-thousand-barrel-per-day oil pipeline

German U-boat attack on U.S. oil tanker off the Atlantic coast

to extend from east Texas through Salem, Illinois, where fifty thousand barrels would be delivered to local refineries and the remainder would be shipped to New York and Philadelphia. The subcommittee also recommended that a products pipeline be constructed from east Texas to Salem, Illinois. If the larger pipeline were built, the subcommittee recommended extending a twenty-inch pipeline from Salem into the New York–Philadelphia area. On April 8, 1942, the chairman of the Petroleum Industry War Council's Temporary Pipeline Management Committee, W. Alton Jones, began planning for the construction of the twenty-four-inch pipeline.[17]

The PAW quickly accepted the Tulsa Plan with only slight modifications, but Ickes still faced skepticism from the War Production Board (WPB, the successor agency to the SPAB). The board was not convinced that the pipeline project merited the large quantities of steel also needed to construct tanks, ships, and airplanes. In June, 1942, Ickes carried his appeal to the House Committee on Interstate and Foreign Commerce, where he noted the heavy loss of oil tankers to submarine attacks and the mounting petroleum shortage on the East Coast. Finally, on June 10, 1942, the long battle was won.

Construction of the Inch Lines (view through pipe)

The WPB allocated 137,000 tons of steel to build the first section of the proposed twenty-four-inch pipeline from east Texas to Norris City, Illinois. When
the private oil companies decided they were no longer capable of financing
the pipeline, this task fell to the Reconstruction Finance Corporation (RFC).
RFC chairman Jesse Jones advised Alton Jones (no relation) that the RFC
stood ready to finance the construction of the initial portion of the pipeline
for $35 million.[18]

With steel and financing finally assured, the eleven private oil companies
which had spearheaded planning for the pipelines met to create an organization
to build them. Ownership would rest with the Defense Plants Corporation
(DPC), a subsidiary of the RFC. But the actual construction and operation
of the lines would be carried out by War Emergency Pipelines (WEP), a private concern that would be under contract to the DPC. The board of directors of the WEP consisted of the top executives of each of the original eleven
oil companies, with Alton Jones as president and Burt Hull, of The Texas
Company, as vice president and general manager. Each of the eleven oil companies contributed personnel to construct and operate the lines.

Pipeline construction: preparing the joint

After several years of arguing, planning, testifying, and lobbying, the businessmen who had finally obtained approval for the Big Inch Line were eager to build. From construction offices established at Little Rock, Arkansas, they pushed the project briskly ahead. The first order for pipe was placed on July 2, 1942; the first shipment left the mill only sixteen days later. On August 3 the first section of pipe was laid by contractors working on a cost-plus basis. The race was on. For the rest of 1942 the emphasis was on completing the first leg of the Big Inch from Longview, in the east Texas oil field, to Norris City, in southern Illinois. Even before the completion of this western section in December of 1943, planning was well advanced for the eastern leg from Norris City to Phoenixville Junction, Pennsylvania, near the eastern boundary of the state. From there, a twenty-inch extension would reach out to refineries in the New York and Philadelphia areas. As work on this eastern project went forward, pipeline crews also began laying the western

TABLE 1.1   Factual Data on Inch Line Systems

	"Big Inch" Crude Line (24" diameter)	"Little Big Inch" (20" products line)
Construction Cost	$78,500,000	$60,000,000
Length in Miles		
Main Lines	1,254	1,475
Feeder and Distribution Lines	224	239
TOTAL MILES	1,478	1,714
Tons of Steel Used		
Pipelines	346,037	278,815
Storage Tanks	20,400	14,800
TOTAL TONS	366,437	293,615
Valves in System		
Main Line	148	197
Others (12" and larger)	826	801
TOTAL	974	998
Pump Stations		
Number of Stations	27	32
Number of Pumps	101	100
Rated HP of Electric Motors	128,450	115,050
Power Used Daily, KWH (Full Load)	2,227,000	1,824,000
Storage Tanks		
Number in System	50	47
Capacity, Barrels	3,867,500	2,884,000
Oil Required to Fill Pipelines		
Barrels	3,791,000	3,018,000
Gallons	159,212,000	126,759,000
Delivery Capacity		
Daily Rate, Barrels	325,000	235,000
Annual Rate, Barrels	118,625,000	85,775,000
Actual Deliveries,		
Barrels (through 8/31/45)	261,862,000	105,960,000

Source: War Emergency Pipelines, Inc., "Fuel for the Fighting Fronts . . . 'Big Inch and Little Big Inch'" (1946), Texas Eastern (TE) Archives, Houston, Tex.

section of the Little Big Inch from the refining centers near Beaumont, Texas, and the Houston Ship Channel area to Little Rock. At that point, the products line met the right-of-way for the Big Inch, which it followed into eastern Pennsylvania before moving on to its ultimate destination, Linden, New Jersey. Thus, there were four substantial pipeline projects going on almost simultaneously: the two legs of the Big Inch and the two legs of the Little Big Inch. Crews completed most major river crossings in advance of the lines. Work went forward at a frenzied pace on all or parts of the Inch Lines from August, 1942, through December, 1943, when both lines were finished.

By any measure, this was an impressive achievement. Table 1.1 gives the vital statistics on the two pipelines. Before the construction of the Inch Lines,

Inch Line construction

most pipelines for carrying either crude oil or products were at eight inches in diameter or smaller.[19] Thus, the twenty-four inch and twenty inch size represented a great leap forward. The Inch Lines were massive by other measures as well. Their combined oil pumping stations were among the largest consumers of electricity in the nation. Pushing more than five hundred thousand barrels per day of crude and refined oil halfway across the country was no easy task. When filled, the two lines together held more than six million barrels of oil. The Big Inch was the nation's largest diameter oil pipeline; the Little Inch its longest.

Yet statistics do not capture either the tone or the human drama of the project. The job of laying the pipelines required a small army at times exceeding fifteen thousand workers. They faced a demanding task on a tight timetable. The route had to be surveyed and cleared, no matter how heavy the underbrush or how steep the grade. Trenches three feet wide and four feet deep had to be dug for a total of twenty-seven hundred miles for the two lines. Forty-foot sections of pipe had to be distributed along the right-of-way, prepared for welding, welded, wrapped, lowered into the trench,

TABLE 1.2   Pace of Pipeline Construction (miles), 1943

Month	Big Inch	Little Big Inch	TOTAL
January	20	—	20
February	49	—	49
March	166	—	166
April	190	3	193
May	164	78	242
June	223	224	447
July	83	333	416
August	10	396	406
September	5	308	313
October	—	171	171
November	—	120	120
December	—	8	8
TOTAL	910	1,641	2,551

Source: A. N. Horne, "Emergency Pipelines—Their Record in Review," *World Petroleum* (June, 1945).

and covered. The work went on in all but the harshest weather. Over, around, or through every natural obstacle in the path, the crews drove the line ahead.[20] Table 1.2 gives some idea of the pace maintained by crews spread along numerous parts of the right-of-way in 1943, when construction of both Inch Lines moved toward completion.

The drive to complete the projects required the crews working on the Little Big Inch to disregard pipeliners' traditions—and their common sense—and tackle parts of the Appalachian Mountains crossing during the severe conditions of winter. Their accomplishment is not easily appreciated in a nation accustomed to interstate highways and populated by growing numbers of citizens who rarely walk across undeveloped "backlands," much less attempt to accomplish demanding work "out in the country." One way to sense the magnitude of the task is to trace the path followed by the Inch Lines on a map and attempt to imagine simply walking the path taken—much less laying pipeline over it. The lines conquered extremely rugged countryside; they crossed the Red, Arkansas, Mississippi, Ohio, and Monongahela rivers, as well as scores of smaller rivers and streams. Construction plowed ahead through swamps, over hills and mountains. Old photographs of the work crews slogging on through bad conditions capture the sense of men on a mission. Such photos still inspire awe at the capacity of highly motivated and well-organized men to accomplish grand things.

As they encountered problems, the work crews improvised to keep the line moving along. At times, experience from the natural gas pipeline boom of the late 1920s came in handy, since natural gas lines up to twenty-four inches in diameter and more than a thousand miles long had been laid in that earlier era. The builders of the Inch Lines borrowed techniques from the gas industry for welding large-diameter pipe. They also used barges as a base to string pipe across wide rivers. Much of the equipment available

Inch Line construction

for use in laying the lines came from prewar petroleum pipeline work, but it often had to be adapted to the new demands of laying much longer and heavier sections of pipe. When machinery for moving the pipe proved too small to handle the heavy weight without tipping over, the solution was not to order new, larger equipment, but rather to rig up makeshift counterweights by attaching any heavy objects on hand to the side of the equipment. Construction crews used the tools at hand to complete their forced march to the oil terminals and refineries on the East Coast.[21]

Nature at times stalled the march. Severe problems arose at several critical river crossings. Just as the Arkansas River crossing was being completed, a flash flood on May 17, 1943, washed away cables and lines, sending sections of the pipeline careening into the river. When the flood subsided, workers had to haul the damaged pipeline from the river, cut and weld the damaged metal, and reinstall it. A similar mishap occurred at the Mississippi River crossing only two days before the deadline for finishing the first leg. There a flood broke the moorings of the barges and other equipment, destroying the original crossing. Serious manmade problems also developed with the pipe used in the Little Big Inch. From the earliest hydrostatic pressure tests, it was evident that the twenty-inch pipe would not withstand the high operating pressures originally contemplated for the line. This required the replacement of long sections of the line and the reluctant decision to operate the products line at a lower pressure than previously planned.

The completed lines quickly became critical to the flow of crude oil and oil products to the Northeast. The lines also took on a certain symbolic importance that transcended statistical summaries. *The Oil Weekly* captured this sense of the undertaking: "Over and above all, the line is more than a metal conduit for moving oil; it is a symbol of American spirit, an expression of determined people whose purpose is freedom."[22] The symbolism was grounded firmly in reality: the Inch Lines were physical evidence for a nation under seige that it could loosen the grip of its foes and reassert control over its own destiny, in this case, by replacing oil tankers vulnerable to German submarines with a secure transportation system beyond the reach of the nation's enemies.

Although the Inch Lines were the most significant pipelines built during the war, numerous other smaller projects played important roles in assuring the flow of oil and gas to the East Coast. Under the guidelines set down in the Tulsa Plan, business and government cooperated in completing thirty-three major projects that built almost ten thousand miles of pipeline at a cost of approximately $290 million. While the government contributed slightly more than $160 million to all of these projects, more than 90 percent of that money went into the construction of the Inch Lines.[23] Most of the remaining projects were privately financed lines built to expand the capacity of existing regional systems of oil production, refining, and transportation. These smaller projects did not enjoy the same publicity accorded to the Inch Lines, but they contributed to the extraordinary expansion of the nation's pipeline capacity for oil, justifying the PAW's claim that the war brought "the greatest pipe line construction period in the history of the industry."[24]

The natural gas pipeline industry was also active during the war. Of special importance in the early history of the industry was the only major natural gas line constructed during the war, Tennessee Gas Transmission Company's 1,265–mile-long pipeline from Texas to West Virginia. This twenty-four-inch line stretched from gas fields in the southern portion of the Texas Gulf Coast to the existing regional distribution systems at Cornwall, West Virginia. Its completion had far-reaching ramifications for the postwar evolution of Texas Eastern, since it brought southwestern natural gas a short step away from the major eastern cities. It also established a strong new company which would subsequently become a forceful competitor in the postwar gas transmission business.

Steel and other materials were made available for the construction of Tennessee's pipeline because of the key role of natural gas in fueling the manufacturing plants located near the Appalachian gas fields in the highly industrialized states of Ohio, New York, Pennsylvania, West Virginia, Mary-

Harold Ickes (seated, left) and W. E. P. President W. Alton Jones at the Big Inch Dedication Ceremony

land, Virginia, and Kentucky. The estimated 660 war factories in this region consumed about 3 million cubic feet of gas each month, and the region as a whole used approximately 400 billion feet of natural and mixed gas each year. The assurance of continued gas supplies in this region was vital to the war effort, but the rapid decline of the Appalachian gas fields raised grave questions about the immediate future. Early in the war, a greatly accelerated drilling program provided a measure of relief, but each new winter brought renewed concern about the adequacy of gas supplies.[25]

In 1943, the WPB responded to this pressing need by authorizing material for the construction of a new natural gas line from the Southwest to the Appalachian region. The board expressed no preference as to which company should build the line. It merely emphasized the urgency of the project by making the permit valid only through September of 1943, which the WPB felt was the last date possible to leave time for completion of the pipeline before the start of the 1944–1945 heating season. The company that took this challenge had to be willing to forge ahead immediately, giving an obvious advantage to those who had already done their preliminary planning.

One such firm was Hope Natural Gas Company, Standard Oil of New Jersey's well-established gas distribution subsidiary in the Appalachian region. Faced by a steady decline in its traditional sources in the Appalachian fields, Hope had previously explored various options for acquiring gas supplies from outside the region. Therefore, when the WPB announced its authorization for a new line, Hope voiced its intention to build one from the giant Hugoton, Oklahoma, field to its existing system, with the connection at Cornwall, West Virginia. Hope's track record of successful operations, its ready access to expertise and capital, and its extensive distribution system in the Appalachian region seemed to give it the inside track in the bidding for the new project.

But as Hope completed its application to the FPC, a relatively new company stepped forward aggressively and won the right to build the pipeline. Tennessee Gas and Transmission Company was the upset winner, in part because it was prepared to move very quickly in a competitive situation. Tennessee had been organized before the war to seek approval for a natural gas pipeline from the Gulf Coast of Louisiana into the Tennessee Valley. Originally based in Chattanooga, the firm had a strong asset in the involvement of Curtis Dall, a former son-in-law of President Franklin D. Roosevelt. Political connections notwithstanding, the firm's prewar application had been unsuccessful. It renewed its efforts to get regulatory approval and financing for its project in the early years of the war. Responding to the WPB's announcement of certification for a new natural gas pipeline, Tennessee Gas submitted a new application for a project quite similar to the one it had planned before the war. After hearings that included testimony from Tennessee Gas and a variety of intervenors on the need for additional natural gas within the Appalachian region, in July, 1943, the FPC granted the company a sixty-day period in which to submit additional evidence of firm commitments for financing. Informed commentators within the industry noted that this ruling "would seem to indicate prospects for getting approval are not very good."[26]

At this critical juncture, another company with holdings in the southwestern gas fields came forward to supply financing, and, in the process, to take control of Tennessee Gas. The Chicago Corporation was a holding company with various enterprises, among them substantial natural gas supplies near Corpus Christi, Texas. Preliminary plans to build a pipeline eastward from these reserves had not come to fruition, but the company now saw an opportunity to move forward in cooperation with Tennessee Gas. The crucial person in the marriage of the two concerns was H. Gardiner

Symonds, who had gone to Texas to manage The Chicago Corporation's gas properties and had stayed to become the guiding force in Tennessee Gas. Symonds had taken his Harvard M.B.A. and several years of experience in banking into The Chicago Corporation, where he started as an assistant treasurer and moved up to vice president in the 1930s. When The Chicago Corporation agreed to help arrange financing for the proposed Tennessee Gas pipeline, Symonds quickly moved to the fore in managing the merged company. The Chicago Corporation acquired Tennessee Gas in 1943, and as the new president of the company, Symonds pushed ahead with plans for the pipeline project. His new proposal called for the line to originate at The Chicago Corporation's reserves in south Texas and to connect into the existing Appalachian distribution system at Cornwall, West Virginia.[27]

The FPC quickly approved this project in September of 1943, in the process abruptly canceling scheduled plans for a hearing on Hope Natural Gas's competing proposal. The commission's haste raised eyebrows. Critics speculated that the political clout of The Chicago Corporation accounted for its sudden success, but less conspiratorial interpretations of this episode seem more plausible. Subsequent events justified the government's urgency. When an especially severe winter in 1944–1945 brought a serious fuel shortage to Appalachia, natural gas from the just-completed pipeline eased the worst effects of the crisis.[28]

Before the next winter, World War II had finally ended, and instead of struggling to meet wartime demands for natural gas, Tennessee Gas Transmission Company began exploring ways to take advantage of its early lead in establishing a Southwest-to-Northeast natural gas connection. The company came out of the war with several clear competitive advantages over potential rivals in the cross-country transmission business. It had a proven leader in Gardiner Symonds. It had excellent access to credit, despite the fact that in 1945 The Chicago Corporation has divested its 81 percent interest in the company's voting stock so as to avoid FPC regulation as an interstate natural gas carrier. Tennessee Gas held large supplies of natural gas in prolific fields located primarily on the coastal plains of Texas and Louisiana. Above all, it had the longest natural gas pipeline from that region to the Northeast. With the return of a peacetime economy, Tennessee held a very strong hand. It would be a player to be reckoned with as the natural gas transmission business sought to recapture the dynamism of the late 1920s.[29]

After a decade of severe depression and four years of mobilization for war, the leaders of the industry were eager to return to peacetime and—they sorely hoped—to prosperity. As all in the industry congratulated themselves on a job well done in meeting the national emergency, the prospects for future expansion seemed excellent. Despite the increased demand for natural gas during the war, proven reserves had actually increased over the period from 1940 to 1945. New discoveries in the Southwest had more than made up for the depletion of the older fields of Appalachia. Markets were likely to be disrupted as the economy demobilized. But the established companies nonetheless looked forward to a return to prewar patterns of supply and distribution.

As they launched into the tasks of reconversion, the industry's leaders recognized that several significant changes had come out of the war. The FPC was now solidly established as an integral part of the industry's decision-making. There could be no doubt that it would take a strong role in planning during the postwar era. An aggressive new company, Tennessee Gas and Transmission, had arisen to take the lead in the race to connect the Southwest and Northeast. The Inch Lines had already won this race, but they carried oil, not gas. Even before the war had ended, speculation had begun about their possible conversion for use in transporting gas. But before the Inch Lines could become a part of the peacetime economy, several big questions had to be answered. How would the government relinquish control of these and other war properties? To what use would the lines be put? Which private investors would take control of the postwar development of the vital eastern markets for natural gas?

Chapter 2

THE WINNING BID

During the two years following the end of World War II, Texas Eastern's organizers threw themselves into a high-stakes, high-risk struggle to gain control of the Inch Lines and thereby win access to eastern metropolitan markets. Buffeted by the political winds of postwar Washington, company executives nevertheless marshalled their resources for the competitive bidding process against other energy companies. Several natural gas concerns, as well as interfuel competitors from the oil, coal, and railroad industries, fought hard to gain control over the lines. The intensity of the struggle reflected the value of the prize; these pipelines promised to be an important force in the development of postwar energy markets. The founders of Texas Eastern displayed considerable "political entrepreneurship" in this battle. They shaped the debate on the pipelines to include the possibility of converting them to natural gas; they explored every avenue of political influence to acquire the Inch Lines, and they deflected aggressive challenges to their new enterprise in confrontational certification hearings before the FPC. Success in the political arena made possible Texas Eastern's subsequent success in the marketplace.[1]

At war's end the Inch Lines became part of a giant inventory of "war surplus properties," or projects built with government funds. Given American business traditions, a return to a peacetime economy meant that the government would liquidate its investments by turning them over to private companies. This was no easy matter. The disposal of almost a quarter of the nation's industrial capacity was bound to raise controversy. How should the properties be sold? Could they be "privatized" without increasing the market power of large companies? What would become of these vital properties in the event of another national emergency? These questions had to be answered quickly, since the American public was impatient after the Great Depression and World War II to get back to a normal political economy.

With an estimated price tag of $146 million, the Inch Lines were among the most expensive individual projects owned by a government which had invested more than $16 billion in war-related manufacturing. The Reconstruction Finance Corporation had financed about half of these government projects, and its holdings at war's end included 450 oil tankers valued at more than $1.8 billion, refining capacity worth some $238 million, more than 50 percent of the nation's aluminum facilities, at least 15 percent of its steel manufacturing capacity, and almost 90 percent of the existing plants for the production of synthetic rubber, aircraft, ships, and magnesium.[2] The disposal of all of these properties promised to generate intense conflict, and the Inch Lines raised particularly troubling issues. Their great value plus their potential impact on postwar competition made them the focus of much political lobbying and public debate.

The tenor of the times placed an edge on these controversies. As American society hustled to return to peacetime life, demobilization became disorderly, even chaotic. The government had used some 165 nonmilitary agencies to manage the war effort, but according to the leading historian of this era, "at the end of 1946 almost nothing was left of that apparatus."[3] There was little system to reconversion. The war had been too long, too draining. Government officials and businessmen in Washington, like the country's soldiers and sailors, wanted to close up shop at once and resume their long-disrupted lives. The haste to dismantle wartime administrative agencies inevitably brought a measure of confusion and even corruption as war-induced cooperation quickly gave way to the pursuit of economic self-interest. An almost frantic tone and intense lobbying accompanied the government's disposal of surplus war properties.

The battle for the Inch Lines went forward on two fronts: public hearings before Congress and behind-the-scenes bargaining. In the public arena, the group that became Texas Eastern faced an uphill struggle. At open legislative hearings witnesses voiced their opinions on the proper use of the Inch Lines in a peacetime economy. Meanwhile, behind the scenes, various lobbyists sought first to shape the rules governing the bidding and then to determine the outcome of the bids. More than a year and a half passed between the time the government first prepared to dispose of the Inch Lines and the date the winning bid was announced in February of 1947. During these months Texas Eastern's founders needed all the political savvy they could muster.

The ground rules for the government disposal of the Inch Lines (and other government-financed properties) were first outlined before the end of the war. Congress set forth general guidelines in the Surplus Property Act of 1944, which required the Surplus Property Administration (SPA) to determine a general disposal policy for war surplus property. The act directed the SPA to consider the competitive ramifications of its sales. The SPA's mandate was to avoid creating monopolies while assisting in development of both new business and a competitive economic base. In addition, the 1944 legislation gave the United States government the authority to repossess and operate the properties during a national emergency.

The RFC, which held title to the Inch Lines, independently seeking to determine the best disposal policy for the system, hired the engineering firm of

Ford, Bacon & Davis to study the options for postwar use. On August 15, 1945, the firm recommended that the Inch Lines be converted for use in transporting natural gas. This nonbinding assessment encouraged the interest of those persons and companies desiring to place the Inch Lines in natural gas service. But all interested parties understood that this was merely the first salvo in what would be an extended battle. There would be no quick and easy government sale or lease of pipelines as important as these. They were too valuable. Their potential for commercial profit was too great. They were attractive to private investors and corporations in both oil and natural gas. Their disposal was also of considerable interest to coal companies whose northeastern markets might be threatened if the lines were to ship natural gas. Many of these parties to the issue could drum up political support for their positions, and that ensured that the struggle would continue long after the submittal of the Ford, Bacon, & Davis report.

The RFC also tested the oil and gas industries' interest in the pipelines. On September 14 it sent telegrams to 135 current and potential users of the pipelines. These messages announced that operation of both the Big and Little Big Inch pipelines would terminate within sixty days. Now that the government no longer needed the lines, the RFC officially invited "negotiations for these pipelines, either on a purchase or lease basis. All inquiries should be directed to the Washington office of the Corporation."[4]

Three days later Washington attorney J. Ross Gamble mailed E. Holley Poe a copy of that RFC release.[5] Poe had closely followed the federal government's plans for the Inch Lines since his work at the Petroleum Administration for War. Gamble, an attorney in the Washington firm of Leighton and Gamble, kept Poe informed of any developments that might influence the lines' disposal. Poe previously discussed his interest in the Inch Lines with Norris C. McGowen, president of United Gas Corporation, whose large gas supplies and extensive distribution system in the Gulf South made United Gas one of the nation's largest integrated natural gas companies. Poe and McGowen had worked together before the war in the American Gas Association, as well as in the gas industry's mobilization program. Poe knew that United Gas owned large natural gas reserves near the originating point of the Big Inch and that McGowen would have a strong interest in the ultimate use of the pipeline. Since at least April, 1945, Poe and Gamble — often working through George Fiser, United Gas's attorney in charge of Washington, D.C., affairs — kept McGowen apprised of congressional deliberation or action concerning the Inch Lines.

Poe had aroused McGowen's interest in the possibility of forming a group to bid on the lines, but no firm arrangements could be made until the RFC, other federal agencies, and Congress decided how to sell or lease them. In particular, Poe and McGowen were following the preparations for the upcoming hearings of the Special Committee Investigating Petroleum Resources, chaired by Senator Joseph C. O'Mahoney, of Wyoming. Congress intended these hearings to consider the fate of all significant government-owned petroleum resources, including the Inch Lines. The explicit purpose of the O'Mahoney hearings was to assist the Surplus Property Administration in determining the best postwar use for particular properties.

The hearings lasted for three days, from November 15 to 17, 1945, and they set the tone and outlined the basic arguments that would characterize the government's two-year-long efforts to dispose of the Inch Lines.[6] Twenty-eight representatives from government and various industries, including railroads, oil, gas, and coal, testified to the effect that the public interest would best be served by satisfying each particular industry's self-interest. Spokesmen for the natural gas industry argued that the Inch Lines should be converted to that fuel. This view found support among those in the petroleum industry who feared that the lines might disrupt existing transportation networks for petroleum products. Some small independent oil producers in the Southwest, however, broke ranks with the larger oil companies. They saw in the Inch Lines a form of transportation that might enable them to bypass the existing systems controlled by the major oil companies. Coal industry representatives strongly opposed the conversion of the Inch Lines to natural gas, which competed with coal and its by-products. Their arguments were seconded by the spokesmen for eastern railroaders, who derived a substantial proportion of their income from the transportation of coal.

At these hearings E. Holley Poe served as an associate member of the Committee on Postwar Disposal of Pipe Lines, which advocated a conversion of the Inch Lines to natural gas, a position he strongly supported. Poe, who identified himself as a partner in the natural gas consulting firm of E. Holley Poe and Associates, testified that a potentially very large natural gas market existed in the Northeast. With studies composed by his friend and business associate, Everette DeGolyer, Poe described how northeastern energy consumers could benefit from southwestern natural gas. He suggested that the Inch Lines could adequately supply natural gas to much of New York, New Jersey, and Pennsylvania. Poe agreed with some of the other witnesses from major oil companies who said that if the lines were not converted to natural gas, they should be held as a military asset and not used at all.

This testimony brought angry rejoinders from spokesmen for the coal industry. Before World War II most northeastern cities had supplied a part of their energy needs with manufactured gas, that is, gas made from coal and coke. But manufactured gas had a substantially lower heating content than natural gas, meaning that less natural gas would be required to supply the same amount of heat. In addition, the prevailing price of manufactured gas exceeded the projected price of natural gas delivered from Texas to the Northeast through the Inch Lines. In direct competition, natural gas would be a more economical and efficient fuel than the manufactured product. Those with a vested interest in manufactured gas — particularly the coal and railroad industries — saw their markets threatened. To attempt to forestall the economic decline of their industry, they lobbied hard for political advantage.

The friends of natural gas were equally adamant. Poe appeared at the hearings as a natural gas consultant without discussing his own interest in the Inch Lines. Other witnesses openly discussed their desire to purchase and operate the system. One of these was Claude A. Williams, an attorney representing natural gas producers in east Texas. Williams was a member of a group of investors who planned to form a corporation to buy the Inch Lines and use them to transport natural gas produced in Texas fields. After briefly summarizing the potential for large-volume natural gas sales to northeastern markets, Williams reviewed his plan to operate the Inch Lines as common carriers so that any producer could transport natural gas on a pro-rata basis. Williams also emphasized the potential role of the Inch Lines in reducing the amount of Texas gas then being wasted through flaring.

Charles H. Smith, a mining engineer, represented a group of businessmen interested in purchasing the Inch Lines and also transporting natural gas through them. During the war Smith served as the chief consulting engineer for the Bituminous Coal Administration; thus, he was actively aware of the coal industry's sensitivity to natural gas competition. However, he believed coal companies could regain any lost domestic market share by increasing coal export to Europe. The war devastated the European coal industry, and Smith believed Europe would require American coal. Generally, he maintained that the natural gas industry would provide great employment opportunities, both directly and indirectly, for returning soldiers and unemployed persons.[7]

Speakers for the coal and railroad interests aggressively challenged these arguments. A representative of the anthracite producers testified that natural gas transported through the Inch Lines would displace six million tons of coal. This figure translated into a loss of 11,650 jobs. He further argued that each of these unemployed workers would receive approximately $780 per annum in unemployment compensation, translating into a $9.1 million annual government expense. The testimony of the general counsel for the United Mine Workers was more general, but equally emphatic: The Inch Lines "should not be leased or sold to private industry or be governmentally operated or subsidized. They should be held intact in reserve against any future national emergency. . . . [Oil or natural gas transportation through the Inch Lines] would certainly tend to seriously interrupt and impede the post-war reconversion and recovery."[8] Spokesmen for eastern railroads left no doubt that their industry would be severely damaged by the conversion of the Inch Lines to natural gas. One such witness estimated that conversion would eliminate at least 20 percent, or seven million tons, of the yearly railroad coal shipments to metropolitan Philadelphia and New York City. Such a reduction in coal shipments would result in a loss in $16,450,000 gross revenues and 3,306 jobs in the railroad industry.[9]

After considering such testimony, as well as the Ford, Bacon & Davis report and its own research, the Surplus Property Administration issued its recommendations in January, 1946. The SPA report—commonly referred to as the Symington Report after SPA administrator W. Stuart Symington—stunned natural gas interests by advising that the Inch Lines be sold for petroleum transportation.[10] The report concluded that the lines were best suited to transport petroleum for small firms that did not own their own lines or have access to oil tankers. The Inch Lines, the report stated, "would be vital in the event of another emergency" and a "careful consideration of all the factors involved leads to the conclusion that the Big Inch and Little Big Inch should be kept in petroleum service."[11] The Symington Report favored allowing a newly created petroleum company to operate the lines.[12]

Disappointed by this report, the proponents of conversion to natural gas intensified their lobbying efforts. The American political system offered numerous channels of influence, and the founders of Texas Eastern explored more than a few of them in their efforts to undermine the recommendations of the Symington Report. While continuing his efforts to put together a group to bid for the Inch Lines, Poe participated in another set of government hearings on postwar conditions in the natural gas industry. These hearings, part of the Federal Power Commission's Natural Gas Investigation, took place throughout the nation between October 9, 1945, and August 2, 1947, with the last hearing in Washington, D.C. The FPC designed the hearings to elicit opinion on practically all aspects of the natural gas industry, hoping that these viewpoints would help the agency administer the Natural Gas Act and perhaps propose new legislation. The hearings gave Poe and others an excellent forum in which to make their case for the sale of the Inch Lines to a natural gas company. Their testimony again cited the great reserves of natural gas in the Southwest and the large unexploited markets in the heavily industrialized and populated Northeast.

Charles I. Francis, a partner in the Houston law firm of Vinson, Elkins, Weems and Francis and a specialist in oil and gas law, had an important role in these hearings. He served as counsel for the Governor's Committee of the State of Texas, as counsel for the American Petroleum Institute, and as an attorney for the Natural Gas Industry Committee. He coordinated and presented testimony at the Washington session. In February, 1946, Francis recommended that the committee hire Poe and his consulting company, E. Holley Poe and Associates, to testify at the hearings. When Francis and Poe met in February to discuss the new hearings, Poe related to Francis his interest in forming a group to bid on the Inch Lines.[13]

When Francis did not sign on, Poe sought to form an investment group with J. Howard Marshall, president of Ashland Oil and Refining Company, and Everette DeGolyer. Marshall had become assistant deputy administrator of the PAW immediately after DeGolyer had left the same position. Marshall's interest in the postwar disposition of the Inch Lines stemmed in part from the desire of Ashland's chairman, Paul Blazer, to keep the lines out of the petroleum transportation business, where they would compete with Ashland's own system. Marshall and Sidney Swensrud, vice president of Standard Oil Company of Ohio, testified at the government hearings in favor of using the Inch Lines for natural gas and even went so far as to bankroll a public relations campaign to promote natural gas use.[14] Marshall's direct involvement in the venture ended, however, when this group's New York–based financial support withdrew from the project.[15]

While Poe tried in vain to organize his investment group, other entrepreneurs interested in using the Inch Lines for natural gas submitted unsolicited informal bids to the War Assets Administration (WAA), an agency of the RFC. Charles H. Smith and Claude A. Williams, both of whom had testified at the November hearings, had already formed companies to bid on the lines. Smith organized Big Inch Oil, Incorporated, and offered $40 million for the Little Big Inch for petroleum transport; he formed a second company, Big Inch Gas, Incorporated, to offer $40 million for the Big Inch, to be used to transport natural gas. Williams and his partners, who had formed Trans-Continental Gas Pipe Line Corporation in February, offered to pay $40 million for both Inch Lines for use in shipping natural gas. The WAA did not officially respond to these informal bids. Instead, the Surplus Property Administration began plans for a public bid to take place within six months of the report date.[16]

Despite continued interest in converting the lines to natural gas, the Symington Report's recommendation to maintain them for oil transportation became official disposal policy. On June 7, 1946, the War Assets Administration announced that it would hold an auction for the Inch Lines. All bids were due by July 30, and they would be read the next day. The WAA placed advertisements for the auction in thirty-eight newspapers and five oil trade journals. The ads clearly indicated that the Surplus Property Administration Report mandated that the Big and Little Big Inch remain in petroleum service, in part so that they would be available during a national emergency. The ads stated that the WAA would give highest priority to bidders who would use the Inch Lines to transport petroleum, but the agency also invited offers from those interested in using the Inch Lines to transport natural gas. In particular, the agency encouraged bids offering small and independent petroleum operators "the opportunity of participating in both the use and acquisition of this facility in whole or in part."[17]

E. Holley Poe responded to these ads by again asking Charles Francis to join him in an effort to organize a group to bid. This time Francis accepted, but with the stipulation that he would have discretion as to the persons who would be asked to join. Poe agreed. As he and Francis began planning their bid, they were also preparing their testimony for the final Natural Gas Investigation hearing to take place in Washington, D.C., between June 17 and August 2, 1946.

Together, Francis and Poe returned to McGowen, who now considered becoming a majority stockholder in their proposed enterprise. With the Inch Lines under his control, McGowen's United Gas would become the dominant natural gas company in the country. United already controlled large southwestern gas fields; the Inch Lines would give the company access to huge northeastern markets. But balanced against this vision was McGowen's fear of antitrust. Of conservative temperament, he seemed reluctant to take the risks involved in what was, after all, an extremely ambitious undertaking. He was comfortable with the enormous system he already controlled and was justly proud that United Gas was already the nation's largest carrier of natural gas.[18] Even before World War II his company had proclaimed its commitment to a strategy of focusing on "the Gulf South," and involvement with the Inch Lines would blur this focus. United Gas was also dealing with the problem of consolidating its diverse holdings to comply with the stipulations of the Public Utility Holding Company Act of 1935. McGowen did not relish entering a new venture that might raise still another series of regulatory challenges. For all of these reasons, he backed away from the opportunity to expand United Gas dramatically by entering the business of the cross-country shipment of natural gas.

Instead of pursuing a direct interest in the Poe group, McGowen pledged to assist indirectly, creating a community of interests. United Gas would thus get the opportunity to sell large quantities of natural gas to the Poe group if they won the bid. In this way, McGowen could be assured of a large market for his company's natural gas without direct exposure to the risks of acquiring and operating two new pipelines.

McGowen cemented this relationship by providing the Poe group with some managerial expertise. The group needed a professional gas company manager to help plan the bid and to manage the company if they acquired the pipelines. Francis's first choice was Reginald H. Hargrove, vice-president of United Gas and second-in-command to McGowen. Poe suggested either J. Howard Marshall or Charles Pratt Rather, president of Southern Natural Gas Company, but Francis prevailed. With McGowen's approval, he asked Hargrove to join the new enterprise. Hargrove initially agreed to assist the group on a consulting basis while on a leave of absence from United Gas. Later, Hargrove would assume the founders' stock interest originally offered to McGowen.[19] Francis also invited into the group J. R. Parten, an independent oil man and former director of the Transportation Division of the PAW. But Parten declined, explaining that his close involvement with the Inch Lines during the war disqualified him from participating in their commercial development.[20] Few others seemed to share such qualms. Washington fairly teemed with "insiders" jockeying for position.

In early June Poe, Francis, DeGolyer, and Hargrove began planning their bid.[21] On June 14 Poe, Hargrove, and Francis met with Frank Andrews in New York, and Andrews joined the group. Andrews was a cousin of Hargrove's wife and president of the New Yorker Hotel. He had close ties with the Manufacturers Trust Company, which owned equity in the New Yorker. He also had potentially valuable financial and political connections. In particular, he was a friend of former hotel man George Allen, an influential lobbyist, a Truman insider, and a director of the RFC.[22] As a director of the RFC, Allen was also a director of the War Assets Corporation, the predecessor agency to the War Assets Administration. As an "insider," his assistance could prove crucial to the Poe group. Through Andrews's introduction, Allen met in New York with Hargrove, Poe, and Andrews to discuss the Inch Lines, and Francis planned "on having a talk with Mr. Allen in Washington next week, after he had conferred here on Monday with Hargrove and Poe."[23]

The Poe group, which still did not have financial backing, was concerned about the economic and political clout of the rival bidders. Hargrove and Francis feared that an alliance of powerful Houston businessmen was also preparing a bid. Francis sought information from his law partner, Judge James A. Elkins. As the dominant figure in one of Houston's leading law firms, Vinson, Elkins, Weems and Francis, and one of its leading banks, City National Bank, Elkins was a powerful, well-connected member of Houston's business and civic elite. Francis wrote to Elkins requesting that he "confidentially ascertain whether or not Jesse Jones is in any way interested in placing a bid for these facilities. Rumor has reached us that along with George Butler and possibly the Brown Brothers and Gus Wortham, he is contemplating making a bid for these same facilities."[24] Jesse Jones, Butler, George and Herman Brown, Gus Wortham, and Judge Elkins were all members of what political commentators called "The 8F Crowd," a coalition of Houston business leaders who regularly met in Herman Brown's suite 8F in the Lamar Hotel in Houston. As the former chairman of the Reconstruction Finance Corporation, Jones's participation — either directly or covertly — in a rival bid would have presented a formidable obstacle.[25]

Elkins's response to Francis's letter is lost to history, but shortly thereafter Francis asked Judge Elkins to contact his friends the Brown brothers to inquire if they would be interested in joining the Poe group as financial backers. This merger offer was accepted, and it proved to be a dramatic turning point in their efforts. George and Herman Brown brought to the group great financial resources, engineering experience, political connections, and — above all — forceful leadership. George Brown quickly became the dominant force in the project, a status he maintained in Texas Eastern until his retirement as the company's chairman in 1971.[26]

George Brown was well prepared by both training and temperament to assume such a role. He was first and foremost an engineer, with training at Rice Institute and a degree in mining engineering (1922) from the Colorado School of Mines. After a near-fatal accident in a Butte, Montana, copper mine, he had returned to Texas to enter the construction firm founded earlier by his older brother Herman. The firm of Brown & Root grew gradually, first by building roads and bridges and later by undertaking a variety

The Texas Eastern Promoters. *Left to right:* E. Holley Poe, Reginald H. Hargrove, George R. Brown, Herman Brown, Charles I. Francis; *inset:* Everette DeGolyer

of public works projects during the New Deal. In this work the Brown brothers honed their engineering skills as well as the political talents that were so much a part of successful bids for government construction projects. With the outbreak of World War II the Browns moved aggressively into defense work by creating a major shipbuilding facility at Green's Bayou, on the Houston Ship Channel — this, despite the fact that Brown & Root had never before built a ship. The company also completed several minor projects on the Inch Lines and experienced firsthand the benefits of natural gas as a fuel in its shipyards.[27]

With the end of the war, Brown & Root was poised to surge forward into the ranks of the nation's major construction firms. The company had a track record of engineering and financial success. The brothers were well connected in Washington, particularly to the up-and-coming politician, Congressman Lyndon B. Johnson. They were prominent in a cluster of Houston businessmen who came to exercise considerable influence on the city's development, and their company was an important part of a nexus of economic institutions

42

that also included First City National Bank, Vinson & Elkins law firm, and American General Insurance.

The move into natural gas was a logical step for George and Herman Brown. While men like Poe and DeGolyer had gravitated toward the Inch Lines from the perspective of the supply and demand for gas, the Browns came to them as expansion-minded, Houston-based engineers. Brown & Root needed new projects to utilize the resources at its Green's Bayou shipyards. There was no more obvious choice to a construction company with a Houston Ship Channel site than the booming oil-gas-petrochemical complex growing along the ship channel. In February of 1946 Brown & Root announced the creation of new petroleum and chemical divisions based at Green's Bayou and focused on the design and engineering of gas compressors, pipelines, and related projects. Brown & Root had built several small regional pipelines for natural gas before World War II, and the company was eager to expand this work. Thus, it was not surprising that the Browns quickly agreed to join the Poe group, whose plans were obviously compatible with their own. Brown & Root could only win.[28]

George Brown brought to the Inch Line bid more than simply an impulse to diversify. He also brought attitudes and an approach to business decision-making which subsequently shaped much of the evolution of Texas Eastern. He was an ardent engineer, one who relished building massive projects: "What was important was the romance of engineering. Engineers were men who went to far places, who built things all over the world."[29] The Brown brothers were twentieth-century Texas variants on the first generation of freewheeling industrialists who had remade the American economy in the nineteenth century. Their aggressive approach to business was best captured in the observations of a friend and colleague during the formative years of Texas Eastern, August Belmont, of the Dillon, Read & Company investment house. Belmont's name recalled the era of "high capitalism" in the nineteenth century. His great-grandfather had been a dominant figure in New York banking in the Gilded Age. When Belmont came down from New York to Houston to work with the Browns on the financing of Texas Eastern, he noted that "they were more or less, like I'm sure a lot of those New Yorkers were in the Civil War — my great-grandfather, and all."[30]

The Browns generated fierce criticism from outsiders and fierce loyalty from their colleagues. The brothers built enduring economic and political alliances on the basis of long-term friendships cemented during quail hunts and football games and protected from public criticism by an almost obsessive unwillingness to talk with outsiders. They helped imbue Texas Eastern with many of his personal traits: a commitment to engineering excellence; a sense of family with colleagues; and an "us versus them" attitude in dealing with outsiders.

The addition of the Brown brothers completed the basic group that Poe had begun to organize in 1945. During June and July of 1946 they acceler-

ated their operations. While Poe, Francis, DeGolyer, and Hargrove participated in the natural gas hearings during the day, they held late-night planning
sessions along with J. Ross Gamble to prepare the bid. Poe and DeGolyer
testified at the hearings on behalf of the Natural Gas Industry Committee,
a committee organized by the Independent Natural Gas Association. Hargrove spoke as a representative of United Gas.

As his colleagues testified, Charles Francis worked with J. Ross Gamble
on the legal and political aspects of the bid. Francis wanted to study the
original contracts authorizing the operations of the Inch Lines. Gamble obtained for him copies of the contracts made between the Defense Supplies
Corporation (an agency of the RFC) and War Emergency Pipe Lines, Incorporated (the operating company of the Inch Lines).[31] In mid-July Gamble
contacted the United States Corporation Company (USCC) regarding the
procedures necessary to incorporate a company to bid on the lines. He requested that USCC reserve the name Colonial Pipe Line Company, and the
name was confirmed on the same day.[32] With this name reserved, the group
would submit its bid through E. Holley Poe & Associates, on behalf of Poe,
DeGolyer, Francis, and the Brown brothers.[33] Poe, who had previously done
other work with the investment firm of Dillon, Read & Company, spent the
latter half of July working with the firm to determine with accuracy the value
of the Inch Lines.

The group labored hard on the intricacies of the bidding process, including
the all-important political aspects. Charles Francis, a legal advisor to Lyndon Johnson, relentlessly pursued the political ties that might ease the way
to a successful bid. The Brown brothers had already formed a close business
and social relationship with Johnson, and Francis talked to the Congressman
about assisting the Poe group in its attempt to acquire the Inch Lines. Johnson reportedly told Francis, "Charley, I can't do that. Tommy Corcoran is
on the other side." Corcoran, an advisor to Franklin Roosevelt and an associate
of Johnson's during the New Deal, had already allied himself with another
group of bidders. Francis said later that "Lyndon took no part in helping
out with the original sale, unless there's something I didn't know. George
Brown and he were awfully close."[34] In addition to those "close" ties, the
Poe group had the assistance of Donald Cook, who subsequently became
a highly trusted advisor to Johnson. Cook helped the group complete its
research for the bid.[35] While political influence is quite difficult to trace, there
can be no doubt that the Poe group included several well-connected, experienced businessmen and lobbyists who explored every available avenue of
political influence. They probably succeeded.

On July 30, 1946, the Poe group submitted a bid for the Inch Lines on
the basis of either a purchase or a lease. For a purchase, the group agreed
to pay $80 million, plus a flat fee for all natural gas transported over 120
billion cubic feet (bcf) per year until a total price of $100 million had been
reached. Alternatively, the group offered to lease the lines for forty years

at a minimum annual payment of $6.5 million. The group indicated that it intended to organize Colonial Pipe Line Company if its bid proved successful.[36]

The Poe offer was one of sixteen valid bids received by the WAA. In a public hearing held on July 31, WAA personnel opened and read bids.[37] The process of choosing the winning entry was problematic, in part because the WAA had not provided a standardized bidding format. The most difficult problem was comparing the monetary value of each bid. The bidders offered a combination of cash, debentures, payments based upon gas sold, and other arrangements. Another difficulty arose because the highest cash offers came from companies proposing to use the lines to transport natural gas, and this was not the WAA's first priority.

The WAA began organizing the bids in terms of their upfront cash component value only, not the total bid price. Using this format, the highest bids came from firms intending to transport natural gas through the Inch Lines. Both Trans-Continental Gas Pipe Line Corporation and the Big Inch Natural Gas Transmission Company offered $85 million in cash. The Poe group had the next highest cash offer, $80 million. The bid of Charles H. Smith, representing Big Inch Oil, Incorporated, adhered most closely to the WAA's disposal policy favoring use of the lines to transport oil, but Smith offered only $66 million in cash. This was significantly less than the value of natural gas use.

Despite the difficulties of comparing the value of each bid, the agency announced on August 2 that it would follow the Symington Report's recommendations in analyzing the bids.[38] Thus, bids proposing to transport oil received highest priority, followed by oil and gas combinations, then gas transmission only, and finally other proposals. The following week, the WAA required all bidders to submit data by September 9 (later extended to September 16) which substantiated their bids. Even with the additional information, the WAA remained unable to choose the winning bid.

In the meantime, Charles Francis and the Poe group lobbied hard for the Inch Lines to be sold for natural gas transmission. Early in August Francis met with Gen. John J. O'Brien, a WAA official, to discuss the merits of his group's bid. After the meeting, he sent O'Brien a letter urging him to consider several points about the Poe bid before he disallowed the bids for natural gas use.[39] The Poe group, he said, would maintain the lines in good condition, ready to be converted back to oil during a national emergency. Francis's main argument was that the Inch Lines could market the tremendous amount of natural gas currently being wasted in Texas. Most of this gas was so-called casinghead gas produced from oil wells. Although some operators reinjected the gas into the well to sustain enough pressure to keep the oil flowing, many more simply flared the gas as waste. Francis argued that it was a travesty to waste natural gas when it could be used to alleviate the fuel shortage in the eastern United States. Francis also met with Col.

Ernest O. Thompson, the head of the Texas Railroad Commission, to discuss the bidding. A few days later, Thompson wrote War Assets administrator Gen. Robert Littlejohn, essentially verifying Francis's information regarding the tremendous amount of gas being wasted in Texas.

Francis pressed the issue on every front. He discussed the bid with H. S. Smith, a special investigator for the House Surplus Property Investigating Committee. Smith met with representatives of each of the sixteen bidders during his investigation. Francis "urged him to immediately commence an investigation of the proceedings that had been followed in offering these lines for sale [and] . . . pointed out that there were no standards for bidding, no good faith deposits required, and that the whole matter had been handled in a very unbusiness like manner, detrimental not only to the best interest of substantial bidders, but also detrimental to the best interest of the Government."[40]

While Francis was on the offensive promoting natural gas, former Secretary of the Interior Harold Ickes attempted to "expose" the Poe group. In his syndicated column, "Man to Man," Ickes published an article titled "'Uncle Jesse's' Bid for Oil Pipelines Seen Loaded Two Ways for Monopoly." Ickes charged that former RFC chairman Jesse Jones was heavily involved in the "so-called E. Holley Poe bid" for the Inch Lines. Ickes advised: "If the story is true, the War Assets Administration had better do some keen sniffing because Uncle Jesse has no peer among horse traders that I have known." Ickes also believed that Houston attorney George Butler, "husband of Jesse's only heir and custodian of many of Jesse's enterprises, both business and political, is one of the E. Holley Poe crowd." After raising doubts about the propriety of Jones's involvement, Ickes gratuitously noted that in general he approved of Poe's bid.

Ickes's article put the Poe group on the defensive. Both Charlie Francis and Poe informed Ickes, by letter and in person, that George Butler and Jesse Jones were not associated with their bid. In addition, Butler issued a personal statement denying his involvement in any group planning to purchase the two Inch Lines. Ickes later replied to both Poe and Francis: "I cannot see that the column did your group any harm. On the contrary, it served notice on Jesse Jones that he was more or less suspect and he might be disposed to keep his hands off. That is really what I had in mind in writing the column."[41] Ickes's article also seemed to raise eye brows at the WAA. The day after his article appeared, the agency requested that all bidders send it a list of the "identity and business connections of all individuals or firms associated with the particular bids."[42] Poe responded tersely to L. Gray Marshall, of the Utilities Branch of the WAA, that his original proposal and additional data contained the names of each person associated with his bid.[43] No known public or private documents ever linked Jones to the Poe group, but his close personal and business relationship with others in the group probably made Ickes's suspicions seem reasonable to some observers — especially those familiar with the Texas style of business.

As it turned out, the Ickes sword cut both ways, against and then for the Poe group. In his correspondence with Poe and Francis, Ickes wrote that he believed the Inch Lines should be used to transport natural gas. Ickes subsequently reaffirmed in his syndicated columns that the Inch Lines should transport natural gas and not oil. An enemy of United Mine Workers chief John L. Lewis, Ickes wrote in one column that natural gas transported by the Inch Lines would "end John L. Lewis' stranglehold on the economy of the United States."[44] Lewis's mine workers went on strike during World War II, thereby aggravating energy shortages throughout the nation, particularly in the Northeast. Ickes shared the belief, along with others in government and business, that the threat of continued mine workers' strikes could be blocked by the availability of alternative fuels such as natural gas.

This entire episode cannot be dismissed as just another example of Ickes's "shoot-from-the-hip" approach to political infighting. More was involved. The Inch Lines had attracted the attention of many prominent figures from business and government, some of whom associated themselves with one of the bidders. "Former Big Names in Government Are Involved in Bids for Pipelines," a contemporary newspaper headline said. This article noted a few of the former government officials most prominent in the bidding. The officers and directors of the Big Inch Natural Gas Transmission Company included former Ohio Senator Robert Bulkley, former Justice Roberts of the Supreme Court, and Admiral Emory Land, former chairman of the Maritime Commission. Thomas Corcoran, a former aid to Franklin Roosevelt, was an attorney for Big Inch, as was William S. Youngman, a former general counsel for the FPC and a former FPC commissioner. Former trustbuster Thurman Arnold and one-time Undersecretary of Interior Abe Fortas were listed as the attorneys for another bidder, American Public Utilities.[45] The revolving door between government and business was spinning rapidly in the years of demobilization, and many once prominent government officials were attracted by the prospect of acquiring the Inch Lines and other war surplus properties. The participation of Jesse Jones — or, for that matter, Harold Ickes — in such activities would have been newsworthy, but not unusual. Those seriously interested in acquiring the lines had no choice but to use all of the political influence they could muster as the bidding process slowly drifted forward.

In mid-October rumors surfaced in the press suggesting that Big Inch Oil, Incorporated, headed by Charles H. Smith, was the front runner in the bid for the Inch Lines.[46] In an article in the trade journal *Gas*, Elliot Taylor claimed that the WAA was likely to declare Big Inch Oil, Incorporated the winner of the auction. Indeed, that firm's bid had the highest cash value of any bid, which also followed the SPA's disposal policy.[47] In Chicago, Poe defended his bid to a reporter and observed that the WAA would be responsible for the continuing waste of natural gas in the Southwest if the pipelines remained in oil service.[48]

By mid-November the WAA had not announced a winning bid. It appeared that natural gas interests in particular were attempting to prevent the agency from awarding the pipelines to Big Inch Oil, Incorporated, or to any other oil company. It was John L. Lewis, however, who inadvertently encouraged the WAA to reconsider its disposal policy for the Inch Lines. Lewis declared void the contract between the government and his labor union, an agreement reached during the previous May. The resulting strike proved short-lived, as the government (which still controlled the properties) forced the workers back to the mines. But the publicity surrounding Lewis's actions and the growing fear of fuel shortages in Appalachia gave the WAA an added rationale for favoring the conversion of the Inch Lines to natural gas.

On November 19 the House Select Committee to Investigate the Disposition of Surplus Property convened in order to examine again the Inch Line issue. During the first day of testimony, WAA chairman Robert Littlejohn announced that the agency would reject all bids for the pipelines. An interagency committee studying the Inch Lines reported that "the interest of national defense could be met regardless of whether the pipe lines be used for natural gas, petroleum and its products, or a combination thereof. . . ." The WAA wanted to start over because "the bids had been invited on a restricted basis, which precluded the government from securing the maximum net cash return."[49] In this regard, Littlejohn noted that the WAA estimated the Inch Lines to be worth $113,700,000. By transforming the bid policy for the Inch Lines from a "best overall bid from an oil firm" to a "highest bid," the WAA was essentially repudiating the Symington Report. The report's legitimacy was already in dispute because administrator Symington told a congressional committee that a young and inexperienced aide, not familiar with the oil or gas industries, had written the document.[50]

During the hearings the worsening energy shortage in Appalachia stirred the committee to consider the stated desire of Tennessee Gas & Transmission Company (the "&" was subsequently dropped) to lease the Inch Lines on an interim basis in order to sell gas in Appalachia.[51] The select committee invited Tennessee's president, Gardiner Symonds, to travel to Washington and discuss a lease. On November 29 Tennessee proposed such a temporary lease, stating that the "sole purpose of its proposal is to attempt to effect a temporary connection of these lines with the existing facilities of the Tennessee company in order to meet the emergent need for natural gas in the Appalachian area. This proposal covers only a short term lease and does not contemplate permanent operation of these lines."[52] In addition to Tennessee Gas, Big Inch Natural Gas Transmission Company, Big Inch Oil, Incorporated, and Trans-Continental Gas Pipe Line Corporation met with representatives of the Department of the Interior, FPC, Army-Navy Petroleum Board, and War

Assets Administration to determine how best to utilize the Inch Lines to alleviate the Appalachian fuel shortage.

Tennessee Gas had not bid on the Inch Lines in July, but it now convinced the government to select its proposal to operate the lines temporarily. The WAA approved its lease on December 3, 1946. Tennessee did not convert the original oil pumping stations to transmit natural gas. The firm flowed gas through the line's compressors, using only the force of the natural gas emerging from the wells. This allowed Tennessee to deliver gas immediately to four major Appalachian customers in dire need of the fuel: Ohio Fuel Gas Company; Manufacturers Light and Heat Company; Kentucky Natural Gas Company; and East Ohio Gas Company. Tennessee had 120 million cubic feet per day (mmcf/d) available for these customers. Tennessee agreed to a sale price of $0.24 per mcf (thousand cubic feet), the firm also agreed to pay the WAA a rental fee of $0.06 per mcf. In addition, Tennessee Gas officials stated that their firm would spend $250,000 to improve the flow of natural gas through the lines. Tennessee's operation of the Inch Lines proved their viability for transporting natural gas and gave that company an apparent edge in the next round of the bidding.

The increasing severity of the Appalachian energy shortage prompted the FPC to set new emergency service rules on another firm, Panhandle Eastern Pipe Line Company. Panhandle's system originated in the Texas Panhandle and southwestern Oklahoma and extended into the large midwestern markets. The FPC required Panhandle Eastern to deliver gas to Appalachian gas distribution companies and curtail its interruptible industrial customers. Natural gas was needed in the Northeast not only for industry but for residential consumers suffering from inadequate existing fuel supplies.

The Poe group did not enter the contest to gain temporary use of the Inch Lines. Instead, it continued to work behind the scenes towards a successful bid. On December 16 Charles Francis wrote Littlejohn and made three suggestions concerning the guidelines for a new round of bidding. Francis suggested that earnest money accompany each bid, that the successful bidder be allowed to acquire an FPC–mandated certificate of public convenience and necessity before paying the full cost of the pipeline, and that the WAA set a time limit for concluding the entire process of acquiring a certificate and financing the lines.[53] All of these recommendations ultimately became government policy, attesting either to the growing influence of Francis or to the fact that he and Littlejohn were thinking along the same lines. At the same time, A. D. Green, of United Gas, submitted a detailed evaluation to George Brown of various estimated purchase prices for the Inch Lines based on a gas sales price between $0.24 to $0.26 mcf and a system capacity of between 80 to 95 percent. Green based his highest figure, $133 million, on a sale price of $0.26 per mcf with the system operating at 95 percent capacity.

On December 18 Littlejohn described the WAA's new disposal policy for the Inch Lines. He stated that the Inch Lines could transport either natural gas or oil, the high bid would be the winning bid, and the new owner of the lines must maintain the oil pumping equipment in case the government decided to repossess the lines in a national emergency.[54] These new provisions put oil and gas bidders on an equal footing. But the provision calling for the maintenance of the pumping stations presented a problem to the bidders. Each bidder would have to determine — without a ruling from the FPC — whether or not they would have to include those stations in their calculation of the line's rate base. An oil bidder could continue to use the existing pumping stations while a gas bidder would have to retain the oil stations and build new gas compressors as well.[55]

The Poe group followed Littlejohn's actions with intense interest because the rules he established might well decide the winning bid. On December 24 J. Ross Gamble reported that Littlejohn and L. Gray Marshall, a WAA executive, were the two persons involved in preparing the new guidelines. Gamble noted that Littlejohn had left the previous night for his home in South Carolina without releasing any information. "For what it may be worth," Gamble wrote, "we are assured that General Littlejohn intends to follow the program which he announced at his last appearance before the Slaughter Committee; that he intends to make it possible for oil and gas bidders to have an equal opportunity; that he expects, subject to action of Congress, to sell the lines to the highest bidder."[56]

Littlejohn moved quickly. On December 27 he announced the mechanics of the new auction. All bids were due by noon on February 8, 1947, at the WAA box located in the Washington, D.C., post office. Unlike the first auction, this time each bidder would submit its offer on a standardized form. There was also a strict timetable, broken down into four payments, set forth for the purchase of the lines. First, each bidder had to submit a $100,000 check with the bid as a deposit. Next, the winning bidder would pay $1,000,000 after the WAA issued a letter of intent to sell the lines. Third, a payment of $4,000,000 would be made on or before the day the winning bidder began transporting fuel through the pipelines. Fourth, the final payment was due within nine months from the date the WAA issued its letter of intent to sell the lines.

At this point, the Poe group reorganized. On January 30, 1947, three incorporators met at No. 100 West Tenth Street in Wilmington, Delaware, and established Texas Eastern Transmission Corporation.[57] The incorporators nominated George R. Brown, E. Holley Poe, Charles I. Francis, J. Ross Gamble, and Warren J. Dale, an attorney associated with Vinson, Elkins, Weems and Francis, to serve as directors of the company for one year. The directors held a second meeting at the Wall Street offices of the law firm Shearman and Sterling and Wright at 20 Exchange Place. At this meeting they elected George Brown as chairman of the board and E. Holley Poe as president. Charles Francis became general counsel as well as resident agent, with offices to be established in Houston. The directors also agreed to make an official request to United Gas Corporation asking that Reginald H. Hargrove be allowed to take a temporary leave from that company to assist in the creation of Texas Eastern.

Now the organizers had to put some money on the line. At Texas Eastern's first board meeting George Brown reported that thirty-five persons were interested in subscribing to the company's initial stock offering of 150,000 shares priced at $1.00 each. The money collected from this stock offering was to be used for the bid deposit. Twenty-eight persons actually subscribed to the stock, although the five directors held 65 percent. George and Herman Brown each purchased 14.25 percent. They also lent $67,500 to nine persons so that they could purchase stock for themselves. The loan required each borrower to grant George Brown proxy for voting of the shares for a period of two years after February 5, 1947. In return, the borrower had one year, or two under an extension, to make repayment, although in the event the bid failed and the money was forfeited, the borrower was not obligated to repay the loan.

The other large stockholders included Reginald Hargrove, who owned about 8 percent. Hargrove also made sure that his three sons would be stockholders; each of them received 3,000 shares, or a 2 percent interest. Reginald Hargrove's cousin by marriage, Frank Andrews, purchased 9 percent of the original Texas Eastern stock. The other original stockholders included Poe, DeGolyer, Francis, Judge Elkins (of Vinson, Elkins, Weems and Francis), J. Ross Gamble, Justin and Randolph Querbes (business associates of Hargrove's), Gus Wortham (a Houston businessman originally rumored to be part of Jesse Jones's group to bid on the lines), and eleven partners of Dillon, Read & Company, including August Belmont.

Belmont, then vice president of Dillon, Read and Company, became an important partner in the early planning and financing of Texas Eastern. He was familiar with Texas business, having done some work for United Gas and N. C. McGowen while with a different investment house, Bonbright & Company, Incorporated, before World War II. After serving in the war he joined Dillon, Read and took up the cause of Texas Eastern after his firm had already begun preliminary work for the new venture. Belmont was the logical choice to take up the financing for the proposal now that a second bid would be held. His name recalled the era of late nineteenth-century capitalism when his great grandfather, August Belmont, served as the correspondent banker for the Belmont family and created the Belmont Stakes horse race; his grandfather had financed part of the original New York City subway system.

Under Belmont's direction the firm's financial resources were quickly enlarged for the bidding process. The board announced that some of the original stockholders, along with Dillon, Read, had loaned $1.35 million to Texas Eastern to assist in financing the bid. This capital was earmarked for the $1 million second payment that would be required if the WAA issued its letter of intent to sell to Texas Eastern. The directors also marshalled letters and reports from United Gas Pipe Line Company, E. DeGolyer, of DeGolyer & MacNaughton, and Dillon, Read to be included as supplementary documentation in support of the company's bid.

On the following day the directors met at E. Holley Poe's office on Pine Street in Manhattan to continue discussions on the upcoming bid, and each director received sample bid forms for inspection and comment. By this time Manufacturers Trust Company agreed to make a $4 million loan to Texas Eastern. This money was earmarked for the prescribed third payment to the WAA to be made at the beginning of the winner's interim lease of the Inch Lines. The loan reflected in part the influence of Judge James Elkins, whose Houston bank maintained correspondent banking ties with Manufacturers Trust, whose president, Harvey Gibson, agreed to help finance the Texas Eastern deal.[58]

Capital had been secured for the first three payments to the WAA, but financing for the fourth payment was another problem altogether and was put off until the company found out whether its bid was successful. Another board meeting took place at the Shoreham Hotel, in Washington, D.C., on the afternoon before the February 8 deadline. Directors Warren Dale and J. Ross Gamble resigned their directorships earlier in the day, and the board elected Herman Brown and Everette DeGolyer to replace them. Five persons attended this meeting: George Brown, Charles Francis, E. Holley Poe, Reginald Hargrove, and August Belmont. Later that evening these five made final preparations for the bid and settled on the total amount to be offered. Although various government reports placed dollar figures on the original construction costs of the Inch Lines, there was considerable uncertainty about their value for the purposes of the auction. The Brown brothers studied engineering data on the lines, but this was not to be a contest in which the company with the most precise evaluation would win. Rather, it was a winner-take-all scramble to be won by the group which placed the highest bid — and then found financing to support its offer.

To get the process going, Charles Francis suggested that each person write on a piece of paper his own idea of the best bid. Texas Eastern's banker, August Belmont, already had his magic number well in mind. Before coming to the meeting, he met with Douglas Dillon "and told him that I felt the Texas Eastern people would come to the meeting convinced that, in my capacity as the banker, I would be the stumbling block against the submission of a truly competitive bid. I told him that I felt they would come up with a price of around $125 million. . . ."[59] Belmont convinced Dillon that "the project could stand a price of $140 million" and received from Dillon permission to propose an offer as high as $135 million and authority to approve one up to $140 million.

During the first round of proposals that night, Belmont's bid was the highest. Just as he had predicted, the other participants were surprised. They had expected their banker to be conservative. As the discussion continued, the participants altered their proposals until finally they had a set of firm propositions, ranging from a low of $135 million (Belmont) to a high of $158,757,000 (E. Holley Poe).[60] At 2:00 A.M., they agreed to bid $143 million. George Brown was concerned that another company might bid the same amount. One of the participants suggested a less rounded figure of $143,123,456. E. Holley Poe wanted his lucky number "7" in the bid. Finally the group agreed on $143,127,000, with the understanding that Belmont would contact Dillon the next morning to get his approval. Ted Wadsworth, an assistant to Belmont, had been waiting for the group to finish their meeting so that he could fill in the amount of the bid on the typed bid form and deliver the papers to the post office the next day. But Reginald Hargrove had other plans. He insisted on sleeping with the bid forms under his pillow that night and keeping them in his sole possession until they were deposited.

The next day was February 8. Four persons, including August Belmont, Ted Wadsworth, J. Ross Gamble, and attorney George Pidot, from Shearman and Sterling and Wright, placed Texas Eastern's bid in the War Assets Administration post office box.[61] To both celebrate the occasion and establish evidence that they turned in their bid before noon, they paid a photographer to snap their picture in front of the clock at the post office. As added insurance, Gamble received permission from the Postmaster General, a personal friend, to sit in the building's gallery and keep an eye on the WAA post office box in order to prevent a competitor from viewing or removing the bids.[62]

On Monday, February 10, the WAA opened the bids.[63] Texas Eastern appeared to win the Inch Lines with the high bid of $143,127,000, an amount only $3 million below the $145.8 million the RFC paid to construct the lines. Claude A. Williams and Associates, representing the Transcontinental Gas Pipe Line Corporation, submitted the second highest bid.[64] Tennessee Gas and Transmission submitted the third highest bid of $123,700,000. The top three bidders were all natural gas companies. The low bid was submitted by J. W. Crotty of Dallas, who pasted a dollar bill on the bid form, allowing sixty cents for the Big Inch and forty cents for the Little Big Inch. The dollar was accompanied with the words, "Payment in full."

In a highly politicized bidding process, Texas Eastern Corporation emerged victorious. After the successful bid Herman Brown told Belmont, "George is just lucky."[65] But of course, more than luck had gone into this victory. E. Holley Poe's vision had attracted others like Everette DeGolyer, Charles Francis, Reginald Hargrove, and George and Herman Brown. This group controlled powerful economic, financial, and political resources, and it proved quite adept at using them to win the Inch Lines. In order to make good use of these properties, the group would now have to prove equally adept at creating and managing a natural gas transmission company.

Chapter 3

CREATION OF A GAS COMPANY

Texas Eastern now had to become an operating natural gas pipeline. Because it purchased the Inch Lines from the government instead of building new facilities, the corporation's early history differed sharply from that of its primary competitors. Other companies planned new lines based on projected patterns of supply and demand. Texas Eastern began its existence with two major lines in place and hustled to gather supplies on one end and extend the lines to prospective customers on the other. Whereas other companies could choose the route and design of the lines they constructed, Texas Eastern had to adapt lines originally built to carry oil and oil products for the transportation of natural gas.

As Texas Eastern sought to create a new company, the Federal Power Commission was busy attempting to define a regulatory regime appropriate to the postwar era. The FPC originally had been created in 1920 to license hydroelectric projects on public lands and navigable waterways, but the Natural Gas Act of 1938 gave it new powers over the interstate shipment of natural gas. In spirit and powers, the newly strengthened FPC was very much a product of the New Deal. Particularly strong in the 1930s was a tendency to define the old phrases "public utility" and "natural monopoly" quite broadly, a tendency which led to new or stronger public regulation of ground transportation, airlines, broadcasting, communications, banking, and energy. The tenor of the times, as well as reformers' easy confidence in their abilities to use administrative agencies to correct the abuses of competitive markets, was summed up in the observation of one of the sponsors of the Natural Gas Act of 1938: "That is what regulation is, monopoly controlled in the public interest."[1]

The newly fashioned FPC embodied both the New Deal's attitude toward regulation and the traditional language of "rates and routes" regulation long applied to the railroads by the Interstate Commerce Commission and to local utilities by state commissions. The FPC's new powers over the interstate shipment of natural gas focused on three areas familiar to all students of rate regulation: (1) control over entry and competition through a certification process; (2) regulation to assure "reasonable" rates based on a fair rate of

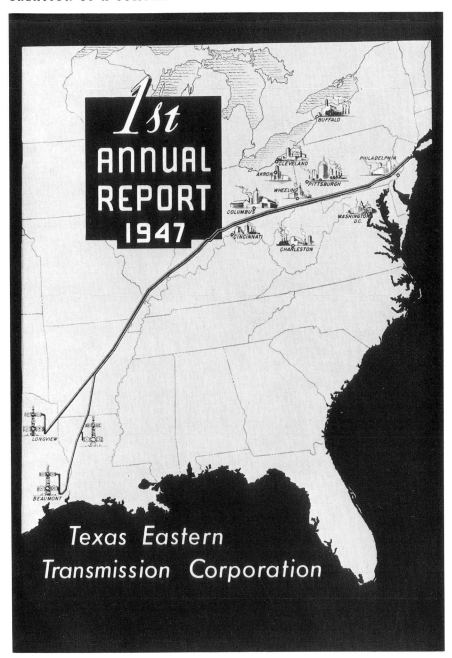

Texas Eastern's first annual report, 1947

return on a fair level of investment; and (3) the imposition of standard accounting practices to simplify both financing and rate setting. The key
mechanism for exercising these powers was the administrative hearing, where
the applicant and supporting and opposing intervenors could present their

cases to the commissioners and their staffs. Such hearings determined if a new pipeline could be built, a new contract could be signed with a supplier or a customer, or a new rate would be allowed. FPC certificates permitting such business decisions would soon become the most valuable commodity in the natural gas transmission industry.

Although given authority to regulate parts of the natural gas industry in 1938, the FPC did little to establish a comprehensive approach to regulation in the brief period between its creation and the onset of World War II. During the war the agency helped oversee the construction of new gas pipelines deemed essential. With the end of hostilities, the FPC set about defining its regulatory approach to the gas industry. Texas Eastern and every other firm in the industry had to learn how to live with this increasingly powerful agency. For natural gas the FPC was the lasting legacy of the Great Depression and the New Deal's approach to regulation. Its choices in the postwar era would go a long way toward determining the tone and the market structure of the emerging system of long-distance gas transmission.

Texas Eastern had to take a "backwards" approach in its initial dealings with the Federal Power Commission. Normally, the founders of a new gas transmission company would first present their plans to the commission for approval. Only after receiving a certificate of public convenience and necessity could the company begin to construct the pipeline. After its successful bid, TE had the Inch Lines, but it did not yet have a certificate. The FPC would issue such a document only after the conclusion of lengthy public hearings during which the applicant would have to prove that it had the engineering resources to maintain and operate the pipeline, that a market existed for the pipeline's capacity, that the company had access to at least a twenty-year supply of natural gas for that market, and that the company's financing plan was feasible.

Texas Eastern had to satisfy the FPC quickly. The WAA had imposed a time constraint that threatened the success of the entire venture. Under the terms of the bid, the company had only nine months to complete its $143 million purchase of the Inch Lines. Although a provision existed to extend this time under certain circumstances, the founders of the company believed that if they missed the deadline, a renewed public debate over the sale of the pipelines would perhaps result in the forfeiture of their bid. Thus, TE had two overriding concerns during its first nine months of existence: the acquisition of a FPC certificate and the arrangement of permanent financing.

As the new company's executives focused on these concerns, however, the smoldering controversy between coal, oil, and natural gas interests again erupted. Initially, some of Texas Eastern's competitors, both in and out of the natural gas industry, did not want to accept the fact that the new company had won legitimately. The firm's attorneys, J. Ross Gamble and Charles Francis, spent the weeks after the bid in February, 1947, dealing with various attempts by competitors to disqualify or otherwise derail TE's winning bid.

Gardiner Symonds, president of Tennessee Gas Transmission Company, was particularly eager to continue the fight. His company was operating the Inch Lines under a temporary lease agreement, and Symonds obviously thought he had the inside track to ownership of the lines. This was evident when WAA administrator Robert Littlejohn ordered the return of the $100,000 deposits posted by the unsuccessful bidders. Tennessee Gas immediately sent its deposit back to the WAA, informing the agency that it intended to keep its proposal for the Inch Lines firm until an actual sale had been made to Texas Eastern.

Tennessee was not alone in its opposition, for many of those who had initially fought the conversion of the Inch Lines to natural gas continued to lobby intensely. The coal and railroad industries carried forward their fight. Tom McGrath, a well known coal industry attorney and lobbyist and a frequent intervenor in government hearings, wrote a letter to the FPC opposing the award of a permanent or temporary certificate of public convenience and necessity to Texas Eastern. On behalf of eight institutions — including coal, labor, and railroad organizations — McGrath repeated the now-familiar argument that natural gas would destroy the manufactured gas industry. As before, these arguments reflected the economic self-interest of well-organized groups; as McGrath knew, such views were not easily ignored in a democratic political system.[2]

While seeking to parry these thrusts, Texas Eastern also faced an investigation by the United States Department of Justice, which had to be satisfied that the proposed operations would not violate the antitrust laws. Since the two Inch Lines were the longest natural gas pipelines in the country and the only pipelines linking the Southwest with the northeastern states of New York and New Jersey, Justice Department officials had to affirm that Texas Eastern would not exercise monopoly power. On this point, Texas Eastern's close relationship to United Gas Corporation attracted intense scrutiny from the government.

In his response to the Justice Department's inquiry on February 20, Gamble stressed that Texas Eastern was not obligated in any way to United Gas and that it had no commitments to purchase gas from any one company. He noted that, as a gatherer, United Gas purchased gas from hundreds of small producers who might otherwise not be able to deliver their product to market. In addition, Gamble wrote, "The United Gas system complements the transmission lines of Texas Eastern more advantageously than any other company's system because no other system so completely covers the 'Gulf Coast Area'. . . ." The Department of Justice required Gamble to list all of the corporate affiliations and stock ownership of the officers and directors of Texas Eastern.[3] Satisfied with Gamble's eight-page response to its questions, the Department of Justice approved the sale of the lines to TE.

Events then began to move quickly. On February 25 Littlejohn mailed a letter of intent to sell the Inch Lines to Texas Eastern. Upon receiving the letter, the company remitted to the WAA its second obligatory payment of $1 million. The date of issuance of the letter of intent marked the beginning of the nine-month period ending November 25, during which Texas Eastern had to submit full payment. With Justice Department approval and a WAA letter of intent in hand, Texas Eastern's directors began to prepare for the FPC's certification hearing.

By this time, Gardiner Symonds had come to grips with the reality that Tennessee Gas would not own the Inch Lines, even though it would continue to operate them through April 30, 1947. Symonds had lost the bid. He would have to contend with a new competitor whose line extended deeper into the customer-rich Northeast than did his own system. Tennessee was suddenly in a weakened competitive position. Symonds's disappointment was tempered somewhat by his knowledge that the potential market in the Northeast was so large that even the combined capacities of Tennessee Gas and its new competitor would not be able to satisfy the demand fully. But he would now have to change course quickly if his firm was going to capture a significant share of that market.

Texas Eastern's founders also had their hands full in the spring of 1947. They first had to obtain a lease and a temporary certificate of public convenience and necessity so that the company would take possession of the Inch Lines from Tennessee Gas. After TE signed an interim lease agreement on March 12 with the Reconstruction Finance Corporation, the FPC issued a temporary certificate on March 21 for the period between May 1 and the issuance of a permanent certificate. As of March 21 Texas Eastern was poised to operate the Inch Lines under lease while actively preparing for the FPC hearings.

Still, an enormous amount of work remained to be done. The company could not take immediate possession of the Inch Lines because Tennessee Gas's temporary lease would not expire until midnight on April 31. Perhaps this was fortunate. Hargrove used the intervening months to build the organization he would need to run the lines. When Texas Eastern signed its lease agreement with the WAA, the company had a total personnel of five: a chairman of the board, president, vice president, secretary-treasurer, and assistant secretary. Quickly Hargrove started to build the team he needed to take over the Inch Lines, prepare for the certificate hearings, and acquire permanent financing.

Hargrove and George Brown now took full control of the operations. Through his own stock purchases and the proxies he held for an additional 67,500 shares, Brown controlled 59 percent of the company's stock. Hargrove, the seasoned natural gas company executive (on loan from United Gas Corporation) had agreed before the bid to become the company's president, replacing E. Holley Poe. Poe's vision had brought the investment group together. His perseverance and his expert knowledge of the industry helped push the company to the edge of its successful bid. But Poe lacked Hargrove's managerial experience. Although the Browns now viewed Poe as an unnecessary outsider, DeGolyer stood up for his business associate and friend and insisted Poe remain as a director of the company.[4]

The new president had spent his entire life in Shreveport and most of his career in the southwestern natural gas industry. Hargrove had left his hometown briefly to attend Rice Institute and then again to join the American Expeditionary Force in France during World War I. But after he returned from the service, he seldom strayed for long from his home base in Shreveport. After managing an abstract company for almost a decade, he joined the land department of a predecessor company of United Gas Corporation in 1928. Over the next twenty years he rose up the ranks of that company, working primarily for the firm's pipeline subsidiary. He was vice president of United Gas Corporation by 1944, but he had only limited prospects of further advancement, since his friend and mentor, N. C. McGowen, was just beginning what would be a long run in the company's top office. Texas Eastern gave Hargrove a chance to build his own empire. He brought to this job a quiet yet forceful demeanor, well suited to the task of organizing a new company. He quickly grew accustomed to the strong input of George Brown and a forceful board, but there was never any doubt that Hargrove was in charge of organizing and managing the rapidly growing company.

Hargrove and George Brown were similar in some respects, but very different in others. Brown was an aggressive entrepreneur who had grown up as a businessman in the rough-and-tumble construction business. Hargrove was more of a professional manager than an entrepreneur. He was conservative in his approach to business decision making, while Brown was accustomed to risk taking. Yet for all these differences, the Browns understood the critical importance of Hargrove to their new venture. He would be the steady hand at the wheel, the day-to-day manager with solid experience in the gas industry. In return for taking on this task, Hargrove and his sons were well rewarded in Texas Eastern's original stock issues. He was also allowed to establish the new company's headquarters in Shreveport, where he had spent his adult life and where his family still lived. Although the Brown brothers sorely wanted their new company to be based in Houston, they understood that Hargrove was more important to the success of Texas Eastern than a central office in Houston—at least for the time being. In Hargrove, the fledgling corporation had a seasoned manager only forty-nine years old and vigorous enough to withstand the pressures that would accompany this new venture.

Hargrove's search for office space, which was scarce in postwar Shreveport, was short and successful. The Hargrove family owned a small office building which seemed to be suitable for Texas Eastern's immediate needs. The Ward building, owned by Mrs. Hargrove and her relatives, was then managed by Jim Hargrove, Reginald's son, who quickly made room there for Texas Eastern. Jim went to work with Texas Eastern in April, assuming

Texas Eastern's headquarters in Shreveport, Louisiana

the role of office manager until later taking a permanent position in the financial department.[5]

The staff for Texas Eastern came from three sources: United Gas, George Brown's associates, and War Emergency Pipeline employees. Reginald Hargrove started by drawing upon the people he knew best, his previous colleagues at United Gas (which was also based in Shreveport). N. C. McGowen, president of United Gas, did not protest as several of his executive and management employees left to go to work for the new business. McGowen had worked at establishing this community of interests, and he knew that Texas Eastern would be a major customer for United's natural gas supplies. From its friendly neighbor in Shreveport, Texas Eastern acquired many of the experienced, competent personnel needed to operate a transmission company.

Texas Eastern's original executive operating staff came almost entirely from United Gas. Hargrove first hired select persons to become department heads at TE, and these persons then became responsible for hiring most of the remaining staff. Hargrove hired E. R. Cunningham, a vice president of United Gas Pipeline Company, to be the new company's vice president and operating manager; George T. Naff, a vice president and general counsel of United Gas, soon thereafter became an executive vice president at Texas Eastern; and Baxter Goodrich, assistant chief engineer at United Gas, became chief engineer. Hargrove also hired Walter E. Caine, an AGA associate with financial and regulatory experience, to serve as treasurer and work on the company's early contracts, and employed S. E. Sentell, a friend of the Hargrove family and a former employee of a regional gas distribution company.

Some of these new employees brought in their own staffs. Baxter Goodrich soon hired Andrew J. Shoup to be his assistant chief engineer. E. R. Cunningham brought with him several other United Gas employees, including chief dispatcher T. B. Kelley and E. C. Aldridge as head of the transportation department. Cunningham also drew upon the staff of the Reconstruction Finance Corporation, from which he hired H. I. Putnam, superintendent of the RFC's Rights-of-Way and Claims Department, and his staff as well.

George and Herman Brown tapped their connections in Houston to help staff upper levels of the financial and accounting departments. Herbert J. Frensley, a long-time associate of the Brown brothers and corporate secretary of many of their companies, including Brown & Root, became secretary and treasurer. Like the Browns, Frensley stayed in Houston instead of moving to Shreveport. Orville "Dick" S. Carpenter, previously associated with both the Browns and Herbert Frensley, became the comptroller.[6]

To assemble an operating staff of field men to live and work along the pipeline route, Hargrove looked first to the men already operating the pipelines for Tennessee Gas. Many of them were original War Emergency Pipeline employees and knew as much about the physical operation and condition of the pipeline as anyone. The men were pleased to know that their jobs would continue when Texas Eastern took over the pipelines, and the company was assured of having experienced staff in place on May 1, 1947.

The earliest employees of Texas Eastern were almost to a man friends or business associates prior to the creation of the new company. This gave the young gas company a sense of family, helping foster a close-knit organization in which employees felt strong bonds of loyalty and shared purpose. George Brown and Reginald Hargrove were strong leaders who commanded the respect of their co-workers. The whirlwind of activities required to create the new pipeline company gave its employees ample opportunity to share a sense of accomplishment in these early years. The company's quick financial success further encouraged pride and confidence. The strong personal bonds built during the company's dynamic formative years would be a valuable asset for Texas Eastern in subsequent decades. The corporate culture forged in this period stressed aggressive action and a straight-ahead approach to management. The organization's self-image was that of a championship team ready to take on the world, if necessary, to become a major natural gas transmission company.

One early challenge to the company's top management was the November 25, 1947, deadline for the completion of arrangements to operate the Inch Lines. By that date Texas Eastern had to obtain a gas supply, customers, and additional financial support. To prove its ability to pay back potential investors, the company had to secure large-scale business customers for its gas; to get these buyers, Texas Eastern needed contracts for supplies of natural gas. With customers and suppliers lined up, the company would be in a position to win the favor of those large institutional investors who had the resources to finance the $143,127,000 cost of the Inch Lines. First they would have to be convinced to commit their support contingent upon a certificate.[7] This support would establish the basis for the FPC certificate, which would be the key to permanent financial backing.

Texas Eastern's officials first moved to secure supplies of natural gas so that they could then convince major customers to sign contracts. United Gas had made a commitment before the bid to supply 25 percent of Texas Eastern's twenty-year requirement. Oil man H. L. Hunt pledged about 25 percent more of the company's maximum requirements. Texas Eastern's connection with Hunt was arranged by Judge Elkins, whose City National Bank had been saved from bankruptcy during the Great Depression with help from Hunt.[8]

Although additional supplies would be needed, the initial agreements with United Gas and H. L. Hunt allowed Texas Eastern to begin writing contracts with customers. Securing an initial customer base presented little problem, since most customers already receiving gas from the Inch Lines wanted to continue purchasing from the new pipeline company. Texas Eastern merely had to keep the system running under the FPC's emergency service formulas.[9] The temporary certificate allowed Texas Eastern to sell gas for not more than $0.23 per mcf in the Appalachian area and the areas served by Panhandle Eastern. Although Hargrove had planned on selling gas for $0.26, the lower sales price was initially acceptable.

The company was soon able to add new customers to its inherited base. As a long-time member in the American Gas Association and its president in 1947, Hargrove had friendly relationships with many of the executives of the northeastern utility companies. Using his contacts, Texas Eastern began to line up prospective sales contracts.

On March 26 Texas Eastern signed its first two contracts with Consolidated Natural Gas. The first agreement covered the period of Texas Eastern's lease of the Inch Lines, and the second one, a twenty-year contract, would begin when Texas Eastern permanently acquired the lines. On the same day, Texas Eastern filed with the FPC for a certificate of public convenience and necessity. Although an interest in making contracts with New England gas distributors had been expressed in the company's bid proposal, Hargrove and his fellow executives decided that Texas Eastern could not at this time afford to build the extra pipeline systems necessary to serve New England. Instead, they focused on making the existing system as efficient as possible. The idea of expanding the customer base and capacity was never far from Hargrove's thoughts, but first he had to create a viable organization.

When the FPC issued the temporary certificate, it advised the company to increase its capacity beyond the current 140 mmcf/d as soon as possible after taking possession of the lines. To facilitate this request, the temporary certificate authorized Texas Eastern to construct and install three conventional reciprocating compressor stations with a maximum of 18,000 horsepower to increase substantially the pipelines' capacity. The company estimated that this would cost about $3.5 million. Even before Hargrove could begin to worry about financing for these three compressor stations. Manufacturers Trust Company, which had already loaned the company $4 million, agreed to finance the cost of the compressors, with the condition that the Reconstruction Finance Corporation buy the compressors from Texas Eastern at five-sevenths of their original cost if the company proved unable to complete its purchase of the Inch Lines. In return, Texas Eastern agreed to invest all of its earnings in the construction of the compressors and pay Manufacturers Trust any funds received from the government for the purchase of this equipment.

As the new company grew stronger and the day neared when it would take over the Inch Lines, relationships with its arch competitor, Tennessee Gas, grew more tense. After it became increasingly likely that the new firm would acquire a certificate and financing for the pipelines, Tennessee entered negotiations with Texas Eastern to transfer operating control of the pipelines on May 1. Tennessee Gas's antagonism toward Texas Eastern was nowhere more evident than in the fact that Tennessee Gas refused to allow any Texas Eastern personnel on the Inch Line property without a guide until the final moment of Tennessee Gas's lease agreement. It took two months of legal maneuvering to settle a disagreement over the amount Texas Eastern should reimburse Tennessee Gas for improvements it had made on the Inch Lines during its temporary lease. Texas Eastern made the necessary payment to Tennessee on April 30, 1947. On the next day, at 12:01 A.M., Texas Eastern became the operator of the lines. One Texas Eastern official later recalled his first entry into a substation as Tennessee Gas held on to the final minute of its lease: "It was like coming into an enemy camp."[10]

The transition was painful but smooth. Since Texas Eastern took over without immediate changes in operating personnel or procedures, the primary change was in paperwork. A conference telephone call between Hargrove and Carpenter of Texas Eastern, Tennessee Gas representatives, and War Emergency Pipeline officials was all that was necessary to complete the transaction. Until the move to Shreveport could be completed, Texas Eastern actually operated the Inch Lines out of the old WEP office in Cincinnati.

The same day it began to operate the lines, Texas Eastern gave the War Assets Administration its third required payment of $4 million, using funds loaned by Manufacturers Trust. As of May 1, Texas Eastern thus had paid only $5.1 million of its total $143,127,000 bid price to the WAA, leaving $138,027,000 to be raised by November 25. Before this could be done, the company had to prove to the FPC that it deserved a permanent certificate by signing up big customers and assuring them a twenty-year supply of natural gas.

Texas Eastern was under considerable pressure to operate the pipeline efficiently, increasing its capacity as soon as possible. The Appalachian region was suffering from a severe fuel shortage, and Texas Eastern sought to prove to the Federal Power Commission that it could efficiently operate the Inch Lines to help ease the region's energy shortage. More generally, TE needed to prove that it could supply gas to the Northeast. To do this, the firm had to clean the lines of petroleum residue from their wartime operation and add compressor stations to increase their gas transmission capacity.

Texas Eastern's new chief engineer, Baxter Goodrich, devised the company's program to convert the Inch Lines from petroleum to natural gas. Goodrich helped develop a plan to use nearly all of the original components of the oil pumping stations (except for the actual oil pumps), including the motors. The company's engineers developed an electrically powered centrifugal gas compressor which would fit into exactly the same bolt holes as the original reciprocal oil pumps. These unique compressors would become the industry standard after Texas Eastern proved their viability. They enabled the company to keep major parts of the original oil pumping stations in the rate base, while at the same time saving development money.

Under the temporary certificate, Texas Eastern made plans to install three compressors to be constructed by Brown & Root. After taking possession of the pipelines, the company quickly decided to build a fourth station and increase the system's horsepower to 28,000, thereby building capacity to 265 mmcf/d. Even basic operational decisions such as the addition of new compressor stations required regulatory approval, necessitating changes in the WAA lease, the temporary certificate, and the construction loan agreement. After clearing these hurdles in early June, Texas Eastern decided in July to expand the system further, even though work had barely begun on the construction of the first four stations. A market in the Northeast clearly existed for as much gas as Texas Eastern could push through the pipelines. With the FPC's concurrence, Texas Eastern amended its lease so that it would now install a total of ten compressor stations, all constructed by Brown & Root, with a combined 71,750 horsepower and 340 mmcf/d capacity. Engineers from Ebasco Services, Ingersoll Rand, and the RFC assisted Texas Eastern in devising plans for the ten new facilities which featured electrically powered centrifugal compressors instead of the standard gas-powered reciprocating compressors originally used when the lines pumped oil. By the beginning of the FPC hearings in early July, Texas Eastern had upped the ante, planning for the installation of twenty-one compressor stations with a capacity of 435 mmcf/d.

While developing these plans, the company set about cleaning out the petroleum products and water left in the pipes from wartime operations. Borrowing techniques from the oil pipeline business, the firm originally used a combination of siphons, drops, and scrubbers to remove fluid from the lines. During the summer of 1947, the company removed almost twelve thousand barrels of liquids from the lines. This system removed enough foreign material to raise the pipeline's efficiency from 67 to 72 percent. Most of these fluids had been present in the pipe lines before Texas Eastern's acquisition, but then natural gasoline (associated with the natural gas being shipped) began to collect, causing further problems. During the next year, Texas Eastern began using a new technique of cleaning, applying "pigs," or scrapers, to remove liquids and dirt in the pipes. The pressure of the natural gas in the lines forced the scrapers through the length of the line in approximately fifty-mile segments, scraping out any sediment. Until TE began using pigs, the traditional cleaning method required the operators to cut the line at two places to insert and then discharge the scraper. This process resulted in the loss of natural gas and required considerable cutting and re-welding of the pipe. The company began using the traps previously installed when the lines carried petroleum. The traps worked just as well with natural gas, and this innovative method of cleaning the lines increased their efficiency to 91 percent in their first year and a half of operations.[11] During 1948 some of Texas Eastern's suppliers helped the company further improve its efficiency by constructing extraction plants which removed natural gasoline from their gas.

The physical condition of the pipeline also posed problems for the company. Serious defects in the Little Big Inch came to light during the late 1940s. During the war the War Emergency Pipelines organization had been forced

Little Rock, Arkansas, compressor station

to make major repairs on the line. Knowing this, Texas Eastern's management decided to conduct an extensive pipe quality testing program on the twenty-inch line. After "many long and exhaustive investigations both in the field and the laboratory," the company and its engineering advisor, Battelle Memorial Institute, decided to test the lines hydrostatically. The injection of water into the pipeline section by section, at pressures much higher than standard natural gas pressures, burst defective welds and joints, making them easy to locate and repair. This was a somewhat controversial plan, though, because many gas pipeline specialists feared that water injected into a pipeline might freeze, either damaging the line or significantly reducing

66

Hydrostatic testing: burst pipeline

its efficiency. To solve this problem, the company pushed a "slug" of alcohol behind the water to dry out the line.

Since the pipe appeared to be in good condition south of Little Rock, testing proceeded from that point to the East Coast. Hydrostatic testing continued well after the company's first year of operation. In 1950, after extensive hydrostatic testing of 824 miles of the twenty-inch pipe resulted in hundreds of breaks and leaks, the company replaced 1 percent, or about eight miles or 968 joints, of the original pipe. Although the testing, rehabilitation, and out-of-service time cost the company $2 million, the improvements increased the long-run profitability of the Little Big Inch and left the firm with a superior system.

Baxter Goodrich was the central figure behind the unique innovations in centrifugal gas compressors, hydrostatic testing, and the use of pigs. Goodrich applied his own formidable skills and knowledge to these engineering challenges and also brought in others from outside the company to evaluate the merits of the firm's innovations. His long record of engineering excellence at Texas Eastern was formally recognized in 1966 when executives of 135 gas distribution and transmission companies acknowledged him as the man who "had contributed the most [to gas transmission] in the last 150 years." Noting specifically his work in pipe research, testing, compressor station design, and "pigging," they praised Goodrich for initiating "many of the technological advancements that have been achieved by the transmission industry."[12]

As Hargrove, Goodrich, and their fellow workers pushed forward on these fronts, Texas Eastern weathered the FPC's public hearings. The hearings began on July 7, 1947, and lasted through September 26, 1947.[13] They brought out a panoply of support and opposition from forty-eight intervenors.[14] Thirty-five supporters of the certificate represented primarily companies which had contracted to receive gas from Texas Eastern, or who hoped to do so. Their eagerness to acquire natural gas spoke well for the new company's future, and the FPC could not easily ignore their testimony as to the attractiveness of natural gas to northeastern utilities. After almost two years of hearings and lobbying and controversy, this was the key point that finally registered with the FPC: natural gas should not be denied to the millions of customers on the East Coast.

Texas Eastern's most determined opposition again came from representatives of the coal and railroad companies. They objected to natural gas sales east of Pittsburgh, where coal and manufactured gas supplied much of the region's energy. Other companies such as Panhandle Eastern intervened against TE's gas sales in the Appalachian area out of fear of losing markets to the new pipeline company. Tennessee Gas Transmission Company presented the same objection to Texas Eastern's certificate application, but this argument did not sit well with the FPC. Noting that "the positions of the Tennessee Gas Transmission Company and Panhandle Eastern Pipe Line Company were not made entirely clear on the record," the commission stated that "we are not persuaded that the certificate herein authorized constitutes any impairment of the markets of these intervenors."

Two closely related issues did temporarily threaten Texas Eastern's certificate application and quickly became the focus of heated debate: TE's desire to sell gas in markets beyond Appalachia and the question of the company's access to rights-of-way for its natural gas pipeline in Pennsylvania. These issues came together in debates over potential sales of gas to Philadelphia-area utilities. In addition to a projected delivery of 340 mmcf/d of natural gas to the Appalachian region, the company planned to sell 80 mmcf/d to two utility companies in Philadelphia, leaving an excess of 13 mmcf/d (providing some sales flexibility). Texas Eastern strongly desired to break into Philadelphia markets. Its lines passed very close to the city, which was among the largest markets for gas on the East Coast. The company overcame several obstacles and signed gas sales agreements with the two major Philadelphia utilities, Philadelphia Electric Company and Philadelphia Gas Works

Inserting a "pig" into a pipeline

Company. But state government officials and representatives of the coal and railroad industries continued to mount a fierce rearguard action against the pipeline. They initally opposed giving TE right-of-way permits for its pipeline system, and Pennsylvania did not yet grant powers of eminent domain to natural gas pipelines.

The problems Texas Eastern faced in Pennsylvania had far-reaching implications for its financing. These problems had attracted the attention of the insurance companies which had pledged to purchase $120 million in bonds to finance the acquisition of the Inch Lines. In the early summer of 1947 the insurance companies as a group advised Texas Eastern that without federal power of eminent domain authorizing rights of way for the interstate transmission of natural gas, they could not go through with their purchase of the pipeline's bonds. The insurance companies feared that without such a law, Texas Eastern would not be able to overcome the intense opposition of Pennsylvania's coal and railroad industries.[15]

Before the FPC hearing, Texas Eastern had sought to satisfy the insurance companies before presenting the financing plan at the hearings. Charles Francis, working with several congressmen, prepared a short statute providing federal power of eminent domain for the transmission of natural gas and had it introduced in both houses of the U.S. Congress. Since this statute appeared so late in that session of Congress, the prevailing rules dictated that it had to pass by unanimous consent. But the first time the statute came to a vote, two senators from Pennsylvania and one from West Virginia voted against it.[16] At this point—according to the later recollections of Francis— John L. Lewis, president of the UMW, allowed his general counsel to work with Francis, who recalled that "when the bill was again brought up there were no votes against the matter in the Senate. . . ."[17] On July 25, 1947, the statute became an amendment to the Natural Gas Act of 1938, giving natural gas companies the right of eminent domain to construct, operate, and maintain gas pipelines. By settling this issue Texas Eastern assured that financing would be forthcoming and that it would be able to sell gas in the large metropolitan areas east of Appalachia, and in Philadelphia in particular.

On October 10, 1947, the FPC granted a certificate to Texas Eastern. As the commission said, there was no "logical justification for providing unlimited gas service in the so-called Appalachian area and at the same time denying service to the Eastern Pennsylvania area."[18] This service would begin on October 1, 1948, when various lines connecting Texas Eastern's pipeline to the utilities would be completed. Meanwhile, the commission allowed the company to use the two twenty-inch sections of the Big Inch and Little Big Inch extending from Skippack Junction to Linden, New Jersey, for storing gas reserved for emergency use in Philadelphia.

With its permanent certificate in hand, TE was at last able to finance its purchase. August Belmont led a large staff of lawyers, accountants, engineers, and financial experts through several weeks of long days, grinding out the paperwork needed to complete the financing. The financing plan involved the sale of $120 million in bonds and about $32 million in stock. Belmont began negotiating with several life insurance companies for their purchase of bonds on September 10, 1947. He had first approached Metropolitan Life Insurance Company, which had conditionally agreed to purchase $36 million in Texas Eastern's First Mortgage pipeline bonds. After Metropolitan agreed to participate in the financing, other insurance companies quickly followed suit. By October 23 a total of twelve major insurors had committed to purchase all $120 million of Texas Eastern's 3.5 percent first mortgage funds at 101 percent of their face value. The prospective buyers conditioned their commitments, however, on Texas Eastern's ability to raise $30 million through the sale of stock.

Originally, the Texas Eastern directors intended to issue preferred as well as common stock. By issuing preferred stock the company could, as Belmont later recalled, "reduce the amount of common stock that had to be sold and therefore reduce the dilution of what we had."[19] When FPC chairman Nelson Lee Smith learned that Texas Eastern was planning to issue preferred stock, however, he forcefully objected in a telegram to both Hargrove and Belmont: "Gravely concerned over reports regarding certain phases of your financing in Docket Number G–880 and considering whether the public interest requires immediate action by it. Please advise earliest you, Belmont and principal counsel can appear in Washington for conference regarding this matter."[20] Belmont and Hargrove realized that this issue could threaten their entire plan. They immediately trimmed their sails to suit the wind from the FPC. They met with Smith and agreed to eliminate the preferred stock. Dillon, Read and TE then worked up a financial plan calling for the issuance of $30 million in common stock. On October 24, 1947, the company filed its registration statement with the Securities and Exchange Commission (SEC). In the fourth and final amendment to the registration statement, a public offering of stock at $9.50 per share was filed on November 10.[21]

The SEC approved the stock issue on November 10, and the next day several newspapers reported the deal. Although the Browns may have wished to avoid public scrutiny, the Texas Eastern story commanded the attention of many reporters. One headline carried the following story: "Texas Eastern Transmission Stockholders Stand to Make $9,825,000 for $150,000."[22] The remarkable part of the financing revolved around the fact that twenty-eight people invested $150,000, some in borrowed money, to purchase a $143,127,000 pipeline (see table 3.1). The transaction received additional unwanted attention when one stockholder, J. Ross Gamble, sold his original shares — which cost him only $2,500 — for $166,250. August Belmont and C. Douglas Dillon of Dillon, Read & Company, attempted to dampen the press reports by holding several press conferences to answer questions about the pipeline purchase. Belmont discussed the transaction with reporters and editors from *Time, Newsweek,* the *New York Times,* and the newspaper *PM.* The next

TABLE 3.1   Original Texas Eastern Stockholders and Their Profits

Name of Purchaser	Number of Original Shares Purchased	Cost of Original Shares	Number of Reclassified Shares	Value on Basis of Offering at $9.50	Paper Profits Available (before taxes*)
Frank L. Andrews	13,750	$ 13,750	96,250	$ 914,375.00	$ 900,625.00
George R. Brown	21,375	21,375	149,625	1,421,437.50	1,400,062.50
Herman Brown	21,375	21,375	149,625	1,421,437.50	1,400,062.50
E. DeGolyer	15,375	15,375	107,625	1,022,437.50	1,007,062.50
12 persons then associated with Dillon, Read & Co., Inc.	18,750	18,750	131,250	1,246,875.00	1,228,125.00
J. A. Elkins +	9,375	9,375	65,625	623,437.50	614,062.50
Charles I. Francis +	9,375	9,375	65,625	623,437.50	614,062.50
J. Ross Gamble	2,500	2,500	17,500	166,250.00	163,750.00
James W. Hargrove !	3,000	3,000	21,000	199,500.00	196,500.00
Joseph L. Hargrove !	3,000	3,000	21,000	199,500.00	196,500.00
Reginald H. Hargrove	12,250	12,250	85,750	814,625.00	802,375.00
Robert C. Hargrove !	3,000	3,000	21,000	199,500.00	196,500.00
E. Holley Poe	10,875	10,875	76,125	723,187.50	712,312.50
Justin R. Querbes	1,500	1,500	10,500	99,750.00	98,250.00
Randolph A. Querbes	1,500	1,500	10,500	99,750.00	98,250.00
Vinson, Elkins, Weems & Francis	1,500	1,500	10,500	99,750.00	98,250.00
Gus S. Wortham	1,500	1,500	10,500	99,750.00	98,250.00
	150,000	$150,000	1,050,000	$9,975,000.00	$9,825,000.00

Notes: *Taxable as long-term capital gains at 25 percent.
   + Member of firm of Vinson, Elkins, Weems & Francis.
   ! Son of Reginald H. Hargrove.
Source: John W. Welker, "Fair Profit?" *Harvard Business Review* 26, no. 2 (March, 1948).

series of articles balanced their accounts of the husky profits of the founders of Texas Eastern with the news that the government was receiving almost its full cost for building the Inch Lines.[23]

The public offering price of $9.50 per share was actually at least $1.00 less than the company originally planned to ask for each share. However, investors became nervous after radio news commentator Fulton Lewis, Jr., devoted parts of two radio broadcasts to his views about the Texas Eastern financing.[24] Lewis charged that the promoters who purchased 150,000 shares at $1.00 per share on February 5, 1947, were making unfair profits. The original stockholders were receiving an additional six shares, at no charge, for each one purchased before the public offering. This was essentially a stock "split" of seven times, as each share became seven shares purchased for the original $1.00 per share — a price of approximately fourteen cents per share. Thus, when Texas Eastern offered to the public its first stock issue at $9.50 per share, the company's stock was priced at sixty-six times the effective price paid by the original investors. Thereby, the original $150,000 investment turned into $9,975,000 (including the original $150,000), at the time of the public offering.

To this Lewis said with sarcasm, "It just goes to show what sweat and toil and preseverance and patience will do for thrifty and hard working men."[25] The next morning, on the day of the closing, Lewis lashed out again at Texas Eastern. He pointed out that the twenty-eight original stockholders would be taxed at less than 25 percent. Lewis also criticized Dillon, Read for its handling of the stock issue. Eleven Dillon, Read partners had purchased one-eighth of the original 150,000 shares, and the company also received a $1.00 per share commission on each of the three and one-half million shares sold. This highly public debate over high finance was later repeated with more subtlety in two opposing articles in the prestigious *Harvard Business Review.*[26]

As with most speculative ventures in relatively new industries, Texas Eastern's close ties with various government officials also fueled speculation that there was more to the sale than met the eye. Even the House Surplus Property Committee began an investigation, as Fulton Lewis said, "to see if there is any possible political implication connected with the sale." Indeed, George E. Allen, the former director of the RFC (who resigned his position in mid-January, 1947) had, as Charles Francis reported to Judge Elkins, earlier discussed with the Poe group the plans for the bid. Allen's precise role in Texas Eastern's bid for the Inch Lines still cannot be pinned down, although many years later Francis commented upon Allen's political abilities; he called Allen "the most *important* & *influential* lobbyist in the U.S."[27] Whatever his services to the enterprise, George Allen indirectly received a healthy share of founder's stock. When Allen published his autobiography—unabashedly titled *Presidents Who Have Known Me*—he dedicated it to literally hundreds of people, including Frank Andrews, Charles Francis, and R. H. Hargrove. In one chapter he discussed his role as a political lobbyist, explaining that "I knew hundreds of people in the executive departments and in Congress." He continued: "The companies with which I am associated sometimes have business to do with the government, as almost every American Company does these days. I am able to tell my associates whom to do business with, how to make their way through the maze of red tape, and how best to conduct themselves, but I can't make a better deal for them with the United States government than any one of their competitors can make."[28] Considering the political forces lined up on every side of the Big Inch and Little Big Inch issue, one should not underestimate Allen's comment.

The early promoters of Texas Eastern reaped substantial profits from this venture. They defended these profits by reminding their critics that while the rewards were indeed substantial, so were the risks. Even forty years after the fact, such arguments remain unconvincing if "risks" are assumed to be primarily economic. In a regulated industry with a guaranteed rate of return, the economic risks were hardly overwhelming. The founders had, after all, put very little of their own money on the line. But even a cursory look at the numerous government hearings and behind-the-scenes lobbying regarding the Inch Lines suggests that the founders of Texas Eastern faced substantial political and regulatory risks in the unpredictable political environment after World War II. The founders had invested their time, energy, and reputations in a venture which did not at first have even a fifty-fifty chance of success. Having brought it nonetheless to a successful beginning, they were handsomely rewarded for that accomplishment.

To the historian of these events, the founders' high profits are of interest because they were one manifestation of a major economic transition. The public's purchase of Texas Eastern's offering at a dramatic premium over the founders' original investments only a year earlier reflected the extraordinary expectations of investors in the future of natural gas in northeastern markets. This major transition in energy use — like the earlier transitions to railroad transportations and to electrical urban transport — destroyed old values, created new ones, and along the way produced entrepreneurial profits for those who bet on the right companies in the right industries. That said, public speculation about the propriety of so-called "promotional profits" of Texas Eastern's founders continued — as well as similar, if less-publicized, speculation about the promotional profits of the organizers of Trans-Continental Gas Pipe Line and other similar companies.[29] Scrutiny by the public and by public officials was a fact of life in the highly regulated natural gas transmission industry.

The public controversy over intrigue, political entrepreneurship, and dramatic profits, gradually blew over, leaving Texas Eastern positioned to close its purchase of the Inch Lines on November 14, 1947. This proved to be a complex undertaking, with 150 representatives of the various parties involved in the transaction. On one side of the table sat representatives of the WAA, RFC, and the Federal Reserve. On the other side, the officers of Texas Eastern, representatives from twelve insurance companies, three banks and investment bankers, the trustee for the bonds, the transfer agent for the stock, and all their respective counsel. The meeting was at the New York Federal Reserve Building, and there Harvey Gibson, president of Manufacturers Trust Co., George Brown, and Reginald Hargrove gave Robert Littlejohn, WAA Administrator, a check for $143,127,000. The WAA then returned Texas Eastern's initial payments totaling $5,100,000. As one of Littlejohn's aides observed: "When we set that deadline, we never thought you or anyone else would be able to meet it."[30]

Texas Eastern Transmission Corporation had met a major challenge and acquired ownership and control of the Big and Little Big Inch Pipelines. The company had evolved from a small group of investors united for the purpose of bidding on the Inch Lines to an established company with its own gas purchase and sales contracts, large scale financing, and regular dealings with both the Federal Power Commission and the Securities and Exchange Commission. During the months since Poe had begun to plan for the bid in November, 1945, to the date of the closing, two years later, Texas Eastern Corporation had become a reality. The founders had brought to this endeavor

Harvey Gibson, George Brown, and Reginald H. Hargrove deliver a check in the amount of $143,127,000 to Gen. Robert Littlejohn of the WAA

a diverse collection of skills and experiences. Their ideas, as well as their resolve, had been tested in a grueling exercise of public hearings and behind-the-scenes lobbying. In the process of defending their views before often hostile intervenors, the company's founders had sharpened their own understanding of the economic and political realities of the cross-country transmission of natural gas. This experience would prove valuable, since similar hearings before the Federal Power Commission would continue to shape the company's planning and operations once the flow of natural gas through the Inch Lines began in earnest.

Chapter 4

RACE FOR EASTERN MARKETS

After two years of testifying Texas Eastern's leaders were more than ready to leave Washington, D.C., and get busy building a natural gas business. The Inch Lines gave them a clear competitive edge versus potential rivals. Texas Eastern was the first—and for a time, the only—company with direct pipeline connections from the Southwest to major northeastern markets. The company stood ready to exploit this advantage to the extent allowed by the FPC. Bold moves were the order of the day, since patterns of supplies and markets established in these formative years for the cross-country gas industry were likely to prove durable.

Texas Eastern was in a high-stakes race with its competitors to claim the ultimate prizes—the large metropolitan markets of the Northeast. The race was not a straight dash to the finish line; rather, it was a marathon whose route travelled through the largely uncharted terrain of the FPC and the various state utility commissions. Competition would be shaped by the choices of the FPC, a relatively young federal agency still uncertain of its powers or even its prime mission. The new natural gas transmission companies would grow up together with this federal agency. Their interaction in the formative years of natural gas expansion into the Northeast would define "regulated competition" as it applied to this dynamic industry.[1]

Like central Africa on the early maps of discovery, the Northeast remained an unexplored gray area on the map of natural gas use after World War II. Most other major population centers in the United States had gained access to natural gas in the pipeline construction boom before the war. The companies most active in this era seemed well positioned to extend their operations into the Northeast. Although these companies did not ultimately win the race for northeastern markets, several of them played important roles in the early histories of the companies that did.

Of particular importance to Texas Eastern was the United Gas Corporation, which parlayed its holdings of excellent southwestern reserves into a status as the world's largest handler of natural gas on the eve of World War II. United had been formed in 1930 through the consolidation of forty gas companies located primarily in Texas and Louisiana. Under the leader-

Texas Eastern's Board of Directors, 1948. *Left to right:* Everette DeGolyer, Charles I. Thompson, Herman Brown, William A. Smith, George R. Brown, Orville S. Carpenter, Charles I. Francis, Reginald H. Hargrove, E. Holley Poe.

ship of Norris C. McGowen, this Shreveport, Louisiana–based company vigorously pursued a strategy based on building an integrated natural gas company serving the Gulf South. The firm's market included most of the big cities in Texas and Louisiana, as well as hundreds of other communities in those two states, Mississippi, southern Alabama, and northwestern Florida.[2] After the war McGowen chose to focus on his company's traditional markets rather than extending pipelines to the Northeast. United Gas nonetheless became a major gas supplier for Texas Eastern and its competitors for northeastern markets.

United Gas was a logical candidate to extend a cross-country pipeline from the Southwest to the Northeast; two other large regional companies — the Columbia Gas System and Consolidated Natural Gas Company — seemed well positioned to make this connection from the opposite direction. Columbia shipped Appalachian gas to Pittsburgh, Cincinnati, Columbus, and numerous other midsized industrial cities in Ohio, West Virginia, and parts of Pennsylvania, New York, Kentucky, and Virginia. By 1940 the company also had a small line all the way east to Paterson, New Jersey, and another line to the outskirts of Washington, D.C. Noting that Columbia's operations reached out toward the lucrative markets of Philadelphia and New York City, *Fortune* magazine speculated in 1940 that "if eastern reserves do not justify serving New York and Philadelphia, another pipe-line connection to the Southwest would do the trick."[3]

Consolidated Natural Gas, which served some of the same cities, had equally strong incentives to search for new gas supplies to use in expanding its markets. Consolidated had the advantage of close financial and operating ties with Standard Oil of New Jersey, the oil giant that had organized Consolidated as its natural gas subsidiary. With established connections to Cleveland, Pittsburgh, and other cities in the region, Consolidated enjoyed excellent prospects for future expansion. Both it and Columbia sold gas retail as well as wholesale to smaller distribution companies. They were the giants of the Appalachian gas industry, and as the reserves in their region declined, they eyed expansion to the eastern seaboard. They began to look to the Southwest for new reserves.[4]

The war disrupted any immediate prospect that either of these companies would extend their trunklines to the Southwest. During the war, Hope Natural Gas Company—a subsidiary of Consolidated—lost out to Tennessee Gas in the contest to build a new pipeline to supply additional gas needed by vital war production factories in Appalachia. After the war, both Columbia and Consolidated became important purchasers of natural gas from Texas Eastern and the other companies which built new lines into their traditional service areas.

Two other potential competitors to Texas Eastern—Panhandle Eastern and El Paso Natural Gas—emerged before the war as long distance transporters of natural gas from the Southwest. But neither of these concerns pointed their lines toward the major northeastern cities, and neither built new lines to them after the war. In the 1920s Panhandle Eastern Pipe Line Company sought markets for its large reserves in the Hugoton and Panhandle fields by extending a line northward through Indiana and into Michigan. Although the company's drive toward Detroit stalled during the Great Depression, it nonetheless became and remained a major competitor in the Midwest. El Paso Natural Gas, using gas reserves in the Permian Basin of Texas, had built lines to serve El Paso in the late 1920s, and this ambitious company had begun work before World War II on lines westward toward Phoenix and, ultimately, Los Angeles.[5] Although both companies remained expansive after the war, neither turned their attention to the Northeast.

Yet there the greatest potential markets for natural gas remained. The decade after World War II witnessed a spectacular expansion in the use of natural gas, and the industry recaptured the dynamism of the late 1920s—and then some. Few industries in American history have grown as rapidly as postwar natural gas, which surged forward into the ranks of the nation's largest economic enterprises. The long-distance transmission companies found these years particularly exciting and profitable, as they constructed major

MAP 4.1 Post WWII Pipeline Construction

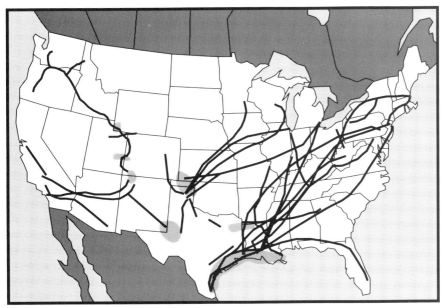

Source: Adapted from Arlon R. Tussing and Connie C. Barlow. *The Natural Gas Industry: Evolution, Structure, and Economics* (Cambridge: Ballinger Publishing Company, 1984), 47.

new pipelines into virgin territories (see map 4.1). This was a golden age for natural gas.

It was also a golden age and a time of great excitement for Texas Eastern and for other interstate gas transmission companies. There was a new industry to be built. Within Texas Eastern, there was a clarity of purpose that could be easily summarized in a single strategic goal: become one of the major suppliers of natural gas to the Northeast. From top to bottom, the company rallied around this goal, gaining unity and resolve from the intense competition with other major companies such as Tennessee Gas and Transcontinental. There was ample work in the gas transmission business to engage the best energies of all of Texas Eastern's approximately one thousand workers. Any impulse to move beyond gas transmission to substantial involvement in related ventures was constrained by economic and political barriers. Integration backward into gas production invited competition from the major oil companies who dominated this sector of the industry; integration forward into gas distribution was illegal under the Public Utility Holding Company Act of 1935. In this sense, Texas Eastern had a single, overriding goal to achieve. It pushed forward with extraordinary vigor and unity guided by a clearly focused strategy.

The company operated within a regulatory system which also maintained a relatively clear and manageable strategy, at least in the years before 1954. The regulatory regime of the FPC in the immediate postwar period of expansion focused on a key issue, the long-term adequacy of gas reserves. It sought to assure that the numerous new users of natural gas would have a reasonably certain and stable supply with minimum risk of future short-ages. To accomplish this goal, the FPC regulated the construction and opera-tion of interstate pipelines, with much emphasis on their access to long-term gas supplies. The production of gas was not subject to price regulation at the well-head. The sale to consumers was subject to state regulation. In this brief but important era of its history, the FPC used its authority to oversee the initial construction of much of the interstate pipeline system which linked supply and demand. In so doing, the commission encouraged the rapid, yet orderly, expansion of the industry.

Both economic and regulatory realities fostered the dynamism of the era. The postwar decade reestablished with a vengeance an old maxim of the natural gas industry: when gas was available, it was the fuel of choice for most categories of consumers. Ample new supplies and the pipeline build-ing boom of the era made more and more gas available to more and more consumers, and the price of this excellent fuel was lower in terms of heating content than either coal or fuel oil. In its *Annual Report* for 1948 Texas East-ern noted "the skyrocketing demand for natural gas," which ". . . is not the result of a trend toward purchasing a superior fuel at a premium price, but rather the result, quite often, of attempts to economize through purchasing natural gas at a cheaper rate than either oil or coal."[6] All segments of the gas industry hurried forward to take advantage of the extraordinary oppor-tunities of an era of postwar economic expansion with a seemingly limitless demand for product.

The most attractive markets were the major cities not yet fully served by natural gas. For companies such as Texas Eastern, Tennessee Gas, and Transcontinental, this meant the cities of the eastern seaboard. The conver-sion of this heavily populated region to natural gas came swiftly and thoroughly in the 1940s and 1950s. Table 4.1 suggests the magnitude of this change by summarizing the growing use of natural gas in major urban areas of the Northeast from 1935 to 1960. During this period Philadelphia, New York, and Boston became the critical targets on the maps of strategists at the major transmission companies.

Natural gas replaced manufactured gas in these cities in a competitive process shaped by regulatory politics. Manufactured gas had spawned a fully developed political economy after almost a century of use in most eastern cities, and its markets and supporting institutions did not simply collapse in the face of competition from natural gas. The major public utilities in the Northeast had hundreds of millions of dollars invested in the large manu-facturing plants and related facilities needed to produce and distribute manu-factured gas. These powerful companies would have to be satisfied that it was in their interest to convert to natural gas. State and local utility commis-sions presided over a comfortable, predictable system. They would have to

TABLE 4.1   Gas Sales of Utilities, 1935–59 (millions of therms)

	Total United States			Total U.S. Residential		
Year	Natural Gas	Manufactured Gas	Mixed Gas	Natural Gas	Manufactured Gas	Mixed Gas
1935	10,635	1,611	678	2,773	1,194	477
1937	13,480	1,535	758	3,365	1,110	512
1939	13,576	1,580	770	3,646	1,118	525
1941	16,358	1,726	925	4,113	1,149	600
1943	20,325	1,967	1,123	5,022	1,261	718
1945	22,563	2,088	1,194	5,601	1,365	769
1947	26,022	2,319	1,481	7,514	1,558	977
1949	32,234	2,274	1,191	9,541	1,526	701
1951	44,718	1,763	1,652	14,009	1,108	1,030
1953	52,800	838	2,351	16,013	478	1,487
1955	63,008	457	3,039	20,086	235	2,011
1957	74,649	215	2,105	24,278	123	1,541
1959	85,518	143	2,196	28,027	79	1,592

Note: 1 therm is equivalent to 100,000 BTUs.
Source: American Gas Association, *Historical Statistics of the Gas Industry* (Arlington: AGA, 1964), 213.

be convinced to introduce a dynamic, and thus destabilizing, new element into this system. Coal companies and the railroads that carried coal had a vested interest in supplying the coal used to make manufactured gas. They would have to be pushed aside with a combination of economic and political force. Gradually, over almost a decade of change, natural gas overwhelmed all of these institutional and competitive barriers with assurances of long-term supplies of a superior fuel at relatively low prices. For a transition period manufactured gas continued to be used as a supplemental fuel, but by 1955 it had gone the way of the horse-drawn carriage.

Interfuel competition was accompanied by intense competition within the natural gas industry. One commentator in this era called the natural gas transmission a "brawling, bawling industry," one in which "brutal fights are waged for gas reserves, for access to new markets or for favored positions within markets too big for one supplier. A high proportion of top executives in the business are Texans; and even if they are not born with an aptitude for cutting throats they perforce acquire it."[7] This tone reflected the high stakes as well as the personalities of the players. All large competitors knew that the first mover into a new market would be in an excellent position to acquire and retain a dominant position. Then the "brawling" and "bawling" would start, as the initial leader and the competitors sought to shape the basic supply picture for the market. The results of these struggles can be easily summarized, but such a summary fails to convey the excitement and the competitive zeal of these formative years.

Executives at Texas Eastern had more excitement than they probably wanted as they launched their competition for new territories. The company's ear-

MAP 4.2 Major Natural Gas Supply Areas

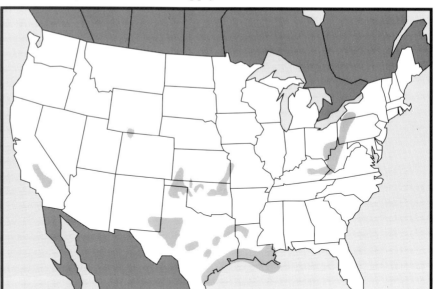

liest choices of markets had been decided in its FPC certificate hearing. The initial certificate authorized the firm to sell gas to Appalachian customers and to two utilities in Philadelphia. Two other regions, the New York City metropolitan area and New England, presented even larger potential markets for natural gas, larger by far than the Appalachian and Philadelphia markets. Texas Eastern's pipeline system already extended into Linden, New Jersey, passing near major metropolitan areas such as Pittsburgh, Philadelphia, and New York City, but it faced intense competition in all of these cities from other transmission companies with pipelines extending to or near them. Philadelphia and Pittsburgh were the focal points of the early conflicts between Texas Eastern and Tennessee Gas. New York City became the key battleground for Texas Eastern and Transcontinental. The New England area was for a time open ground, since no natural gas pipelines served the region in the early 1950s. But the tranquility of New England was soon shattered by a bitter, no-holds-barred fight between Texas Eastern and Tennessee Gas. This struggle climaxed an era of corporate wars of territorial expansion.[8]

Throughout these struggles the FPC was an intrusive and powerful referee. To expand, a gas transmission company had to apply for a certificate and participate in public hearings, just as it had done for its original authorization. The FPC could divide markets between competing lines and determine the volume and rates at which each of the companies could sell its gas. Thus, while privately owned gas transmission companies provided the impetus for natural gas, the FPC shaped this drive along what it considered expansion "proper" competitive lines.

During its first seven years of operation, Texas Eastern pushed hard to expand, fighting its competitive battles in both the marketplace and the regulatory arena. The company first increased sales in its original market area, the Appalachian region. Next, it began selling gas to utilities farther along its pipeline system, first in the Philadelphia area. It next tried to crack the New York City market, but it lost the bulk of this trade to Transcontinental. Finally, it struggled for over five years to break into New England, the last northeastern market without natural gas. All of these corporate efforts were accompanied by the sort of conflicts and even confusion which inevitably arises when a new company is in competition with other aggressive businesses — all under the close watch of an agency that was itself exploring new regulatory frontiers.

Texas Eastern's chief engineer, Baxter Goodrich, was in charge of the company's expansion program. In order to keep up with growing demand, Texas Eastern steadily expanded its system, keeping the company's engineering staff constantly at work. Expansion involved much more than just contracting for increased sales and supplies of natural gas. For Texas Eastern it meant regularly adding compressor stations and horsepower, cleaning the pipeline, and examining the possibility of utilizing old and depleted northeastern natural gas fields for storage areas. In addition, the company began planning to build a third major pipeline into the Northeast. First, however, the company had to use its existing Inch Line system to push more gas into Appalachia and the huge northeastern market.

Texas Eastern had started to work out its expansion programs as soon as it had acquired the Inch Lines. As the hydrostatic testing and cleaning work progressed, the firm developed plans to increase the capacity of its system. But regional demand for natural gas was so high that before one expansion plan could be completed, an additional one had to be developed. Under Texas Eastern's original expansion plan — referred to as both the New England plan and the "433 Program," because it would boost the capacity of the Inch Lines to 433 mmcf/d — the FPC approved the installation of twenty-one compressor stations with a total horsepower of 153,000. In February, 1948, Texas Eastern decided, pending FPC approval, to boost capacity an additional 75 mmcf/d. The FPC gave its temporary approval in June to this "508 Program," which did not require the installation of new compressor stations. It did, however, call for a substantial increase in system strength from 153,500 to 239,900 horsepower. The pipeline capacity reached 508 mmcf/d by early 1949.

This expansion was needed just to supply the growing demands of Texas Eastern's primary Appalachian customers, Consolidated Natural Gas and Columbia Gas System. These two companies, which operated the major distribution systems in Appalachia, were hungry for gas. They absorbed almost all of Texas Eastern's gas in the late 1940s, and they remained very significant customers even after the company began serving broader markets in the Northeast.

Soon after Texas Eastern and the Consolidated companies accepted the "508 Program" (February, 1948), Texas Eastern agreed to sell more gas to three other, smaller Appalachian distribution companies under an agreement signed on May 21 with Texas Gas Transmission Corporation. According to this contract, Texas Eastern would sell Texas Gas up to 200 mmcf/d at a delivery point near Lisbon, Louisiana. In return Texas Gas would sell to Texas Eastern near Middletown, Ohio, up to 235 mmcf/d, of which 210 mmcf/d would be sold to the three Appalachian companies. Thus, before the "508 Program" had even received FPC approval, Texas Eastern had made firm plans for the "740 Program." This new effort was the company's first expansion within its Appalachian service area in which it relied upon the pipeline facilities of a potential competitor to increase its own sales. It also marked the beginning of a long alliance with Texas Gas, on Owensboro, Kentucky–based company serving markets spread through western Tennessee, Kentucky, Indiana, Illinois, Ohio, Arkansas, Louisiana, and Mississippi. The company's gas supplies came from fields in Texas and Louisiana, as well as from purchases from United Gas, Texas Eastern, and other companies.

The 740 plan called for the construction of 177 miles of twenty-six-inch line to "loop" the Big and Little Big Inch lines from Lebanon, Ohio, to a point west of the West Virginia border. Also, thirty-six miles of twenty-inch pipe would be run parallel to the Little Big Inch in northern Louisiana and thirty-three miles of a twenty-inch loop would run from Baytown to Beaumont, Texas. In addition, 112 miles of new sixteen-inch pipe would run from Houston to supply fields in Lavaca County, Texas. This plan required both construction and modification of compressor stations. Texas Eastern would construct three new reciprocating compressor stations – one each in Ohio, Texas, and Louisiana – convert two former oil-pumping stations to centrifugal gas compressors, and modify four existing stations in Ohio and Pennsylvania.

This agreement was important for both Texas Eastern and Texas Gas. Its origins dated back to January, 1948, when Texas Gas President J. H. Hillman, Jr., met with R. H. Hargrove to discuss gas purchases. Since United Gas did not have enough supply to support Texas Gas's expansion, the latter firm needed ties with Texas Eastern. Originally, the agreement called for Texas Eastern to deliver gas near Lisbon, Louisiana; it was amended in the summer of 1948 to provide for an extension of the Texas Gas system in Ohio to connect there with Texas Eastern. The agreement enabled Texas Gas to continue the planned expansion of its own system, and it allowed Texas Eastern to increase its system capacity. There were other advantages as well. J. H. Hillman also owned Pittsburgh Coke and Chemical and controlled several coal, coke, and iron companies, and in return for assistance with his gas supplies, he was able to make scarce steel piping available to Hargrove for

Texas Eastern's pipeline expansion. Little wonder, then, that during the following two years, the original agreement was enlarged several times.[9]

The two companies developed very close ties. To gain FPC approval and financing for its own expansion, Texas Gas at times relied upon some of the same persons who had been instrumental in forming Texas Eastern. August Belmont, through Dillon, Read, supervised the financing for Texas Gas's expansion. J. Ross Gamble, Texas Eastern's Washington, D.C. attorney, assisted Texas Gas in some of its Washington dealings. The ties between them steadily grew stronger. Texas Gas came to rely on TE for much of its supply. In February, 1950, Texas Eastern and Texas Gas signed a twenty-year supply agreement and also entered into the so-called Carthage contract, which called for Texas Eastern to deliver 100 mmcf/d before November, 1951, and 200 mmcf/d thereafter. The two contracts were important for the future of both firms.

These deals helped Texas Eastern increase sales in its original market area, providing the company with a solid base as it anxiously reached out to new customers farther east. The first target was Philadelphia, where Texas Eastern had signed contracts with two utilities, Philadelphia Electric Company and Philadelphia Gas Works Company. Sales to these companies began in September of 1948, making Philadelphia the first major eastern city to begin receiving gas from the Southwest. Once cheaper natural gas began to flow into the region, Philadelphia quickly converted from manufactured gas to mixed gas.

Like most other utilities after World War II, Philadelphia Electric had confronted a growing demand for gas, due in large part to a dramatic rise in residential housing construction and an increased interest in gas home heating. The rising price of coal made manufactured gas more expensive than natural gas, even after the addition of transportation charges from gas fields more than one thousand miles away in Texas. Along with most other northeastern utilities, Philadelphia Electric found it difficult to keep on hand adequate supplies of all the necessary components for the production of manufactured gas. In the summer of 1946 the company had faced serious problems. It had received nine thousand orders for gas installations, but only 1,721 could be made that year due to the limited supply of manufactured gas. Despite determined attempts by the coal lobby to keep natural gas out of Pennsylvania, the growing demand in Philadelphia and the proximity of the Inch Lines encouraged the utility to go after this new fuel. Once regulatory approval had been received and the short lateral pipelines connecting the Inch Lines to Philadelphia Electric Company's own pipeline system were completed, the process of change accelerated.

In September, 1948, when Texas Eastern began delivering natural gas to Philadelphia Electric's Tilghman Street Gas Plant, the new supplies were used for reforming and enriching the utility's current manufactured gas production. Philadelphia Electric's President, Horace P. Liversidge, had even larger plans for the future. He noted the rapid increase in customer applications for natural gas and said that ". . . the supply of natural gas to Philadelphia Electric will permit it to increase its capacity and bring nearer the time when all applicants for gas services may be accepted and adequately supplied."[10] First, natural gas (which has an average heating content of about 1020 Btu) was added to the manufactured gas, with a heating content typically about 520 Btu, to transform it into mixed gas, with a heating content of 801 Btu. This change required adjustments in all residential appliances designed to use manufactured gas.

Philadelphia Electric hired four hundred men to make the needed adjustments to each residential consumer's gas appliances. This four-hundred-man conversion team adjusted 380,000 appliances in the homes of 170,000 customers. Adjustments were made to 220 various kinds of gas ranges, 160 styles of water heaters, and numerous kinds of house heaters, exclusive of commercial or industrial gas appliances. As demand continued to increase, Philadelphia Electric and other local utilities contracted for even more supplies from Texas Eastern. By the end of the 1950s the Philadelphia utilities had eliminated all the manufactured gas from their distribution operations, and the manufactured gas business in Philadelphia disappeared.[11]

The Philadelphia sequence was repeated in other major eastern cities in subsequent years.[12] Natural gas was simply too good a fuel to be long held out of the market by either short-term economic or political considerations. Although the conversion process was demanding, it was not prohibitively expensive; the higher heating content of natural gas promised considerable long-term savings that far exceeded short-term conversion costs. Expensive expansion of distribution mains could be pushed far into the future because tasks traditionally fueled by manufactured gas could be accomplished with about half the volume of natural gas. The experience of Philadelphia confirmed what was increasingly evident to utility executives throughout the Northeast: Natural gas was the wave of the future.

The most significant single utility market was the New York City area, the largest market for natural gas in the nation. Millions of potential consumers in and around New York City awaited the coming of this new fuel, and the company that got there first would enjoy an immediate and lasting bonanza. Thus, it was not surprising that all the major Southwest-to-Northeast transmission companies had an eye on that market.

During 1949 Transcontinental Gas Pipe Line Corporation (Transco) began construction of a pipeline from the Rio Grande Valley in Texas into Manhattan to serve several large customers, including Consolidated Edison and Brooklyn Union Gas Company. Texas attorney Claude A. Williams, who had once served as a district attorney in the East Texas oil field, led the enterprise. His close associate was Rogers Lacy, who owned substantial oil and gas reserves in Texas. Williams had submitted the highest cash bid in the initial government auction for the Inch Lines; he had been the runner-up to Texas

Eastern at the second bid. Even before the War Assets Administration had completed its deliberations on the disposal of the Inch Lines, Williams had applied to the FPC for permission to construct a new pipeline from Texas to New Jersey in the event he failed to obtain the government lines. This tactic proved critical to Transco for it gave the company a head start through the regulatory maze which confronted any other competitors who might decide to build a new system parallel to the Inch Lines.[13] The path chosen went from the Texas-Mexican border, through Houston, across Alabama and Georgia to the north of Atlanta, through the heart of North Carolina and Virginia, near the outskirts of Washington, D.C., to Baltimore, and on to New York City. Williams's choice of New York City as the eastern terminus for his line was an obvious one, since neither Texas Eastern nor Tennessee Gas had made it into this giant market. In reaching it, Transco — unlike Texas Eastern or even Tennessee Gas — could choose its route based strictly on peacetime commercial considerations. Along the way, its line penetrated numerous virgin markets, giving it excellent opportunities for future expansion.

Transco moved forward rapidly while Texas Eastern was consolidating its position in the Appalachian region and Philadelphia in the late 1940s. Williams's quest for supplies led finally to agreements with producers along the Texas-Louisiana Gulf Coast. His search for firm purchase contracts was given a boost by a long-term agreement with Sun Oil to supply its Marcus Hook (Pennsylvania) refinery. As this work went forward, Transco survived an arduous nine-month-long FPC certification hearing in 1948, complete with the predictable parade of intervenors. After finally winning FPC approval and obtaining financing, Transco began construction of its thirty-inch, thousand-mile main line in the summer of 1949. In January of 1951 the $233 million pipeline began to transport gas "from the region of the world's greatest natural gas reserves to the world's richest market."[14]

Texas Eastern had sought to protect its competitive advantage by filing a motion asking the FPC to dismiss Transco's application. Jack Head, counsel for TE, argued that the line was not necessary because ultimately his company would serve the New York area. He asserted further that the Transco project would disrupt the orderly development of Texas Eastern's system. But the FPC did not buy this argument. It was moving toward a de facto policy of assuring that each major gas market was served by more than one major pipeline, thus providing a measure of protection against possible future abuses.

In this sense, the FPC was beginning to treat gas transmission as a "natural oligopoly" (with competition among several large firms) rather than a "natural monopoly," which had been the traditional watchword in utility regulation. In denying the appeal to block Transco's entry into New York, the commission took occasion to chide Texas Eastern about the values of competition. The commission pointed out to the company that its purchase of the Inch Lines did not bestow a monopoly in the Middle Atlantic area and that "it should go out and fight for business."[15] This foray into the tricky world of regulatory warfare taught Texas Eastern's leaders a valuable lesson. The acquisition of the Inch Lines had marked their company as a leader in its industry. As such, it could expect little protection from an agency committed to fostering a new brand of regulated, oligopolistic competition.

An opportunity soon came for Texas Eastern to follow the FPC's advice at Transco's expense. As Transco neared completion of its main transmission line near New York City, one of its prospective New York area customers, the small New York and Richmond Gas Company, became restive. It wanted to convert its distribution system entirely to natural gas, but in order to receive any gas from Transco, the company requested that the FPC include it among the other retail gas distributors stated to receive that firm's gas. The FPC granted the small company only 2.5 mmcf/d out of Transco's initial capacity of 340 mmcf/d. The pipeline's larger customers, including Consolidated Edison of New York, Public Service of New Jersey, and Brooklyn Union Gas, had many more customers themselves, and they received most of Transco's gas supply.

Frustrated with its low allocations from Transco, the New York and Richmond Gas Company turned to Texas Eastern. Since Texas Eastern had transmission lines to the south in nearby New Jersey, and a connection to the New York and Richmond's service area, including Staten Island, the New York utility applied to the FPC to be served by Texas Eastern. The commission agreed to switch Richmond's gas supply to TE, which made the first delivery of southwestern natural gas to New York City. In a public ceremony marking the delivery, New York Mayor William O'Dwyer lit on Staten Island the first flame produced from southwestern gas. During 1949, the first year of operation with natural gas, New York and Richmond made a net profit of $200,000, compared to a loss of $45,000 in 1948, and passed on to its customers an 11 percent rate reduction. In this instance, Texas Eastern had served notice that an initial loss did not mean it would halt its "fight for business."[16]

Texas Eastern was the first pipeline company to deliver gas to New York City, but it did not become the major supplier to the city's utilities. Transcontinental Gas Pipe Line's grip on Consolidated Edison and Brooklyn Union Gas Company, which required tremendous volumes of gas, remained firm. Although Texas Eastern and Tennessee Gas both made subsequent inroads into the vast New York City market, Transco consolidated its early lead in this area and remained the dominant supplier. This development assured Transco's status as one of the nation's major cross-country natural gas transmission companies.

The competition with Transco primed TE for its next battle with Tennessee Gas for the New England market. Texas Eastern's overall plan for expansion in early 1948 identified New England as an important target. The company made official its "New England Plan" in March, 1948, when it filed an application to the FPC to construct a third pipeline parallel to the Big and Little Big Inch lines. This third line was to be twenty-six inches in diameter and to extend from Longview, Texas, to a point near the town of Wind Ridge in southwestern Pennsylvania. It would be over a thousand miles long with 314,740 horsepower and a capacity of 425 mmcf/d, and it would cost approximately $152,131,000. The proposed line would increase Texas Eastern's total capacity to approximately 933 mmcf/d, and the plan allocated part of the 425 mmcf/d to various customers in New England.

E. Holley Poe had led Texas Eastern's first change on the New England market. Shortly after the company began operations in 1947, Poe attempted to develop a natural gas distribution company in New England. Minute Man Gas Company would supply the New England market with gas delivered by Texas Eastern. Under Poe's plan, Texas Eastern would retain a controlling interest but join in partnership three large regional gas distributor companies: Eastern Gas and Fuel Associates, New England Gas and Electric Association, Providence Gas Company, and several smaller firms. While in Boston to complete the arrangements for this venture, Poe received a phone call at his hotel before leaving to meet with the other partners in the deal and sign the papers. A representative of the financial institution told him that the firm had been pressured to back out of the deal.[17]

Whether the pressure came from a competing company or from the other utilities is uncertain. But when the local companies involved came to believe that their share of the proposed profits might be insufficient, the deal quickly broke down. One journal vividly described the situation: "This proposal got a freeze-out which is memorable even in New England, where the fiscal climate has long been adverse to outsiders who propose to make money New Englanders might be making themselves."[18]

With Poe's effort derailed, the company modified its plans to construct the additional twenty-six-inch line. Texas Eastern was still determined to enter the New England market, but bitter competition forced the company to reassess its strategy. Since the New England situation remained confused, the company amended its FPC application, reducing its request from an additional 425 to only 200 mmcf/d. The company's market research indicated that New England would require approximately 250 mmcf/d in natural gas at the end of a five-year development period. Since some portion of that demand would undoubtedly be allocated to Tennessee or other successful competitors, Texas Eastern lowered its sights. The prospects for the New England market remained bright, but the company's effort to become its dominant supplier was stalled.

For a time, Texas Eastern tried to revitalize a version of the original Poe deal. The company proceeded carefully and discreetly, for it knew that similar plans were being laid by Gardiner Symonds at Tennessee Gas and Transmission. Soon, however, discretion went overboard as open warfare erupted between Tennessee Gas and Texas Eastern. The battles, which raged for more than five years, took place before the FPC and spilled over into several state governments. The troops included a cohort of highly paid Washington lobbyists and a corps of attorneys. The nation's press viewed the affair as proof that natural gas was, indeed, a "brawling, bawling industry."[19]

Reginald Hargrove's first move in this campaign involved an effort to form a pipeline company, Algonquin Gas Transmission Company, with the same three large New England distributors Poe had aligned in the earlier unsuccessful deal. Texas Eastern would remain as Algonquin's major supplier of natural gas. Hargrove's approach succeeded. The corporate partners established Algonquin Gas Transmission on September 28, 1949 (see map 4.3). On January 24, 1950, the new company applied to the FPC for a certificate to construct and operate the new pipeline. It would connect with Texas Eastern facilities in New Jersey and extend north to Boston.[20] But Tennessee Gas Transmission Company was not about to back away from this challenge.

In popular perceptions — especially in the business press — the ensuing struggles became a man-to-man duel between Reginald Hargrove and Gardiner Symonds. Their contrasting public images made the struggle all the more interesting. Symonds was an Easterner with a banking background. Hargrove's strong ties to Louisiana made him "almost" a native Texan; virtually his entire career had been spent in the gas industry. Journalistic accounts tended to emphasize the differences in their personalities. Early accounts of the New England controversy depicted Symonds as a "bland, affable citizen [who] typifies the newer element in gas-pipeline management," while later articles emphasized that he was "famed as a scrapper in this industry of scrappers," an "acknowledged 'enfant terrible'," "hard fighting," and "vindictive" toward his industry adversaries.[21] Hargrove's media image was more subdued. One account described him as the "finest witness in the country . . . whose belligerence tends more to the tart quip than the rap of a fist," but nevertheless portrayed him "as one of the shrewdest and toughest pipeliners of the bunch."[22] The personal element spiced up this battle for New England gas markets, and the ongoing struggles remained a topic of general interest in the region and the industry.

Symonds was intent upon capturing the New England market before Texas Eastern and Algonquin. Several weeks before the incorporation of Algonquin, Tennessee Gas organized a wholly owned subsidiary, Northeastern Gas Transmission Company, to serve the New England market. Symonds then announced plans to build a gas pipeline from existing Tennessee Gas terminals at Buffalo, New York, to New England and applied for FPC certification of this project. Thus in a matter of weeks, two major companies put forward competing proposals to supply natural gas to Boston and the remainder of New England.[23]

The contest then moved to the Federal Power Commission. Eschewing the approach it had adopted in the New York case, the FPC initially expressed the opinion that a single company, or supplier, should supply natural gas

MAP 4.3 Algonquin Gas Transmission Co., 1953

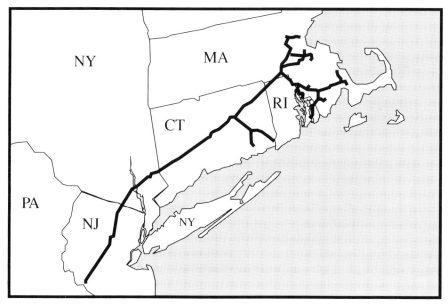

to the entire New England market. But the commission soon developed doubts about the ability of a single company to fulfill the area's long-range market demands. It urged the two companies, Algonquin and Northeastern, to seek an agreement to share the New England market. Acknowledging that this proposal had merit, Algonquin suggested "peace talks" with Northeastern. But Gardiner Symonds was adamantly opposed. He argued that "in the interests of the people of New England . . . the one essential is single management responsibility concerned only with selling natural gas." He charged that Eastern Gas and Fuel Associates, a major stockholder in Algonquin, was controlled by those "whose primary interest is the coal mining industry"; they could not be trusted to act as an impartial seller of natural gas.[24] This charge was not easily dismissed, since in 1947 Eastern Gas and Fuel had indeed intervened in Texas Eastern's certificate hearings and opposed the sale and use of the Inch Lines for natural gas. Indeed, the Koppers Company, a coke manufacturing concern, once owned Eastern. Yet, Reginald Hargrove clearly believed the company's dedication to natural gas was complete. He told regulators that the investors in Algonquin, including Eastern Gas and Fuel, had already invested a great deal of money in natural gas and "no company is going to throw $3½ million away for a front."[25]

After its efforts to promote cooperation proved fruitless, the FPC conducted further hearings on the matter. Then the commission decided to force rather than to persuade the companies to share New England. In November, 1950, the FPC ruled that Gardiner Symonds's Northeastern should serve 54 percent of the New England region, with the remainder reserved for Algonquin. Texas Eastern's affiliate thus claimed slightly less than half the regional market, but its share included the largest city in the area, metropolitan Boston. In a separate decision a few months later, the FPC implemented its decision by authorizing Algonquin to begin constructing its pipeline.[26]

Symonds would not accept the FPC ruling. He appealed for a rehearing but found that body unsympathetic. The commission dismissed his plea, pointing out that it had been "untimely filed" and refusing further hearings. Symonds then bypassed the regulation and filed suit at the U. S. Third Circuit Court of Appeals. Symonds claimed that the FPC denied Northeastern due process. The court agreed with Symonds, nullified the commission's earlier decision to split the market, and required the FPC to reopen the hearings on New England. Algonquin and Texas Eastern appealed the Third Circuit Court's decision to the U. S. Supreme Court via writ of certiorari, but the Supreme Court denied these motions. The FPC, thus charged with a complete review of the matter, set new hearings for November, 1952.[27] In its effort to find an equitable solution for bringing gas supply to New England from at least one of two competitors, the FPC and the courts, rather than the pipelines, became the focus of corporate activity.

The Federal Power Commission reopened hearings on the New England matter in November. Somewhat ironically, it discovered that public opinion favored FPC's original proposal that Algonquin and Northeastern share the market. As early as 1950 Massachusetts Governor Paul Dever had announced that he favored a dual supply. After Northeastern had rejected this proposal, Dever sought to mediate a compromise, but Gardiner Symonds ignored his efforts. As the FPC began its rehearing in 1952, Dever reaffirmed his support of the dual supply plan, along with Massachusetts Congressman Henry Cabot Lodge and Senator Leverett Saltonstall. One month later, Christian Herter, Massachusetts governor-elect, endorsed the dual supply approach.[28]

This support reflected the fact that New England, with its severe winters, required all the natural gas that the two firms could supply. Reginald Hargrove made several speeches to New England business groups in an effort to assure them that adequate gas supplies would always be present. In an earlier speech before the New England Council, he pointed out that the projected capacity of Algonquin alone would be able to satisfy the New England demand during all seasons.[29] Yet natives better acquainted with the harshness of New England winters apparently wanted the assurances that would be provided by two suppliers.

Another New England concern was the "foreign" control of Northeastern. Gardiner Symond's formation of that company as a wholly owned subsidiary of his Tennessee Gas Transmission aroused resentment of the wealthy outsiders shaping New England's energy system. By contrast, Texas Eastern's project was designed to include local interests. Eastern Gas and Fuel Associates and New England Gas and Associates together owned over 70 percent of Algonquin. Texas Eastern owned only 28 percent of the venture, and

Reginald Hargrove often pointed this out in talks given in New England. He described Algonquin as "a joint venture — one-fourth ours, three-fourths New England's."[30] Meanwhile, press accounts of the time criticized Northeastern for being owned and managed by outsiders and cited the need for "keeping New England for New Englanders." Characteristically, Gardiner Symonds ignored the criticism. He actually inflamed the controversy by stating that "we had no intention of giving away part of [Northeastern] for the privilege of doing business in New England."[31]

As this debate surged back and forth, the FPC's new hearing on Algonquin droned on, from November of 1952 through the next June. By the late winter of 1952 Northeastern had completed its New England line. Algonquin's line, on the other hand, remained one hundred miles short of completion, due to the court's decision throwing out the FPC's earlier approval of Algonquin's application. Algonquin charged that this delay was costing as much as $32,000 per day and adding a substantiated cost overrun to its estimated $50 million price tag. Algonquin requested an "emergency certificate" from the FPC to at least finish construction of the line, but the commission replied that Algonquin would have to wait for the rehearing. One magazine article covering these events noted that if the FPC refused to grant a certificate to Algonquin, the company "faced the gloomy prospect of trying to sell its premature pipeline for what it could get to the only possible bidder: its No. 1 enemy, Gardiner Symonds and Northeastern."[32] Texas Eastern's 1952 *Annual Report* expressed a similar concern for the future of Algonquin. Texas Eastern reported that although it had invested $4 million in Algonquin, it did not "consider the extent of such exposure after tax credits to be particularly significant in relation to the size of the Company's other assets and investments."[33]

Sensing victory, Symonds continued to attempt to pressure the FPC into giving him the entire New England market. He argued that Algonquin's increasing cost — due to the delay he was causing — would later be translated into higher gas prices. Northeastern, he stated, would not have as high a rate base as Algonquin and could charge lower rates. Symonds also relied on the assistance of Washington insiders. He employed Thomas G. Corcoran, the Washington attorney and lobbyist, who had apparently been involved in a rival bid for the Inch Lines. "Tommy the Cork," as he was called in his New Deal days, worked hard to gain political support for Symonds. *Life* magazine reported that Corcoran and Massachusetts Rep. John McCormack, Democratic majority leader and Corcoran's friend, had "convened a meeting which has never been matched in FPC annuals. Four of the five commissioners and several of the staff attended. New England representatives and senators rawhided the commissioners for upward of two hours, telling them in effect to quit stalling and get gas into New England — or else. Corcoran, apparently overcome by good taste, did not attend."[34]

While Symonds employed Washington heavy hitters to swing opinion in his favor, the Texas Eastern–Algonquin group either worked behind the scenes or had few allies. The article noted that only Secretary of Labor Maurice Tobin, of the prominent Boston family, openly supported their project. Apparently, his efforts remained limited ". . . to four or five introductions at the commission and elsewhere."[35]

Despite efforts to sway opinion in political circles, only the FPC could solve the dilemma. But the commission was groaning under the huge volume of information presented at the hearings; the hearings included eighty-three daily sessions and 125 witnesses.[36] The months of hearings gave the appearance of fair play and due process, but the price for thoroughness was high. The FPC firmly pushed for compromise, and Symonds and Hargrove began to realize that compromise was the only option.

Testifying in March, 1953, Symonds sounded uncharacteristically gracious when he noted that even if only Northeastern received permission to sell gas in New England, it would purchase gas supply from both Tennessee Gas and Texas Eastern.[37] Hargrove moderated his position also when he cited surveys which indicated a rapid increase in New England gas demand which would "rapidly outdistance the ability of . . . one [company] service to be adequate for New England."[38]

Soon thereafter both Algonquin and Northeastern agreed the hearings would end on June 3, 1953, followed by closing arguments within fifteen days. The FPC would issue its final decision on July 1, 1953. The proposed settlement subsequently accepted by the parties reflected this mood, and it won the approval of the FPC.[39] On July 1, all parties involved agreed to a dual supply for New England, based largely on the FPC's earlier decision. Algonquin would serve the Boston area, but in return for giving up that major market, the FPC certified Tennessee Gas to serve two local distribution companies previously served by Texas Eastern in Louisville, Kentucky, and Pittsburgh, Pennsylvania, as well as several other small Tennessee towns.[40] Obviously, the long, drawn-out legal battle had worn them down, making compromise seem more attractive. Regulatory battle fatigue encouraged all participants to leave the hearing room and return to the right-of-way.

Symonds gained one additional and unexpected concession. Tennessee Gas had another application pending before the FPC to deliver gas to Niagara Gas Transmission Limited for resale in Canada. He tied final acceptance to FPC approval of an export license to sell gas in Canada. The commission initially did not rule on this issue and scheduled further hearings for its consideration. *Time* magazine then reported that Symonds was in "no mood to carry out the original agreement [the Algonquin-Northeastern settlement] until his Canadian market is guaranteed."[41] However, the FPC granted Tennessee's export permit within a few weeks, and Symonds supported the New England settlement.[42] Symonds gambled that the commission's desire to conclude the New England controversy and avoid a politically explosive dispute involving gas exports to Canada gave him leverage in gaining last minute concessions. Although he did not receive the entire New England market, his overall gains while stalling gave him entry into the Canadian market.

In early July Algonquin and Northeastern submitted their official settlement offer to the FPC. In August Algonquin finally received a certificate of public convenience and necessity to finish construction of its pipeline, which it did in only one month. And on September 2, 1953, Algonquin began delivering gas to its New England customers. The intense and lengthy competition for the New England market was not rewarded with profits. The financial returns to Texas Eastern proved mediocre in comparison to the company's record in other markets. In the New England case, both individual and corporate pride were at stake as two aggressive competitors fought for dominance, or at least equity, in the last major northeastern gas market remaining to be served with natural gas.

The fight for New England was the last of the series of all-out scrambles for new territories that had marked the era after World War II. Texas Eastern had won on some fronts, lost on others, and negotiatied settlements on still others. Its major competitors could all say the same. The FPC hearings were the most visible settings for these struggles; outside of these heated public confrontations proceeded the hard work of laying pipe, securing purchases and sales, and obtaining the financing needed for expansion.

The New England episode marked the conclusion of an impressive era of entrepreneurship in the natural gas industry. Three interstate pipeline companies, Texas Eastern, Transco, and Tennessee Gas had fought for the opportunity to sell southwestern natural gas in northeastern markets. Although the FPC shaped this struggle, hard-driving businessmen — notably George Brown and Reginald Hargrove at Texas Eastern, Gardiner Symonds at Tennessee Gas, and Claude Williams at Transco — had been responsible for marshalling the financial and technical resources needed to operate their pipelines and push large quantities of natural gas into the northeastern states for the first time. They had created an entirely new industry. In the process, they had built three major Houston-based companies which would dominate this segment of the natural gas industry for decades to come.

The ascent of the natural gas industry in the Northeast occurred at the expense of manufactured gas. By 1953, with natural gas flowing into New England, leaders in the regional manufactured gas industry clearly understood that their long reign over the northeastern gas market was coming to a quick end. By the end of the decade their industry was gone, routed in the marketplace by a superior product. As the statistics indicate, natural gas did not simply take the traditional markets for manufactured gas; as more natural gas became available, it created entirely new markets for itself, becoming the fastest growing fuel in the post–World War II decades.

Texas Eastern's president, Reginald Hargrove, stepped back from the action to observe the state of industry during the early 1950s. Noting that the

Reginald H. Hargrove

era of rapid expansion was over, Hargrove commented upon the future prospects of the industry: "If the era of territorial expansion of our industry is coming to end," he told a group of investment bankers, "that of developing the potentialities of our present areas has scarce begun."[43] Texas Eastern certainly had the management it needed to confront this new era. At the top, George Brown, now an experienced gas man, was a firm, shrewd, and often imposing strategist, lobbyist, and financier. As a partner of Brown & Root, he brought an engineer's acumen to his job as chairman. Of course, he also brought along Brown & Root itself, as Texas Eastern's primary contractor for its expansion programs. Reginald Hargrove managed the company's strategy and its day-to-day operations, with expert pipeline engineering supplied by Baxter Goodrich and his co-workers. By the early 1950s Texas Eastern had created a strong organization, one bonded together by the shared experiences of building a company from the bottom up. Its employees had met the challenges posed by determined competitors and aggressive regulators.

One can excuse a touch of nostalgia for the company's formative years, "the good old days." The firm had a sharp, narrowly focused strategy, a small, close-knit work force, and opportunities for fun, advancement, and profit presented by a dynamic industry. Blessed with strong leaders who had aggressively and successfully pursued the "main chance" presented by the government's disposal of the Inch Lines, Texas Eastern surged forward as a major new company in a high-growth industry. Those who came later would look back with envy as they grappled with a more complicated array of problems amid great economic and regulatory uncertainty. But as Texas Eastern moved out of its formative years, its founders had every reason to be confident, even cocky, about their company's future.

Part Two

THE LURE OF DIVERSIFICATION
1954–71

Chapter 5

CONSTRAINED EXPANSION
OF THE GAS SYSTEM

The end of the era of rapid territorial expansion in the early 1950s did not mark the end of growth in the gas transmission business. During the next two decades, the industry continued to expand, as Texas Eastern and its competitors responded to consumer demand in existing markets by building new trunk and gathering lines, by improving service with extensive new storage facilities, and by searching for new supplies of gas. Texas Eastern, like most other gas transmission companies after 1954, sought pathways around growing regulatory constraints on its operations, constraints which were most readily apparent in the acquisition of adequate gas supplies.

Constrained growth was the keynote in a closely regulated industry that was clearly maturing. In the company's core industry, natural gas transmission, the Federal Power Commission was the source of much uncertainty. In the life of the FPC, and indirectly in the evolution of the gas industry as a whole, 1954 was a pivotal year. In that year, the Supreme Court's *Phillips* decision pushed the FPC reluctantly into the business of the regulation of gas prices at the wellhead. Instead of spending most of its scarce organizational resources overseeing the expansion of the gas pipeline system—as had been the case in the immediate postwar era—the FPC now had to focus its energies on the highly political problem of the case-by-case determination of prices. Texas Eastern had prospered under the FPC's expansion-minded regulatory regime before the *Phillips* decision. As the commission subsequently focused more and more of its efforts on wellhead pricing policies, the company confronted new problems in securing long-term gas supplies. The uncertainties posed by price regulation encouraged Texas Eastern to diversify both its sources of natural gas and its basic mix of business activities. Indeed, the FPC's ultimately unsuccessful effort to develop an effective system of price regulations was the major factor shaping the strategies of Texas Eastern and its competitors during the 1950s and 1960s.

Despite these problems, Texas Eastern steadily expanded its capacity to gather, store, and deliver natural gas by investing hundreds of millions of dollars in new facilities. While expanding capacity, the company also explored every available avenue for securing increased supplies of natural gas. These initiatives often involved creative efforts to avoid the FPC's price regulations, and they resulted in several protracted disputes with the commission. Texas Eastern also sought to acquire both gas supplies and new markets via a major acquisition. In 1967 it purchased Transwestern Pipeline Company, an important supplier of gas to southern California.

Taken as a whole, Texas Eastern's various strategies were successful. They enabled the company to grow steadily despite constraints imposed by regulatory policies. But Texas Eastern and its competitors could not forever escape the basic problem of the gas industry, the growing imbalance between the surging demand for natural gas and the declining supplies available for interstate shipment. Nor could the firm always deal effectively with the tensions that developed within its own organization. At Texas Eastern internal tensions mounted between those who had built the highly profitable gas business and those who sought to build diversified subsidiaries in unregulated industries. But as long as the company remained profitable, these tensions were tolerable.

One of the first snags Texas Eastern hit in the early 1950s was the inadequacy of its existing pipeline system. The twenty-inch Little Big Inch line posed special problems. It had been designed to transport petroleum products, and its size limited its gas-carrying capacity. By the early 1950s most new lines were at least thirty inches in diameter. These larger lines had substantially greater capacities and operating efficiencies. With demand surging, the obvious solution was to build a new pipeline.

As part of its original plan to expand into the New England market, Texas Eastern's managers had projected just such an investment. In addition to pushing the company into a new territory, the system would facilitate increased sales in existing northeastern markets. These plans took on an important symbolic meaning, as well, because the firm had purchased, and not built, its existing system. For the first time, Texas Eastern's engineers had an opportunity to design and construct a line that would meet their company's specific needs. Under the direction of Baxter Goodrich, vice president and chief engineer, they would build a modern, large-diameter line to supplement or even replace the existing Inch Lines.

Coming up to this challenge, Goodrich and his engineering staff took great pains to insure the line's structural integrity and operating efficiency. This was a significant, long-term investment. Accordingly, they built a line that would perform well over the long term even though it was not the least expensive in the short term. Because of the company's previous success in determining the precise strength of its pipe through hydrostatic testing, they applied this test to all of the pipe. Knowing the exact rating of the pipe allowed Texas Eastern to operate its system above the voluntary ASME pressure ratings. The Federal Power Commission approved Texas Eastern's application to build the system on February 27, 1951. Dubbed the "Kosciusko

Orville Carpenter and Baxter Goodrich

Line" after its point of origin at Kosciusko, Mississippi, the 791–mile, thirty-inch line extended to Connelsville, Pennsylvania.

The Kosciusko Line was the centerpiece in Texas Eastern's expansion plans (see map 5.1). The development of this system, the construction of six new compressor stations, and the building of thirty-five miles of thirty-inch line to the storage field rounded out an ambitious expansion program which gave Texas Eastern forty-two hundred miles of pipeline, thirty-five compressor stations, and a system capacity in excess of 1.2 bcf/d.[1] By the late 1950s the Kosciusko Line extended all the way to the Texas-Mexican border, where it could pick up Mexican gas under an agreement negotiated with Pemex (see chapter 7).

Texas Eastern relied upon Brown & Root, its chairman's company, for much of its engineering and construction work, including the Kosciusko expan-

MAP 5.1 The Kosciusko Pipeline

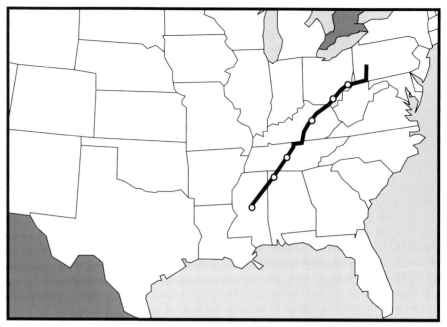

sion. Of course, George and Herman Brown had recognized from the start that Texas Eastern would require vast amounts of engineering and construction; this doubtless whetted their interest in the pipeline. Now their efforts were coming to full fruition. The Kosciusko pipeline was one of the first major projects Brown & Root undertook for its closely "allied" pipeline company. Other construction work followed. Between 1947 and 1984 the Browns' engineering firm completed at least eighty-eight major pipeline, compressor station, and related jobs for TE. In these years Brown & Root, as the firm's primary contractor, completed $1.3 billion in work for Texas Eastern.

George Brown's potential conflict of interest as both chairman of the board of Texas Eastern and partner in Brown & Root did not escape the scrutiny of the FPC. Charles Francis, TE's General Counsel, discussed the problem in a letter to Dick Carpenter, president of the company, during the 1950s: "Both the Federal Power Commission and the Securities Exchange Commission regard Herman and George Brown as controlling partners. We have always denied this but such is a matter open to debate. In rate cases, the Commission Staff takes the viewpoint that all contracts with controlling partners or directors are presumed to be unfair and inequitable and the burden of proof rests upon Texas Eastern to prove the fairness. . . . Hence, it is essential for our next rate case that these contracts be carefully scrutinized, legally approved and adopted by the Board of Directors, without the vote of Messrs. Herman and George Brown. Even with these safety provisions,

Kosciusko Line construction

the difficulties in a rate case in matters of this kind are very great. . . ."[2] Brown & Root nevertheless continued as a major contractor for Texas Eastern in the Kosciusko and other expansion projects, even though the pipeline firm was throughout walking a narrow line under the hostile eye of regulatory authorities.

Texas Eastern also had close relationships to United Gas, but these ties raised fewer questions of conflict of interest. Indeed, they proved extremely beneficial insofar as the company's gas supply needs were concerned. The new line was designed to tap United Gas's sources of supply, connecting directly with United Gas at Kosciusko. As the sole original supplier to the line, United Gas agreed to sell 387 mmcf/d to Texas Eastern. Later, other suppliers such as Southern Natural Gas also linked up with TE at Kosciusko.

Oakford storage field compressor station

Near the line's northern termination point at Connelsville, the Kosciusko Line passed by the Oakford Storage Field. This facility helped TE increase the capacity and improve the reliability of gas deliveries to northeastern markets. Storage fields offered a partial solution to the problems of meeting high winter peak loads. While limited use had been made of them for years, they were now employed to store huge amounts of natural gas. By purchasing a large volume of natural gas at a steady rate on a year-around basis, the pipeline could qualify for a discount from its suppliers, who valued the opportunity to sell gas all year. The Oakford storage facility, Texas Eastern's first, was developed by the New York State Natural Gas Corporation (a subsidiary of Consolidated Natural Gas Company) and by Texas Eastern as a co-owner.

The gas originally contained in this field (about 30 miles east of Pittsburgh) was nearly gone, but as Texas Eastern and its partner began to use the field, they encountered serious problems. The original operators at Oakford had drilled extensively. As Texas Eastern discovered, "No one had any records of where the wells had been drilled. No one had plugged the wells

Natural gas scrubber

and when the wells went dry, they just forgot about them. So, when we started pumping gas into that old abandoned formation, all of a sudden, gas started springing up all over the countryside from those abandoned wells, and it took months for us to find all the wells."[3]

Once these holes had all been plugged, gas could be injected into the facility and saved for future use. Texas Eastern originally planned to use Oakford mainly to support its sales in the New England area, but even after New England expansion was placed on hold, the storage facility was useful to the company's other service areas. Texas Eastern and Consolidated first injected 45 bcf of "cushion gas"—that is, gas that remained in storage to help provide pressure for the removal of the remaining gas—supporting 60 bcf of "top" or "circulating" gas that was available in equal shares to the two firms. Deliveries began in April, 1951.[4]

To further utilize the Oakford Storage field, Texas Eastern formed the Texas Eastern Penn-Jersey Transmission Corporation, a wholly owned subsidiary. This organization had a 265-mile system of twenty-four-inch pipelines, extending from the Oakford storage field to Texas Eastern's compressor station number 26 near Lambertville, New Jersey. It provided a capacity of 204 mmcf/d. With this addition to its network Texas Eastern had excess storage capacity, some of which it leased to one of its competitors. But its long-term plans for expansion clearly justified the investments it was making to increase the capacity and the efficiency of its system.[5]

Even before service to New England markets had begun, Texas Eastern began searching for increased supplies of natural gas. Some came from new properties in Texas. The enterprise augmented its supply by acquiring a majority interest in Wilcox Trend Gathering System, Incorporated, a southwestern Texas operation capable of delivering 100 mmcf/d. Wilcox Trend was the brainchild of Dallas oilman Harry W. Bass and attorney John C. Jacobs, Jr. The Wilcox Trend company built gathering lines to gas wells in the area and sold all of its product to one customer, Texas Eastern. In order to receive Wilcox Trend gas, TE extended its Big Inch system southward by building a 315-mile, twenty-four-inch pipeline from Provident City, Texas, to Castor, Louisiana (see map 5.2). After acquiring Wilcox Trend, the parent firm also brought John Jacobs—who proved to be an important addition to the executive ranks—into its management.

Texas Eastern's expansion was jolted by two events in 1954, one internal and the other external. The first was the sudden and unexpected death of Reginald Hargrove, who had directed its operations through its great expansion and who was expected to provide strong leadership for at least another decade. A group of friends and business associates, including Hargrove, N. C. McGowen, of United Gas, and Thomas Braniff, of Braniff Airlines, took a trip to the Louisiana coast to go duck hunting in early January of 1954. McGowen, who provided the transportation, had two planes ready for the return flight to Shreveport. Amid cold, wind, and ice, the group boarded the planes, continuing in one plane a poker game they had begun during the hunt. Some of those not involved in the game, including McGowen, flew back in the luggage plane. About ten minutes from Shreveport, the pilot of the plane carrying Hargrove and Thomas Braniff radioed that ice had formed on his plane's wings. He was losing altitude and would attempt an emergency landing on a lake. Unable to negotiate the landing, the plane crashed, killing its ten passengers and two pilots. In addition to Hargrove and Braniff, the crash claimed the lives of Justin and Randolph Querbes, two original stockholders in Texas Eastern.[6]

The crash stunned the company. A friend and a colleague who had been with the firm from its birth was dead at fifty-six. Hargrove's sudden death left the company with an unanticipated void at the top. Forced to replace its well-respected leader, the board named George T. Naff as the new presi-

MAP 5.2 Wilcox Trend Gathering System, Inc.

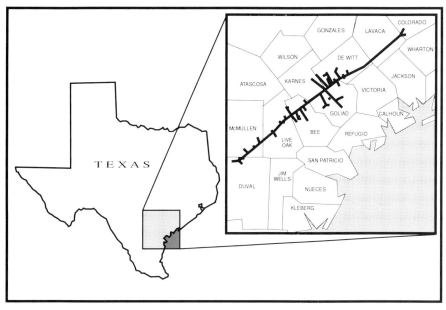

dent. Naff, like so many others at Texas Eastern, had come to the company from United Gas. He originally worked on the public financing of Texas Eastern and gradually rose to the position of first vice president (in charge of internal administration) before assuming the company's top post. Unfortunately, Naff did not stand up well to the pressures of his new job and remained as president for only two years. Texas Eastern's banker, August Belmont, recalled the confused state of affairs at Texas Eastern after Hargrove's death. "It was," he said ". . . a peculiarly headless thing for a while. . . . The fact that it was able to hold together, just meant that it was a real business, it was pretty hard to choke it."[7]

The second major blow to Texas Eastern came from outside the company. Far-reaching regulatory changes imposed a new operating environment on the entire gas industry. The coming of FPC price regulation at the wellhead altered the basic rules governing the production and sale of gas, setting off long-term trends which threatened to choke off growth in the industry. Since 1938 the FPC had regulated interstate natural gas pipelines but not the independent producers from whom the pipelines purchased their natural gas. Although a provision of the Natural Gas Act stated that the act "shall not apply . . . to the production or gathering of natural gas," other sections of the act seemed to leave open the possibility that the FPC could expand its powers over the production of natural gas. In 1951 the commission eschewed that course, ruling that the Phillips Petroleum Company, an independent gas producer and not an interstate pipeline company, was not subject to FPC

George Naff

regulation. Nevertheless, the state of Wisconsin filed suit against Phillips in an attempt to have it declared a natural gas company subject to FPC regulation. On June 7, 1954, the United States Supreme Court in *Phillips Petroleum Co. v. Wisconsin, et al.*, ruled that the FPC had authority over Phillips gas production sold into interstate commerce. Suddenly, the FPC found itself thrust into the netherworld of case-by-case rate-making for all natural gas sold in interstate commerce.

The natural gas industry as a whole lobbied hard against regulation of producers. In early 1956 Congress considered the Harris-Fulbright Gas Bill, which would have exempted natural gas producers from direct federal control. Pipeline companies generally approved of this bill because it allowed for the determination of a reasonable market price for gas (as opposed to cost-based utility regulation). Many producers, however, opposed the bill precisely because it gave the FPC authority to supervise contract prices. The political debate over the bill was intense, but Congress appeared ready to approve the measure. Then, on the very day the Senate voted on the bill, Senator Francis Case (R–North Dakota) publicly stated that an oil industry lobbyist had offered him $2,500 to vote for the measure. The Senate passed the bill, but President Eisenhower, sensitive to the emerging scandal, vetoed it on February 17, 1956. As a result, two decades of price regulation would pass before a political consensus for deregulation again emerged.[8]

With the drive toward legislative reversal of the *Phillips* decision stalled, industry attention again focused on the FPC's efforts to define a coherent regulatory policy in case-by-case decisions. One of the key problems associated with this sort of price regulation was the FPC's dramatically increased case load. From 1938 to 1954 the commission handled approximately 1,900 gas cases; between 1954 and 1958, it handled 14,500.[9] Although the commission routinely approved many of these requests for rate increases, producers often felt that they were being hamstrung by the long delays caused by bureaucratic procedures. They often thought they were being deprived of an opportunity to receive higher prices. After a period of depressed prices in the late 1940s, "a seller's market prevailed" as pipeline companies began to bid up the price of new gas supplies. Price regulation threatened to reverse this trend.[10] Producers had very strong incentives to fight price regulation. Their ongoing efforts to find ways around the regulations were a crucial aspect of business policy in the natural gas industry after 1954.

Even though Texas Eastern was not a major gas producer, the enforcement of price regulations significantly affected its operations. Since producers selling gas in interstate commerce now had to sell their gas at a regulated price which generally proved lower than a market-determined price, they began to look for opportunities to sell in intrastate markets. The fact that gas produced and sold within the same state was not regulated by the FPC opened the possibility that producers would begin to seek higher prices by targeting markets within the major gas-producing states such as Texas. Moreover, the *Phillips* decision altered gas pricing in another significant way. The Natural Gas Act of 1938 had discouraged gas pipelines from either owning their own reserves or controlling subsidiary production companies. It did so by providing for the regulation of the wellhead price of gas sold by a pipeline's affiliated production company to the line, while leaving unregulated the sales of gas from an unaffiliated producer to a pipeline firm. After the *Phillips* decision, however, the FPC was regulating the price of both affiliated and unaffiliated wellhead gas production sold to pipelines. This stimulated natural gas transmission and distribution companies to integrate vertically into the production business.

Texas Eastern had to reexamine its existing strategy. It had focused its energy and resources on a prolonged effort to establish a strong presence in the major northeastern cities. Now more attention had to be given to the previously routine issue of gas supply. With gas producers seeking routes around price regulation, TE and other major interstate pipelines had strong incentives to lend a helping hand. Otherwise, they might be unable to maintain a steady flow of gas in interstate commerce through their lines and thus be unable to protect their substantial investments.

The natural gas transmission companies quickly entered some phases of the production business. Panhandle Eastern Pipe Line Company and Tennessee Gas Transmission Company created their own production businesses and purchased reserves. Panhandle Eastern's subsidiary was Anadarko Production Company. Tennessee Gas's production company purchased 1 trillion cubic feet (tcf) of gas for $159 million.[11] Texas Eastern tried to adopt this strategy but achieved only limited success. Despite the commitment of considerable resources to production, the firm was unable to find large sources of natural gas.

Texas Eastern was more successful in securing adequate gas supplies through innovative new contractual arrangements. Since these adaptations to FPC regulation required careful legal footwork to ensure that the firm's actions were consistent with federal policy, lawyers with special expertise in this area became a valuable commodity. At TE, Jack Head shouldered much of the burden of developing these creative responses to price regulation. As the company's General Counsel, he spearheaded several important initiatives to increase gas supply. As a partner in the Houston law firm of Vinson & Elkins, Head had represented Texas Eastern since its founding in 1947. After Charles Francis's resignation from the position of general counsel, Head became the company's vice president and general counsel in 1958. The following year he resigned from Vinson & Elkins to work full-time at Texas Eastern. For years he spent most of his time on a number of important cases dealing with gas supply arrangements between the company and various producers.

The first of these involved the Rayne Field case, in which Texas Eastern sought to avoid FPC price regulation by purchasing leases to a gas field, not the gas itself. Located in southern Louisiana near the town of Opelousas, the Rayne Field contained estimated recoverable reserves of 989 bcf, making it one of the few remaining large natural gas fields not already committed to a buyer. Texas Eastern executives were anxious to use this field to supplement the company's supplies. Their initial entry came in early 1957 with the negotiation of standard gas purchase contracts with Continental Oil Company, Sun Oil Company, M. H. Marr (Marr), and General Crude Oil Company. The twenty-year contract term paid $0.226 per mcf, plus a $0.013 tax reimbursement on an additional 101 mmcf/d to be sold to eleven of Texas Eastern's existing northeastern customers. In order to connect the Rayne

Field to the Kosciusko Line, Texas Eastern planned to build a twenty-two-mile extension of fourteen-inch pipe from its trunkline to the field (at a cost of $48.6 million). The company presented its original certificate application to the FPC, and it was confident that the commission would approve the application.[12]

The FPC's presiding examiner issued an initial decision to authorize the proposed project, but the FPC staff counsel, the New York Public Service Commission (NYPSC), and three of the company's customers filed exceptions to the proceedings. This resulted in a continuation. Their primary objection to the deal involved the price Texas Eastern agreed to pay for the gas. The NYPSC claimed that Texas Eastern's gas costs, and therefore its rate base, under existing gas purchase contracts would increase substantially as a result of the Rayne Field contracts. According to the NYPSC, this might result in higher prices for all of Texas Eastern's gas, and the cost ultimately would be paid by its customers.

As a result of this attack on the application, Texas Eastern launched a new series of negotiations with the same producers. These discussions yielded an innovative contract which became the subject of a thirteen-year controversy with the FPC. Ultimately the U.S. Supreme Court decided the issue.[13] Texas Eastern's contract was indeed of a new sort, because the firm purchased the leases for the Rayne Field property. By buying the leases instead of the gas, Texas Eastern hoped to avoid FPC regulation, which in the company's view applied only to direct purchases of gas.

Texas Eastern formed the Louisiana Gas Corporation to acquire all of the leases to oil and gas properties in the Rayne Field. On December 4, 1958, the company agreed to pay $134.4 million for these leases, including a down payment to the producers of $12.4 million in cash and monthly installments through 1975 to cover the remaining $122 million. At the reopened certificate hearing, Texas Eastern asserted that its average cost of producing Rayne Field gas under the lease-purchase arrangement would be $0.2059 per mcf ($0.0201 less than the original price). Management believed that this was a satisfactory response to the complaints of the NYPSC and others that it was paying too much for the gas. The participating producers also should be satisfied, company officials said, because they would receive more money up front than in a gas sale. The FPC also seemed satisfied. It acknowledged the modified agreements and granted Texas Eastern a certificate based upon its modified lease-purchase agreement pursuant to its initial decision of April 15, 1958.

But during April of 1959 Texas Eastern's president, Orville Carpenter, learned that the NYPSC was considering an appeal of the FPC's decision. Carpenter, Jack Head, Baxter Goodrich, and Keith Pyburn (manager of TE's Washington, D.C., office) then decided "to go to New York and talk to our friends there to see if anything could be done toward avoiding such an appeal."[14] Their "friends" included both industrial and political associates.

As was so often the case in negotiations surrounding the regulation of business, political pressure, both favorable and unfavorable, became a part of the regulatory process.

Carpenter and others brought all of the firepower they could muster to bear on the NYPSC. Carpenter called Ed Clark, Brown & Root's legislative aide in Austin, and Baxter Goodrich discussed the situation with executives at Consolidated Edison, one of Texas Eastern's customers. Con Edison helped set up an appointment with a representative of the New York commission. Support from even more highly placed political figures was also discussed. Ed Clark called Carpenter and suggested that Governor Dewey of New York be contacted to support Texas Eastern's purchase of the Rayne Field leases. Con Edison's representatives argued, however, that "it would not be wise to bring in Governor Dewey or any other outsider. . . . It was their suggestion, to which I readily agreed, that we should await the outcome of this meeting before taking any other steps."[15]

In June the company received some very good news. The FPC had reviewed Texas Eastern's application for a certificate and concluded that it did not have jurisdiction over the sale of leases. The regulatory agency had "no objections to Texas Eastern's acquisition of the Rayne Field leases of such materiality as to offset the public benefits thereof and justify denial of Texas Eastern's project in this proceeding. Needless to say, a large number of natural-gas companies rely to a considerable extent for their supplies of gas on company-owned reserves, and the manner in which Texas Eastern's arrangements for the purchase of the leases were consummated is not unique in the gas and oil business. . . ."[16] In addition, the FPC noted that the terms of the transaction appeared to be cost effective and required by the public convenience and necessity. The FPC granted a certificate by confirming its earlier decision. Soon thereafter, August Belmont penned a letter to Carpenter: "Congratulations on your Certificate on the Rayne deal. This is certainly a real feather in Texas Eastern's cap. Certainly every other pipeline company is on the phone this morning to their lawyers wanting to find out just how the whole thing was done."[17] Texas Eastern was not the first pipeline company to purchase leases, but its acquisition of the Rayne Field lease seemed at the time to mark an important departure which might enable a pipeline company to acquire natural gas and avoid FPC price regulation. By August 1959 gas was flowing from the Rayne Field through Texas Eastern's pipeline system to customers in the Northeast.

But Texas Eastern struck out in its efforts to dissuade the New York Public Service Commission from opposing the Rayne Field deal. The NYPSC filed an application with the FPC in July, 1959, for a rehearing. The commission denied the application, but instead of accepting defeat, the NYPSC then filed a petition for a review of the decision in the U.S. Court of Appeals. Finding that the FPC had not adequately determined what the consumer's ultimate cost for this gas would be, the court essentially directed the commission to

Texas Eastern natural gas dispatching office, 1962

inquire into the reasonableness of costs of the Rayne Field leases. Even though the commission did not have jurisdiction over the sale of leases to a pipeline, it did have responsibility to regulate the pipeline's purchase price as it related to the sale of the leases. The court remanded the case back to the FPC, which reopened hearings on the Rayne Field in the summer of 1961.

In the hearings, Texas Eastern sought to justify the lease-purchase, using the precedent of a lease-purchase arrangement between Panhandle Eastern and its production subsidiary.[18] Texas Eastern argued that in *FPC v. Panhandle Eastern Pipe Line Co.* (337 U.S. 498), the court concluded that "the transfer of undeveloped gas leases" was "an activity related to the production and gathering of natural gas beyond the coverage of the [Natural Gas] Act." But the FPC countered that "the present case [Rayne Field] is distinguishable from that involved in the Panhandle case. In that case the leases were undeveloped so that the transfer did not resemble a sale of gas as did the sale of developed leaseholds here." In addition, the commission argued that the gas sold via the leases in the Panhandle transaction was dedicated

for the unregulated intrastate market and consequently not subject to federal regulation in any case. The FPC, prompted by the court's action, thus
applied new standards to the contract, and this boded ill for TE.[19]

Under pressure, the FPC essentially reversed its original decision. On
February 6, 1963, the commission rescinded the lease-purchase agreements,
finding that "what is objectionable here is the attempt to disguise a transaction which in effect is a sale of gas by casting it in the form of a sale of
leases with provisions that would make it difficult if not impossible to subject to regulatory control the price for the sale to an interstate pipeline of
this large body of gas."[20] By reversing its own decision, the FPC subjected
itself to intense criticism. The Rayne Field case became a nationally discussed
example of commission indecision.[21]

For the FPC, however, the important point was its jurisdictional authority. Normally, it would not have jurisdiction over the sale of leases, and for
that reason it had issued its original certificate. Once the court had determined that the Rayne Field transaction was actually a sale of natural gas
disguised as a lease transaction, the FPC took the opportunity to extend its
regulatory authority. On July 12, 1963, the commission ordered Texas Eastern and the producers to renegotiate a gas purchase agreement for the Rayne
Field gas.

Whatever one's assessment of the correctness of the ruling, it is hard to
escape one conclusion: the new FPC–style regulation posed dilemmas for
strategists at Texas Eastern. The commission had strong institutional incentives to "close up" the system of price regulation by blocking any efforts
to escape its reach. The costs of achieving that goal were high. Almost as
troubling as the outcome of the case to Texas Eastern were the stops and
starts along the way. The original decision had been subjected to court review, as well as to the objections of determined intervenors such as the
NYPSC. As a result, Texas Eastern had to fight a series of battles on a number of fronts—all this, only to lose in the courts. As a result, it had now
to devise a different strategy, one that would take into account the new regulatory setting.

The FPC accelerated this adjustment by requiring Texas Eastern to "file
a revised application for a certificate to put into effect a 'new arrangement'
for the sale of gas to Texas Eastern from the Rayne Field." The commission
warned that if its order was not carried out, all involved parties would be
in violation of the Natural Gas Act. Texas Eastern unsuccessfully appealed
the recision of the lease-purchase agreement, eventually taking this decision
to the U.S. Supreme Court. But to no avail. The Court supported the FPC
by ruling that the sales came under the commission's jurisdiction, and finding
that the Rayne Field transaction was a sale of developed leases and, therefore, a sale of natural gas rather than leases.

Texas Eastern and the producers had no choice but to renegotiate the purchase of the gas. In early 1966 the four Rayne Field producers applied for

a certificate with the FPC to approve a revised lease-sale arrangement. During the summer of 1967, the commission consolidated Texas Eastern's application with that of the four producers. During a prehearing conference, the examiner made a tentative decision to abide by the earlier FPC rulings rescinding the lease-sale arrangement and setting the price of all Rayne Field gas sold to Texas Eastern at $0.185 per mcf, a price based upon the area rate-pricing formula in use by the FPC. All charges above $0.185 would have to be refunded to customers.[22]

Proceedings in the case continued in an effort to clarify the cost of gas to Texas Eastern. Ultimately, the FPC approved a modified version of the lease-sale arrangement, provided that the arrangement reflected the regulated area price of gas. Thus in August, 1969, the FPC approved the lease-sale arrangement but ruled that by concentrating its gas payments for the leases through 1975, TE was essentially paying $0.235 per mcf of gas. The FPC felt this price was excessive. It ruled that Texas Eastern should pay $0.20 per mcf for gas produced between 1959 and 1967 and no more than $0.185 per mcf for Rayne Field gas produced after October 1, 1968. The commission ordered the producers to refund $31.4 million to Texas Eastern for the excessive gas charges, and required the company in turn to refund $30 million of that amount to its customers and reduce its system-wide rates. After one more regulatory skirmish, this ruling was invoked.[23]

Eleven years after the original agreements between Texas Eastern and the four Rayne Field producers, the Federal Power Commission seemed finally to have closed the case. In September of 1970 the commission ruled that Texas Eastern could not pay a lump sum of $134.4 million for an unknown quantity of gas through the purchase of leases. The commission required the company instead to pay for only the gas it actually used. Producers hailed this decision as a victory, since it was expected to increase substantially the amount of money they would receive for the gas they sold to Texas Eastern.[24]

Several lessons emerged from the Rayne case. Most obvious were the perils of FPC–style price regulation for the interstate transmission companies. The FPC could change its mind years after making its original decision in a particular case. While this case was an especially convoluted one, the commission's inability to act quickly and decisively suggested that it did not have the capacity to regulate the natural gas industry effectively. Price regulation was particularly susceptible to political pressures. In any highly publicized case, the commission was likely to be swayed by the political logic of low consumer prices. Discussion of long-term supply problems was not a high priority in a regulatory system sensitive to consumers. Texas Eastern's efforts to buy leases instead of the gas itself was perhaps too clever and was certainly too obvious a circumvention of the price regulations. But what got lost in the controversy was the firm's pressing need to secure long-term gas supplies at reasonable prices.

Thwarted by the FPC in the Rayne Field, Texas Eastern changed course. Now it attempted to increase its gas supply by contracting for substantial offshore, as well as onshore, reserves. The company had a strong regulatory incentive to look offshore in federally controlled leases for new sources of natural gas, since existing rules classified the sale of such gas as an "interstate" transaction. Thus, Texas Eastern could seek new supplies from offshore fields without fear that their owners might be tempted to avoid price regulations by restricting sales to intrastate markets.

During the 1950s and 1960s the lands lying off the shore of southern Louisiana yielded a series of new discoveries that marked this area as one of the nation's most promising sources of natural gas. During its early involvement with the Rayne Field, TE had also investigated other gas reserves in southern Louisiana, including those in nearby Bastian Bay. The firm's executives had as well learned of an even more promising prospect, a tremendous volume of gas for sale in offshore Louisiana leases. On November 16, 1960, James Allison, president of Warren Petroleum Company (a subsidiary of Gulf Oil Corporation), invited John Lynch, Texas Eastern senior vice-president, Oil Division, to come by and discuss Gulf's interest in selling its gas production from a recent discovery in Block 27 offshore of southern Louisiana. Allison told Lynch that the estimated reserves of the find were four trillion cubic feet and that Gulf owned and operated the block in conjunction with Humble Oil and Refining Co., a minority owner. Allison also told Lynch that Gulf wanted to keep the find quiet for now, in part to give it more time to secure additional leases surrounding the new discovery. But Gulf intended to request bids for the gas from both Texas Eastern and United Gas Corporation, the only pipeline companies in the area capable of handling that volume of gas. In subsequent discussions, William K. Whiteford, the CEO of Gulf, told Lynch that Gulf would not be interested in a sale of gas in place (perhaps referring to the Rayne Field deal), but that the corporation would be willing to participate in the construction of a pipeline to connect its reserves with Texas Eastern's Kosciusko Line.[25]

While Texas Eastern was interested, the company had already begun plans to expand its system through the purchase of gas from Bastian Bay. But Gulf wanted Texas Eastern to make a proposal for a purchase of its gas by December 12, and John Lynch called Allison to tell him that Texas Eastern could not put together a proposal to purchase a minimum of 400 mmcf/d until it completed a market survey to discover if this quantity of gas could be sold. Although Texas Eastern was currently investigating markets for the gas from the Bastian Bay field, the Gulf gas represented a substantial increase and would require a new market survey. During most of 1961, Gulf and Texas Eastern continued to negotiate. Initially, however, Texas Eastern expressed interest in purchasing only 1 tcf of Gulf's total estimated reserves of 4 tcf.

Frustrated over the slow pace of the negotiations, Allison called Carpenter on December 13, 1961, and told him that "he thought we may be doing just a lot of talking and that there really was not much chance of putting these two deals together."[26] Allison urged Carpenter to consider purchasing the entire 4 tcf from Gulf. Eager to make a major sale and tiring of Texas Eastern's failure to commit, Gulf pressured its potential buyer.

Carpenter's main concern was keeping the price down and at the same time acquiring the gas through an agreement other than a straight gas purchase contract. Carpenter and Allison discussed both a sale of reserves in place and a sale involving a cash down-payment and non-interest bearing notes over a sixteen-to-seventeen-year period. On the smaller purchase, Gulf would not budge on the price, but the negotiations nevertheless continued.[27]

Herman Brown had already asked Charlie Francis whether he thought a joint Texas Eastern–Gulf Oil pipeline deal would disrupt any future business possibilities between Texas Eastern and its customers. Francis responded that he did not believe it would except perhaps with Humble, "whose Katy reserve we someday would like to be afforded the opportunity of acquiring."[28] Carpenter received a copy of Francis's letter and quickly informed both Francis and Herman Brown that Humble would almost certainly agree to participate in the joint Texas Eastern–Gulf pipeline since it also owned a portion of the Block 27 gas.

Negotiations plodded on for two more years. One of Gulf Oil's primary concerns throughout was avoiding public disclosure of the magnitude of its discovery. At one point, Jack Head suggested to James Allison that Texas Eastern could purchase the gas through a warranty contract so that Gulf would warrant to sell Texas Eastern a particular amount of gas during a specific time period. By signing a warranty contract, Gulf could avoid disclosing the total quantity of natural gas reserves in the field. Again negotiations stalled. But within a few weeks of his meeting with Head, Allison reported back that Gulf's chief of production believed Gulf could warrant 4.4 tcf and a deal could be consummated. On February 27, 1963, negotiations were far enough along to persuade Baxter Goodrich to outline a proposed agreement to the Texas Eastern board of directors. Texas Eastern would receive 200 mmcf/d from Gulf for a four-year build-up period needed to replenish its field reserves; it would also expand its current system for deliveries by an additional 274 mmcf/d, and transport 23 bcf for Gulf to the Philadelphia area. Texas Eastern agreed to pay (at 80 percent load factor), the area price of $0.195 in offshore and $0.2125 in onshore areas for the first ten years. During the entire life of the twenty-six-year contract, the delivered price to Texas Eastern could not exceed $0.24 per mcf. Texas Eastern agreed that Gulf would have a five-year period in which to begin delivering the full 500 mmcf/d of gas.[29]

By the summer of 1963 Texas Eastern had completed negotiations for one of the largest purchases of gas in history from a single field. By this time Algonquin Gas Transmission had entered the agreement as the primary distributor of the supply purchased from Gulf. In order to connect with the reserves, Texas Eastern constructed a 172–mile, thirty-six-inch pipeline from Venice, Louisiana, near the mouth of the Mississippi River, to New Roads, Louisiana, near Baton Rouge. There the new extension linked up with TE's thirty-inch Kosciusko Line from Louisiana to New Jersey.[30]

The only hurdle left to clear was the FPC, and events there initially took a threatening turn. Company representatives went to Washington to discuss with commission staff the possibility of the Gulf warranty contract being recommended to the commissioners for a certificate hearing. Ominously, the staff refused to recommend the contract. Pushing ahead, Texas Eastern and Gulf nevertheless filed an application on July 5, 1963, for a certificate, as did Algonquin. Then the proceedings turned in Texas Eastern's favor. Without opposition, the FPC combined the applications into one. FPC Chairman Joe Swidler was favorably impressed that Texas Eastern had negotiated this unusually large, long-term contract. Indeed, he gave the Texas Eastern–Gulf–Algonquin application a "Frannie," that is, a certificate without a hearing. This time, TE would not have to put up with regulatory delay, nor would it have to fight off hostile intervenors. The "Gulf Warranty Contract" guaranteed a substantial new supply equal to some 20 percent of the company's total. As General Counsel Jack Head aptly observed, this "was one of the most important contracts that Texas Eastern ever had."[31]

To deliver its new gas supplies, Texas Eastern undertook an ambitious expansion program, "the largest in company history." The FPC again granted a "Frannie." Over a four-year period, the firm built a connecting pipeline, as well as another seven hundred miles of pipe looped along the system's current thirty-inch line in order to increase its overall capacity. The company also acquired another major underground storage reservoir.

The firm purchased the unfortunately named "Accident Storage Field," located on thirty-four thousand acres in western Maryland in 1962. TE converted it into one of the industry's first completely automatic, high-pressure storage fields. When the company purchased the field, it had gas reserves of 38 bcf, with a total reservoir capacity of approximately 64 bcf. This storage facility, like the one in western Pennsylvania and the Leidy Storage Field in north central Pennsylvania, improved the company's ability to serve the growing northeastern population during the winter months.

As Texas Eastern began purchasing gas under its new contract, Gulf Oil made a startling discovery. Its original estimate of 5 tcf total in its offshore field was wrong; the field contained only about 2 tcf. Under the warranty agreement in the contract, Gulf faced the disturbing prospect of having to find other sources of natural gas — almost certainly at higher prices — to make up the difference in the amount actually contained in its field and the amount promised to Texas Eastern. At one point, Texas Eastern offered to amend the original contract to give Gulf price relief, if in return, Gulf would extend the contract for an additional 2 tcf. Gulf refused. But it had few practical

alternatives except to "swallow" the existing contract. At one point in its annual report, Gulf noted that it was considering invoking the Louisiana version of force majeure in order to break the contract. Gulf ultimately chose,
however, to abide by the agreement despite its high cost. As a result, Texas
Eastern remained extremely competitive in the 1970s and 1980s. Under the
Gulf Warranty contract it bought as much as 625 mmcf/d at $0.21 per mcf
while other pipelines were purchasing much of their supply in the $1.75–
$2.50 per mcf price range. As gas available to the interstate market dwindled,
this contract helped buffer TE from changes in the market.

Texas Eastern's negotiations with Gulf Oil and its subsidiary, Warren Petroleum, led indirectly to another major strategic choice, a decision to enter
the West Coast gas market. Perhaps Texas Eastern's most dramatic venture
in the natural gas business between 1954 and 1971 was its acquisition of
Transwestern Pipeline Company, which was partially owned and supplied
with gas by Warren Petroleum (see map 5.3). The acquisition moved Texas
Eastern into the California market for the first time. For the company this
was a major shift in policy. It had been from its creation identified with major markets in the Northeast. Indeed, its name reflected this basic orienta-
tion. Expanding its natural gas system to markets on the other side of the
continent was a long step away from the company's traditional strategy. At
the time of Texas Eastern's acquisition of Transwestern, no other gas transmission company served markets on both coasts.

In entering the business of gas sales in the southern California market,
Texas Eastern was moving into an environment with its own distinctive economic and regulatory history. California's natural gas industry was a relatively old one. In 1909 the Los Angeles area received natural gas from the
Buena Vista Field in the San Joaquin Valley, and early California gas consumers were predominantly in areas near local natural gas fields. This changed
after World War II, when El Paso Natural Gas Company expanded its pipeline system with a twelve-hundred-mile link from the massive gas fields of
the Permian Basin in west Texas to the southern California border.[32] There
the El Paso system connected with the Southern California Gas Company,
which transported the gas to southern California utilities. In 1950 El Paso
and Pacific Gas and Electric Company (PG & E) constructed additional facilities to bring gas from northwestern New Mexico and Colorado into the
San Francisco metropolitan area.

The most distinctive aspects of the California market resulted from the
California Public Utility Commission's determined efforts to prevent interstate pipeline companies from entering the state. The commission required
El Paso's pipeline (which alone brought out-of-state gas to the California
market) to stop at the California border, where California-owned pipelines
picked up the gas. Texas Eastern or any other transmission company which
wanted to serve the booming California market would have to learn to play
by these unique regulatory rules. Californian officials at times seemed to

MAP 5.3 Transwestern Pipeline Company

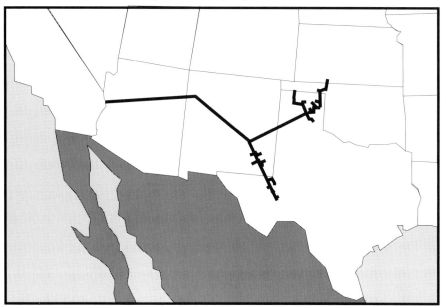

relish their reputation as the most antibusiness regulators in the nation. Texas Eastern knew that a decision to buy Transwestern would place the company in a more hostile regulatory environment, but the potential rewards seemed to justify the aggravations that would undoubtedly arise.

Texas Eastern recognized that southern California was one of the most promising markets for natural gas in the nation. By 1961 California's consumption of natural gas sold by utilities had surpassed that of Texas; the volume sold in that state made it the largest natural gas consuming state in the nation.[33] The state's own reserves were not sufficient to supply its needs. El Paso Natural Gas had dominated the supply of gas from outside the state before the 1960s, but it was uncertain in the early 1960s that it could satisfy the growing demand. As dependence on out-of-state natural gas increased dramatically, other producers and pipeline companies began to show an interest in this large market. It was estimated that approximately 80 percent of the state's requirements would now have to be met with gas produced elsewhere.

Texas Eastern executives followed with interest the efforts of several pipeline companies to obtain FPC certificates to serve the California market. One of El Paso's emerging competitors was Transwestern Pipeline Company. It had been organized on March 11, 1957, by Warren Petroleum Corporation, a subsidiary of Gulf Oil, J. R. Butler and Associates (Houston), and Monterey Oil Company (Los Angeles). Texas Eastern had a connection to the project even then, as Mills Cox, a vice president of Texas Eastern, resigned to join the Transwestern project. Cox became "about the only full-time, salaried director and officer of Transwestern Pipeline Co. for a couple of years."[34] He served as Transwestern's first president.

The FPC gave Transwestern its certificate of public convenience and necessity on August 10, 1959. W. K. Warren, Chairman of the Board and CEO of Warren Petroleum, was also chairman of the board of Transwestern. His interest in Transwestern was partly based on the large west Texas natural gas reserves held by Warren and by Gulf. The California market needed that gas, and the Transwestern pipeline linked Texas supply with California demand. Transwestern began delivering gas to the southern California market on August 9, 1960. Drawing upon gas fields from both the Texas Panhandle and the Permian Basin and delivering it to the California border at Topock, Arizona, the thirteen-hundred-mile, twenty-four to thirty-inch pipeline offered a strong measure of competition for El Paso. At about this same time, El Paso's position in the San Francisco area market was being threatened by the introduction of Canadian gas. Pacific Gas Transmission Company began using a fourteen-hundred-mile pipeline owned by PG & E to transport natural gas from the Alberta "foothills" belt in Canada to PG & E's distribution system in the bay area.

Although market surveys predicted substantial long-term growth in the demand for gas in California, Transwestern faced intense competitive pressures there in the short term. Transwestern could only fill its pipeline to 60 percent capacity during its first years of operation in the early 1960s. El Paso Natural continued to be the state's major supplier, providing 75 percent of the area's imported natural gas. Like Transwestern, El Paso delivered gas to Pacific Lighting Corporation (the largest distributor in the nation), which sold to various customers, including the Los Angeles Department of Water and Power and Southern California Edison.[35]

Although the California gas market seemed at this time near saturation, another tenacious competitor, Tennessee Gas, soon entered the competition. Tennessee Gas had been interested for years in cracking the West Coast market, but Pacific Lighting Corporation's control of distribution to southern California utilities and its gas purchase ties to El Paso Natural and Transwestern seemed to preclude entry. Ignoring these difficulties, in December of 1960 Tennessee announced its plan to build a new pipeline from Texas through Mexico to the southern California border in order to serve Southern California Edison. Tennessee hoped that this project—which came to be known within the industry as the "Enchilada Inch Line"—could avoid Federal Power Commission regulation since no state lines would be crossed. Both Southern California Edison and the Los Angeles Department of Water and Power expressed interest in the new long-term supply of natural gas that might become available through this undertaking. But the FPC was skeptical. It was not enthusiastic about the prospect of a major new pipeline "skirting" its control with a long detour through Mexico. Thus, Tennessee's proposed new pipeline faced an uphill political struggle from the beginning.[36]

Then, too, its competitors aggressively responded. El Paso proposed a new venture of its own to increase its presence. Called the Rock Springs project, this plan involved building a pipeline from the Rocky Mountains into southern California. Seeing what El Paso was doing, Tennessee Gas decided to fight on the regulatory front. It intervened in the FPC hearings to oppose the Rock Springs project. As the battle for California heated up, the struggle came to resemble the war Texas Eastern and Tennessee had fought for the New England market.

This new round of competition came complete with espionage and intrigue. On November 14, 1961, a lawyer for Tennessee Gas revealed that he was in possession of a letter written only nineteen days earlier by PG & E's vice president, James Moulton, to Howard Boyd, president of El Paso. In the letter, PG & E indicated that it would not purchase a 200 mmcf/d block of gas from the pipeline. This disclosure seemed to weaken the Rock Springs application, since it suggested that California's demand for out-of-state natural gas was considerably less than previously believed. El Paso executives cared less about the content of the letter than about the fact that their rival had somehow obtained copies of confidential correspondence.[37]

Five months later the struggle produced another startling episode of intrigue. As El Paso Natural Gas officials met in a Washington hotel suite, they discovered by chance a bugging device. Although the listeners were arrested and prosecuted, investigators never conclusively identified the persons behind the bugging. Nor could El Paso be too self-righteous, because the investigation also revealed its leader, Paul Kayser, had hired a private investigator to keep tabs on Tennessee Gas. For many months, stories of bribes and secret lobbying poisoned the atmosphere of the FPC hearings.[38] Finally, in July of 1963 the FPC rejected the project on the grounds that there was no need for an additional pipeline to supply gas to the California market.

Meanwhile, Tennessee Gas's proposal was the subject of hearings held by the California Public Utility Commission. The original proposal — also known as the Pemex plan — called for the construction of a pipeline to purchase natural gas from Mexico and deliver it through Mexico into southern California. Unfortunately for Tennessee, neither the government of Mexico nor California was enthusiastic about the proposition. In Mexico, nationalists feared that the U.S. pipeline company might seek to control northern Mexican gas supplies on behalf of its two customers in California. In California, opposition focused on Mexico's previous history of expropriating American energy companies and on the more practical problem that the proposed price of the delivered gas would be higher than that of existing supplies.[39] After realizing that the project had little prospect of gaining approval, Tennessee abandoned the Pemex plan in November, 1962.

As an alternative, Tennessee proposed constructing a pipeline from Texas to the California border, wholly within the United States. Based on its new plans, Tennessee was able to sign up Southern California Edison and the

Los Angeles Department of Water and Power for deliveries of 865 mmcf/d of gas for boiler fuel. Tennessee's new venture was known as the Gulf Pacific project. In response, both El Paso and Transwestern proposed increases to their own system capacity. El Paso filed a counterproposal stating that for an additional $50 million investment, it could increase deliveries by 250 mmcf/d (for $134 million it could build a new pipeline). Transwestern stated that by spending $46 million it could increase its sales volume to 640 mmcf/d. Taken together, the proposed expansions of the two systems would exceed the capacity of Tennessee's proposed line to the west. This left to the FPC the job of sorting out these various complex approaches and defining "the public interest."

The commission consolidated all three proposals and began hearings. Tennessee asserted that Gulf Pacific would remove the potential of monopoly power by Pacific Lighting. It also argued that year-round supplies of natural gas to Southern California Edison would lower pollution by eliminating that utility's need to burn fuel oil during the winter months. The possibility of reduced air pollution seemed to give Tennessee's proposal an edge on the others. Nevertheless, in December of 1965 the FPC's presiding examiner, Alvin Kurtz, surprised everyone by abruptly recommending that Gulf Pacific be constructed. His recommendation was subject to review by the entire commission, but Tennessee seemed to have won the war.[40] But then the hearings began again, dragging on for several months. Tennessee Gas pressed its case, as did Transwestern and El Paso. On July 26, 1966, the FPC formally turned down the Gulf Pacific proposal, stating that Gulf Pacific would lead to higher gas prices while not significantly alleviating southern California's air pollution problems. Instead, the FPC endorsed the proposals of both Transwestern and El Paso to expand their existing systems (while denying El Paso's application to construct an additional pipeline). This decision guaranteed both Transwestern and El Paso a large stake in the current and future California market.

Transwestern's future as a gas pipeline company now seemed assured, but the collection of corporate investors who controlled the company were not committed to the long haul. The company's largest stockholder was Warren Petroleum Corporation, a Gulf Oil subsidiary which owned about 32 percent of the outstanding stock. The second largest shareholder, Northern Natural Gas, owned about 16 percent of the total. Holding some 15 percent were investors from the oil and gas consulting firm of Butler, Miller and Lents, whose partner J. R. Butler served as a director of Transwestern. Gulf, which had the controlling interest, became concerned about the implications of an FPC ruling prohibiting profits to affiliates of natural gas pipelines.[41] That news sent Gulf in search of a way to divest its holdings in Transwestern.

Texas Eastern was an obvious possibility. The two firms had maintained a close working relationship since the beginning of their negotiations for the warranty contract. Knowing of TE's interest in expanding its pipeline system, Gulf executives inquired whether it would consider buying a stake in Transwestern. The answer was yes. After the FPC ruled in the summer of 1966 that El Paso Natural and Transwestern would remain the major suppliers of natural gas to the southern California market, Texas Eastern's management saw a ripe opportunity to expand through the acquisition of Transwestern and its pipeline to California.

Several Texas Eastern executives, including president Baxter Goodrich and vice president and comptroller Jack Bixby, led the negotiations for the acquisition. They brought the proposal before a special meeting for the board of directors on March 17, 1967. Goodrich discussed the company's plans, recommending a $16 per share offer. The directors approved a tender offer for three million or more shares of Transwestern's common stock for $16 per share, which yielded a minimum purchase price of about $48 million. In reality, Texas Eastern hoped to purchase all of Transwestern's nearly six million shares for a total cost of approximately $100 million, but first the financing had to be arranged. To fund the acquisition, Texas Eastern arranged a revolving credit agreement for $100 million with six banks; twelve days later the company was able to double its credit line.

On March 23, 1967, Texas Eastern publicly offered to purchase all of the outstanding stock of Transwestern for $16 per share, approximately $6 to $7 over current book value. The offer was set to expire on April 7. Texas Eastern's only condition was that it receive at least three million of Transwestern's nearly six million outstanding shares. This was a friendly offer. TE noted that "the Board of Directors of Transwestern has unanimously recommended acceptance of the tender offer by its stockholders."[42] Texas Eastern also stated that holders of more than 2.5 million shares had already agreed to tender their stock. These shares included those controlled by Gulf Oil.

One major shareholder temporarily held out. Northern Natural Gas Company, which held 16 percent of Transwestern's stock, delayed making a statement of its intention to sell. By the April 7 deadline, shareholders had tendered approximately 65 percent of Transwestern's outstanding stock to Texas Eastern, but Northern Natural had not yet turned over its holdings. Texas Eastern extended the offering through April 18, and at last Northern Natural sold its stock.

Texas Eastern's original plan for Transwestern was to allow it to operate independently and retain its current employees. Several of Transwestern's directors quickly resigned, however, and were replaced by Texas Eastern officers, including Jack Bixby, vice president and comptroller, and A. J. Shoup, senior vice president. Later, Texas Eastern executives filled most of the top positions. Still, TE did not want to consolidate the two firms completely, if only to minimize regulatory problems. The parent firm hoped thus to keep Transwestern's FPC certificate valid.

With this purchase completed, Texas Eastern had links to both the West and East coasts. The acquisition boosted its daily deliveries of natural gas

Texas Eastern pipeline expansion

approximately 20 percent, while also giving the company access to more than six trillion cubic feet of proven gas reserves located primarily in west Texas and the Texas Panhandle. The purchase had been possible because the company's credit was strong, its operations unquestionably efficient, and its management experienced in the transmission business. Texas Eastern had benefitted from a working relationship initially established during negotiations leading to the Gulf warranty contract; that relationship yielded an excellent opportunity for expansion. In taking advantage of this opportunity, TE redrew the map of its gas transmission business.

The company's leaders had good reasons for optimism in the late 1960s. The acquisition of Transwestern was the most visible symbol of Texas Eastern's prosperity, and the gas transmission business as a whole seemed buoyant and expansive. The system had experienced a long phase of almost uninterrupted expansion. From the early days immediately after the winning bid for the Inch Lines to the recently completed bid for Transwestern, the company had surged forward into new markets, constructed new pipelines, and acquired new gas supplies. This expansion had made Texas Eastern one of the nation's largest gas transmission companies.

By the late 1960s Texas Eastern's position among the major pipelines in the industry seemed secure. It was one of the largest suppliers of gas to both the Northeast and to California. It could boast that it was the first and only coast-to-coast natural gas pipeline company operating in the United States. The firm's long-term prospects were sustained by its excellent gas supply contract with Gulf (which more than offset the disappointment of the failed Rayne contract). Despite the constraints imposed by price regulation and the growing difficulties in obtaining secure sources of natural gas, Texas Eastern had prospered and grown. The FPC's regulations were frustrating, but the company"s business remained highly profitable. Some of these profits were reinvested in the gas industry. But returns from gas transmission increasingly found their way into non-gas ventures as Texas Eastern sought to avoid the impact of regulation by moving into other businesses.

Chapter 6

DOMESTIC DIVERSIFICATION

By the mid-1950s Texas Eastern had reached a sharply defined transition point. The initial scramble to reach the major northeastern markets had ended, and the possibilities for domestic territorial expansion were diminishing. As the company prospered on the returns from its transmission of natural gas within the United States, it sought to define an appropriate strategy to sustain its prosperity in coming decades. While gas transmission would clearly remain the core business, the company had powerful incentives to diversify into other activities. From the 1950s forward Texas Eastern was ever alert to opportunities to enter new businesses. Management examined many prospects while choosing a handful of new ventures. Most were energy-related, although in the early 1970s the company went farther afield, moving into real estate development. Some moves were domestic; others, notably the lucrative movement into North Sea oil and gas production, were outside the United States. Taken together, these diversified enterprises fundamentally altered the management, the business, and the corporate culture of Texas Eastern.

Strong incentives to diversify were built into the regulations governing the gas transmission business, and all companies in the industry responded, in varying degrees. The FPC guaranteed gas transmission companies a fair rate of return on a fair level of investment, but standard accounting procedures used in determining the rate base included depreciation on investments in physical plant. The resulting phenomenon of "declining rate base" presented a dilemma to executives in the business. Depreciation steadily decreased the figure used to calculate a reasonable return on investment. The decline in the value of the existing rate base was masked by the expenditure of new investment funds during the expansive postwar decades, but managers reasoned correctly that at some time in the future mature pipeline systems would experience declining revenues as their fixed costs were depreciated. The desire to establish a position in related activities not subject to rate regulation spurred managers to look hard for opportunities to diversify. This was particularly true as the rate of inflation rose, for the FPC did not rush to adjust the rate of return allotted to gas transmission companies, leaving it hovering around 6 percent for many years.

Other considerations helped convince Texas Eastern to diversify. The firm's culture stressed entrepreneurship. Texas Eastern's early history reflected its impulse to do things on a grand scale. But the dynamism of the industry in the decade after World War II could not be sustained as the opportunities for territorial expansion declined. By the mid-1950s many commentators were beginning to take note of the tendency of managers in the regulated industries to become conservative and cautious; they were constrained, in this view, by the mountain of paperwork and the unending administrative hearings associated with rate regulation. Of all the managers in regulated industries, those in natural gas seemed most restless in these years, perhaps in part because most of them had come of age professionally amid the entrepreneurial energies of a young, dynamic industry. Executives in the gas industry no doubt also were influenced by their close association with oil men, who prided themselves on their industry's rough-and-tumble — and largely unregulated — traditions. One oil man who became a Texas Eastern executive playfully captured this sentiment: "I've always felt that in a natural gas transmission company, you could turn the management over to a bunch of chimpanzees, but it would take ten years for them to ruin it, because the Federal Power Commission is looking over your shoulder all the time and they won't let you make any bad mistakes. Neither will they let you make any good decisions."[1] Diversification out of natural gas promised managers new chances to try their hands at making entrepreneurial decisions and opportunities to compete more aggressively for profits in challenging new business.

While providing natural gas transmission companies with strong incentives to diversify, regulation also assured the cash flow that made diversification possible. With a guaranteed rate of return on huge investments in cross-country pipelines, the gas transmission companies still had large, predictable sources of revenue. The regular construction of expensive new facilities also made them familiar and valued customers of major investment banks. As one former company executive explained, "Since we have such a good record in expanding that pipeline, we could go to the financial community and get most any amounts of money we had asked for."[2] When Texas Eastern and other gas transmission companies decided to embark on strategies of diversification, they seldom lacked investment funds. Indeed, readily available credit was one of the company's great strengths in this era.

No two gas transmission companies responded exactly the same way to these incentives. The most aggressive practitioner was Tennessee Gas Transmission Company, which became one of the nation's first large conglomerates. It entered a variety of businesses, some of which were completely unrelated to natural gas. By the early 1960s, this company had substantial holdings in oil production and refining, an extensive chain of gasoline service stations, and an expanding assortment of other investments in chemicals, real estate, life insurance, and banking. In 1966 the company created Tenneco, Incorporated, as a holding company to coordinate the varied activities of its subsidiaries. It was already well onto the path of aggressive conglomeration that ultimately led it to become a major force in shipbuilding and farm implements.

On the other end of the spectrum was Transcontinental Gas Pipe Line Corporation (Transco). When questioned about the strategy of Tenneco and other companies in diversifying to spread both risks and rewards, the president of Transco summarized his company's attitude: "We decided to let the stockholders diversify on their own."[3] This company avoided non-gas ventures on principle, choosing instead to focus its energies exclusively on developing gas transmission and closely tied activities.

Clearly there were choices to be made, not just formulas of diversification to follow. Although Tenneco's example often put pressure on executives at competing companies to diversify or to be prepared to explain to shareholders and stock analysts why they had not done so, each company charted a different course over these relatively unexplored waters. Texas Eastern initially chose a middle course, somewhere between the two extremes exemplified by Tenneco and Transco. It sought to diversify into areas where its existing resources could be put to new uses. In George Brown's words, TE looked for opportunities to diversify "where we can bring something to the party."[4]

The company inched into the new strategy. Its earliest decisions to diversify involved oil and gas production and the shipment of liquid petroleum products, two businesses closely tied to natural gas transmission. The poor results of these early ventures and the appearance of numerous other potentially profitable endeavors persuaded the company it could ultimately succeed if it would more systematically approach diversification. In 1956 it created a new department, Plans and Economic Research, "to consider new areas of business and diversification and to make long range plans for the future."[5] In 1958, renamed the Coordinating and Planning Department, this small group reported directly to the president and became the staff for a newly formed management committee.

During its first decade of existence, the department investigated three or four prospects for diversification each year, focusing on the chemical industry, mining and metals, and oil. It considered numerous major investments in the oil industry, including a merger with Pure Oil Company. It also studied the idea of purchasing all or part of the stock of American Motors, but decided this venture was "too large in concept and the problems of the business are too different from those with which we are familiar." A similar undertaking in electronics was rejected "because it is felt that Texas Eastern has no real management capability for the electronics industry." Joint ventures in synthetic rubber and ammonia production fell through because the company was unsuccessful in forging alliances with experts, and the company was unwilling to rely "upon its own resources in these fields."[6] Despite the strong urge to diversify, TE's management proceeded cautiously, recognizing that the risks of diversification increased as the company moved farther away from its base of operations in the gas industry. By examining many opportunities but pursuing only a select few, the company sought to avoid potentially unprofitable forays into unfamiliar fields.

Texas Eastern's initial move grew out of its search for gas to fill its pipelines and out of the oil found in association with natural gas. While the company was still in the midst of completing its system in the late 1940s, George Brown had already decided to enter the oil and gas production business. Oil offered the chance to operate outside the purview of the FPC. Gas production, as we saw in the previous chapter, was needed to protect the company's supplies over the longterm.[7] United Gas and most of the other major regional distribution companies had substantial holdings of oil and gas reserves, and Reginald Hargrove had moved Texas Eastern toward their model of backward integration into production.

The company entered this business in April, 1950, when it formed Texas Eastern Production Company. The company's directors gave Mills Cox, the gas supply manager, responsibility for running this wholly owned production subsidiary. Cox had worked in the oil and gas production business for much of his adult life; he had first learned about the business while working for his uncle, Mills Bennett, in the Texas Panhandle. Before the new company was even formed, debate began over the location of its headquarters. While Hargrove had persuaded the Brown brothers to base Texas Eastern Transmission Corporation in Shreveport, the Browns insisted that Texas Eastern Production Company establish headquarters in Houston. So it did in 1951. The company was organized separately to give maximum autonomy to the exploration specialists and to keep the company's regulated and unregulated parts distinct.

Unlike its parent firm, the production company got off to a very slow start. It acquired a block of oil and gas leases in the tidelands area of the Gulf of Mexico, where another company had drilled one dry hole and a producing gas well which it subsequently closed. Unfortunately, litigation between the United States and the state of Texas over the ownership of offshore lands temporarily stalled further exploration on this tract. While waiting during 1951 for the resolution of this dispute, the production company drilled onshore in Texas two additional test wells, both of which were dry. By the end of the year the company held 34,751 acres under lease in Texas and Louisiana and 11,070 in the tidelands area of the Gulf of Mexico. It had built up a staff of experts in geology and geophysics to enhance its exploration efforts. But it failed to score. Even after offshore drilling commenced, the company had very little success in finding oil or gas.

The lackluster performance of Texas Eastern Production Company forced the directors to make some mid-course adjustments. In search of a more experienced oilman who might be better able to guide the fledgling production effort to success, they hired Herbert "Bert" Hemphill. Hemphill had a track record of finding oil in the Permian Basin of west Texas, and his hiring signified that Texas Eastern was still committed to the expansion of its production company. Instead of cutting back, the directors pumped more resources into production in an effort to turn around the subsidiary's performance. This same pattern would be followed in each of the company's subsequent efforts to diversify.

Texas Eastern's executive staff decided to raise additional capital by selling an interest in the production company directly to the public. The firm's officers and directors believed that the hiring of Hemphill and the strengthening of the support staff would convince investors to discount the poor performance of the production company and purchase its stock. Working through Dillon, Read, Texas Eastern arranged a New York public offering and sent Hemphill to present the prospectus to an audience of potential investors. Alas, his presentation foreshadowed the performance of the production company. Having been primed by officials from Dillon, Read and Texas Eastern to avoid reading the prospectus, Hemphill seemed ready to give a lively performance. Instead, he gave the public-speaking equivalent of a dry hole. He began by noting that he was from Midland, Texas, where it was dry and never rained, but that Texas Eastern had hired him and stuck him in the Gulf of Mexico where he was unfamiliar with the geology. Following this brief personal apologia — which could not have been particularly encouraging to investors — Hemphill read the prospectus.

Whether or not his poor presentation had a decisive effect on stock purchases is uncertain. Some stock was sold to the public, but it gradually lost value until Texas Eastern finally purchased back all the outstanding shares. The production company's *Annual Report* for 1952 unwittingly provided a symbol of its poor performance. A photograph on the first page showed only the empty chairs of the company's board room, aptly symbolizing the lack of direction in a subsidiary that had not lived up to expectations.

The enterprise nevertheless continued to grow. By the end of 1952 it had thirty-five employees. In addition, it acquired several new undeveloped leaseholds and producing properties. One transaction included a one-fourth working interest in eight blocks of leases in west Texas, amounting to 23,400 acres. Several test wells drilled in this area indicated that they would be significant enough to become producers. In May of 1952 the company also purchased seventeen gas wells "capable of production" from Delhi Oil Corporation. The company bought these wells to connect with the Wilcox Trend system already acquired by the company to augment its natural gas supply. The production company and Delhi entered into a joint-venture agreement for the exploration and development of oil and gas leases in eight southwest Texas counties.

Despite these initiatives, 1952 was a bad year, and production losses mounted to more than $1 million. In the *Annual Report* George Brown and Bert Hemphill tried to explain the losses: "In a sense the 1952 loss is a logical reflection of the 'pains' of a young company rapidly beginning an extensive exploration program. When a production company initiates operations, unproductive exploration costs become an immediate charge against earnings, whereas revenue from successful exploration lags during a period of field development, and even after that the resulting revenues and profit normally are spread over a period of years."[8] This was all true, but it was not what investors wanted to hear.

Believing that success was still just a matter of time, TE decided to invest more funds in oil and gas exploration and production. At the same time, the company moved ever deeper into production-related activities in an effort to protect its initial investment. To improve its ability to locate oil fields, Texas Eastern acquired an 83.5 percent interest in the voting stock (representing a 50 percent interest in the common stock) of a fledgling geophysical company having only eight employees, Georesearch, Incorporated. Like many other corporations trying to diversify, Texas Eastern decided it simply needed greater expertise and attempted to buy it. But this, too, had disappointing results, and the company finally divested its holdings in Georesearch in 1955.

Next TE's management considered the acquisition of a number of small, established oil companies. In August, 1957, the firm acquired La Gloria Oil and Gas Company by exchanging one share of Texas Eastern common stock for each of the one million outstanding shares of La Gloria common. La Gloria had extensive gas and oil reserves, a modern twenty-five-thousand-barrel-per-day refinery at Tyler, Texas, and one of the largest natural gas processing plants in the industry. Organized in 1940, La Gloria's original mission had been to build and operate a large natural gas cycling plant in the La Gloria gas field in South Texas. The company had grown and diversified, so that by 1957 it held both oil and gas reserves and had capable managers of great value to Texas Eastern.[9]

Interestingly, this acquisition went forward outside of Texas Eastern's established planning system. President Orville "Dick" Carpenter did the background research and financial preparation himself, with little help from others except Mills Cox. The company's president from 1956 to 1965, Carpenter was TE's diversification strategist. He brought an experienced accountant's perspective to his job. Before joining the firm as comptroller in 1947, he had practiced as a certified public accountant and served as an auditor for several Texas state agencies and as executive director of the Texas Unemployment Compensation Commission and of the Texas Old-Age Assistance Commission. During World War II he had served in the Army as the executive officer of the Texas Selective Service System before going to the European theater. After leaving active duty as a lieutenant colonel, he was brought into Texas Eastern by the Brown brothers, and he quickly moved up from his comptrollers position to a vice presidency in 1950. His experience in ac-

La Gloria refinery, Tyler, Texas

counting, auditing, and managing organizations gave him an edge in evaluating potential acquisitions.

Carpenter summarized his approach to diversification as follows:

> Up until a short time ago, the question of what type of company Texas Eastern is could have been answered very simply—we were a natural gas pipeline company. Well, we are still that in a bigger way than ever but in addition we are now in the field of producing and refining, petroleum products pipelining and gas processing. . . . We are diversifying—yes—but we are diversifying with direction and in accordance with a new and tremendous concept—the pipeline transportation of energy.[10]

In subsequent speeches and publications, Carpenter shortened this summary of his company's strategy into a forceful phrase: pipeliners of energy. In practice, this meant that the company remained interested in exploring opportunities in all phases of the energy industries—including gas, oil, and coal — with an emphasis on the transportation of energy in its various forms via pipelines.

Carpenter's managerial style was sparse and direct. At the beginning of one meeting of the officers, he simply announced that Texas Eastern had acquired a new company. None of the other officers had even known that a deal was in the works. But Carpenter himself had examined the financial aspects of the agreement in detail, and he felt that "Acquisition of La Gloria fits perfectly with Texas Eastern's planned expansion and diversification program. La Gloria, a long supplier of natural gas to Texas Eastern, is a well-managed, successful company. In addition to its many millions in assets, it will bring into the Texas Eastern organization an extremely capable management-employee group with an outstanding record of achievements."[11]

Obtaining capable managers has always been an important aspect of acquisition, particularly when the company was diversifying outside its traditional areas of experience. One of La Gloria's able executives was John Lynch, who subsequently took a strong role in the management of Texas Eastern. Lynch had entered La Gloria in 1944, after fifteen years of oil industry experience with Shamrock Oil Company and later with Fletcher Oil, of Los Angeles. A substantial investor in La Gloria, he had become that company's president in 1947. After TE purchased La Gloria, Lynch became a senior vice president and a director of the parent enterprise.

Orville Carpenter thought that La Gloria would improve the company's record in production. He was convinced that Texas Eastern Production Company was too small to be successful, since a production company needed enough resources to withstand the inevitable dry holes in between the good finds. Carpenter felt that the acquisition of a fairly large company with greater in-house capabilities and a larger, more experienced staff would quickly and dramatically enhance Texas Eastern's performance. La Gloria seemed to be a sure thing. But its initial attempts to find oil and gas in the Midland area, the Gulf of Mexico, and the Black Warror Basin of Alabama proved disappointing. At one point the company was on the verge of purchasing a large acreage in the Lake Washington Field in South Louisiana from John Mecom, but that deal fell through as well.

As Texas Eastern grappled with these problems, it faced similar issues in its efforts to build strength in another field, the shipment of petroleum products. For a natural gas transmission company, diversification into the shipment of petroleum products did not appear to be a major step. But once begun, the process of diversification can and often does take on a logic of its own, pulling the firm down paths far removed from the considerations that prompted the original choice. Strategic decisions to diversify which seem to involve straightforward choices to enter a new venture often subsequently require more complicated considerations of how best to protect the initial investment with other, related acquisitions. Thus Texas Eastern's involvement in the shipment of petroleum products began as a way to utilize existing resources more efficiently but ultimately led to a major acquisition which made the company a dominant force in the liquid petroleum gas business, an enterprise which differed sharply from natural gas transmission.

The path looked inviting at first. Early in its history, Texas Eastern had recognized the disadvantages of using the Little Big Inch as a natural gas line. Its twenty-inch diameter had been a decided leap forward in the size of petroleum product lines in the 1940s, but larger diameters were commonplace in the postwar natural gas industry. The construction of the Kosciusko Line in 1952 gave the company a modern line that replaced the Little Big Inch, and Texas Eastern focused its attention on expanding the capacity of the Kosciusko Line, not the Little Big Inch, during the 1950s. The smaller line was simply not competitive as a gas pipeline. It was better suited for its original purpose, the shipment of petroleum products. Its origins in the nation's largest refining center, the upper Gulf Coast of Texas, gave it ready access to potential shippers. By the early 1950s Texas Eastern had begun to explore the prospect of converting the line to its original purpose in the interest of increased profits, diversification into an allied but FPC–free field, and the strengthening of its gas business.[12]

The first step in this direction was to commission an outside consultant to study the potential markets for petroleum products, the technical problems involved with reconversion, and the economics of the proposal. These initial investigations came back quite positive, complete with projections of increased profits for the corporation from reconversion. The project was attractive in its own right. But it also made sense as part of a package which included the continued expansion of the Kosciusko Line to serve the markets then being served by the Little Big Inch. The company's leaders were convinced. They decided to diversify into petroleum products transportation through the Little Big Inch, while pushing to expand natural gas capacity through new construction.

Texas Eastern moved into this new area as it would subsequently move into others, by investing in a small company already engaged in products shipment. This gave Texas Eastern a toehold and experienced managers to take charge of further expansion. The initial step came with the acquisition of the Triangle Pipeline Company in early 1954 for about $3.2 million. George Brown reasoned that once the Little Big Inch was converted to products, it would need additional pipelines to provide inputs for the main system. Triangle gathered petroleum products in a ten-inch system serving east Texas, north Louisiana, and south Arkansas gasoline plants and refineries. It carried the products to a water terminal on the Mississippi River at Arkansas City, Arkansas, then moved them by barge to more distant markets. Texas Eastern also acquired an option to purchase a minority interest in Triangle Refineries, a small refining company.

Along with the deal came J. B. Saunders. This colorful oil man had previously known both the Browns and Reginald Hargrove, who negotiated the purchase of Triangle just before his death. Saunders had built a reputation as a good marketer. He became a vice president of Texas Eastern with responsibility for marketing and managing the products pipeline's services.[13] Saunders took charge of planning for the reconversion of the Little Big Inch.

The system as subsequently proposed to the FPC made use of the line's connections to its original products-gathering system, which included ties to refineries in the Houston–Texas City and Beaumont–Port Arthur areas. The original 1.2 million-barrel batching terminal located near Beaumont, Texas, had also been retained by Texas Eastern and could be reemployed. As a products carrier, the twenty-inch line would be able to deliver 235,000 barrels per day to its northern terminus at the Ohio River near Moundsville, West Virginia, where storage terminals would be constructed and lateral lines built to Pittsburgh. Along the route of the pipeline additional laterals would be constructed to connect Louisville and Cincinnati with the products line. Since the Little Big Inch crossed the Mississippi near Cairo, Missouri, it could deliver products to barges on the Mississippi as well. Early in the planning, future extensions to both Chicago and the East Coast were contemplated.

Before plans got very far, Texas Eastern encountered stiff opposition from a predictable source, the oil companies and barge owners who transported refined products up the Mississippi River. These same interests had fought hard in the lobbying over the postwar disposal of the Inch Lines to assure that the lines were not used to transport petroleum. Now, with their victory in danger of being reversed, they attacked Texas Eastern's proposal with all the weapons at their disposal.

When the FPC opened hearings on the reconversion project in December of 1954, Texas Eastern faced determined opposition from intervenors with a strong economic incentive to defeat the proposal. The relatively short hearing came to an end in late January, 1955. As in the original postwar hearings over the use of the Inch Lines, the intervenors questioned the need for reconversion while also asserting that it would have negative economic consequences for an existing transportation system. The FPC delayed its decision, although Texas Eastern seemed confident that its plans would be approved. But the intervenors were determined to exhaust all avenues of challenge, for even if they ultimately lost the battle, a delaying action would buy them time. They would retain temporary control of their markets while preparing for the day when the Little Big Inch would become a competitor. With their prospects dim at the FPC, the barge owners and the oil companies that supported them turned to the courts for relief, or at least for further delay. They appealed the FPC's authority to allow Texas Eastern to withdraw the Little Big Inch from gas service. The U.S. Court of Appeals in Washington, D.C., remanded the case back to the commission for further hearings in January of 1956.[14]

The court's order did not apply to other parts of Texas Eastern's proposal, which included the completion of its new thirty-inch gas pipeline. The com-

Welding 30-inch sections of the Kosciusko Line

pany forged ahead with the construction of a southern extension of the Kosciusko Line to Beaumont, Texas. The completion of this 382–mile, thirty-inch line more than replaced the Little Big Inch's 200 mmcf/d of natural gas. The new line allowed gas to be shipped from the large fields on the Gulf Coast to Kosciusko, Mississippi, where it entered the previously completed thirty-inch gas line for its eastward journey. Included in the construction of this Beaumont extension was the addition of approximately 125,000 horse-power in compressors to the Kosciusko Line, and approximately one hundred miles of small lateral lines in Texas (along with 2,200 horsepower in compression). After the completion of this work late in 1955, the Little Big Inch would no longer be missed if Texas Eastern received permission for its reconversion.

As the courts and the FPC deliberated, Texas Eastern proceeded with work on the facilities needed to handle petroleum products in the Little Big Inch. Once the FPC granted permission, no further regulatory approval would be required, since the Interstate Commerce Commission did not certify common carriers. Confident of the FPC's ultimate approval, Texas Eastern pushed ahead. At one level, the company was playing a form of "regulatory chicken," wagering that the expenditure of large sums on reconversion and related endeavors (an estimated $67 million for the new thirty-inch replacement line and $31 million for reconversion) would make it difficult for the FPC to block the project.

On October 9, 1956, the FPC finally decided that the public interest would indeed be served if Texas Eastern removed the Little Big Inch from natural gas transportation service and constructed substitute facilities. But on October 29 the commission reconvened hearings, in compliance with a federal court ruling that further study was necessary to determine the effect of the reconversion on other petroleum product carriers such as barge lines. The hard-pressed intervenors also claimed that reconversion would violate antitrust laws and be inconsistent with national defense policies. Three oil company operators, Harry Jordan, a barge company owner, Paul Blazer, of Ashland Refining Company, and Fritz Ingram, owner of a major barge company, filed a lawsuit against the conversion plan. Claiming violation of the Sherman and Clayton acts, the three charged that Texas Eastern and Triangle sought to monopolize the petroleum products transportation business. In this, the three plaintiffs had found an effective delaying tactic, one which promised to keep the conversion in limbo and allow the barges additional time to operate without competition.

The opponents' legal delays were testing TE's will to continue the fight, but the company finally broke through with a strong counterattack: it filed a suit against the barge owners for conspiring to restrain trade, thereby subjecting them to the same legal expense and financial exposure to treble damages that they had imposed on Texas Eastern. Within two weeks of the company's counterclaim, Harold Levanthal, an experienced attorney for the barge owners, contacted Texas Eastern's general counsel, Charlie Francis, to settle all claims. Within days a settlement was reached.[15] With this legal action dismissed, on January 22, 1958, the FPC finally authorized Texas Eastern to convert the Little Big Inch.

As this episode indicated, managers who were trying to innovate in a regulated environment were severely constrained. A corporate decision based on sound technical and economic reasons was bottled up in the regulatory and legal process for more than six years. The reconversion of the Little Big Inch was not held up because of any regulatory concern about the broad public interest in oil and gas transmission. Rather, determined rivals used guerilla warfare before the FPC and the courts to buy several more years of freedom from competition. Management at Texas Eastern had to fight legal battles on several fronts for six years to gain the right to carry out a strategic choice that promised to introduce a healthy dose of competition into the transportation of petroleum products.

As the FPC hearings and the court challenge went forward, J. B. Saunders decided to leave Texas Eastern; the company began at once to search for another experienced oil executive capable of managing the operations of the Little Big Inch and building up the products business. At the recommendations of Saunders and others in the oil pipeline industry, Texas Eastern brought in Millard Neptune, who had more than twenty years' experience with Phillips Petroleum, the PAW, and subsidiaries of Continental Oil (Conoco).

Neptune had grown up in the heart of the midcontinent oil fields in Bartlesville, Oklahoma, and had helped pay his way through college and law school by working in the oil fields for Phillips. After a stint at the PAW, he had worked in production in Venezuela for Phillips before taking a job as manager of the foreign department of Continental. After returning to the company following a stay with the Petroleum Administration for Defense in the Korean War, Neptune supervised the construction of a crude oil pipeline from Montana to Illinois. He then spent three years managing an oil exploration company in Egypt for a consortium that included Conoco.[16] Neptune thus brought to Texas Eastern extensive experience in both oil pipelines and foreign and domestic oil production. His contacts within the oil fraternity ultimately proved quite valuable as he undertook the difficult job of building shipments for the Little Big Inch and helping to guide the company in its early moves into international ventures in oil and gas exploration and production.

As the effort to build traffic on the products line commenced, the organization and management of this and other efforts to diversify began to exert a strong influence on the company's structure and style of operations. When Orville Carpenter became president of Texas Eastern in 1956, he inherited a company that previously had little need for decentralization of authority. The company's single focus on natural gas transmission had made the lines of authority relatively simple. Nor had early involvement in oil and gas exploration and production disturbed this setup, because the new operation had been organized as a separate subsidiary. But the acquisition of Triangle Pipeline, the reconversion of the Little Big Inch, the acquisition of the production subsidiary by Texas Eastern, and the acquisition of La Gloria in 1957 all pointed to the need for alterations in management structure. In 1958 Carpenter introduced reorganization along divisional lines. The Little Big Inch Division, under the leadership of Millard Neptune, was responsible for oil products. In practice, Neptune enjoyed considerable autonomy. Within certain rough guidelines, he could do whatever he felt was necessary to build traffic on the line, and he could depend upon receiving support from Carpenter and several board members.

Decentralization was not achieved without tensions, if only because the "secondary" division competed with natural gas for resources and status within the organization. At times, oil and gas did not mix well. Early in his tenure at Texas Eastern, Neptune crossed swords with Baxter Goodrich, head of engineering in the Gas Division, over issues raised by reconversion of the Little Big Inch. From Neptune's perspective, Texas Eastern's engineering group

> had been doing engineering work for the gas pipeline and they did not under-stand the difference in the regulatory climate of an oil pipeline versus gas pipeline. In a gas pipeline, if it cost an extra million dollars, well, that's just an extra million rate base that you earn on. Under the Interstate Commerce Commission, which regulates oil pipelines, they have standard rules of thumb by which they establish values of a pipeline and they say you can earn on that rate base, which they set by formula. So if we'd save a million dollars, it's a million dollars saved.[17]

Tiring of struggles with the company's engineering department, Neptune fi-nally created his own engineering department within the Little Big Inch Divi-sion. He was able to do this because of Carpenter's dual commitment to the concept of decentralization and to the Little Big Inch Division. One cost, however, was continuing tension with the Gas Division and with Goodrich, who later became president of Texas Eastern.

High expectations for the reconverted pipeline added a sense of urgency to the search for shippers. The early consulting reports on the feasibility of reconverting the Little Big Inch had been overly optimistic in their assessments of potential traffic for the line. These projections had been echoed by the company throughout the long struggle to gain regulatory permission for the project. A statement to shareholders in the company's *Annual Report* for 1957 captured the prevailing sentiment: "After a reasonable development period, operation of this system is expected to contribute substantially to company earnings."[18] The definition of "reasonable" was left open in the *An-nual Report*, but in practice this period stretched out for almost five years.

Part of the problem was a downturn in the general economic condition of the domestic oil industry in the late 1950s. After booming in the early 1950s, expansion tailed off, and the basic economic assumptions underlying the earlier projections proved overly optimistic. Another problem was the lack of initial interest from the major oil companies, which had been counted on heavily by TE's planners as sources of products. Since many of these com-panies had consistently opposed the use of the Little Big Inch for products shipments, it was a tricky job for Texas Eastern to persuade them to consider using its newly available capacity to ship products. The Little Big Inch Divi-sion "both served the major oil companies and competed with the major oil companies. . . ." As John Jacobs later noted "that's a very narrow line to walk and we walked it very carefully."[19] If the line could not be walked, the Little Big Inch faced a bleak future as a products carrier.

Another, quite different sort of pressure was much on the minds of the divisional managers in the first years of products shipments. Until the line could be utilized, its operators faced the task of assuring sufficient pressure in the line to push batches of products to their destinations. Neptune and his operators came up with a novel approach to this problem: they developed methods for pushing these products to market using shipments of natural gas. A pig—a device to separate different shipments and prevent their intermingling—went into the line after batches of products, and natural gas was then used to fill the line and send the products on their way. At the end of the line, the natural gas could be separated and reinjected into gas lines or used for other purposes. Implemented with the approval of regulatory authorities, this procedure proved quite useful as the company gradually expanded its products traffic.[20] Operators kept close tabs on the size of the "gas bubble," that is, the amount of gas in the Little Big Inch Line at any one time. The steady decline in the bubble as petroleum products replaced gas marked the division's slow climb to profitability.

Shrinking the bubble required aggressive marketing in an industry with which Texas Eastern was unfamiliar. This division had to expend considerable effort to attract customers. The task initially fell to J. B. Saunders and then to his replacement, Millard Neptune, both of whom had experience in petroleum marketing. One of their initial marketing tools was a festive weekend gathering, held in French Lick, Indiana, of those in charge of supply and transportation at the major oil companies. With golf, trap shooting, gin rummy, and fishing as the immediate attractions, Texas Eastern sought to "let them know we are ready to do business and see what we can do about developing business."[21] Neptune also took the more direct route of approaching old contacts within the oil industry, including his brother, at Phillips Petroleum, and management at Ashland Oil, the long-time opponent of the reconversion of the Little Big Inch. Once a shipper had begun to make small commitments of products to the Little Big Inch, its operators sought to encourage expanded use by juggling shipments through the line to provide the most timely service possible. In these and other ways, diversification into products shipment called for new skills and a new approach to business at Texas Eastern.

One thing that did not change, however, was the crucial fact of life for any pipeline business: the primary marketing tool was having the best possible connections between the points of supply and demand. Shippers might be swayed by excellent service or even by weekends in French Lick. But they ultimately based their shipping commitments on the costs and convenience of using pipelines rather than other types of transmission. This meant that a pipeline had to extend as near as possible to major shipping points. Recognizing this, Texas Eastern embarked on an expensive program to build extensions and feeders for the Little Big Inch. Well before receiving final permission to reconvert, the company built the first, a 233–mile, fourteen-inch line connecting Seymour, Indiana, with the major markets in the Chicago area. Almost as fast as one extension could be completed, another was begun in the ongoing effort to tie potential shippers into the system. Growth also required the construction of new terminals and storage facilities. The products pipeline steadily reached out into the Midwest and on to Philadelphia. By 1962 the system could ship products from the Gulf Coast to the Atlantic seaboard. By 1964 it reached into upper New York state and New England. All of this construction required substantial new investments, adding pressure to improve profitability.

By the late 1950s liquefied petroleum gas (LPG)[22] had become one important target of the Little Big Inch Division's efforts to attract additional traffic. From the time of the first shipment of LPG in 1958, this group of products seemed to be particularly suitable for the Little Big Inch, which promised to reduce transportation costs dramatically in comparison to the batch shipment methods commonly used in the LPG industry. But before the division could take on heavy shipments of LPG, new storage facilities were needed at each end of the line. On the south end, the company built a salt dome storage facility at Mont Belvieu, in the middle of giant refining and petrochemical complex on the Gulf Coast near the Houston Ship Channel. By circulating fresh water through salt domes some thirty-seven hundred feet underground, the company created a giant cavity capable of storing more than seven million barrels of LPG. The expansion of storage on the northern end of the Little Big Inch posed more difficult problems. Here the solution was a mined cavern storage facility at Todhunter, Ohio. The construction of this series of "criss-crossing, catacomb-like tunnels" some four hundred feet underground, required drilling a four-foot shaft down into underground caverns surrounded by impermeable rock and then lowering down the shaft the men and equipment needed to excavate the cavern. When this work had been completed, Texas Eastern had the largest mined-cavern storage terminal in the world, with a capacity of almost 1.5 million barrels. Mont Belvieu and Todhunter cost the company approximately $11 million, but these facilities gave the Little Big Inch distinct competitive advantages over other shippers of LPG. Indeed, the combination of the Little Big Inch pipeline system and these large storage caverns altered the basic economics of the LPG business by dramatically lowering transportation costs for long-distance shipments.[23]

By 1962 Texas Eastern had invested more than $100 million in its Little Big Inch Division and related facilities. This endeavor had not proved particularly profitable, and the company struggled to increase its return on this investment. In several lengthy reports to the board in 1961 and 1962, Millard Neptune discussed various ways to "cure the ills of the Little Big Inch," which still had not attracted sufficient traffic to produce the profits originally projected. Neptune carefully reviewed the prospects for recouping as much as possible of the company's stake in the line by selling all or part of it to a major oil company. Using a company-by-company approach, Neptune suggested why each would not be interested, at least at a price acceptable to

Texas Eastern. He further reported that a series of overtures to various oil companies had produced no serious responses. If "disinvestment" was not an option, then further expenditures would almost certainly be needed to protect the capital already spent on the division.

The most attractive target for future diversification was the LPG business, which had already become a growth area for shipments through the products line. Neptune became a strong supporter of deeper involvement in propane, and he gained the support of president Orville Carpenter and the company's board by moving his division gradually in this direction. The case for propane was strong. It would make the best possible use of Texas Eastern's existing resources and market position. The primary consideration was the company's highly developed storage facilities at Mont Belvieu and Todhunter, which gave TE a competitive advantage over all existing propane retailers and over all who might enter the business, including major oil companies. Another attractive feature was the fact that the large oil companies had not yet moved into propane in a big way. Texas Eastern might be able to forestall such a move in the future by providing a ready outlet for large refiners who produced LPG as a by-product. As Texas Eastern contemplated its move into propane retailing, management noted with interest that the business remained in the hands of hundreds of small firms, none of which had access to the resources of a company the size of Texas Eastern or to transportation which was cost competitive with the Little Big Inch.[24]

Along with these specific reasons for diversifying into this new area was a general sense that such a move fit easily into the company's overall strategy as a "pipeliner of energy." Propane was simply another form of hydrocarbon, used largely for the same purposes as natural gas. The key difference was that the propane business served primarily those not yet connected into the nation's grid of natural gas pipelines. Although strikingly different from natural gas on the marketing side, LPG was quite compatible with natural gas in such areas as production, transportation, and storage.

It was to the problems of retailing that Neptune and his division turned in their efforts to persuade TE to enter the propane business. One essential step was to learn as much as possible about the business. This was done through a series of in-house studies, contacts with propane companies using the Little Big Inch Line, and, finally, through the acquisition of a small propane company. Neptune had initially invested personally in a small propane retailer, operating it for a brief period to get a better feel for the business. He then went to the board in 1961 and requested and received a $2 million appropriation to begin to establish a small, Texas Eastern–owned propane marketing company, the Texane Gas Company (based in Newark, Ohio). At the time of this appropriation, Neptune also suggested that Texas Eastern explore seriously the acquisition of an established propane retailer. He felt that diversifying through purchase would be superior to gradually building up the company's own small business and that there were excellent potential acquisitions in this industry.

The target of opportunity in propane retailing was Pyrofax, one of the nation's oldest, best known, and largest retailing companies. After its founding in 1922, Pyrofax had grown steadily, with major markets in the upper midwestern, northeastern and southeastern United States, and eastern Canada (see map 6.1). Having established a reputation as "the Tiffany of bottled gas companies," Pyrofax built an operation with 134 bulk distribution stations and $30 million in annual sales of 100 million gallons sold to approximately 500,000 individual customers. The company was "a wholly-owned, semi-autonomous subsidiary of Union Carbide." Pyrofax had experienced a rough period of adjustment to new competition in the period immediately before 1962. Having just weathered that crisis, Union Carbide seemed open to a proposal to sell this subsidiary.[25]

Despite Carpenter's support, Neptune encountered skepticism from most of the board in his efforts to convince them of the wisdom of purchasing Pyrofax. The key issue was the appropriateness of entering a business so markedly different from Texas Eastern's natural gas business. In company debate, the argument became: how can a company accustomed to serving about 70 customers be expected to perform well in an undertaking with 500,000 customers? Also troublesome was the fact that only about one-third of Pyrofax's marketing area was served by the Little Big Inch. Neptune countered these objections with a variety of arguments, including the fact that Pyrofax's presence in New England might facilitate the planned expansion of the products line into that potentially lucrative market. While admitting that retail marketing would generate new demands, he held out the prospect that Texas Eastern's transportation and storage facilities would make the company a dominant force in propane. He also used statistics developed by several detailed studies of potential propane markets to argue that Pyrofax had ample room for growth and that its acquisition could provide an excellent return. Over and above all such arguments, however, was the contribution that this venture might make to the building of the traffic and profitability of the Little Big Inch.

With the board's approval, Carpenter entered price negotiations with Union Carbide, which had earlier indicated its willingness to consider an offer for Pyrofax. These talks continued during the last half of 1962. Union Carbide had a strong incentive to close any deal for Pyrofax before the end of the year, and the sale was finally completed on New Year's Eve, 1962. The total price was approximately $30 million, including $22 million for the company's assets and $8 million for its cash and accounts receivable.[26] This completed a major step forward in implementing Texas Eastern's new strategy. A decision made almost a decade earlier to reconvert the Little Big Inch pipeline had led Texas Eastern down a path that produced the purchase of a major propane retailing and distribution company.

Map 6.1 Little Big Inch Division and Pyrofax

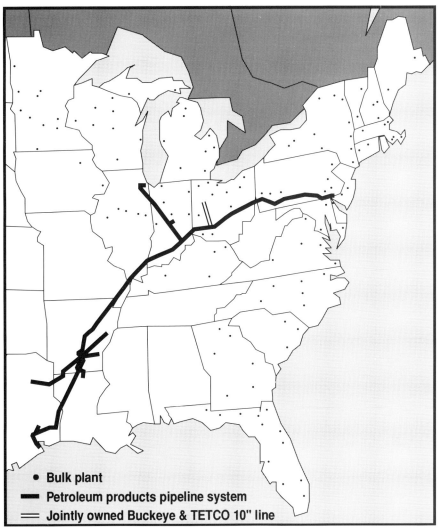

- **● Bulk plant**
- **▬ Petroleum products pipeline system**
- **═ Jointly owned Buckeye & TETCO 10" line**

The new acquisition now had to be fitted into the company's existing operations. The use of the Little Big Inch gradually altered the traditional business of Pyrofax, assisting this wholly owned subsidiary in expanding its bulk distribution while also helping to lower its transportation costs. Texas Eastern moved to take full advantage of its new business in 1964 with the extension of the Little Big Inch into New England, one of the Pyrofax's traditional strongholds. The completion of a 384-mile, eight-inch pipeline from Greenburg, in western Pennsylvania, to Selkirk, New York, gave the company the capacity to ship LPG from the southwest all the way to the doorstep of New England. LPG could be shipped into New England via tank cars or trucks from the modern terminal constructed at Selkirk, a small town just south

Little Big Inch products storage plant, 1962

of Albany, New York, near the intersection of the New York State Thruway and its connection to the Massachusetts Turnpike. The facility was also adjacent to the New York Central Railroad's main switching yards. Good storage facilities along the pipeline assured the company of adequate supplies of LPG throughout the year. As projected before the acquisition of Pyrofax, the combination of pipeline shipment and large modern storage facilities gave Texas Eastern's propane business a distinct competitive edge over many of the smaller retailers, and the company steadily expanded both its shipments of LPG through the Little Big Inch and the profitability and sales of Pyrofax.[27]

The long struggle to reconvert the Little Big Inch had been a difficult ordeal for Texas Eastern. From the earliest efforts to build traffic on this line, internal opposition to large new investments in the products line had grown, particularly among those in the gas transmission end of the company's business. The opponents of this path toward diversification became more vocal

148

after the purchase of Pyrofax. One prominent TE executive of this era summarized the tensions: "We went from a business where we generated hundreds of millions of dollars of revenues in a gas pipeline with about 75 customers. We went to a business where we generated doodly-squat and had a half million customers." Much of this criticism focused on Millard Neptune: "Damned and determined he [Neptune] was going to do it. The guy had been hired to run the products pipeline and we bought Pyrofax from Union Carbide on a damn-the-torpedoes basis." Neptune was much aware of the opposition to his division. For a few years, he was shielded by Carpenter. With the retirement of his staunch supporter, however, and the subsequent promotion of his old nemesis, Baxter Goodrich, to the presidency, Neptune's position became untenable. He left the company in 1965.

Although the organizational tensions generated by the purchase of Pyrofax often focused on the individual personalities involved, tensions ran much more deeply into the corporate culture. Texas Eastern had begun as a natural gas transmission company. This core business remained far and away the dominant producer of profits, despite diversification. Those who had built the pipeline system and then daily grappled with the frustrations of managing under FPC–style regulations in the 1950s inevitably resented newcomers from outside who used profits generated by gas transmission to "play" in unregulated ventures. Just as inevitably, these newcomers viewed the conservative gas men as unnecessarily afraid of risks. The resulting tensions were more annoying than threatening in the early stages of diversification, but they were bound to grow as more non-gas ventures were added. They pitted old versus new; core industry versus periphery; regulated versus market-driven.

Tensions of another sort blocked Texas Eastern's efforts to diversify into another type of energy transportation, the coal slurry pipeline. Befitting a company whose proclaimed goal was to become a "pipeliner of energy," Texas Eastern's policy was to take the lead as an innovator in the shipment of treated coal via pipeline. Here, however, it encountered political obstacles that could not be overcome. It never was able to defeat the well-organized opposition of railroads fearful that this new technology would cut into their traditional traffic in coal. As in the case of the reconversion of the Little Big Inch, the company's competitive impulses had to be played out in several legal, political, and regulatory arenas before having a chance to succeed or fail in the marketplace. Beginning in 1960 W. T. Thagard, vice president, directed the company's coal pipeline activities and continued to do so through 1967. Thagard, who had been employed at Texas Eastern since 1947 (after leaving his previous position as rate consultant with Ebasco Services, Limited), had a tough job. The slurry project faced strong, well-connected opponents determined to block Texas Eastern's innovative technology.

In 1958 Texas Eastern had begun investigating pipeline transportation of coal with Consolidation Coal Company, the nation's largest coal producer.

Consolidation had begun research and development on slurry technology in 1949. In February of 1959 TE joined Consolidation in planning to build a 350-mile, $100 million coal slurry line from the West Virginia coal fields to a number of eastern electric utilities in the New York–Philadelphia area (see map 6.2). The single most important customer for coal was the electric utility industry. For its pipeline to be successful, TE had to demonstrate that it could deliver coal to a utility at a lower cost than could railroad transportation. The company also had to prove that coal delivered by a slurry pipeline could be used effectively to generate power. During June, 1960, Babcock and Wilcox Company began a research and development program to "find a simple, reliable method of firing coal slurry."[28] In June, 1961, after experimentation and development of a five-foot diameter cyclone furnace boiler in which slurry could be injected, the Jersey Central Power and Light Company, Consolidation Coal Company, and Texas Eastern agreed to participate in a test of the equipment from October 1 to November 10, 1961. The demonstration seemed successful, and Texas Eastern and Consolidation Coal looked forward to a heavy demand for coal slurry by utility companies.[29]

But before that could happen, the two innovators had a legislative task to accomplish. Eminent domain for coal pipelines was not covered under the Interstate Commerce Act. Since such pipelines were a new technology, there had never been a need for national legislation. The longest existing coal slurry pipeline was a 108–mile line owned by Consolidation Coal and located completely within Ohio (which had passed a state law granting eminent domain for such projects). Completed in 1957, this short line had produced excellent results, including a dramatic reduction in the transportation costs of coal.[30] But the new, longer line proposed by Texas Eastern would of necessity go through several states, and a federal eminent domain law would almost certainly be needed to complete the line.

The lack of established law governing this new technology gave opponents an opportunity to block its introduction. The major railroads quickly agreed not to allow the new pipeline to cross under their existing rights-of-way. Without cooperation from the railroads, the pipeline's builders would be forced to depend on government coercion of the roads to obtain needed rights-of-way. But a complex federal political system characterized by checks and balances and laced with procedural safeguards presented many opportunities for a determined opponent to veto the introduction of a new technology by "delaying it to death." The railroads focused on Texas Eastern's weakest point, the fact that there was no law granting slurry pipelines the right of eminent domain. If such a law could be kept off the books, the innovation could be stymied.

The railroads built a powerful coalition to achieve that purpose. The AFL–CIO came out against the pipeline, fearing that this project would bring about a substantial loss of revenue to the railroads, producing layoffs of up to fifteen thousand railroad workers.[31] Texas Eastern countered these charges

MAP 6.2 Proposed Coal Slurry Pipeline

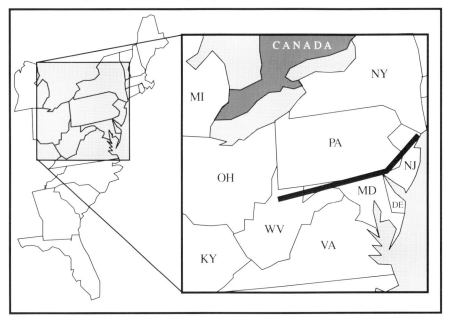

by arguing that the slurry pipeline would help certain coal producing areas of the country. Appalachia, in particular, was not able to develop fully its coal resources because of high railway transportation costs. As had been true in several previous hearings involving the transportation of energy, such estimates (for and against the coal pipeline) could not easily be compared to reach a clear decision. Much more than the economics of coal pipelines was at issue. Potential job losses registered heavily on the scales of electoral and regulatory politics. These scales also at times seemed biased on the side of the status quo, since innovation almost by definition disrupted existing patterns of economic activity. Those hurt by such changes had a strong incentive to use the political system to protect themselves, and they did so with great vigor.

Texas Eastern tried to recharge its old political contacts to gain eminent domain for its coal slurry project. Charles Francis contacted Donald C. Cook, who had helped with the research when Texas Eastern bought the Inch Lines and who was now president of the American Electric Power Company. Cook believed that slurry pipelines would benefit the electric power industry. He agreed to help. Ed Clark, also an associate of Vice President Lyndon B. Johnson, was heavily involved with Texas Eastern in the coal pipeline matter. Johnson himself was a strong supporter of Texas Eastern's proposal and the eminent domain bill. On January 16, 1962, the vice president met with Secretary of Commerce Luther Hodges about the coal slurry issue. The following day, Orville Carpenter, noting Johnson's meeting with Hodges, sent to

Texas Eastern's Board of Directors meeting, 1963. *Left to right, standing:* James W. Hargrove, George A. Butler, John F. Lynch, Ralph S. O'Connor, John S. Ivy, Gus S. Wortham, William A. Smith. *Left to right, sitting:* Herbert J. Frensley, George R. Brown, Orville S. Carpenter, and Charles I. Francis.

the vice president information regarding coal slurry. He emphasized that all Texas Eastern wanted was eminent domain power for coal slurry pipelines, something the railroads opposing the bill already had.

One of Texas Eastern's strongest arguments in building greater popular support for its project was the idea that the pipeline might help relieve poverty in Appalachia. Late in 1962 *LOOK* magazine published an article titled "Portrait of an Underdeveloped Country."[32] After describing the extreme poverty in the region, the author concluded that this problem cried out for solutions like coal slurry, which would reduce the delivered cost of Appalachian coal. Noting that "transportation accounts for over half the retail price of coal today," the author concluded: "It is absurd that the coal industry is today being prevented from using all available techniques for meeting competition in the national fuel market . . . While the Big Inch carries petroleum [*sic*] and Little Inch gasoline and other products from Texas to the East Coast, West Virginia coal operators can't get "slurry" past their own state line."[33]

In response to the article Vice President Johnson wrote to Daniel Mich, editorial director of *LOOK*, and discussed the eminent domain bill for coal pipelines. As Johnson observed, "President Kennedy has called upon Congress to enact legislation granting coal pipelines the same right of eminent domain that oil and natural gas pipelines, and the railroads themselves, enjoy."[34] Johnson said of Texas Eastern's proposed pipeline, "I am convinced that this legislation will be passed and that coal pipelines will soon be in operation in the Southern Appalachian area. Already plans have been drawn for a privately-financed $100,000,000 coal pipeline from West Virginia to Philadelphia and New York City. This pipeline alone will provide thousands of new jobs for unemployed miners. It will be followed by others and more thousands of miners will find work and dignity again."[35] President John F. Kennedy had previously voiced similar sentiments in a conservation message sent to Congress in March, 1962. Kennedy included a section on coal slurry pipelines, describing their value to the energy industry and promising that "I will shortly send to the Congress proposals to facilitate the construction of pipelines to transport coal slurry in interstate commerce."[36]

As the slurry measure appeared to be moving closer to reality, the oil industry began to worry about the ramifications of the bill. On March 6 Jack Head and Millard Neptune, of Texas Eastern, met with three representatives of the legislative committee of the Association of Oil Pipe Lines. They feared that the bill might somehow jeopardize the certificate-free status of oil pipelines, and they vowed to oppose the measure if it appeared that it would be used against their lines. Head and Neptune assured them that if the bill became a threat to oil pipelines, they would withdraw their support, since Texas Eastern, too, was an oil-oriented company.

In March, 1962, in the Eighty-Seventh Congress, Second Session, Senator Wayne Magnuson, by request of President Kennedy, introduced a bill to amend the Interstate Commerce Act to grant any carrier of coal by pipeline the right of eminent domain. Texas Eastern and Consolidation Coal Company had largely written the measure. Although Lyndon Johnson and Kennedy were working for the bill, Charles Francis was not completely confident that it would pass. He wrote Carpenter about Kennedy's favorable position on the pipeline and added, "I think, however, that we must give earnest thought to securing a good Republican Lobbyist to help us with those Senators and Congressmen who are across the aisle from the Democrats. We may need them, and it might take some well known Republican Lobbyist (such as General Persons) to help us in this matter."[37]

While open to this suggestion, Texas Eastern management became nervous as to whether it was overstepping its bounds in lobbying for the bill. Jack Head, the company's general counsel, investigated the matter. He wrote to Carpenter on May 24, 1962, "I have reviewed the provisions of the Federal Lobbying Act, and, in my opinion, the Act cannot be construed to cover either your activities or the activities of Texas Eastern as a corporation in attempting to influence the passage of S. 3044."[38] Head's study of precedents convinced him that the act applied only in cases where a person solicited, collected, or received contributions of money to influence the passage of an act. No one at Texas Eastern had stepped over that line.

Encouraged by the promise of political relief, Texas Eastern and Consolidation Coal Company also began investigating the possibilities of operating a five-hundred-mile coal slurry pipeline from Utah's coal fields to industrial centers in southern California. The lack of powers of eminent domain would obviously block this project too, but if such powers were forthcoming, this second line seemed promising. In the 1962 *Annual Report* George Brown and Orville Carpenter addressed this problem. They discussed the bill sent to Congress by President Kennedy, noting that this measure gave coal pipelines the right of eminent domain and made it possible for them to pass under railroad rights-of-way. According to the *Annual Report*, "a large number of our shareholders wrote their legislators on behalf of the bill and your management is grateful for this support."[39]

On such controversial issues, however, Congress never moved quickly, and sometimes it proved politically expedient to take no action at all. Congress did not address eminent domain for coal slurry pipelines during that session, and the company was forced to wait until Congress reconvened the next year. The wait proved deadly. Interest in coal slurry projects and the eminent domain bill waned in the interim. Although several states considered legislation giving eminent domain to coal pipelines, few passed the measures — with the notable exception of West Virginia. The interest of Texas Eastern and Consolidation Coal in coal pipelines also flagged after several of the railroads began a frontal economic assault by lowering coal freight rates considerably. In addition, several utilities, including Niagara Mohawk, Consolidated Edison of New York, and Central Jersey Power, announced plans to build nuclear generating plants, a prospect that dampened enthusiasm for coal slurry by suggesting that the heyday of coal-fired power plants of any kind had ended.

The fate of coal slurry pipelines had been sealed by the railroads. After lobbying hard to block passage of a federal eminent domain bill, the roads lowered their rates enough to offset any economic advantage of coal slurry. This one-two punch proved devastating to the new technology. Not even Consolidation Coal could resist. During the debates on its project with Texas Eastern, the giant coal company felt the pull of new economic forces. As the railroads made drastic cuts in their rates for coal shipments, Consolidation suspended the operation of its existing coal slurry pipeline in Ohio and began to ship coal to the plant by rail.[40]

The proponents of the new slurry line had failed. In a highly regulated economy and a political system susceptible to influence by well-organized, entrenched economic interests, the new technology had been denied a chance to prove its worth in the marketplace. Despite a concerted effort by a major natural gas company, a major coal company, and numerous supporters among the nation's largest utilities, the coal slurry pipeline project had to be suspended, at least for the time being. As a result, Texas Eastern was not successful in diversifying into the pipeline transportation of coal. The company had embarked on a strategic path that held great promise for a self proclaimed "pipeliner of energy," as well as for a coal-rich nation in search of domestic energy. Yet potential competitors in related fields had succeeded in turning aside Texas Eastern's strategic thrust with very effective political lobbying. Texas Eastern withdrew from the field, convinced that politics had blocked a technically and economically sound initiative.

By the late 1960s Texas Eastern had a report card on diversification that was not particularly encouraging. While its gas pipeline transmission business had continued to expand, its ventures into related fields had produced disappointing results. Domestic oil and gas exploration and production had been launched with great confidence in the early 1950s, but despite several significant acquisitions and a long effort to build up the company's capabilities in this area, little oil or gas had been discovered. The products pipeline business had become a paying proposition only after a different struggle involving large new investments in improvements and extension of the Little Big Inch, storage facilities and terminals, and also including acquisition of Pyrofax to help build shipments for the line. In this field, the company had responded to mediocre financial performance by moving much more deeply into the industry, not by cutting back as had ultimately been the case with domestic exploration and production. Finally, the impulse to move into the shipment of coal through slurry pipelines had been blocked by the political efforts of competing shippers. Texas Eastern was by no means finished with diversification, but through sometimes bitter experience, it had learned of the costs, as well as the benefits, of this strategy.

Chapter 7

FROM TEXAS TO
THE NORTH SEA

Texas Eastern's strategy of diversification also led the company to look overseas. Beginning in the early 1950s, the firm made several attempts, not all successful, to enter natural gas development during its formative stages in other countries. Many nations in both South America and Europe began to develop their own natural gas industries in the years following World War II, and Texas Eastern's management calculated that the firm's experience could be of value to these countries. As the gas revolution got underway throughout much of the world, Texas Eastern offered its services in foreign natural gas industries as purchaser, transporter, and producer. The company was the first major United States pipeline to purchase natural gas from Mexico after World War II. In the North Sea, TE became an active partner in the original seismic testing, development, and production of oil and gas. Sandwiched between these two successful ventures were abortive attempts to build a natural gas pipeline in Argentina and one crossing the Mediterranean from Algeria to France.

From a strategic perspective, international expansion made sense. With the end of the first flush of territorial expansion in the United States, domestic opportunities for large-scale pipeline construction waned. Texas Eastern saw itself as the sort of company that could complete ambitious projects in any political or geographical environment. The company also needed supplies of gas, and one place to look was outside the United States. By moving outside the nation, Texas Eastern would escape the often stifling authority of the FPC, which stopped at the American border.

Yet when Texas Eastern crossed that frontier, it soon learned that the United States was not the only nation with a constraining regulatory environment. Indeed, the political systems of many foreign lands made the regulators at home seem predictable and business oriented. In the United States, Texas Eastern at least clearly understood the rules of the game. In other nations, the company had to learn as quickly as possible how literally "foreign" political economies operated. There was a learning curve in this process. The company had little choice except to forge ahead as best it knew how, hoping that in each subsequent venture the experience gained would be cumulative and international operations would be more manageable.

In its initial ventures abroad Texas Eastern looked for political assistance from a carefully chosen "ally" in the country involved. Often this was an American national with some familiarity with the foreign government and close personal ties to at least one of the top executives at TE. When this approach failed to produce acceptable results, more tightly organized teams of company executives and representatives of interests native to the country in question were employed. This approach proved more successful. As the company gained international experience, it became more skillful in its dealings with foreign governments.

Texas Eastern's earliest attempts to enter foreign natural gas markets illustrate just how complex this process could be. Its first international venture involved the purchase of Mexican-produced natural gas for resale in the United States. This arrangement commenced with a long series of complex negotiations with Petróleos Mexicanos (Pemex), the Mexican government's oil and gas agency. Pemex had been created in 1938 to manage the nation's recently nationalized petroleum industry. From Mexico's first oil production in 1901 and through 1938, many foreign oil companies, most of them from the United States, had located and produced Mexican oil. By 1921 the country's production of 530,000 barrels per day represented one-fourth of total world oil output, and Mexico was then the second largest producer in the world. Although significant quantities of natural gas were found along with the oil, most of the gas was simply flared. During the late 1930s Mexico's oil production declined fairly rapidly to about 100,000 barrels per day. Due in part to this decline and to related political exigencies, Mexico expropriated nearly all petroleum exploration, production, and transmission companies operating in the country and created Pemex, a government agency, to manage the industry.[1]

After World War II Pemex increasingly viewed natural gas as an important domestic fuel, but one which might also be exported to the United States. With the goal of becoming energy independent, Pemex began producing gas from the Reynosa fields in northeastern Mexico to serve industrial and commercial markets in nearby Monterrey. By the early 1950s Monterrey's natural gas requirements were filled almost entirely by Reynosa gas, but a surplus remained. Pemex began to investigate the possibility of selling it to United States pipeline companies.

At that time the demand for natural gas in the United States was growing at a tremendous pace, and U.S. pipeline operators were attracted by what they hoped would be relatively inexpensive Mexican gas. Understanding that northern Mexico had an oversupply, these companies believed that the government might be willing to sell at a low price. During late 1951 TE's Reginald Hargrove read with interest several newspaper articles citing Mexico's interest in selling natural gas to United States companies. During late December, 1951, and early January, 1952, several of these articles quoted Antonio J. Bermudez, then General Managing Director of Pemex, to the effect that Pemex was currently negotiating with several firms.[2] One article said that Sinclair Oil and Gas Company, which had retained its oil and gas concessions in northern Mexico after nationalization, was considering purchasing Pemex's surplus gas in the Reynosa area and reselling it to Tennessee Gas Transmission Company.

As Hargrove knew, Texas Eastern had the perfect liaison with Pemex and the Mexican government in board member and founder Everette DeGolyer. As a young geologist, DeGolyer had gained fame in Mexico and throughout the oil fraternity as the discoverer of two major Mexican oil fields. His standing in Mexico was untainted by any residue of bad feelings from the controversy over the expropriation, since DeGolyer had sold his holdings and left Mexico before World War I, well before events had begun to move toward the bitter climax of 1938. Later, DeGolyer had renewed his contacts in Mexico when, during World War II, he returned on a U.S. government–sponsored mission to survey Mexico's oil and gas reserves.

At Hargrove's request, on January 7, 1952, DeGolyer sent a letter of introduction to Antonio Bermudez. DeGolyer conveyed Hargrove's interest in meeting to discuss "the possibility of contractual relationships between his company and Petróleos Mexicanos [Pemex]."[3] DeGolyer told Bermudez that Hargrove would soon be contacting him directly. Hargrove wrote Bermudez on January 11 requesting a meeting sometime during the week of February 11, 1952. Bermudez did not reply. More than one year later, Hargrove asked DeGolyer if he, during his own trip to Mexico City, would follow up on his letter of one year ago.[4] On January 16, 1953, DeGolyer wrote to Bermudez again, reminding him of their previous correspondence and reiterating Hargrove's interest in setting up a meeting.

The second round of letters brought results. In February, DeGolyer received a reply from Bermudez's associate, Raul Medina Mora, who conveyed Bermudez's interest in meeting with Hargrove during the first half of March. Hargrove replied, and they met on March 2. This discussion was successful, and Hargrove afterward wrote Bermudez a three-page letter describing Texas Eastern's south Texas system and emphasizing his interest in buying gas from Mexico at $0.11 per mcf (which was $0.05 more than Texas Eastern's south Texas subsidiary, Wilcox Trend Gathering System, Incorporated was currently paying). Hargrove noted that Texas Eastern could extend its current pipeline system (terminating in Lavaca County, between Houston and San Antonio) to the McAllen-Reynosa area, or it could extend its Wilcox Trend system to the Mexican border. Hargrove invited Bermudez to visit parts of Texas Eastern's system, particularly the Oakford storage facility in Pennsylvania.[5]

On August 25 Bermudez wrote to suggest that they begin talking about a contract for 100 mmcf/d to be increased later to 200 mmcf/d at prices between $0.14 and $0.16 per mcf. Bermudez's own market research indicated that these prices corresponded with those for the natural gas sold by local producers in south Texas to other transmission lines. Hargrove then sent a representative, Oscar Chapman (whose firm had done work for Texas Eastern on other matters), to meet with Bermudez. Chapman had been undersecretary and later secretary of the interior, and he already knew Bermudez. Under Chapman's guidance a contract was drafted and presented to Pemex as a basis for negotiations.

These talks dragged on for the next eighteen months, and during that interval, competition for northern Mexican gas began to increase. The U.S. investment company of Baruch Brothers and Company thought it had an agreement with Pemex to purchase from 200 to 400 mmcf/d. But Pemex rebuffed Baruch Brothers, while continuing to negotiate with Texas Eastern. There were several problems with the proposed contract. Discussions continued in late 1953 and 1954 over the exact terms of the price redetermination clause and over the quantity of gas to be sold. While this was going on, press reports began circulating that Pemex and Texas Eastern had made a deal. Both organizations denied that they were on the verge of signing an agreement or had already done so.

On September 28, 1955, however, after more than three tedious and uncertain years, Texas Eastern and Pemex signed a twenty-year contract for 115 mmcf/d at $0.142 per mcf, rising to only $0.182 by the end of the period. As new gas supplies in the Gulf Coast region were becoming more expensive, this long-term agreement assured Texas Eastern of a reasonably priced supply. In contrast, Tennessee Gas had recently contracted for offshore gas at $0.214 per mcf. Three of Mexico's twenty-two producing fields in the northeastern section would supply the gas for the Texas Eastern contract. The gas would be processed through Pemex's new Reynosa gasoline absorption plant, which had a capacity of 300 mmcf/d.

Having agreed at last with Pemex, Texas Eastern had to receive authorization from the FPC to purchase this gas for its expansion program. With Pemex gas contracted, Texas Eastern had to extend its thirty-inch line 422 miles from Beaumont, Texas, to the Mexican border, halfway across the Rio Grande River. The initial part of the expansion would cost $82 million out of an expected total of $147 million. This time the negotiations with the commission went smoothly. The FPC authorized TE to import the Mexican gas on October 9, 1956, allowing the firm to expand its present system. The company used its new pipeline network to carry natural gas produced in south Texas as well, including gas from a substantial contract with California oilman Edwin Pauley, who had developed leases in Hidalgo County.

On August 22, 1957, Texas Eastern sponsored a valve opening ceremony at McAllen, Texas, to inaugurate the first importation of Mexican natural gas into the United States. Ingenieno José Colomo represented Mexico. He and Orville Carpenter opened the valve at the United States–Mexico border. This new supply initially increased TE's capacity by 18 percent. Although

TABLE 7.1   Imports of Natural Gas
(millions of cubic feet)

Year	Total	Mexico
1955	10,892	7
1960	156,843	46,988
1965	456,694	52,007
1966	480,591	48,636
1967	564,228	50,972
1968	651,885	47,423
1969	726,952	46,845
1970	820,781	41,336
1971	934,547	20,689
1972	1,019,495	8,140
1973	1,032,903	1,632
1974	959,285	222
1975	953,007	0

Note: Significant imports resumed in 1980.
Source: American Gas Association, *Gas Facts: 1981* (Arlington, Va.: AGA, 1982).

this source subsequently declined in importance (see table 7.1), the contract with Pemex was a major accomplishment for Texas Eastern, which emerged from its international experience flushed with success and eager to pursue other opportunities outside of the United States.

The contract was valuable to Pemex as well. Before this agreement, Pemex's policy was to keep all of its gas in Mexico for domestic use. For a time, the company shipped much of the product into the northern industrial region of Mexico; but domestic demand lagged, and Pemex badly needed markets. It benefitted from the sales to Texas Eastern and then to other foreign firms. Pemex used the contract, which guaranteed it a minimum annual income of $5 million, to obtain credit for its own expansion, including the construction of refineries.[6]

Two other international ventures attracted Texas Eastern's attention during the late 1950s and early 1960s. One involved the construction of a natural gas pipeline in Argentina, and the other, the construction of an underwater pipeline crossing the Mediterranean from Algeria, with an ultimate destination in France. The two projects were similar in certain respects. Argentina and France were only beginning to develop their natural gas industries, and Texas Eastern was attempting to get in on the ground floor—as it had in the United States. Both pipelines were to be used to bring gas from large outlying fields to heavily populated residential and industrial centers. Both looked feasible on the basis of reports from consultants, Norbert A. McKenna in Argentina, and H. Steele Bennett in France.

In the first of these endeavors, Texas Eastern entered a joint venture with Dallas-based Dresser Industries. The Argentinian pipeline proposal offered a promising opportunity for Texas Eastern to export its expertise. Gas del Estado, the government-controlled distribution agency, had advertised the fact that it wanted a foreign company to finance and build a pipeline which would be owned jointly, 50 percent each, by Argentine and foreign investors. The proposed one-thousand-mile line would deliver gas from the large fields at Comodoro Rivadavia to Buenos Aires. The most unusual aspect of the venture was the provision that the company selected to build and finance the pipeline would own it for a period of only fifteen to twenty years, at which time the Argentine government would take over the line.

On June 4, 1959, representatives from Dresser met with the president of Yacimientos Petroliferos Fiscales (YPF), the agency controlling oil and gas production in Argentina, to outline the Texas Eastern–Dresser proposal. After the meeting they mailed him a written version of their initial proposal. The two corporations were concerned that three conditions be met before the deal could be made: "1) Exclusive invitation from the Government of the Argentine to do so, 2) Acceptance by the Government of the Argentine of the general concepts outlined herein, and 3) Evidence, satisfactory to us, of adequate gas reserves and markets."[7]

After having received a less than encouraging report on the natural gas reserve situation from DeGolyer and L. W. MacNaughton, a group of Texas Eastern and Dresser officials met with Argentine President Arturo Frondizi on February 18. Frondizi was the first elected president of Argentina since the overthrow of Juan Perón in 1955. A controversial figure, Frondizi's economic development policies were quite different from those he had espoused before being elected president. A scholar who studied Frondizi described this transition president as follows: ". . . once regarded as Argentina's most articulate spokesman for economic nationalism, [he] invited foreign companies and foreign capital to participate in the development of Argentine petroleum and heavy industry."[8] Texas Eastern was a beneficiary of Frondizi's new-found enthusiasm for foreign investment.

Frondizi's administration gave the American company the distinct impression that it would get the contract, even though the government might hold a bid for the pipeline job. The Texas Eastern–Dresser team was encouraged. But already it was clear that negotiating with a foreign government agency did not resemble in any way the task of building a pipeline under FPC regulation. During a conference on June 4, Petroleum Minister Alsogaray told the team's representatives that a public tender would be made, with a minimum of eight weeks during which bids could be entered. Alsogaray mentioned that " that was the break he was giving us."[9] Although there was some concern at Texas Eastern that the Argentine government might end up rejecting a plan in which the pipeline would be privately owned, Alsogaray assured the group that the government was leaning toward private ownership.

At this point in the negotiations, Dresser's H. Neil Mallon expressed his concern to John Lynch that if they did get approval to build the pipeline, "we will fall on our face when it comes to raising the money."[10] The problem was the reluctance of the Gas del Estado to give the two companies a letter

161

of intent which they could use to arrange firm financial commitments in the United States. Without the letter, they could only pursue the pipeline deal under the risky assumption that financing could be arranged later. Of course, without a firm financial plan their bid for the pipeline would probably be inadequate.

Concerned now about the unfamiliar Argentine political environment, Texas Eastern and Dresser hired Norbert A. McKenna, who had initially brought the project to Dresser, to begin working for their interests in Argentina. A promoter and one-time banker, McKenna had worked on previous projects for multinational corporations. In Argentina he had good contacts and was useful in pressing the pipeline proposal. With McKenna's assistance, Dresser and Texas Eastern formed an Argentine company named Gasodar, and under this name the two United States companies bid for the project.

On November 4, 1960, McKenna filed Gasodar's bid with Gas del Estado. Although McKenna had originally felt that his client would be the only bidder, the government also received several other offers. Two of these, along with that of Gasodar, were accepted for further consideration. Saipem (E.N.I.), a subsidiary of the Italian national oil company, submitted one, and Tipsa, an Argentine company, submitted the other. The Saipem bid proposed a much lower cost for building the pipeline than did Texas Eastern–Dresser. But McKenna felt that the Italian's bid was unrealistic and that Texas Eastern would still win.

At this juncture, McKenna sensed a need for the expression of American political support for the project. On November 27 McKenna sent a telegraph to Texas Eastern's Dick Carpenter, suggesting that "you and George Brown urge Lyndon Johnson fly here before home [from London] as dramatic proof interest [sic] new administration in Latin America. . . ."[11] Although the Johnson visit did not materialize, McKenna continued to exercise his influence through various Argentine political and governmental connections. He was able to have several newspaper articles written in Argentina favoring the development of the natural gas industry, the pipeline project, and the Gasodar bid in particular.

As became apparent, however, the Italians wielded strong political influence of their own, and their position was strengthened by the existence of an influential Italian "colony" in Argentina. McKenna nevertheless reassured Texas Eastern that the Italians were not well liked by the present administration and would surely not get the bid. One official told McKenna that Texas Eastern's bid would not be chosen until after the upcoming visit of the Italian president in order not to sour this event. Despite the continued inaction by the Argentine government, McKenna seemed relatively confident. In the early spring of 1961 he wrote Carpenter "just a brief note to tell you that I've never been so convinced that the business is ours. It's been no cinch keeping one's patience and also explaining away the enormous differential between our top price and the memorandum price of the Italians."[12]

Frustrated by the slowness of the process, McKenna made inquiries among certain government officials, through his Argentine attorneys, and reported that he had encountered what he interpreted as a need for a bribe to smooth the way for the project. Although such payments to government officials were considered a standard form of doing business in much of Latin America, Texas Eastern faced an uncomfortable choice. Would it "play by the rules" of the host nation, or risk losing a major project? As McKenna wrote, "In any event, this is something we have to think about right now. I did not ask Juni directly, rather I asked De Colombi [the Argentine lawyer he was using] to ask Juni [government Minister] whether a political contribution was going to be necessary to grease this deal through on *our terms.* His response was that the deal was big enough to get through without that sort of thing but he felt that in all probability the new combination would need money to combat the Peronists and the opposition."[13] McKenna went on to say that all industries in Argentina contributed regularly to all of the political parties. They just gave a little more to the ones that could help them the most.

After reading McKenna's report, Texas Eastern's general counsel, Jack Head, wrote Carpenter in longhand on his personal notepad paper, "Dick, I think the attached letter from McKenna is inexcusable. . . . I believe we should call McKenna back to this country."[14] Although McKenna was not called back immediately, later in May Carpenter requested through an intermediary that McKenna return to New York for a visit with his family and a meeting. Perhaps sensing what was afoot, McKenna decided to stay in Argentina, suggesting that a decision on the pipeline was imminent and his presence there a necessity.

A decision was forthcoming, but it was not the one McKenna had predicted. On the evening of July 21 he learned that the Argentine government had rejected Texas Eastern's certificate of finance. Officially, the TE proposal had been turned down because of its lack of solid financial backing. Although company officials had been dealing with both the Development Loan Fund and the Export-Import Bank, trying to get financial commitments, there was little encouragement. Without a letter of intent from the Argentine government, the team's officials could not arrange financing. The Italians had the job.

At this point, Dick Carpenter ordered McKenna to break off all communications in Argentina. Texas Eastern then sent its vice president for finance, Jim Hargrove, a son of the late Reginald Hargrove, to Argentina to conduct a post-mortem. Hargrove met with various government and industry representatives as well as with the U. S. ambassador to discuss the circumstances surrounding the rejected certificate. After the meetings Hargrove concluded that for unknown reasons President Frondizi had personally rejected Texas Eastern's bid at the last minute.[15] Nearly two years of often intense and certainly expensive work had been for naught. Texas Eastern sold its 50 percent interest in Gasodar to Dresser Industries and pulled out of the country.

The company had learned several lessons about the perils of foreign politics. Without strong Argentine business or political allies, the company was quite vulnerable to the shifting winds of a political system it was poorly equipped to "manage." It was uncomfortably dependent on a single operative, Norbert McKenna, who did not even have close colleagues with the company. Despite its technical qualifications and its enthusiasm for the job, Texas Eastern had not done a particularly good job of coping with this unfamiliar political setting.

Rebuffed in South America, Texas Eastern looked to the African and European continents. The next foray into overseas exploration and production stemmed in part from the contacts of Millard K. Neptune, Texas Eastern's senior vice-president, Little Big Inch Division. Before coming to Texas Eastern, Neptune had worked for Continental Oil. He had helped manage a joint venture with Marathon Oil in a petroleum concession in Egypt, where he spent three years as president of the Sahara Petroleum Company. After joining TE, Neptune learned that a South African named J. A. Christiansen wanted to sell an option on a concession he held in Southwest Africa. It would apparently expire soon unless he made a $15,000 payment to extend it. Despite TE's initial geological studies that downplayed the prospects for finding oil in Southwest Africa, Neptune decided to pay for the extension of the concession.[16]

He then contacted Joe Hargrove, another son of Reginald Hargrove, to assist him in developing the venture. Neptune had previously employed Hargrove in late 1959 to try to "get several companies to support a joint program of overseas exploration and development in the manner in which Conorada performs for the Continental, Ohio and Amerada oil companies."[17] To explore the prospect of producing oil in Southwest Africa, Neptune and Hargrove travelled to Africa to examine the so-called LeRiche Concession. Neptune wrote to Carpenter, "Since Mr. Lynch has been occupied on the Argentine project, I have been doing most of the planning and negotiating with Joe, in a pattern which Mr. Lynch and I had previously agreed upon."[18] Hargrove presented a formal proposal to Neptune for Texas Eastern's involvement in the LeRiche Concession. Although at least one previous concession had already been granted to another oil exploration group, Hargrove believed that no drilling activity had yet occurred. Despite a precarious political environment in which the Union of South Africa currently was attempting to bring Southwest Africa into its polity as a fifth province, the area seemed ripe for oil exploration and development.[19]

The LeRiche Concession, an area of approximately sixty-four million acres in the northern portion of Southwest Africa, had previously been issued to Mr. Reho LeRiche, "a prominent farmer and rancher, who is a Nationalist Party Member of Parliament from South West Africa."[20] As outlined in the Hargrove proposal, Texas Eastern would assume J. A. Christensen's option payments on the concession and pay him bonus fees under certain conditions. According to Hargrove, "the total obligated expenditures required by ultimate acquisition of the concession should be no more than $75,000 excluding internal expenses. This represents a cost of acquisition of approximately $0.00117 per acre, plus a total royalty of 7%."[21] In 1960 Texas Eastern formed the Etosha Petroleum Company (named after the Etosha pan of salt in this area) to conduct the work at the LeRiche Concession. Instead of instituting a major core drilling operation with a large rig, Etosha Petroleum hired a two-man crew to live at the site and drill cores. Neptune also hired John Cooke to supervise the Etosha operation. After drilling many core samples over a several year period, however, the company found no trace of oil. Finally, it stopped all drilling activities in 1964, transferring the Etosha Petroleum Company's stock back to Christiansen, as stipulated in the agreement.

While these disappointing results were being achieved in the southwest, Texas Eastern had also been developing projects on the north African coast. The company attempted to join a venture to transport natural gas from Algeria to France by way of a Trans-Mediterranean pipeline. Texas Eastern's interest in European natural gas stemmed from at least 1956, when a mission of the French natural gas industry scheduled a tour of several American companies. During the summer of 1957 Millard Neptune had hired H. Steele Bennett, Jr., a petroleum geologist and promoter based in France, to keep Texas Eastern Transmission Corporation informed of any "matters relating to petroleum concessions, petroleum exploration and petroleum development in Europe and Africa, with particular emphasis in metropolitan France and north and west Africa."[22] Bennett was another geologist who had worked for Neptune in Egypt. He had married a French woman and remained in France after his work in Egypt ended. A timid yet tenacious man, Bennett had strong ties to French petroleum officials.

In late 1958 Bennett reported to Millard Neptune that the Compagnie Française du Sahara was investigating the possibility of producing and transporting natural gas and liquids from the Algerian Hassi R'Mel Field to northern Africa and possibly into metropolitan France. This field, then one of the world's largest, contained natural gas reserves estimated to be between fifteen to thirty-five trillion cubic feet. Some 130 miles south of Algiers, the field had been discovered in 1956 by the Société Nationale de Recherches et d'Exploitation des Petroles en Algerie (S. N. REPAL). Hassi R'Mel provided energy for the expansion of the Algerian industrial and electric utility businesses, and the discovery of the massive field also stimulated much interest among European and American gas companies in Algerian gas. Texas Eastern and Brown & Root were both attracted by the opportunities to enter the African-European natural gas industry and pipeline construction business. What attracted Texas Eastern most was the possibility of constructing a pipeline crossing of the Mediterranean to transport gas from Algeria into France.

On October 15, 1958, Neptune wrote H. Henri Bonnet, president and general manager of the Compagnie Française du Sahara, expressing Texas Eastern's interest in pursuing opportunities in the North African region. Interest was so great that George Brown, Orville Carpenter, and Millard Neptune flew to Paris and Algeria in early 1959 to investigate the situation themselves. Subsequently, Neptune made another investigative trip to Paris. He learned that "lots of groups are maneuvering to get a position in this project. . . . Soundings have been taken of all of the Western Mediterranean including the Straits of Gibraltar and soil samples have been gathered and tested. From these surveys it has been concluded that the best crossing is from Mostaganem in Algeria to Cartagena in Spain."[23]

Although Texas Eastern was interested in participating in any facet of the North Africa industry, the Mediterranean pipeline crossing seemed to be the most logical venture for the company. Eventually, two possible routes were developed for the crossing. One of these was at the Straits of Gibraltar, a distance of eighteen miles and a depth of fourteen hundred feet. Technically, this crossing seemed to have the best chance for success; the underwater route would be relatively short and the shallower waters would put less extreme pressures on the line. Another proposal was to cross the Mediterranean between Mostaganem, Algeria, and Cartagena, Spain, a distance of 125 miles at depths up to five thousand feet. Although this plan posed problems in laying and maintaining the line, several hundred fewer miles of pipe would be needed in the total project than at the Straits of Gibraltar. Both proposals were made by the Société D'Étude du Transport et de la Valorisation des Gaz Naturel du Sahara (SEGANS), as well as other companies working with SEGANS. Texas Eastern entered negotiations with SEGANS, seeking to join in these projects.[24] The several groups of companies interested in the undertaking had proposed different methods of transporting the gas from Algeria to Europe. One group, known as CAMEL (a venture composed of S. N. REPAL and Conch, a company formed by Comstock Methane and Shell) proposed to liquefy the natural gas for transport to French and British markets.

But then, just as the project appeared to be underway, the French-Algerian war and technical considerations slowed progress. It became clear that the sub-Mediterranean proposal could not be acted upon immediately. While Texas Eastern remained interested in the project and received invitations to join some of the other ventures proposing to transport liquid natural gas from Algeria to Europe, the prospect of long delays turned the company's attention elsewhere.

Texas Eastern, along with much of the energy industry, began looking to northern Europe. In August, 1959, at Groningen, Holland, a Shell-Esso group discovered a major natural gas field, one of the largest in the world. The Groningen Field put a damper on plans to transport Algerian natural gas because the new discovery was very large and very close to European markets. Groningen was also important because it stimulated increased exploration in the territory off the northern coast of Holland, the Netherlands, and throughout the North Sea.

Texas Eastern's involvement in the North Sea developed through various industry contacts, including those of Millard Neptune. His previous work for Continental had included a stint with Conorada, a joint venture of Conoco, Marathon, and Amerada formed to look for international business. As manager of Conorada's foreign department, Neptune had worked closely with Chris Dohm, who had been hired away from Standard Oil of New Jersey (Exxon) to get the group moving.

Like Neptune, Chris Dohm left the Conorada group and went to work for Amoco, organizing its foreign department. In the early 1960s Amoco joined with the British Gas Council (the British government's gas distribution monopoly), Amerada Petroleum, and Mobil in a joint venture to search for oil and gas in the North Sea.[25] As Amoco was getting its North Sea venture organized, Neptune met Dohm in New York on a social occasion. Dohm complained that Mobil seemed less than eager to push forward as a partner in the project. Neptune suggested that if the group had prospects for finding natural gas, the inclusion of Texas Eastern might prove beneficial to the group. Neptune then consulted with Jim Hargrove and Dick Carpenter, both of whom supported the idea of participating in this venture. Carpenter placed the matter before George Brown, who also favored the proposition. The next week senior vice president John Lynch, John Cooke, and William Kendall, one of the company's lawyers, flew to New York to meet with Dohm. Quickly, Texas Eastern replaced Mobil in the Gas Council–Amoco group.

On March 27, 1963, Neptune reported to the Texas Eastern board of directors that the designated operator of the group, Amoco, had formally invited Texas Eastern to participate. Amoco would be responsible for the plans and operations, and the other members would participate by assisting the operating company both financially and operationally. Neptune also reported that TE's initial participation in the seismic studies would be approximately 30 percent, although this would be subject to a reduction later if the British Gas Council decided to increase its own stake. Neptune told the board that the total cost of the survey would be $1 million and that this meant a $300,000 investment for Texas Eastern. The board approved the proposal, and an agreement was signed among the four participants to conduct seismic tests. These tests indicated large geological structures under the North Sea seabed. It was still not clear if North Sea oil and gas reserves actually promised a worthwhile long-term investment, but the possibility encouraged the company to investigate further.

During 1963 the Management Committee sent John Jacobs and Jim Hargrove to Europe to evaluate all of the European opportunities, including the seemingly thwarted Algerian pipeline proposal and the feasibility of continued involvement in the North Sea venture beyond the initial survey work. Visiting France, Germany, The Netherlands, Great Britain, Spain, and Algeria during a six-week tour in the months of June and July, company representatives accomplished two goals. First, they evaluated "prospects for Texas Eastern's participation in the energy market in Western Europe, particularly with respect to (a) utilization and transportation of Saharan gas and (b) exploration for oil and gas in the North Sea."[26] Second, they decided what form of organization Texas Eastern should use to achieve that goal. When Jacobs and Hargrove returned to Texas Eastern, they recommended that one person "be made responsible for the supervision of all foreign operations and charged with the task of presenting additional specific proposals."[27] Although they advised that the firm should continue in the Algerian project, they saw that the French-Algerian conflict was dimming prospects for the pipeline. On December 23, 1963, Hargrove wrote Bennett: ". . . it appears to me that the French are giving careful consideration to a change in their overall policy regarding petroleum, including both oil and gas. It seems to be that this is brought about by the increasing show of independence by [Algerian Premier] Ben Bella and also by the greatly increased gas reserves in Holland."[28] As there was an increasing likelihood that Ben Bella would nationalize the Algerian oil and gas reserves, the outlook for the sub-Mediterranean pipeline began to fade.[29]

At the same time, Texas Eastern learned that France had contracted for natural gas for its northern market from Dutch reserves. Although a pipeline would be constructed for the transmission of this gas, only Gaz de France could own transmission facilities in that country. Restrictions against foreign pipelines in Europe made it unlikely Texas Eastern would be able to participate in that part of the energy market. Although demand for Algerian gas remained high in Spain and southern France, Paris and northern France would now be supplied by Holland's Groningen Field. The time had passed, at least for now, for the sub-Mediterrean project.

Texas Eastern investigated other non-gas projects in the French energy market. One of these was a proposal to build a pipeline to transport sulphur from the Lacq Field in southern France to the port of Bayonne, where the sulphur would be shipped to other European ports. A representative of the Société Nationale de Petroles D'Aquitaine (SNPA), the regional petroleum agency, told Hargrove that if Texas Eastern could transport sulphur by pipeline at a 15 to 20 percent reduction from current costs, they would be interested in pursuing the matter. Hargrove asked Tom Thagard at Texas Eastern to determine the feasibility and costs of constructing such a line. But this deal never materialized. It fell through, as did investigations of the Acquitane Basin near the Lacq Field (for oil and gas) and of the natural gas situation in Germany.

By this time Texas Eastern was increasingly focusing its attention on the North Sea. There, seismic studies of the basin showed promising signs for oil and gas development, and TE began to consolidate its energies on this potential source. It also centralized these operations under John Lynch and terminated its contract with Steele Bennett at the end of 1964.

That same year the nations bordering the North Sea facilitated development by agreeing on boundaries for their respective countries. On May 14, 1964, they accepted the Continental Shelf Act, which was based on the 1958 United Nations Conference on the Law of the Sea and the Geneva Convention on the Continental Shelf. The agreement essentially divided up the North Sea continental shelf so that the United Kingdom had rights to about 40 percent, Denmark, 10 percent, the Netherlands, 11 percent, and Norway, 27 percent; West Germany later received sovereignty over a part of the Continental Shelf as well. With boundaries legally defined, concessions could be granted to drill in these waters.

As it was becoming increasingly clear that the North Sea contained substantial volumes of natural gas, Texas Eastern brought its industrial expertise and experience into play. Here the firm was entering the industry during a phase somewhat analogous to the one that had existed in the United States when the company had broken into the northeastern gas market. In both cases the existing industry relied heavily upon manufactured gas, although Britain in the 1960s was even more dependent on this source of supply than the northeastern United States had been in the late 1940s. By 1963 there were 12.7 million gas customers in Britain, 94 percent of whom were residential. Britain's gas consumption in 1963 was 286 billion cubic feet, with natural gas supplying only about one percent of this total. The British Gas Council was responsible for the distribution of gas in the entire nation.

Texas Eastern hoped to assist in the production and transportation of natural gas as well as in the conversion from manufactured to natural gas. Jim Hargrove reported to the Texas Eastern Management Committee that "it is apparent that a great deal of conversion from manufactured gas appliances to higher BTU appliances must take place in Europe over the next several years."[30] Hargrove noted that due to the discovery of the Groningen Field, all of Holland would be converted. Only Stone and Webster and a small Dutch company were presently converting furnaces, and neither company was being particularly aggressive. Hargrove recommended that Texas Eastern acquire all or part of the Dutch conversion company. In addition, he thought Texas Eastern might engage in the natural gas appliance manufacturing business to profit from the increased sales of those appliances.

The North Sea exploration and production venture now looked very promising indeed. The seismic tests were so favorable that TE executives began to smell their first big find. Although clearly the junior partner in the group, Texas Eastern's expertise in the natural gas business was valuable to all of the members of the consortium. As the press officer of the Gas Council stated: "Most of the experience gained over the last twenty-five years of marine drilling has been from America, and it is from this No. 1 oil country that 'know-how' will largely come to help conduct drilling operations in the North Sea."[31] The same was true for natural gas production and transport.

The Gas Council–Amoco group, including Texas Eastern, participated in the United Kingdom's first licensing round for exploration concessions in the North Sea. The British government awarded the group exploration licenses covering approximately thirty-six hundred square miles, or approximately 2.3 million acres, off the coasts of Scotland and England. At this point, Texas Eastern organized a new wholly owned subsidiary, Texas Eastern (U.K.) Limited, through which the company managed its North Sea operations. The following year the North Sea group obtained additional exploration rights and acquired licenses on fifty-one blocks covering 2.8 million acres. Texas Eastern held an 11 percent interest in the newly acquired acreage.

Texas Eastern gave John Jacobs the task of overseeing North Sea operations. On January 1, 1965, he assumed this responsibility under the title of vice president and general manager of the Oil Division. He reported to John Lynch, who was in charge of all petroleum activities. Even though significant volumes of oil had not yet been located in the North Sea, most of the companies involved were confident that significant oil as well as natural gas deposits would be found under the seabed. Texas Eastern finally appeared to be on the verge of success overseas.

Texas Eastern's George Brown saw even larger opportunities in the North Sea. Brown & Root's general experience in construction work and in pipeline construction in particular made it a strong contender to develop North Sea oil and gas facilities. Texas Eastern's role gave Brown & Root good access to the various construction jobs, and that firm ultimately became one of the major contractors for the construction of pipelines, pipe laying barges, and oil platforms. It did "the lion's share of North Sea pipe-laying."[32] The Texas-based construction company had platform fabrication yards on the east coast of Scotland, and it also became involved in a group with J. Ray McDermott and SEDCO that constructed a semisubmersible barge designed to lay pipe in up to four hundred feet of rough seas.

In 1965 Texas Eastern began exploration in the Norwegian sector of the North Sea as a member of a group of private companies, including Amerada Petroleum Corporation, American International Oil Company (a subsidiary of Amoco), and a consortium of Norwegian industrial companies, the NOCO Group. No longer was the company even entertaining the idea of going it alone. These projects were too large and too tightly controlled by their respective governments. Besides, Texas Eastern had learned during more than a decade of international projects that it was always wise to work with "locals" in any substantial foreign ventures. In unfamiliar political environments, a partner with a solid sense of history, culture, and politics was invaluable. Participation by nationals gave the group legitimacy, as became apparent when the Norwegian government awarded this group of American and Norwegian interests licenses on 1.2 million acres. Texas Eastern acquired a 28⅓ share. The company's first Norwegian sector oil and gas production began in 1978 from the Tor Field.

By that time, the British Gas Council–Amoco group had already drilled eleven wells in the United Kingdom sector, nine of which contained commercial quantities of natural gas. TE participated in the development of two of the major North Sea gas fields, the Leman Bank and the Indefatigable. When the British government held a competitive bid to determine which company would win the contract to build a pipeline from these fields to the mainland, TE's wholly owned subsidiary, Texas Eastern Engineering, Limited, won the engineering and management contract; Brown & Root performed the construction work for the subsidiary. It designed and constructed a thirty-eight mile, thirty-inch pipeline from the Leman Bank field to a processing plant at Bacton, England, 112 miles northeast of London.

Texas Eastern had scored in a big way. Its strategy of seeking international gas production and transmission had failed initially, but now the company was successful in a truly outstanding venture. On December 19, 1968, the Gas Council–Amoco group signed a twenty-five-year contract with the British Gas Council to deliver gas from the Leman Bank field to Bacton. On the following April 18 the group began delivering gas from three drilling platforms in the North Sea to the British mainland, and by the end of the year these deliveries averaged more than 450 mmcf per day.

The group began developing a second large field, the Indefatigable, in 1970. The original thirty-inch gas pipeline did not have sufficient capacity to transport gas from both the Leman Basin and Indefatigable fields, so a connecting line between the two fields, a second thirty-inch line to Bacton, was built in a joint venture with the Shell-Esso group, which also had an interest in both fields. These developments moved forward rapidly. By 1975 these two major fields supplied approximately one-third of Britain's natural gas needs.

In the 1970s Texas Eastern had finally established a strong beachhead in international gas production. The company had hit the jackpot after a series of unsuccessful foreign adventures. By doing so, Texas Eastern had escaped the strict oversight and regulation of the FPC and other domestic regulatory agencies, but it had encountered new and equally challenging political constraints as it learned to conduct business in other nations and other cultures. These foreign ventures upheld one long-established company tradition: they were conducted on a grand scale. They were ambitious entrepreneurial endeavors of a sort not readily available in the maturing U.S. gas transmission business.

Along the path that led from Mexico to the North Sea, the firm had gained valuable experience and contacts for other foreign projects. While these undertakings absorbed a great deal of management's energy and time, the profits from the North Sea bonanza would ultimately more than compensate for these costs. Success in the North Sea rewarded the company in prestige as well as dollars, for Texas Eastern could now lay claim to a new status as an "international energy company."

Chapter 8

THE LEAP INTO HOUSTON
REAL ESTATE

With diversification into North Sea production promising to be extremely profitable, Texas Eastern's management was encouraged to look for other opportunities to broaden the firm's mission. It found one close to home in a booming Houston real estate market. The decision in the late 1960s to develop Houston Center, a thirty-two-block area in downtown Houston, into a futuristic, billion-dollar platform city was a dramatic strategic choice. Flushed with cash and confidence, the company placed a large bet on its capacity to master a new field in a competitive market. Announced amid much fanfare, this innovative departure seemed to offer great prospects for enhanced profits and visibility in Houston, the site of TE's corporate headquarters.

Above all else, this decision to make a major commitment of resources to a new field of endeavor was a wager on the long-term future of Houston. George Brown and others in the firm's top management had strong ties to the city, which had become one of the fastest growing real estate markets in the nation in the decades after World War II. These personal ties more than the managerial or monetary resources of Texas Eastern shaped the company's initial planning for Houston Center. Confident of both the continued prosperity of Houston and the firm's capacity to master new challenges, Texas Eastern leaped hard with both feet into the development business. The plan was to learn from experts in this field as the program got underway.

The strategy of diversification into real estate promised to make use of two of the company's historical strengths, its ready access to financing and its engineering expertise. Large investments in the gas pipeline business gave the corporation a steady rate of return while also making it a regular and welcomed visitor to the nation's major investment banks. Table 8.1 shows the record of the company's major borrowings in the 1950s and 1960s; the firm would not be begging among strangers for the large sums of investment capital needed to finance a major real estate development. The top executives felt that their company's leverage in financing would provide a distinct competitive advantage over the much smaller firms that traditionally domi-

TABLE 8.1   Texas Eastern Long-Term Debt, 1947–71
($1,000.00)

Year	Amount
1947	$120,000
1948	140,783
1949	140,938
1950	132,888
1951	195,000
1952	240,231
1953	236,098
1954	251,131
1955	294,852
1956	299,092
1957	451,664
1958	485,413
1959	503,688
1960	458,169
1961	522,851
1962	530,008
1963	545,968
1964	605,369
1965	570,192
1966	575,849
1967	732,566
1968	743,416
1969	791,095
1970	849,957
1971	917,461

Source: Texas Eastern Financial and Statistical Summary, 1956, 1960, and 1971.

nated Houston-area real estate. These financial resources promised to give the company the clout to enter this new field very aggressively and then to "wait out" the periodic downturns that plagued real estate markets. Company executives had no reason to doubt the long-term prospects for real estate in a booming city. They felt confident that their company was well positioned to take and hold a substantial position in this potentially lucrative market.

Engineering expertise, including that available through the company's old friends at Brown & Root, also seemed readily transferable from the construction of pipelines to the building of giant office buildings. The construction work which would recast downtown Houston would be challenging as well as profitable. Brown & Root was deeply involved in the planning and contracting for Houston Center. From the perspective of TE's planners, "the decision to turn to large-scale urban development in the corporation's home city was a natural outgrowth of Texas Eastern's long experience and success with all aspects of large scale engineering construction. . . ."[1] Some of the more ambitious advocates of diversification reached even further in their efforts to show that Texas Eastern had engineering resources that could be transferred into this new field. The large office buildings planned for Houston could, they felt, make use of variants on the technology developed by Texas Eastern to control the flow of products through its pipelines.

These sorts of advantages seemed to counterbalance the project's disturbing, if seldom mentioned, downside. For the venture to succeed, the company's access to big league financing and engineering expertise would have to compensate for its total lack of experience about real estate.[2] Much of the discussion of the "natural ties" between Texas Eastern and real estate development reflected the determination to justify on every level possible a decision which was, in essence, a gut-level choice by top managers. Certainly, inherited resources in financing and engineering could be brought to bear on aspects of the new endeavor. But still, the step into real estate was a long one for a gas transmission company — even one that had previously moved into a variety of energy-related endeavors.

From a strategic perspective, the move out of energy transportation and production was a decisive break with the company's previous policy of diversification. The economic rationale that Texas Eastern was, after all, a construction company was unconvincing. The other justifications for this departure were more to the point. One was the strong pressure to find new investment opportunities for the company's profits. A second was the strong ties the company's founders had to Houston, a city that they understood very well. A third was the firm's tradition of undertaking large-scale challenges. Under George Brown's leadership Texas Eastern had always found new challenges worthy of its ambitions. Rebuilding half of downtown Houston promised a new outlet for the firm's entrepreneurial energies.

Texas Eastern was not alone among large American corporations in seeing grand opportunities in real estate in the late 1960s. Indeed, diversification into this area was "in the air." As major corporations sought hedges against inflation and new uses for investment funds, they increasingly turned to real estate. One detailed study of this phenomenon identified 140 U.S. corporations taking this route in the real estate boom years from 1967 to 1972. The motivation for their decisions differed from company to company, but several broad patterns marked much of this activity. Most of these companies entered the field with high expectations similar to those of Texas Eastern. They hoped to use existing corporate resources to ease their entry into real estate, which they saw as a promising investment. In the process, most hoped to make better use of their existing land holdings. The returns on investment projected for real estate would, the companies assumed, counterbalance the downturns they experienced in their traditional industries. Texas Eastern's management could see in the action of other managers justification for its break with the past. Annual reports, public pronouncements, and articles in leading business journals made this move a popular one for managers seeking a "more balanced" package of investments in the late 1960s and early 1970s.[3]

Charles I. Francis and George R. Brown

Like most of the large corporations that diversified along these lines, Texas Eastern began to consider real estate when it examined the prospects for constructing a new headquarters building. The company's primary offices had been established in Shreveport, although the Browns and members of their staff were located in Houston. Hargrove's death in 1954 hastened the company's move to Houston, which was the center of oil- and gas-related activities on the Gulf Coast. In the early 1950s the offices of the struggling Exploration and Production Division were established in that city. By the late 1950s the corporation had decided to relocate its executive offices and the offices of the Little Big Inch Division in the larger city. The growing need for space prompted the company to search for an acceptable location for its permanent headquarters.[4]

After settling briefly at several temporary locations, George Brown acquired a permanent site as a result of his close friendship and business ties with Gus Wortham, of American General Insurance, and Judge James A. Elkins, of First City National Bank. These friends shared a common interest in a wide variety of economic activities, including real estate. Wortham, who was then on the board of Texas Eastern, had previously taken an option to buy the First City National Bank building at McKinney and San Jacinto streets as a new headquarters for the offices of American General. First City was at the time completing construction of new offices nearby, and Judge Elkins was eager to complete the transition by disposing of his bank's former building. Wortham and Elkins had agreed upon a package which included an option to buy the building with financing guaranteed at a specified interest rate. But Wortham had begun to favor an alternate location, on the west side of the city, slightly removed from downtown. He no longer wanted to exercise the option on First City's building. After Wortham explained his position to George Brown, Brown and Elkins agreed that Texas Eastern would take over the Wortham option. TE now had a site for its headquarters.

Through other personal contacts the company acquired additional lands adjacent to this property. Texas Eastern director Charles Francis, a graduate of the University of Texas and a former regent of that institution, knew through this association that the university owned a portion of land adjacent to TE's new property. Francis no doubt encouraged W. W. Heath, a University of Texas regent, to approach the company's president, Orville Carpenter, about the company's interest in purchasing this property. Another group of Houston investors had offered the university $1 million dollars for the land, and in October of 1960 Heath wrote to Carpenter to ask for his opinion about this offer (equivalent to approximately $40 dollars per square foot). Carpenter took the bait. He responded that the offer seemed appropriate, at least as "a trading figure" for further discussion. He then promptly arranged for Texas Eastern to purchase the property. The company next negotiated the purchase of the remainder of the block from two other owners, completing the transaction by October of 1961, at a cost of approximately $2.65 million. Texas Eastern now had ample room on which to build its headquarters.[5]

There matters rested for almost a decade, as the company focused its energies on extending its pipeline system and implementing its strategy of diversification. In the late 1960s, however, Carpenter returned to the issue of the need for suitable offices. Like other CEO's, he wanted to construct a major office building to symbolize the company's standing as an economic force in its city. Carpenter had read a description of the ten tallest buildings in Houston, and he noted with dismay that his company did not make the list. At that time, the Humble Building led the way at 605 feet from sidewalk to rooftop; number two on the list was the relatively new headquarters of the company's long-time rival, Tennessee Gas, at 502 feet. "Where are we?" was Carpenter's inquiry after reading the article, and the answer was disappointing: "The top of the concrete slab forming the roof of the center tower section is 286' 6½" above the Main Street sidewalk. The tip top of the Terra Cotta Spandrels is approximately six feet higher."[6] His company was out of the running, but Carpenter was not going to allow that disturbing situation to persist.

In the late 1960s Houston was booming. The demand for additional office space was surging, with no obvious long-term limit in sight. Texas Eastern had an excellent piece of property, a market for office space, and a desire to diversify. Carpenter began to think about a building worthy of Texas Eastern, but shortly those plans gave way to a far more formidable undertaking.[7]

This happened in the late 1960s, when Shell Oil, U.S.A., began soliciting proposals for a new building in Houston in which to relocate the bulk of its corporate staff from New York. Texas Eastern entered the competition for this ambitious project, which ultimately produced the tallest building in the city. Of course, the major gas transmission company turned real estate developer was not the only company to enter the bidding for the building which became One Shell Plaza; indeed, most of the experienced developers active in Houston were interested in gaining a role in this project.

Texas Eastern hoped to convince Shell to build on the east side of downtown, on the land which had been acquired earlier as a site for the company's own headquarters. Although this approach proved unsuccessful, TE gained valuable experience while losing the project to Gerald Hines, Interests. Hines ultimately built a fifty-story office building for Shell in a fast-growing section on the west side of downtown.

Hines was a formidable competitor. Over the previous twenty years, he had learned the business from the bottom up by developing a series of larger and larger projects in and around Houston. One Shell Plaza was the climax of the first phase of his career as a developer. This project marked his most ambitious entry into downtown office construction. At roughly the same time he was beginning work on the Galleria, a path-breaking mixed-use development outside of the city's central business district. In competition with a strong developer with the local experience and reputation of Gerald Hines, Texas Eastern proved unable to parley its financial and engineering strengths into a winning proposal.[8]

The first lesson TE learned from this experience was a variant of the three guiding principles of the real estate business: location, location, location. Texas Eastern's property was on the east side of Main Street. The thrust of development in the postwar years was westward. Shell had displayed a strong preference for the more popular and thus more expensive sites in the growing sections of the city to the west of Main. To succeed in countering this bias and developing a major office building on its property, TE had to do something special, something that would compensate for its poorer location. It was unable to come up with a suitable approach. The central business district was steadily moving in the other direction, and such trends are not easily overcome in office construction. When a major investment and a long-term commitment to a location were involved, few companies were willing to gamble that the city's previous pattern of development would change. The stakes were simply too high, the risk too great, to bet that the city's pattern of development would be reversed.

After this unsuccessful bid Texas Eastern's management could see just how much time, energy, and money could be consumed in real estate. This was not an enterprise that could be entered on a shoestring. To be successful, TE would almost certainly have to own substantially more land. Then it could offer a major client flexibility in the design of its central structure and the adjoining facilities. Planning and negotiation would in any case require considerable work by high level executives, and the firm had to be prepared to make a long-term commitment of managerial resources in order to maintain a presence in the markets it had targeted. The start-up costs, the risks, and the opportunity costs began to spiral upward as the company set forth to become a serious competitor in this new field.

Confronting this situation directly, top management made a dramatic choice: real estate development made sense only on a grand scale. The company could not successfully diversify into this new field one small step at a time. From the perspective of President Baxter Goodrich and Chairman George Brown, real estate was attractive only if it would "make a difference on the bottom line." Since Texas Eastern was a multi-million-dollar corporation, its future initiatives in real estate would have to be on a scale in keeping with the company's experience in its core industry of natural gas transmission.[9]

The move into real estate was thus similar to the diversification into liquid petroleum products. In both cases, planners decided that their company's scale of operations would yield clear advantages over competitors who did not enjoy the same access to credit and the same level of engineering and management expertise. In the LPG business, TE used these advantages to become the first company to operate cross-country pipelines and build giant storage facilities, achieving economies of scale. In the case of real estate, however, it was less obvious that competitive advantages would accrue from scale. Moreover, by deciding that it should enter this new field in a manner consistent with its resources, organizational values, and history, management assured that TE would have to move up the real estate learning curve very quickly. There would be virtually no opportunity to learn by developing a series of projects of increasing size, as Gerald Hines and others had done in this particular market.

Instead, Texas Eastern jumped into real estate much as it had into gas transmission, with a big investment in a bold, innovative project. Management decided to develop thirty-two blocks of land in the central business district! It would embark on "the biggest privately owned real estate development project ever," yanking the city's attention toward the neglected east side of Main Street.

Management's leap from two to thirty-two blocks of development was one that generated numerous explanations and some widely repeated stories that may or may not have been true. According to the company legend — which eventually was published as fact in a local newspaper — the bold move into big-time real estate stemmed from a dramatic flash of inspiration by George Brown. In this version of history, Brown and the president of Texas Eastern, Baxter Goodrich, were talking about company matters in Goodrich's office. As they pondered the proper extent of the company's involvement, Brown reportedly looked out the window at the largely undeveloped land which stretched out before him, all of the way to the elevated section of Houston's "inside loop," U.S. Highway 59. Inspired, Brown "remarked that the property could be put to better use. 'Let's see if it can be bought.' They agreed and went to the Texas Eastern board and got approval."[10]

Whether literally true or not, this often-repeated story captures both the tone of the time and the optimistic mood of the company. The setting was ripe for this sort of decision. Others in the company had been contemplating a broader commitment to real estate since the time of the Shell proposal. Texas Eastern's holdings looked to the east, toward Highway 59. Although this general question had been kicked around in the company for some time, of course only Brown and Goodrich could make this sort of decision. They did. Then the legend of "Brown at the window" galvanized the company into action behind a unifying symbol of bold leadership. George Brown was already a symbol of the company's success in the good old days. The image of Brown and his hard-driving, hand-picked lieutenant, Goodrich, making an inspired choice to conquer new territory was comforting when so much was at stake, when so much had to be learned and done so quickly. Once again, it seemed, strong entrepreneurs would cut through the red tape and get on with the business at hand. Corporate legend and corporate culture thus coalesced as the firm pushed forward in this new and challenging venture.

The first step toward remaking the east side of Houston was to purchase the big chunk of real estate Texas Eastern needed. This had to be done without forcing up property values. The company relied on the Houston real estate firm of Laguarta, Gavrel & Bolin to purchase the land. Partner George R. Bolin was the son of L. T. Bolin, a top executive at Brown & Root and an associate of George R. Brown. Brown's namesake could be trusted to handle the delicate matter of accumulating many separate parcels of land without arousing rumors that would raise prices. Bolin's original task was to make a detailed survey of the area bounded by Highway 59 on the east, Rusk Street on the north, Dallas on the south, and San Jacinto on the west. He determined that this seventy-four acre section included 127 separate land holders, with property valued at approximately $20 to $25 million at going prices. When Texas Eastern responded to his survey by giving the go ahead to buy the properties, Bolin initially asked "Which piece?" The answer, "All of it," took a while to sink in as Bolin slowly realized that he was to be the point man in the largest land purchase in the history of downtown Houston.[11]

What followed was subsequently described by the *Houston Chronicle* as "a fascinating story of secrecy, intrigue, tough bargaining frustration, humor, and a little luck. . . ."[12] Bolin worked closely with Texas Eastern officials Gordon Jennings and Charles Staffa to organize an efficient and secret operation. They started by preparing a detailed abstract for each separate plot of land. Then a month-long planning session helped establish priorities in approaching the various owners, while suggesting the best avenues to use in opening discussions.

As they prepared to hit the pavement, they set up a "command post" in a TE office overlooking the entire section of land. A large "battle map" depicted the location of each desired piece of property, and as the negotiations got underway, updated reports on their status were added to the map. From this vantage point, they could literally look over the shoulders of Bolin's realtors as they maneuvered to acquire the properties. "Bolin's Brigade" included some twenty-four real estate brokers, eight title company representatives, seven people to work on abstracts, and a number of lawyers. This crew negotiated 127 separate transactions without scaring off any of the property owners in the area. To assure a measure of secrecy, they purchased the various properties in the name of "George R. Bolin, Trustee." They had to remain discreet, to keep their efforts coordinated, and above all to move with speed. Within eleven months, they had about 95 percent of the targeted land in hand, for a price estimated at $50 million.[13]

On April 26, 1970, Texas Eastern went public. Baxter Goodrich announced that the company had "acquired a major portion of an area comprising 32 contiguous city blocks, bordering directly on Houston's business district." As Goodrich explained, "to Texas Eastern, one of the nation's leading natural gas companies, this represents an entirely new area of diversification." With considerable pride, he added that "we know of no project of this magnitude ever undertaken in a central business district." The land would be used, he said, for a major development to be known as Houston Center, and specific plans for this "long term project" would be released in the near future. Goodrich noted that "plans for development will be carried out in consultation with William L. Pereira Associates, of Los Angeles, California. Brown & Root, Incorporated, of Houston, will be associated with us for consultation on construction and development." The announcement pointed out that Texas Eastern "brings a wealth of financial experience to the project," which would make a "real contribution to a growing Houston" by attracting companies and industries across the nation.[14]

The project was a public relations coup. Both major Houston newspapers gave the undertaking a front page headline. The *Houston Chronicle* said "Big Downtown Area to be Rebuilt," while the *Post* was even more enthusiastic, proclaiming "Growing Houston: Up, Up, Up." The *Post* labeled the land transaction the "largest single deal in city's history." Newspapers throughout the nation picked up the story, often emphasizing that there was a "Texas brag" element in the project. The *Cincinnati Enquirer* said: "Gas Firm Buys Downtown Houston." The *Wall Street Journal* more accurately reported "Texas Eastern Buys a Substantial Chunk of Central Houston." Publicity throughout the country outlined Texas Eastern's plans to double the size of downtown Houston while creating a magnet for new businesses and jobs.[15]

Texas Eastern's executives had every reason to smile. After making a hard choice to move aggressively into this new field, they had mobilized their managerial and financial resources to carry out a successful campaign to purchase land on a scale previously not considered possible, at a price not likely to be repeated. As the company's top managers basked in the warm glow of favorable national publicity, they could be excused their pride. Now, they could plan a futuristic development worthy of the project and their company's history.

The choice of William L. Pereira Associates assured that the plans for the Houston Center would be visionary. Actually, one of Texas Eastern's primary criteria for choosing Pereira had more to do with equity than vision; the company decided not to choose one of the "equity types," companies which would not participate in projects unless they could have an ownership interest. By avoiding such a financial partnership, Texas Eastern kept strict control of its venture and of the profits that would be generated by Houston Center. In so doing, the company missed an opportunity to reduce its risks by forming an alliance with a seasoned developer. But that was consistent with its earlier decision to go for a very large undertaking and to do so at once.

The chosen planner, William L. Pereira, was a well-known Los Angeles–based architect who had designed several highly publicized projects. He came recommended by Brown & Root, which would be the project manager for Houston Center. Pereira's international reputation had merited a place on the cover of *Time* magazine in 1963. He had been the principal designer of the Transamerica Tower in San Francisco, three campuses in the University of California system, the Lost Angeles County Museum of Art, the Los Angeles International Airport, and the planned community of Irvine, California. This much publicized project involved the creation of a master plan for an entire community on the ninety-three-thousand-acre Irvine Ranch south of Los Angeles. To Texas Eastern's managers, Pereira appeared to have a vision of the future as ambitious as the company's projections for the east side of Houston.[16]

The company gave William L. Pereira Associates leeway to design "a truly large scale, high quality, innovative development, new to the fabric of the city, made possible by multi-block planning and the use of air rights over streets."[17] This was a formidable challenge to Pereira, who had considerable experience in planning communities but had never before tackled a central business district. The firm took up the task with a passion. William Pereira cast his design in phrases that depicted it as the next stage in the evolution of cities. "A city," he said, "is like a living organism . . . and depends on its heart for survival." He was interested in "shortening the desire lines of the people, to provide within a compact attractive city all the products and services its residents want and need." His design, he hoped, would make downtown Houston a magnet for future growth, reversing the steady stream of people and resources out into the surrounding suburbs. All of this he would accomplish by careful planning in a city long noted for its lack of zoning and its unwillingness to plan. To Pereira, "the main problem with today's cities is not with single buildings; it is with the total environment and the complex relationships and linkages of buildings and functions to each other and to the overall complex." In the heart of the city's unplanned sprawl, Pereira was planting a development that would "make Houston a precedent and a prototype for the cities that are to come in the third millennium."[18]

When the architectural plans for Houston Center were announced on October 11, 1970, the third millennium seemed to have arrived. Photographs of a model of this astonishing, $1.5 billion master plan were included in the *Houston Chronicle*'s story "'City of Tomorrow' Planned Here." The sheer size of the undertaking was newsworthy. As was the fact that it was a "privately" led example of urban renewal. The design itself was incredibly bold and newsworthy. Houston Center would cover over most of the thirty-two-block area on the east side of downtown Houston. Pereira's innovations included

———four levels of parking under the development to "tame the automobile" by providing ample parking;

———the widespread use of "people movers" of various sorts to whisk pedestrians around the complex, reducing automobile traffic;

———long stretches of landscaped plazas five stories above the existing street level so that pedestrians might enjoy a pleasant, parklike environment as they moved within the complex;

———a mixture of buildings to include at least twelve high-rise offices, four hotels, major apartment buildings, and shopping and entertainment facilities.

These breathtaking plans would create a futuristic city combining elements of the Astrodome with an air conditioned shopping mall. The master plan offered flexibility to meet future changes and the consistency of design that would give the entire project a sense of unity. From transportation system to utilities, the plan topped the most advanced thinking about the needs of a large-scale planned city.[19]

As Texas Eastern announced with pride, the development would "virtually double the size of the present urban core . . . [and] . . . provide some 23 million square feet of new buildings, . . . and enclosed parking for approximately 35,000 to 40,000 cars." George Brown and Baxter Goodrich were enthusiastic about the architects and designers. They were excited about this "totally integrated community development to serve all the people of Houston and Harris County."[20] The company mounted a public relations blitz for its "platform city."

The blitz succeeded. In a city long enamored of economic growth, Houston Center was seen as the latest phase of the Sunbelt boom that had pushed Houston into the ranks of the nation's major cities. Mayor Louie Welch foresaw sweeping effects as "a major part of our city that has long lain fallow will be recovered for more productive use." Like most mayors, Welch was a booster. "The planning is beyond anything that's ever occurred as far as

Texas Eastern land purchase in downtown Houston

I know in any city; it dwarfs Rockefeller Center in New York. It will, again, set Houston ahead of anything."[21]

Outside of Houston, too, the publicity campaign found a ready audience. Papers throughout the nation took note of the "billion-dollar development" and the "Texas-size plan for Houston." Accompanying many of these accounts was a striking artist's conception of the fully developed Houston Center superimposed on an existing photograph of downtown Houston. A city councilman caught the general tone: "After all, this looks like a Buck Rogers development."[22] Although the master plan noted that Houston Center would not be completed for some fifteen to twenty years, the public vision was of a fully constructed, futuristic enterprise.

Of course, even in the first flush of excitement not all Houstonians reacted with either awe or enthusiasm. One city councilman said of the trend of

184

Downtown Houston with Houston Center design

connecting downtown buildings with bridges over streets, "If such bridges are allowed to proliferate, Houston will become a grotesque city, with air, sky, rain and sunshine cut out. . . . To me this is eye pollution. . . . I am disturbed about what could happen to the city if this is allowed to proceed." A prominent local columnist also voiced reservations: "It all sounds a little preposterous — everything up in the air, connected by malls and people movers with cars relegated to the basement. But the construction sounds even more like pie-in-the-smog considering that the parent company . . . is not a real estate development firm but a giant gas pipeline company. . . ."[23]

Adding to this undercurrent of criticism were the published comments of several architects and architectural critics in other cities. Perhaps the most stinging commentary came from another city developing its downtown, Seattle. There a columnist proclaimed "Houston's Monster Not for Us" and described the Center as "a five-story Chinese wall across one quarter of the city of Houston." He said, "It is what could happen only when the aberration which is a company's ego meets the peculiarity of Houston which is that it has no zoning ordinance."[24]

This was just the sort of mixed reception one would expect, given the nature of the media and the crossroads at which the city stood in the early 1970s. New voices were beginning to be raised in opposition to unrestrained development. New challenges were being issued to the business leaders who had long charted the city's course. George Brown and friends had led Hous-

185

ton's extraordinary growth after World War II as a "free enterprise city."[25] Private initiative led the way; urban amenities would follow. From their point of view, the imperative was to move forward aggressively in a manner befitting a Texas city on the rise; Houston Center's scale, its private financing, and its futuristic look were all much in keeping with the attitude of the boosters who had done so much to push their city into the national limelight. But now an opposition had developed to what the boosters called "Texas style urban renewal." The critics had a quite different vision of Houston's future. They saw the center as a symbol of development out of control. Where, they asked, was the input from ordinary citizens or regulation by the government? Why was there no low income housing in the master plan? Should they attract still more automobiles into a central business district struggling to absorb existing traffic?

Much of the opposition to Houston Center focused on legal and political challenges to Texas Eastern's proposal to cover a section of the city's streets. In the planning process, the company had acknowledged the need to clarify its access to air rights, and it had done so with aggressive legal work and political lobbying. Under Texas oil law the owner of the surface land was assumed to own subsurface rights down to the center of the earth. This principal offered legal support for the conclusion that the land owner also owned rights to use the air above this property, at least to the extent that this use did not interfere with the rights of others. But air rights above city streets were another matter, since citizens had a legal right to access to streets. The city administered these rights through the granting of easements, and Texas Eastern argued that the city could abandon such easements and grant air rights to the owner of the property on each side of a street. Under a new ordinance passed at TE's request, the city granted these rights and executed a "quit claim" deed giving the company complete ownership of certain specified air rights, subject to restrictions on noise and air pollution. The speed with which these negotiations were carried out provided a good measure of the relative strengths of the boosters and their critics. Houston was still essentially a city dominated by the developers' mentality. The city government was quite sympathetic to George Brown's real estate project.[26]

Despite the continuing criticism, Texas Eastern boldly announced that it was launching the first phase of construction. The company declared its intention to move ahead with the development of a nine-block section. Included would be a major hotel, three high-rise office towers clustered around a great enclosed plaza, retail stores and low-rise office blocks flanking the pedestrian open spaces, and cascading garden apartments along the eastern perimeter (along with parking facilities). These early plans retained the visionary quality of the master proposal. The twenty-first century was coming to Houston.

As the official groundbreaking for Two Houston Center—the project's first major building—took place in January of 1972, Texas Eastern could look back with satisfaction on a long era of success. Its profitable, expanded gas pipeline system was continuing to generate the revenues needed to sustain the strategy of diversification. The company had established strong positions in several industries outside of natural gas transmission, notably LPG and North Sea gas production. The launching of Houston Center amid national fanfare added still another source of strength and seemed to herald the continued growth of the company and its city. With much of the rest of the American economy, the company had enjoyed a heady period of postwar prosperity. As the 1970s began, Texas Eastern had every reason to be confident in its future.

Part Three

THE LIMITS TO STRATEGY
1971–89

Chapter 9

RESPONSES TO GAS SHORTAGES

Texas Eastern's leaders did not have long to enjoy the national publicity generated by their plans to recast downtown Houston. The 1970s and 1980s brought a new set of challenges, as an unprecedented series of regulatory and economic changes buffeted the company. Deregulation in natural gas dramatically transformed that industry. The process of change was halting and unpredictable, leaving managers uncertain about the basic rules under which they operated. Drastic swings in the price and the availability of natural gas and oil made planning for supply at best problematical. Those uncertainties exacerbated the day-to-day problems of managing an increasingly diversified company, and the threat of hostile takeovers at times deflected the energies of executives from long-term planning.

There is no easy way to analyze the variety of choices faced by managers at a diversified natural gas transmission company such as Texas Eastern during these years. After the energy crisis of the early 1970s the world of oil and gas changed rapidly and often with little obvious direction. The scholar looking back on this period has an option not available to managers hard pressed to meet real world pressures. The historian can simplify reality by reducing the chaotic press of events into more easily understood categories. We have chosen to do that by examining events in the natural gas industry separately from events in the remainder of Texas Eastern's diversified holdings. We have also decided to treat 1971–89 as two separate periods, the first marked by sharp rises in energy prices and the second introduced by a dramatic decline in prices in 1985 and 1986. But as you read these pages, bear in mind that these periods and patterns were unclear at the time. Event tumbled over event, undermining the capacity of planners in business and government to project future patterns of supply, demand, or price.

As this era began, growing oil revenues encouraged further diversification aimed at building strengths outside of the natural gas business. TE had good reason to believe it should continue to develop such areas as oil and gas production, real estate, LPG, and oil services. But falling energy prices after 1985 forced a reevaluation of this strategy as the company sought to simplify its operations by refocusing on a smaller number of core industries.

The process of adaptation was abruptly ended in 1989, when the company was acquired by Panhandle Eastern Corporation. The new company simplified things with a vengeance by selling off all of Texas Eastern's holdings except its natural gas transmission system, thereby focusing quite clearly on the business which had always remained central to the company's growth.

Acquisition by another gas transmission company was a part of an ongoing, industry-wide effort to come to grips with the vast changes of the 1970s and 1980s. During the two previous decades the natural gas industry had been marked by relative stability in regulation, pricing, and supply. But dislocations unleashed by the energy crisis set off a search for a new equilibrium, a new order that still remained undefined as the gas industry entered the 1990s.[1]

The earliest signs of the impending breakdown of the old order were gas shortages. By the late 1960s Texas Eastern could no longer assume that adequate gas supplies could be obtained at the price levels which had prevailed for several decades. As the company's 1972 *Annual Report* proclaimed, "the national energy shortage" had thrown Texas Eastern into "a new corporate era."[2] This new era involved fundamental changes in the natural gas transmission business.

Political and regulatory forces shaped these changes, and Texas Eastern joined others in the industry in lobbying for relief from the price regulations which had helped create a shortage of natural gas. As these spirited debates about regulatory reform continued, the company's executives had to chart strategy for their business in spite of the existing uncertainty about the rules that ultimately would emerge. Even after the passage of the Natural Gas Policy Act of 1978 replaced traditional price regulation with a complicated form of phased deregulation, considerable uncertainties remained. A confusing period of adjustment hampered the best efforts of public as well as private planners.[3]

While awaiting legislative and regulatory relief from gas shortages, Texas Eastern explored a variety of projects designed to supplement traditional sources of natural gas. These ventures included several rather expensive proposals to produce gas from new sources. Liquified natural gas (LNG) transported from foreign fields, extraordinarily long pipelines to reach vast gas fields in Alaska and Canada, and different technologies for producing gas from coal and liquid hydrocarbons all captured the attention of management in these years. Government policies shaped all of these ventures, leaving Texas Eastern's planners juggling political as well as economic considerations. None of these projects ultimately produced significant new supplies of supplemental gas; yet all absorbed considerable executive energy at a critical time in the company's history.[4]

At this critical juncture in its history Texas Eastern was also struggling to cope with problems of management succession. After Orville Carpenter reached retirement age in 1965 and George Brown stepped down as chairman in 1971, TE sought to continue its tradition of "home-grown" leadership by appointing Baxter Goodrich as president in 1965 and as chairman in 1971. Goodrich, who had joined the company in 1947, had been a prime mover in the expansion of the pipeline system. He was a well-respected and hard-working engineer. For a loyal Brown lieutenant such as Goodrich, the opportunity to replace Brown as the top executive at Texas Eastern was the crowning achievement of a long, successful career.

Alas, it was not to be. History dealt Goodrich and Texas Eastern a bad hand. Just as Goodrich took charge, the long wave of crises began. Battered by these events and beset by health problems, Goodrich struggled unsuccessfully to remain effective before retiring in 1974. Suddenly, the organization had to search for new leadership again in the midst of a rapidly changing political economy.

For the first time in its history, Texas Eastern looked outside for new management. George Kirby had come to the company in 1970 as an executive vice president after thirty years at the Ethyl Corporation.[5] A chemist by training, Kirby had first attracted the attention of George Brown and others at Texas Eastern in preliminary discussions concerning the possibility of a merger between the company and the Ethyl Corporation. Although these meetings failed to produce a merger, they did help to identify a promising executive. Kirby joined the TE board in 1969. He became president in 1971 and chairman in 1975. The coming to power of an outsider—and one with limited exposure to the natural gas industry—heralded other departures in company history.

Given his long experience in the chemical and petroleum industries, Kirby quickly set out to strengthen Texas Eastern's position in each of these businesses. He had little interest in real estate ventures and at times seemed to view natural gas as an industry with discouraging long-term prospects. With strong backing from George Brown, Kirby might have changed the face of Texas Eastern had he been able to exert strong leadership for a decade or more. Yet, as had been the case with Baxter Goodrich, fate was unkind to the company. Kirby had barely begun to put the stamp of his personality on the organization before he fell victim to serious health problems which sapped his energies. He died in 1980 at the age of 63. For the third time in less than a decade, TE had to replace its top manager and experience the sort of reorientation that inevitably accompanies a change in command.

Even in the best of times, rapid turnover at the top places strains on an organization, and the 1970s were not the best of times for Texas Eastern. During no decade in the company's existence was there a more pressing need for strength and continuity in the executive suite. As the economic, political, and financial pressures mounted, the firm needed a clear vision of the future and forceful communication from the top. What it got was frequent changes in top management during a pivotal period in its history.

None of the transitions was more pressing than the growing shortage of

Dr. George F. Kirby

natural gas. At the heart of this problem was an imbalance between supply and demand at the price allowed by the Federal Power Commission. As shown in table 9.1, from the 1940s through the 1960s rising demand had been met by the nation's gas producers at relatively stable prices. They provided an excellent, clean-burning fuel at regulated prices below the prevailing prices for comparable heating units of coal and fuel oil. Given these conditions, demand surged upward year after year.

Until the mid-1960s Texas Eastern had been able to expand its pipeline system and its commitments to deliver gas (see table 9.2) without too much concern about long-term supplies. Indeed, as late as 1966 the company had joined with the American Gas Association and other transmission companies to fund advertising that promoted gas use. These ads and the announcement of a major $195 million dollar expansion program in the mid-1960s suggested that Texas Eastern was not yet deeply concerned about potential gas shortages. In 1965 the company reported to its stockholders that there was a bright future, with "adequate reserves" for expansion. Others saw a similarly rosy picture. Public officials and other managers in the gas industry projected steady growth in demand and supply well into the future. Table 9.3 juxtaposes the company's widely publicized projections of gas consumption against the actual usage for those years. This comparison highlights the transformation that took place as price controls finally began to choke off growth in gas supplies.

194

TABLE 9.1   Natural Gas Prices and Demand, 1945–72

| Year | Marketed Production | | Average Wellhead Price (cents per mcf) |
	Millions of cubic feet	Trillions of Btu	
1945	4,042,002	4,481.7	4.9
1950	6,282,060	6,753.0	6.5
1951	7,457,359	8,016.7	7.3
1952	8,013,457	8,614.5	7.8
1953	8,396,916	9,026.7	9.2
1954	8,742,546	9,398.2	10.1
1955	9,405,351	10,110.4	10.4
1956	10,081,923	10,838.2	10.8
1957	10,680,258	11,481.0	11.3
1958	11,030,248	11,857.5	11.9
1959	12,046,115	12,949.5	12.9
1960	12,771,038	13,728.8	14.0
1961	13,254,025	14,248.1	15.1
1962	13,876,622	14,917.4	15.5
1963	14,746,663	15,852.7	15.8
1964	15,462,143	16,621.8	15.4
1965	16,039,753	17,242.7	15.6
1966	17,206,628	18,497.1	15.7
1967	18,171,325	19,534.2	16.0
1968	19,322,400	20,771.6	16.4
1969	20,698,240	22,250.6	16.7
1970	20,920,642	23,564.7	17.1
1971	22,493,012	24,180.0	18.2
1972	22,531,698	24,221.6	18.6

Source: American Gas Association, *Gas Facts,* 1974. Adapted from U.S. Bureau of Mines.

While optimistic about future supplies, Texas Eastern favored a number of adjustments in the FPC's regulatory procedures. It did not yet acknowledge that the most realistic solution would be the deregulation of gas prices at the wellhead.[6] After all, the company was a buyer, as well as a transporter, and the price controls worked to its advantage in the short term.

The FPC at this time was also searching for a more efficient form of price regulation, not deregulation. One of the most prominent commissioners of the 1960s, Joseph Swidler, captured the prevailing sentiment in a speech to gas representatives soon after becoming FPC chairman in 1964: "It is unthinkable that this country's 35 million captive consumers of natural gas could be abandoned to the unequal market forces of the field."[7] Swidler's basic assumptions about the future availability of gas were shared by many in the industry, including the management of Texas Eastern. In fact, Jack Head, the company's general counsel, recalled that years later Swidler chided him about the gas industry's attitudes in the 1960s:

TABLE 9.2   Growth of Texas Eastern Corporation, 1947–88

Year	Miles of Pipeline	Natural Gas Delivered (bcf)	Total Assets (millions)	Operating Revenues (millions)	Earnings Per Share
1947	2,848	40	$ 156	$ 9	N/A
1950	3,395	300	245	74	$1.78
1955	6,613	499	580	163	2.11
1960	5,617	744	897	317	2.07
1965	10,922	867	1,106	422	1.59
1970	11,792	1,260	1,748	653	2.66
1975	12,172	1,024	2,554	1,298	3.13
1980	12,655	1,436	3,314	4,273	8.72
1985	N/A	996	5,075	5,250	0.05
1988	10,567	1,016	5,444	3,481	2.85

Source: *Texas Eastern Financial and Statistical Summary,* various years, and Texas Eastern Corporation, *Annual Report,* various years.

'Now, Jack, the industry lied to me when I was chairman of the Commission. You told me there was just an immense amount of gas. . . . Had I known that gas would become in short supply, I would have regulated in an entirely different manner. . . . I was regulating to see how far I could reduce the price of the gas and still keep it flowing in interstate commerce. . . . Had I known that a shortage was just around the corner, honestly, I would have been establishing prices that would have given the producers some incentive to continue to explore.'[8]

Swidler and many others in the industry were blindsided by the shortages which swiftly developed in the late 1960s.

Relatively rigid prices had discouraged exploration, and supplies began to lag behind demand. New gas was becoming increasingly expensive as producers moved offshore and drilled deeper into the earth in search of new deposits. Once discovered, much new gas increasingly flowed into intrastate markets, where unregulated prices pushed above those in the interstate field. The FPC remained responsive to consumers' traditional desire for low prices. Soon, however, the economic value of new supplies of natural gas began to exceed the political value placed on them by the FPC.[9]

This posed an immediate and pressing problem for Texas Eastern and other interstate pipelines. Their giant transmission systems had been built under the assumption that gas would continue to be available. These lines had been financed on the basis of operations at full capacity, so the supply problems threatened the financial health of the pipeline companies. As a small producer of natural gas and a substantial purchaser of supplies for interstate markets, Texas Eastern's future was endangered by the continuation of these regulatory policies.

The dramatic trend toward intrastate gas sales in the late 1960s and early 1970s was the most pressing threat. The FPC's authority in these years still

TABLE 9.3   Total Reserve Additions: Interstate versus Intrastate, 1966–75

Year	AGA Reserve Additions Excluding Revisions	Interstate New Supply[a]	Percentage	Inferred Intrastate New Supply[b]	Percentage
1966	14.8	10.0	68	4.8	32
1967	14.8	9.9	67	4.9	33
1968	9.8	6.4	65	3.4	35
1969	9.6	6.2	64	3.4	36
1970	11.3	3.5	31	7.8	69
1971	11.1	2.2	20	8.9	80
1972	10.7	5.0	47	5.7	53
1973	10.1	1.7	17	8.4	83
1974	9.7	2.4	25	7.3	75
1975	10.0	1.3[c]	13	8.7	87

Note: Trillions of cubic feet.
[a]Form 15, FPC, excluding revisions.
[b]Derived by assuming that intrastate reserve additions are equal to the difference between total AGA reserve additions and the reserve additions committed to the interstate market.
[c]Preliminary.
Source: Richard H. K. Vietor, *Energy Policy in America since 1945* (Cambridge: Cambridge University Press, 1984), p. 289. Adapted from FPC, Docket No. RM 75–14, *Opinion No. 770–A* (Washington, D.C.: FPC, 1976), p. 116.

extended only to interstate sales. The "natural" thing for a regulatory agency to do in this situation would be to seek to extend its power, bringing intrastate gas under control. But that policy seemed both constitutionally questionable and politically unachievable. So producers still had the option to seek unregulated prices in intrastate markets. Before the late 1960s the markets in producing states had not been very large. But as Sunbelt growth spurred industrial demand, more and more gas could be sold in those markets. As the higher prices in Texas and other producing states drew off scarce supplies, Texas Eastern was blocked by the FPC from raising its own bids in an effort to compete for new supplies. Interstate pipelines could and did compete by offering producers a more attractive package of services, notably contractual guarantees of higher takes and pledges to extend pipelines to the wellhead. Smaller intrastate pipelines seldom matched such offers. They usually did not have to, because they could offer substantially higher prices.[10]

Texas Eastern watched in frustration as aggressive intrastate lines pulled in more and more production from areas long considered the best suppliers for interstate markets. This development imperiled the firm's traditional mission: the shipment of southwestern gas to the Northeast. Over the long term the growth of intrastate sales could well destroy the company and deal a blow to those northeastern customers who depended on natural gas as a basic source of fuel.

Texas Eastern — never coy about the politics of economic life — lobbied the FPC for regulatory relief. Along with other interstate pipelines, TE sought ways to "loosen up" the commission's hold on gas prices and supplies. The business sought three goals: new policies for checking the movement of gas into intrastate markets; a higher rate of return for gas pipelines; and higher rates at the wellhead to encourage the search for new gas reserves.

The last of these objectives placed Texas Eastern and other pipelines in the somewhat awkward position of trying to persuade the FPC to allow them to pay higher prices for newly discovered reserves. Thus, when the commission announced its area price for Louisiana's on- and offshore gas in 1968, Texas Eastern joined five other major pipelines in filing a motion to reopen hearings in order to consider raising the price allowed. The intervenors justified this "extraordinary step" on the grounds that rates ordered by the FPC were too low to attract "the vast sums of money needed for exploration and development of these reserves on a scale sufficient to produce enough gas for the nation's burgeoning gas markets." In support of this position, spokesmen for the pipelines cited the growth of intrastate sales. The lack of adequate financial incentives, they said, might convince the major oil companies which dominated gas production to divert potential investment funds out of gas exploration and into other, more profitable endeavors.[11] The FPC ultimately reopened its hearings on the area rate for southern Louisiana. Under the cumulative pressure of these sorts of pleas, the commission also began to reconsider its basic pricing policies.

Texas Eastern took a second line of attack in 1969, when it applied for the certification of a new project with the stipulation that the undertaking would not go forward unless new supplies were forthcoming. The firm had already warned that it would have to begin saying "no" to future requests for more gas. Now, in 1970, it said in frustration: "The Company did not expand either system [eastern and western] on a scale comparable with former years because large, new gas reserves to support additional deliveries were not available. Furthermore, Texas Eastern plans to undertake no new gas sales commitments until it is able to purchase under long-term contracts additional proven gas reserves in adequate volumes."[12] Texas Eastern and its competitors hoped that such statements would convince the FPC that the wolf was now at the door of the gas transmission companies — and of gas consumers.

Curtailments of gas shipments to established customers were potent political messages that the wolf was inside the door. By the early 1970s sufficient natural gas was not available at prevailing prices to meet demand in some interstate markets. When suppliers were unable to acquire the gas needed to fulfill contracts, they had no choice but to curtail deliveries. In an industry long accustomed to expansion, such cutbacks signalled a major crisis. The FPC now had powerful evidence that there was need for regulatory reform.

Texas Eastern first began curtailments in 1970, after one of its suppliers informed the company that it could no longer meet its contractual obliga-

TABLE 9.4   Texas Eastern System Curtailments

Year	TE Eastern System	TE Western System
1971	3–7 percent	— percent
1972	3–7	—
1973	13	—
1974	21	13
1975	27	22
1976	27	31
1977	17	32
1978	18	39
1979	Curtailments virtually eliminated	

Source: Texas Eastern *Annual Report*, 1971–80.

tions. As a ripple of such actions spread through the industry, more and more companies began the agonizing process of curtailing shipments. By the mid-1970s Texas Eastern was making regular and extensive cutbacks in deliveries on both its eastern and western pipeline systems (see table 9.4). Curtailments imposed hardships on consumers and were a source of frustration for gas company executives. They were as well a daily reminder to the FPC that something had to change.

Curtailments were tricky for a private firm to implement. Who was to have their supplies cut? By how much? By whom? The first wave of cutbacks were directed by the managers of the individual gas supply companies. Texas Eastern executives joined others in the industry in attempting to stretch available gas to meet the essential needs of its customers. But these private curtailment plans quickly found their way into the regulatory agencies and the courts, as those harmed by curtailment sought redress.

After much controversy arose over the proper design and enforcement of privately managed curtailment programs, in 1973 the FPC imposed its own set of guidelines and procedures. The commission put forward an end-use curtailment program which assigned priorities for eight different categories of customers.[13] Industrial consumers of boiler gas received the lowest priority; residential consumers the highest. This had been the case in most of the private plans, since traditional contracts with large industrial consumers such as electric power plants had contained clauses making shipments "interruptible" under certain conditions. But unlike private companies, the FPC could use the authority and the sanctions of government to require compliance and to extend curtailment to customers without interruptible contracts. FPC–backed curtailment policies remained effective until gas shortages eased in the late 1970s, and they enjoyed the support of most of the gas industry. Not everyone agreed that these policies were perfect. But most saw the benefits of cooperation among all parties to get through a bad situation.

Such could not be said of the efforts to reform natural gas regulations.

199

During the 1970s highly divisive and heated partisan debates erupted over natural gas policy. Most participants in these debates agreed on the weaknesses of existing FPC regulations, but there was no consensus on answers to the key questions facing reformers. What was the proper price of natural gas? Should the existing division between interstate and intrastate markets be retained? Were end use controls needed for natural gas? But as the debates made evident, these questions were far from easy to answer.

They raised fundamental issues regarding the proper role of government in regulating the economy. They caused deep divisions that made political compromise almost impossible. Particularly evident were tensions between producers and consumers, both of whom sought to sway the legislature through well-organized interest groups. Regional divisions further complicated matters. Representatives from the Northeast and the Southwest grappled over issues of pressing importance to their constituents. Divisions also emerged within the industry. Given these deep fissures, the nature of interest group combat, and the inflamed political environment of the 1970s, the debate over natural gas policies was bound to be volatile, long-lasting, and impossible to resolve to the satisfaction of all of the different political factions.[14]

Texas Eastern was, of course, up to its armpits in this struggle. As had been the case from its origins, the company had much to lose or gain from the political process. In the Washington of the 1970s — with its focus on energy policy and its newly assertive public interest groups — Texas Eastern and other representatives of "Big Business" had to compete with many other points of view. David Bufkin and Jack Head spent considerable time lobbying in the company's interest. They testified. They talked with congressmen. They worked closely with Houston-area representatives such as Bob Eckhardt. They also joined in "education" campaigns with industry groups such as the Interstate Natural Gas Association. They did all they could to assert their company's legitimate interests. But Texas Eastern's voice was merely one in a cacophony of competing choruses. Their political influence was offset by that of numerous other groups with quite different interests. The struggle over gas policy was one of the most hotly contested political contests of the 1970s, and its outcome was far beyond TE's control.

Texas Eastern sought to expand its influence by joining a formidable alliance of likeminded companies. The firm joined in the call for a coordinated federal energy policy relying primarily on private enterprise to "maximize domestic production" under "realistic environmental, health and safety standards." The company also supported government encouragement of synthetic gas production and imports of foreign gas.[15] On the more specific issues of natural gas policy, Texas Eastern strongly advocated higher prices to provide producers with incentives to expand exploration. The company also sought reforms that would stem the flow of gas into intrastate markets. Both of these changes would involve fundamental alterations in the FPC's policies. Although the commission had allowed natural gas prices to move up sharply in the 1970s, Texas Eastern and most of the other businesses in the industry now favored a more basic move toward some form of deregulated, market-sensitive pricing. They had concluded by this time that the FPC's brand of price controls had created a long-term disaster.

After a long series of intense interest-group battles, a compromise gas bill finally made its way out of Congress. The Natural Gas Policy Act of 1978 was the most significant reform of natural gas policy since the original act in 1938. It bore the scars of the political bargaining that had accompanied its passage. It was a bundle of unlikely compromises which tried to offer something to everyone — and thus provided nothing coherent for anyone. On every major issue the act incorporated compromises among producer and consumer groups and among regional interests (see table 9.5). The "phased deregulation" authorized by the act moved the nation gradually away from price controls while leaving ample opportunity for Congress or the Federal Energy Regulatory Commission (which had assumed most of the powers of the FPC in 1977) to step back in at a later date and revise the pace or direction of deregulation.[16]

Texas Eastern could find some consolation in at least two aspects of the act. The new law breached the wall between intrastate and interstate markets, removing one of the most difficult obstacles to increased gas supplies for the interstate companies. In addition, the law promised gradual increases in prices for gas producers, a change which might reasonably be expected to enhance gas supplies from conventional sources in the long run.

But in the short term the 1978 law did little to end the regulatory uncertainly facing strategists in the natural gas industry. The act's complicated formula for the pricing of various types of natural gas was far from a straightforward deregulation of prices. Its stipulation that new gas prices should be freed of price regulations by 1985 guaranteed a period of confusion as decontrols were "phased in." The uncertainties embodied in the Natural Gas Policy Act were capable of confounding the best efforts of planners in the industry. Many of the questions raised by the new law ultimately had to be answered in hearings before the Federal Energy Regulatory Commission. Thus an act which held out the promise of deregulation in the long term fostered an era of intense regulatory uncertainty in the short term.

So Texas Eastern and its major competitors had no choice but to continue to develop supplemental sources of gas. The firm was still in a strong position to launch these bold initiatives. Its corporate culture stressed "doing big things," and this reinforced the impulse to enter into ventures that promised to develop important new sources of energy at costs often reaching billions of dollars. The returns from its gas transmission business and growing revenues from North Sea oil and gas production kept the company on a solid financial footing. Its easy access to capital made even the most ambitious projects seem feasible; for engineering expertise it could always look to Brown & Root.

TABLE 9.5   Key Provisions of the Natural Gas Policy Act of 1978
and the Power Plant and Industrial Fuel Use Act of 1978

PRICING:	——phased and partial deregulation
	——26 categories of natural gas created based on the year gas was first committed to sale and on other characteristics.
	——"new" gas (including gas from Outer Continental Shelf; old leases if discovered after July 26, 1976; reservoirs from which gas was not produced before April 20, 1977; gas from new onshore wells 2.5 or more miles from "marker wells"; and reservoirs closer than 2.5 miles from a marker well if 1,000 feet deeper) to be relieved from federal price controls by January 1, 1985.
	——"old" gas brought into production before the date of enactment of the new law to remain under price regulations.
	——"deep" gas from reservoirs below 15,000 feet to be exempt from price controls immediately.
COVERAGE:	——all natural gas production within the United States, including gas produced and sold in intrastate markets.
END USE CONTROLS:	
	——new electric power plants may not use oil or gas as a primary energy source; existing electric power plants must end natural gas use as a primary fuel by 1990; the Secretary of the Department of Energy is further impowered to prohibit non-boiler uses of natural gas in new major units.

One of the efforts involved liquefied natural gas (LNG). Natural gas cooled to a temperature of at least 260 degrees below zero (Fahrenheit) could be transformed into a liquid with only 1/625 of the volume of the natural gas. It could thus be transported in relatively small, supercooled containers. In tankers equipped with these containers, LNG could be transported across oceans. This process was quite expensive. It required the construction of plants to cool the natural gas; cryogenic tankers which cost approximately $100 million each; and giant storage and regasification facilities. But despite their high cost, LNG–tankers promised to revolutionize the transportation of gas by connecting vast fields in Africa, the Middle East, and the Soviet Union to major new markets around the world.

In the United States, however, the history of LNG utilization had not been a success story. The product had been developed initially as a means of storing large volumes of gas, not of transporting it. In 1941 the East Ohio Gas Company constructed in Cleveland the first commercial LNG plant to be operated in the United States. In 1944 this plant exploded, killing 130 people. This disaster "brought a halt to the domestic LNG storage business for almost twenty years."[17]

But in the 1960s and 1970s countries that were still wasting flared gas at the wellhead began to explore means of using LNG to get this product to markets in Europe and elsewhere. Algeria, in particular, aggressively pursued plans to liquefy much of its natural gas production and sell it to England, France, Japan, and other countries. By the early 1970s LNG tankers were transporting the fuel from Brunei, Libya, southern Alaska, and Algeria to Japan, continental Europe, and the United Kingdom.[18]

Texas Eastern had watched these innovations with interest. It had investigated the effects of cryogenic temperatures on various types of material which could be used to contain LNG. Texas Eastern joined efforts with Battelle Memorial Institute to evaluate the technical and economic feasibility of large-volume LNG storage. Together, they "studied 19 different kinds of insulation materials and 27 types of liners, all having properties that would undergo a wide range of heating and cooling cycles over a long period of time."[19] After several years of experimentation and the construction of a twenty- by twenty-eight-foot demonstration tank, Texas Eastern decided a commercial-sized tank was feasible.

In August of 1965 the company filed an application with the FPC for authorization to construct and operate a large LNG storage facility on Staten Island. The proposal attracted immediate opposition. The Bureau of Mines, the New York City Marine and Aviation Commission, and the New York City Fire Department all opposed the plan. Spokesman for these agencies argued that the proposed facility would create potential hazards which could not be effectively controlled by the local fire department. Nevertheless, the FPC issued its certificate in December of 1966. The New York Board of Standards and Appeals approved the construction permit, with the condition that the Fire Department and the Commission on Marine Aviation had to monitor the construction of the terminal.

Brown & Root was the design engineer for the storage facility, which had a capacity of six hundred thousand barrels of LNG, the equivalent of approximately two billion cubic feet of natural gas. After about 80 percent of the insulation had been installed, the New York City Fire Department's Fire Prevention Bureau, "discovered that the material was not self-extinguishing, contrary to design specifications." Nevertheless, it was determined "that it would be more dangerous to remove and replace the insulation than to go ahead with construction."[20] On that somewhat ominous basis, the tank was finally completed in late 1969. It was the world's largest operating, above-ground facility, and it could receive LNG directly from tankers or from Texas Eastern's pipeline system; there was equipment at the site to convert natural gas to liquefied natural gas for injection into the tank. Alternately, the LNG could be returned to its natural state for transport via Texas Eastern's pipeline. In March, 1970, the company filled the tank with liquid nitrogen, which was kept there fifteen months for testing purposes.

Texas Eastern's first contract for LNG was made principally through British Methane, a joint venture of the British Gas Council, Conch Methane International, and Sonatrach, the National Algerian Hydrocarbon Company. Texas Eastern contracted for three shipments of Algerian LNG. The FPC initially approved the first shipment while postponing its decision on subsequent orders. On April 3 Texas Eastern received its first load of LNG.

While Texas Eastern and other companies were pushing these plans along, however, new opposition to LNG arose. Some oil and gas companies, as well as northeastern utilities, argued that LNG imports would actually aggravate domestic shortages. Superior Oil summarized the thrust of this attack, asserting that "displacement . . . of domestic natural gas by imported LNG would aggravate an already critical deficiency in the domestic gas exploratory program of independent producers and will create a dependency on foreign production."[21] Despite these complaints, regulators refused to block further LNG imports, and Texas Eastern continued to receive tanker shipments of LNG at its Staten Island facility.

Late in 1970, however, operators at the storage facility noted an apparent leak through the interior tank liner into the insulation space. By that time, the level of LNG had reached 52 feet, 2¼ inches. The tank continued to be used, but it operated under the restriction that the liquid level be kept below 51 feet, 6 inches. In February of 1972, all of the LNG in the tank was withdrawn, the tank was cooled, and it was then purged with gaseous nitrogen. Finally, continuous air circulation was begun. In mid-April repair work began in the interior of the tank and continued for the following ten months.

But what had begun as a routine repair job ended in tragedy. On February 10, 1973, "a fire broke out in the tank and in a very short time the self-supporting concrete dome of the tank lifted from the pressure produced by the heat of combustion and collapsed into the tank."[22] Forty-two workmen were in the tank at the time the fire erupted. Two escaped, but the remaining forty men perished. Most of the deaths occurred from the inhalation of fumes from the burning lining and insulation of the tank.

In the aftermath of the worst industrial accident in its history, Texas Eastern faced probing questions about the safety of its storage facility and about the entire LNG technology. Since no LNG had been present in the tank at the time of the disaster, the accident could not be attributed directly to this relatively new technology. Yet to the media, this episode lent credence to the fears of those who had opposed the initial construction permits. Given its history, LNG raised concerns which only a long period of accident-free operations could soothe. The Staten Island catastrophe brought into question the safety of Texas Eastern's LNG facilities, giving a black eye to the company and the LNG industry as a whole. The company was subsequently indicted on forty counts of criminally negligent homicide by the Staten Island grand jury. The case was settled out of court, but it apparently convinced Texas Eastern not to rebuild the storage facility. What had begun as an innovative effort to make use of a promising new technology concluded as one of the saddest chapters in the company's history.

While moving out of Staten Island, the company still did not give up on LNG. It had for some years joined with several other U.S. companies in negotiations to import large volumes of natural gas from the Soviet Union.

This project proposed to liquefy natural gas produced in Siberia and ship it by LNG tankers to the East Coast of the United States. Such an undertaking was ambitious even by Texas Eastern's standards. To complete this extraordinary venture, the firm would have to introduce some creative technical innovations, handle large financial risks, and juggle the demands of an unfamiliar Soviet political system while experiencing the unpredictable swings of international diplomacy.

Texas Eastern's previous international projects had given it valuable exposure to foreign politics, convincing management it could handle the complications of superpower diplomacy. The opportunity to enter negotiations with the Soviet Union was an offspring of "detente," the thaw in relations between the United States and the USSR during the early years of Richard Nixon's presidency. Nixon's pursuit of improved relations and increased trade with the government of the USSR opened the way for TE and other U.S. energy companies. With gas becoming more scarce in the United States, they were attracted by the abundant supplies in the Soviet Union. So, too, were several western European countries, which were attracted to the extraordinary and relatively undeveloped Soviet gas reserves.[23]

By that time many large American oil and gas companies were gaining new expertise in the exploration, production, and transportation of oil and gas in arctic conditions on the North Slope of Alaska. Several of them felt that this technical knowledge could be put to good use in the Soviet Union if political barriers could be surmounted. By the early 1970s two major joint ventures involving American companies had reached the stage of serious discussions about the possibilities for massive LNG shipments. In the eastern Soviet Union, Occidental Petroleum Company and El Paso Natural Gas Company put forward a $10 billion proposal to build a two-thousand-mile gas pipeline from Yakutsk to Vladivostok, where a giant liquefaction plant would prepare LNG for shipment to the West Coast of the United States in cryogenic tankers.[24] Texas Eastern entered an equally ambitious joint venture to ship LNG from the western Soviet Union to the East Coast.

After exploring alone the prospects for such a project, Texas Eastern had joined forces with two other Houston-based companies, Tenneco and Brown & Root. Herbert Brownell, attorney general in the Eisenhower administration who had worked for TE briefly in 1947, represented the consortium along with John B. Connally, former governor of Texas and U.S. secretary of the treasury.[25] Texas Eastern was well represented in the joint venture by its president, George Kirby, lawyer William Kendall, LNG–specialist Nevil M.E. Proes, and assorted technical experts. Joining these men in numerous trips to the Soviet Union were their counterparts from longtime competitor Tenneco and longtime ally Brown & Root.

After much preliminary planning, this consortium came up with a proposal that seemed to fit their needs for more gas and the Soviets' need to generate an increased flow of capital and technology from the West. On

July 2, 1973, the U.S. companies signed a "protocol of intent" that amounted to a preliminary agreement with the Soviets "to discuss the development of a major natural gas export-import project."[26] About a month earlier a similar agreement between the USSR and the Occidental–El Paso consortium had been announced. Texas Eastern seemed poised to take part in a historic development in East-West relations.

The Texas Eastern–Tenneco–Brown & Root project came to be called "North Star." It would acquire its natural gas from the Urengoiske gas field in Central Siberia and then transport it by pipeline fifteen hundred miles to a LNG plant one hundred miles west of Murmansk. Converted to liquid, the gas would be shipped by tankers four thousand miles to Philadelphia, regasified, and sold to northeastern customers through existing pipelines. Over a twenty-five-year period, two billion cubic feet per day would be delivered every year.

The North Star proposal faced many potential problems, but adequate reserves was not one of them. Proving the reserves of the Urengoiske Field was much easier than arranging for the financing. During the early 1970s international sources confirmed this gas field as one of the largest in the world. It contained an estimated minimum proven reserves of 141 trillion cubic feet and a potential maximum of nearly twice as much. The field was substantially larger than any of the largest outside the Soviet Union, including the Groningen Field. Urengoiske alone contained quantities of gas equivalent to between 50 and 80 percent of total U.S. proven reserves. This lure was strong enough to draw Texas Eastern to the forbidding physical environment of Siberia and the equally daunting political setting of Moscow.[27]

Because the entire project came with a staggering $6.7 billion price tag, financing was a problem. About 30 percent of the total cost would be spent on the construction of the twenty LNG tankers — at an estimated cost of $131 million per vessel. To put such figures in perspective, in the early 1970s the book value of all of the property, plant, and equipment of Texas Eastern was less than two billion dollars. The company's long-term debt was less than one billion dollars.[28] Although the other two members of the consortium would share this financial burden, Texas Eastern had never participated in a project of this size.

There were also complications over the precise route of the pipeline from the Urengoiske Field to the sea. The Soviets originally wanted the line to terminate at a Baltic port. But this route would pass near both Moscow and Leningrad, and the American companies feared that the Soviets might someday decide to expropriate the line to supply gas to these two cities. In light of the financial risks of the project, the companies felt compelled to minimize the risks associated with the choice of a pipeline route. After extensive negotiations involving geographical as well as financial considerations, the Soviets agreed finally to a port near Murmansk (see map 9.1).

It appeared that "by June, 1974, all substantive issues were agreed upon,

MAP 9.1 The North Star LNG Project

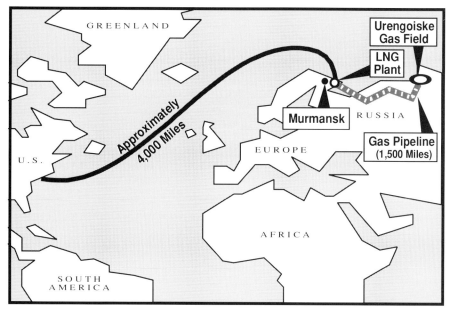

except price, between American and Russian negotiators."[29] The Trade Act of 1974 gave the Soviet Union most-favored-nation status so long as it did not unduly restrict emigration of its citizens, and this measure facilitated the negotiations. Thus, by the summer of 1974 Texas Eastern and its partners seemed on the verge of completing an extraordinary agreement. A final meeting was scheduled to be held in Moscow.

There was, of course, the matter of U.S. government approval, but the consortium apparently had that well in hand. Experienced and politically astute, the North Star partners had employed Herbert Brownell to arrange the Washington side of the contract. The North Star participants had already sought to create favorable opinion about the project by holding a series of educational press conferences and "by contacting senior officials of leading companies representing potential suppliers . . . in order to solicit support for the project."[30] In addition, there were public disclosures that officials of Texas Eastern, Brown & Root, and Tenneco contributed "substantial" sums of money to President Nixon's reelection campaign in order to help the deal through.[31] Just before the Americans were to leave for Moscow, they received permission from the secretary of state through Brownell to consummate the deal.[32]

The meeting in Moscow started well but ended with a stunning defeat. After the morning session there was a break for lunch, and during that time an American government representative telephoned a Soviet official and informed him that the deal was off. The U.S. government would not approve it. The American participants were shocked to hear this news from the Soviets first. Only hours away from an official and successful conclusion, they abruptly terminated the negotiations. The U.S. government never told the company why it had scuttled the project, nor did it explain its continued opposition. North Star stayed alive for four more years in various altered forms, but it never gained U.S. government approval. The obituary for this formidable project appeared in 1978 in a newspaper account of its final collapse: "Politics Derail U.S.–Soviet Deal."[33] Texas Eastern and its partners had found a potentially profitable opportunity to break into a new and significant source of gas, but Cold War diplomacy had thrown up political hurdles that North Star never quite cleared.

Paradoxically, the fate of other pipeline companies which invested heavily in LNG suggests that Texas Eastern was fortunate when it failed to get into this new business. One company in particular, El Paso Natural Gas Company, suffered severely, losing its corporate independence in part because of problems with a massive project to import Algerian LNG. That venture left El Paso heavily in debt and vulnerable to a takeover by Burlington Northern, Incorporated. As it turned out, LNG technology enabled a company to transport gas from one continent to another, but it was too costly so long as natural gas was selling for regulated prices. As gas prices rose in the late 1970s, LNG became a more cost-effective investment. Then, most major transmission companies took hard looks at LNG as a potential means of acquiring new supplies. But until deregulation LNG was too costly to be competitive, forcing Texas Eastern to look elsewhere for gas.

One appealing prospect was Alaska. Amid the mounting gas shortages of the late 1960s, industry attention had turned towards a discovery of large quantities of natural gas in that state. In 1968 Atlantic Richfield Company (Arco) "stumbled upon the biggest hydrocarbon discovery then known in North America."[34] Arco located both oil and gas at the Prudhoe Bay Field, where the estimated total gas reserves exceeded twenty-six trillion cubic feet.

These prospects stimulated intense interest among the major oil companies. Primary developers Arco, Humble Oil and Refining Company (Exxon), Standard Oil of Ohio (Sohio), and British Petroleum (BP) joined forces with several other companies to design and construct the Trans-Alaska Pipeline System (TAPS). This line stretched from Prudhoe Bay, on the northern Alaskan coast, eight hundred miles to a point on the southern Alaskan coast at Valdez, where tankers could take on the oil. After numerous delays, the consortium finished the TAPS line in 1977. Meanwhile, U.S. natural gas companies were eagerly exploring the means of exploiting the field's massive natural gas reserves.

They investigated the possibilities of transporting the gas to markets in the lower forty-eight states by using either pipelines or LNG tankers. In either case, this would be an ambitious undertaking. Arctic conditions posed challenging construction problems, as did the technology for shipping gas long distances at extremely low temperatures. The unprecedented length and cost of the proposed pipeline created complex financial and legal problems. Indeed, by one estimate, the total cost of an overland line would exceed the cumulative total investment in all interstate pipelines in the United States.[35] Yet the time seemed ripe for an Alaskan gas project by the mid-1970s. TAPS was making its way down the length of Alaska. President Nixon's call for energy independence after the Arab oil embargo of October 1973 indicated that political support would probably be forthcoming.

During the next several years three groups of companies, Canadian and American, took shape and presented competing proposals for bringing Alaskan gas to market[36] (see map 9.2). Arctic Gas, a consortium of Canadian and U.S. energy companies, submitted the first proposal to the FPC in March, 1974. Arctic was originally conceived by the Alberta Gas Trunk Line Company in May, 1970, and Texas Eastern announced its participation on December 21, 1970. By 1974 Arctic Gas included sixteen Canadian and U.S. firms. It planned to construct a twenty-five-hundred-mile, forty-eight-inch line originating at Prudhoe Bay, travelling along the coast of the Beaufort Sea into Canada, and then passing through the Mackenzie River Delta gas field in Canada. The line would pick up and deliver Canadian gas to customers and to pipeline connections in Alberta, with gas entering the United States at two places along the Idaho and Montana borders. There the gas would feed into pipelines that would move it into eastern and southwestern markets. The entire system would cost approximately $10 billion.[37]

Environmentalists quickly attacked this proposition. They criticized the fact that the proposed route crossed the Arctic National Wildlife Range and could destroy or damage part of the coastal environment along its route. Arctic Gas executives contended that the system would not endanger wildlife and that the consortium would actually clean up the existing trash along the route, particularly on the coastline.

El Paso Natural Gas Company proposed a very different system for transporting Alaskan gas. El Paso's eight-hundred-mile pipeline would not cross Canadian soil because it would follow the right-of-way of TAPS. At its terminus on Prince William Sound, El Paso would construct a liquefaction plant and transport the LNG to southern California, using a fleet of eleven tankers. Because this $7.9 billion project would finesse negotiations for a Canadian right-of-way, El Paso thought it could be completed quickly.

The Northwest Energy Company submitted the third proposal to the FPC on July, 1976. Northwest was originally a member of the Arctic Gas consortium but had decided to offer its own proposal after environmental problems stalled that group's plans. Since the FPC's environmental group had already suggested that a desirable route would be along the Alcan Highway corridor, Northwest proposed a sixteen-hundred-mile pipeline on that route. In Alaska the line would follow the TAPS right-of-way, then veer toward the southeast along the Alaskan Highway, entering the United States in Montana. Alcan's proposal was similar to that of Arctic Gas, except that it would

Map 9.2 Artic Gas Pipeline Route

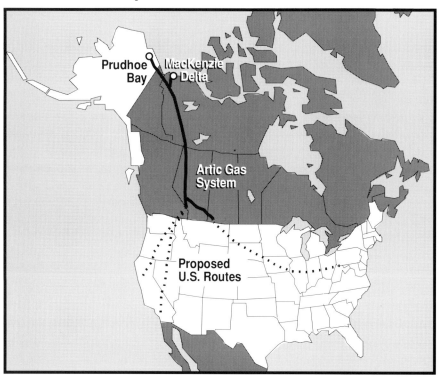

not rely upon the TAPS right-of-way and would take a more direct path towards the U.S. border. Its estimated cost was $6.7 billion, substantially lower than the competing proposals. From the regulators' point of view, one of this proposal's strengths was that its sponsors initially asked for no special considerations such as federal loan guarantees or promises of an "all-events tariff" (that is, one which would protect the owners against all unforeseen costs of construction and operation).

Public support was quickly mustered for the undertaking—whichever route was chosen. Having learned from the TAPS experience, Congress implemented a legislative timetable for the construction of Trans-Alaskan natural gas pipeline. The Alaskan Natural Gas Transportation Act (ANGTA) required the FPC to recommend one of the three systems to the president by May 1, 1977. In addition, the United States signed a treaty with Canada, the "Transit Pipeline Agreement," which would apparently ease the way for an overland pipeline crossing through that nation.

Despite all of this pressure for quick action, the FPC's initial consideration resulted in a split vote. There was support for both the Arctic Gas and the Alcan proposals. The commissioners agreed that if the Canadian MacKenzie Delta gas field was not going to be developed, there was less reason to approve the Arctic Gas plan; they would then choose Alcan. However, if gaining Canadian right-of-way proved difficult for Alcan, the FPC would provide a certificate for El Paso's plan. For Texas Eastern this was deja vu, a return to the firm's origins and the bids for the Inch Lines. Once again, the company's fate rested on a complex government bidding process that was likely to result in an all or nothing-at-all decision.

At first it appeared that TE would end up with "nothing at all." President Carter cast the deciding vote for Alcan. The consortium then reorganized and renamed itself the Alaskan Northwest Pipeline Company. In 1977 the government issued a conditional certificate of public convenience and necessity for the project, which (in accordance with the congressional act) was renamed the Alaska Natural Gas Transportation System (ANGTS). As it turned out, all was not lost for Texas Eastern. In this case — unlike the Inch Lines bid — the winner and the losers all joined hands to develop the giant system. Texas Eastern cast its lot with ANGTS, as did most of the other companies which had submitted proposals.

ANGTS needed all the support it could get, if only because of the formidable environmental, technological, and financial problems it was facing. First, the project had to solve the financial puzzle. The pipeline had to attract sufficient financing at prevailing interest rates. This was a problem because it was not obvious that the undertaking ultimately would pay for itself at the projected prices for natural gas. The stakes were very high. Miscalculations on standard cross-country pipeline construction projects could place an individual company at risk. Miscalculations on a project the scale of the Alaska system could devastate a substantial segment of the entire industry.

For the company's planners the only certainty was that the old rules no longer applied. Adequate supplies at low prices could no longer be assumed. Beyond that, there was no bedrock on which to stand. If gas prices continued to rise and if construction costs for the Alaska system did not escalate, then the project might continue to make financial sense. But the price of gas was by no means predictable. Supplemental gas would face competition from existing sources, as well as from other fuels. Conservation measures prompted by higher prices or by regulatory restrictions might reduce the demand for gas and send the Alaskan venture plunging into the red.

As planning inched forward, the companies involved nervously watched their key indicator, the price of natural gas. As shown in table 9.6, gas prices did not follow the upward course needed to make this very large investment a success. Gas prices softened, in part because of the surge in discovery that followed passage of the Natural Gas Policy Act of 1978, in part because of regulatory constraints on demand, and in part because all energy prices sagged as OPEC's hold on oil prices weakened in the 1980s. By 1982 the consortium of which Texas Eastern was a member had to put on hold its plans for the construction of ANGTS. Lower prices for gas and competing fuels had undercut this important project.

TABLE 9.6   Gas Prices before and after Deregulation

Year	Wellhead ($/Mcf)	City Gate[a] ($/MMBtu[b])	Cost to the Ultimate Consumer ($/MMBtu[b])
1965	$0.156	$0.339	$0.618
1966	0.157	0.333	0.612
1967	0.160	0.330	0.612
1968	0.164	0.328	0.607
1969	0.167	0.334	0.616
1970	0.171	0.354	0.641
1971	0.182	0.389	0.681
1972	0.186	0.429	0.730
1973	0.216	0.463	0.788
1974	0.304	0.573	0.953
1975	0.445	0.798	1.285
1976	0.580	0.984	1.599
1977	0.790	1.308	1.974
1978	0.905	1.466	2.184
1979	1.178	1.812	2.522
1980	1.588	2.414	3.134
1981	1.982	2.885	3.650
1982	2.457	3.598	4.456
1983	2.593	4.041	5.121
1984	2.655	3.890	5.128
1985	2.511	3.821	5.017
1986[R]	1.942	3.579	4.602
1987	1.710	3.339	4.315

[a]Resale prices approximate city gate prices.
[b]Mcf and MMBtu prices are roughly comparable. On a MMBtu basis, the wellhead price would be slightly less.
[R]Revised.
Source: American Gas Association, *Gas Facts, 1988*, p. 112.

Several other supplemental gas projects undertaken by Texas Eastern encountered a similar fate. Most prominent among these were the efforts to develop "synfuels," that is, gaseous or liquid fuels made from coal or other hydrocarbons. The promise of synfuels had tantalized the energy industries in the United States since at least the 1920s. Great personal and societal gain seemed to await the developer of a commercially viable process to convert the nation's vast deposits of coal and shale oil into a gas or liquid fuel. Texas Eastern had been involved in coal slurry pipelines in the 1960s, and since then its management had kept track of developments in the synfuels field. In 1968 Texas Eastern voiced an optimism common at the time that gas could be produced from coal at a cost only "a few cents per thousand cubic feet above the delivered pipeline price of natural gas in many regions of the United States."[38] Synfuels seemed to be "just around the corner." Other oil and gas companies and prominent government officials joined the effort to build this new industry. The welfare of the nation and of the individual companies and agencies involved seemed to call for an aggressive synfuels program. Texas Eastern answered the call.

Despite formidable technical, environmental, and financial barriers, synfuels became a favorite of government officials and pipeline strategists alike. Government officials embraced synfuels as an important part of a national energy policy. They desperately needed domestic energy to replace imported oil. Gas transmission executives saw synfuels as a promising avenue for developing supplemental gas supplies, an avenue which would be paved with government subsidies.

Texas Eastern launched its program by sponsoring a coal gasification research program at the Institute of Gas Technology in Chicago. As the technology for gasification improved and as gas shortages mounted, Texas Eastern became ever more enthusiastic about this particular type of synfuel. Citing President Nixon's message to Congress on June 4, 1971, which noted the seriousness of the shortage and called for "an expanded program to convert coal into a clean gaseous fuel," TE's executives began planning to construct a commercial synfuels plant. During late 1971 they helped organize a joint venture of Transwestern Coal Gasification Company (a subsidiary of Texas Eastern Transmission Corporation) and the Pacific Coal Gasification Company (a subsidiary of the California based Pacific Lighting Corporation). The new business, called Western Gasification Company (Wesco), set out to build a coal gasification plant in northwestern New Mexico.

The proposed site of the Wesco plant was approximately thirty miles southwest of Farmington, New Mexico, on land owned by the Navajo tribe. Wesco chose this site because of its proximity to Utah International Incorporated's coal reserves, which also lay in the Navajo Indian Reservation. The site was also convenient to Texas Eastern's existing pipeline system, which would need only a sixty-seven-mile extension to reach Transwestern's line. The company quickly reached a tentative agreement with Utah International to furnish the coal and water it needed. On this basis, Wesco announced its intention to build a $1.3 billion facility capable of producing 250 standard mmcf/d of synthetic gas.

When Wesco filed its application for a FPC certificate on February 7, 1973, it became the first gasification project to receive full consideration by the commission.[39] One key to the proposal was the company's request for a cost-of-service rate. If granted, this would guarantee the viability of the completed project by assuring that any unforeseen increases in the cost of completing the plant would be included in the final rate structure. Such a stipulation would calm the fears of investors, who would probably not support this risky innovation without some sort of guaranteed return. The FPC granted Wesco a certificate of public convenience and necessity in 1975 but did not authorize a full cost-of-service tariff. Instead, the FPC mandated an initial price of $1.38 per mcf. This decision significantly increased the risk and made investment in the new technology much less attractive.

Texas Eastern also hit a snag in its negotiations for coal. Since the reserves were located on Navajo land, the company had to deal with both the Indian nation and Utah International. Unfortunately, the Navajo government and the coal company could not agree. A TE planner involved with synfuels projects recalled that "from what I saw, the Navajos were not totally unreasonable; they just wanted a fair royalty for their coal, and our guys [Utah International] basically had some ideas and they weren't going to budge off of them."[40] Unable to get the two parties to settle their differences and unwilling to live with the FPC ruling, Texas Eastern dropped its first venture into synfuels.

The regulatory treatment of costs continued to be a central issue in the growing national debate on synfuels and on energy policy as a whole. Should the government promote domestic energy production? To what extent should the financial risks in developing new synfuels technologies be assumed by the government? Texas Eastern and the other interstate transmission companies had grown up with price regulation and were comfortable with the idea of using that system to reduce the risks of innovation. But for the FPC this was a question that went far beyond the rate-of-return regulation to which it was accustomed.

Texas Eastern's executives and their counterparts in other companies argued for government subsidies. From their perspective, synfuels were more than a means of providing gas to private companies facing shortages. They represented an important step toward long-term energy independence for the United States, a nation with abundant coal reserves. In their view, government support for synfuels would encourage the efficient efforts of private companies to develop innovations in an area vital to the nation's energy security. The large sums of private money needed to fund commercial synfuels projects would not be forthcoming without government backing. Thus, while engineers sought to improve the manufacturing processes needed to produce synfuels, lobbyists in Washington sought to build a consensus for government subsidies ranging from loan guarantees to cost-of-source rates for the synfuels. The political debates ultimately shaped this effort as much as did technical considerations.

During the Carter administration, national support for federal funding for synfuels was forthcoming. Spurred forward by a second energy crisis spawned by the Iranian Revolution in 1979–80, Congress funded the Synthetic Fuels Corporation (originally named the Energy Security Corporation) to subsidize commercial synfuels projects. The corporation (SFC) was a controversial agency perceived as a "message to OPEC" by supporters and "just another boondoggle" by critics.[41] With a potential long-term budget of up to $88 billion, the SFC promised massive levels of financial assistance to both ongoing and new synfuels projects. During July of 1980 the U.S. Department of Energy (DOE), through its synthetic fuels commercialization program, distributed $200 million, and Congress anticipated making available more than $5 billion during the next several years.

As the rush to subsidized synfuels got underway, the government made a large award of $22.4 million to the Tri-State Synfuels Company (Tri-State), a joint venture between Texas Eastern and Texas Gas Transmission Corporation. This grant was for the first phase in the construction of a coal liquefaction and gasification facility to be located in Geneva (Henderson County), Kentucky. The Tri-State partnership would contribute $20 million to the total first-phase cost of $44.1 million. If, after the first phase, Tri-State decided to go forward with the $4 billion plant, the DOE would continue to support the project. Once completed, the plant was expected to produce the equivalent of fifty-six thousand barrels of oil per day, with 44 percent of the output being synthetic gas and the remainder consisting of transportation fuel and chemicals.[42]

Texas Eastern had learned many lessons from the abortive Wesco project, and it applied some of that knowledge to Tri-State. First, Texas Eastern chose Texas Gas Transmission Corporation, headquartered in Owensboro, Kentucky, as its partner. The close historical relationship between the two companies facilitated their cooperation. In addition, Texas Gas owned West Virginia coal reserves which it dedicated to Tri-State. Kentucky was a major coal-producing state, and by pledging to use high-sulfur coal in its plant, Tri-State attracted political support from state officials, including Governor John Brown. Since the state had its own department of energy, Tri-State worked closely with that agency to determine the best plant site and to resolve other potentially troublesome issues.

Texas Eastern designed the plant to utilize a unique technology borrowed from South Africa, which had perhaps the world's most developed synfuels system. With few energy resources of its own, South Africa had been producing synfuels since the mid-1950s. The South African Coal, Oil and Gas Corporation (SASOL) built its first synfuels plant in 1955, using technology initially developed in Germany during World War II. This plant utilized steam and oxygen placed under extremely high pressure to convert coal to carbon monoxide, carbon dioxide, hydrogen, and methane. Some of the gas was then liquefied to produce a synthetic oil similar to natural crude. After the 1973 Arab oil embargo, SASOL intensified its synfuels program, stepping it up again when Iran's Ayatollah Khomeini stopped selling oil to South Africa after the Iranian Revolution. South Africa's highly advanced synfuels program attracted interest throughout the world, and SASOL began exporting its technology to U.S. companies, including Texas Eastern.[43]

It was not evident at first that the SASOL process would work on the high-sulfur coal which Tri-State intended to use. The state government agreed to pay for a test to ensure that the coal could be used, so Tri-State shipped twenty thousand tons of high-sulfur coal to South Africa. The results were favorable. Despite its high sulfur content, Kentucky coal could be processed.

Shortly, however, the Tri-State project began to encounter other technical difficulties. While SASOL technology allowed coal to be broken down into both gas and liquids, the process required substantial amounts of energy. It was not clear that the undertaking was energy-efficient so long as alternative fuels were available. This was especially true after the price of both gas and fuel oil began to fall in the 1980s. Without a high price for its end products, the Tri-State project simply could not be justified economically. As one company executive concluded, "There [were] so many more efficient global solutions that synfuels didn't make sense."[44]

Neither the economic nor the political environment in the 1980s favored the synfuel projects, most of which went under. All of these efforts had to have high prices for their products if they were to be commercially viable. When energy prices collapsed in the early 1980s, so did the prospects for synfuels. Changes in the political environment further undermined the nation's resolve to produce synfuels. President Ronald Reagan brought to Washington, D.C., a determination to remove the federal government from activities which he felt should be performed by private industry or state governments. With the so-called "gas bubble" of the early 1980s dampening fears of shortages, the Reagan administration slashed synfuel subsidies. Most private support then quickly evaporated. In a breathtaking turn of events, synfuels – which had been heralded as the key to the nation's domestic energy policy in 1980 – had all but vanished from the nation's energy mix by 1984.[45]

In April, 1982, after the expenditure of $20 million, Tri-State placed its synfuels project on indefinite hold. Paul Anderson, then head of synfuels development for Texas Eastern, noted that investors were no longer interested in synfuels because of the risks involved and the poor outlook for profits. Tony Roeger, manager of technical services for Texas Eastern, echoed Anderson: "The technology is available today. Unfortunately, the world economy is not such that we can afford to do it."[46] Only a renewed oil and gas shortage and much higher energy prices could spur another round of investment.

Texas Eastern's Wesco project was also put to rest. Wesco had received a $3 million grant from the DOE's initial distribution of funds for research. But a study of the resulting project reached the gloomy conclusion that the "economics of the plant during its operating life are anticipated to be poor. . . ."[47] While technically feasible, that form of synfuel production was economically inefficient. Along with it went down practically every synfuel plant in the nation.

Texas Eastern nevertheless remained active in research and development on supplemental fuels. In July, 1982, the firm acquired a scientific research and design company, the Halcon SD Group, which specialized in energy-related work. Subsequently, Halcon won a contract to model the Great Plains

MAP 9.3 Coal Slurry Pipeline: Arkansas and Texas Routes

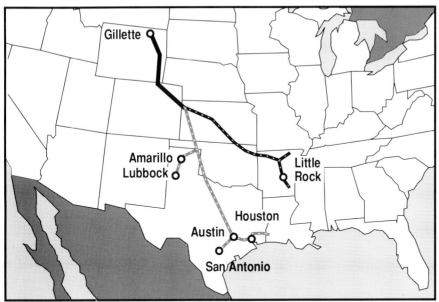

coal gasification plant in Beulah, North Dakota, one of the few coal gasification plants actually built and put into operation. The model was used to study the specific gasification processes to be used in the plant. Halcon also won a $250,000 contract for a technical and economic feasibility study of a project for NASA to produce rocket fuel through coal gasification.

Although national interest in producing gas from coal was waning, the company continued to pursue this research and began to look again at the prospects of transporting coal through a slurry pipeline (see map 9.3). This would require the construction of a new pipeline system that would differ significantly from the company's existing gas lines. In 1979 TE tried to float a proposal to transport slurry from Wyoming to Texas. Two of the project's toughest problems were obtaining access to water and acquiring rights-of-way. The uses of scarce western waters remained a sensitive issue, and in May of 1979 the governor of Wyoming stopped TE in its tracks by rejecting the company's request to purchase, from the Little Bighorn River, the water needed to transport up to twenty-five million tons of coal annually.

Rather than give up on the plan, Texas Eastern joined another more firmly established venture, the Energy Transportation Systems, Incorporated (ETSI). This four-billion-dollar joint venture originally had four partners, Bechtel Corporation, InterNorth, Incorporated, Kansas-Nebraska Natural Gas Company, and United Energy Resources Corporation. Texas Eastern purchased United Energy Resources's interest in 1980. The original ETSI plan called for the construction of a fourteen-hundred-mile, forty-inch coal slurry pipeline extending from Gillette, Wyoming, to points in eastern Arkansas.

Since Wyoming rejected ETSI's proposal to purchase water, the firm had turned to South Dakota, which signed an agreement for use of water from that state. In return, ETSI agreed to transport large volumes of water annually to communities and rural water systems along the pipeline route.

But soon ETSI ran into the same sort of obstacles that had blocked Texas Eastern's venture in the early 1960s. Railroad company opposition, right-of-way restrictions, and problems in acquiring water and potential customers plagued nearly all of the coal slurry proposals. The project promoters countered by emphasizing that the new technology would weaken the railroads' hold on coal transportation. The new lines would create thousands of new jobs, they contended, and would deliver coal at cheaper rates.

The railroads fought back on all of these issues. The roads had led the way in blocking the attempts to pass a federal law granting coal slurry pipelines powers of eminent domain, powers enjoyed by the railroads and oil and gas pipelines. The most publicized attempt was the Coal Pipeline Bill of 1977, which was put forward by the Carter administration. When that measure failed to pass, the pipelines sought eminent domain legislation within the states through which the line would pass. There the companies achieved some success. In 1977 Oklahoma, Texas, and Louisiana passed such legislation, joining the seven other states that had these statutes.

Backers of the ETSI venture discovered an effective method for dealing with the opposition of the railroads. ETSI was expected to cross as many as seventy different tracks belonging to ten different railroads, nine of which refused to grant permission to the pipeline. After intensive research into the original right-of-way grants to those specific railroads, ETSI discovered that while many of the railroads had easement rights, they often did not have subsurface rights, which typically still belonged to the original land owners. ETSI simply bought the subsurface crossing rights from the original land owners, thereby avoiding the necessity of negotiating with the railroads. There were sixty-five suits contesting these issues, and ETSI won every case.

Still, that left the pipeline without certain important rights-of-way.[48] Fortunately, Congress took up the eminent domain issue again in 1983, and Texas Eastern and the other ETSI partners strongly supported a bill which would allow them to acquire the remaining rights-of-way necessary to build their line. This bill (the Coal Distribution and Utilization Act) was introduced by Senator Bennett Johnston (D–Louisiana), while Morris Udall (D–Arizona) sponsored similar legislation in the House. Despite an intensive lobbying campaign for the measure, the House rejected this legislation. Once again, the railroad interests were able to use their political clout to defeat an attempt to introduce a new technology in coal transportation.

The defeat was not a death blow to ETSI, but the railroads' continued opposition finally wore down the project's supporters. ETSI's original plans called for sales to Arkansas Power and Light Company, but a group of railroads undercut ETSI's proposed sales price and left the pipeline without its primary customer. ETSI then proposed a new route quite similar to the one earlier put forward by Texas Eastern. The pipeline would now terminate in the Houston area, where Houston Lighting and Power, the biggest coal consumer in the Southwest, would buy its slurry. But there, too, the railroads could undermine the proposed pipeline by cutting prices. Tiring of the long ordeal, Bechtel withdrew. Texas Eastern finally gave up on August 1, 1984.

When ETSI announced the termination of its project, its partners fired a parting shot in the form of a lawsuit alleging that certain railroads that blocked ETSI's pipeline proposal were in restraint of trade. In early 1989 a jury in Beaumont, Texas, agreed with ETSI, awarding a $1 billion judgment against the roads. This award soothed the frustration and replenished the balance sheets of the ETSI partners, but it did not change the fact that after almost three decades of controversy, coal slurry pipelines were little used in a nation still searching for cost effective ways to use coal, its primary domestic energy source.

All of the supplemental gas projects of the 1970s met a similar fate. Their high expectations were undercut by changing economic conditions in the energy industry. Much effort had been expended but little fuel produced. These projects all required massive investments and employed new and unproven technologies. They badly needed government subsidies, which were often promised but never sustained at a level sufficient to assure the development of commercial production in competition with traditional fuels. All were extremely vulnerable to the bust that took place in gas prices after the early 1970s. By the late 1980s these various projects were historical relics of an era that had passed. Although Texas Eastern had invested substantial energy and money in these ventures, it emerged from the debris with no life-threatening wounds. It also emerged with a growing sense of the difficulties inherent in an industry in flux. In light of economic and political constraints in the gas transmission business, Texas Eastern's leaders redoubled their efforts to find new opportunities outside of natural gas.

Chapter 10

OIL-DRIVEN DIVERSIFICATION

In the 1970s and early 1980s an extraordinary surge of profits from North Sea oil fed a new wave of diversification at Texas Eastern. Increased revenues gave the company the resources to move aggressively to expand its existing ventures or to explore new ones. Oil-related investments were especially attractive. Texas Eastern's growing oil reserves combined with the rising price of oil in these years to make petroleum as important as gas within the company. Diversification into oil-related activities was a logical strategy, one that continued to shape the company's evolution until the sharp decline in oil prices in the mid-1980s.

As Texas Eastern continued to diversify, its management redefined the corporate mission in an effort to preserve a sense of unity among its various businesses. The phrase adopted to describe Texas Eastern in the 1970s was "an international diversified energy company." This description could have applied to any of several hundred oil and gas companies, and it did not provide the clarity of purpose that had existed when TE had characterized itself as "a major gas transmission company" or later when it referred to itself as a "pipeliner of energy." When pressed, the company's executives stressed the "common denominator of energy" to explain how the various parts of the company fitted together. This common denominator applied, at least indirectly, even to the company's Houston real estate venture, since property values and the leasing of office space in the city were dependent on conditions in the oil and gas industries.

Those conditions were especially favorable to investments in oil in the 1970s and early 1980s. The industry was experiencing sharp increases in prices in the 1970s. Almost all of the projections indicated higher and higher oil prices for decades to come (see chart 10.1). Seen in the historical context in which it moved forward, oil-led diversification seems natural, almost inevitable. Planners at Texas Eastern joined their counterparts in most oil-related companies in pursuing strategies based on the assumption of steadily rising prices for oil. This assumption proved true through the mid-1980s, and Texas Eastern enjoyed an era of heady expansion.

In the North Sea the company's spectacular success encouraged manage-

CHART 10.1 U.S. Oil Prices, 1930–1985
($/42 gallon barrel)

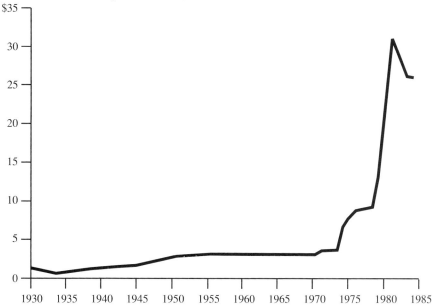

Source: Adapted from Walter L. Buenger and Joseph A. Pratt, *But Also Good Business* (College Station, Texas A&M University Press, 1986), p. 308.

ment to follow this course. TE had entered this area in the 1960s, originally to exploit its expertise in transporting natural gas. The company remained an important producer and pipeliner of North Sea gas. But in the late 1960s the firm also entered joint ventures aimed at developing North Sea oil. The company acquired promising leases, and its investments in acquiring, exploring, and developing these leases proved quite profitable.

Texas Eastern made its first crude oil discovery in 1969 off Scottish waters in a joint venture with Amoco and the British Gas Council. Earlier that same year Phillips Petroleum had announced the discovery of the first major oil field in the North Sea, the giant Ekofisk Field on Norway's continental shelf. Since the early spring of 1969 the Gas Council–Amoco–Texas Eastern group had been drilling on block 22/18, close to the border with the Norwegian sector, and 180 miles east of Aberdeen, Scotland. Using the rig "Orion," they remained on the block through much of the remainder of the year while issuing no status reports. In December they moved the rig to a new location after the expenditure of over £2 million. Some competitors then speculated that the group had made a major find, but in fact they abandoned the site because it did not meet their expectations.[1] Still, the North Sea oil discoveries in 1969 and 1970 were impressive enough to stimulate increased drilling that resulted in new discoveries of oil and natural gas.

During the early 1970s the consortium of which Texas Eastern was a member brought in wells that more than met their expectations. They discovered oil in both the Norwegian and United Kingdom sectors of the North Sea. In 1970 the company discovered oil in Norwegian waters at Torfelt No. 1 near the large Ekofisk oil field. In 1971, after Texas Eastern completed a confirmation well at Torfelt No. 2, it began producing more than 3,900 barrels of crude per day, of which the firm owned 28.33 percent. In 1971 in the U.K. sector 135 miles east of Aberdeen, Scotland, they also brought in a well that tested 4,000 barrels per day of high quality crude oil and 2 mmcf/d of natural gas. This well lay only six miles north of Texas Eastern's first North Sea oil discovery.

The pace of North Sea development quickened in the early 1970s, as the energy crisis pushed up oil prices, hastening further exploration and drilling. The North Sea was particularly attractive to major oil companies because it was one of the most promising oil frontiers not controlled by OPEC.[2] The harsh weather conditions in the North Sea had initially slowed development, but higher oil prices provided a powerful incentive for companies to risk millions of dollars searching for oil beneath as much as four hundred feet of water in cold, windy conditions.

Texas Eastern participated in the development of oil and gas in seven major North Sea fields in both the British and Norwegian sectors: the Indefatigable, Leman Bank, Torfelt, S. E. Torfelt, Montrose, and the Beryl Fields (see table 10.2). Through the 1970s Texas Eastern generally remained primarily an investor in joint ventures with large oil companies, but these investments nonetheless began to have a profound impact on the company.

In 1972 Texas Eastern owned 20 percent of the lease on which the Beryl Field was discovered. This giant field became the source of a significant portion of the company's North Sea profits. According to results from the confirmation well, the Beryl Field was initially expected to produce more than one hundred thousand barrels per day of good quality crude. Oil production began in July, 1976, and in November Texas Eastern shipped its first tanker load of crude, 440,000 barrels. This operation was unique because the field's developers used the world's first "Condeep" drilling, production, and storage platform, known as Beryl "A." Condeep, which was constructed at Stavanger, Norway, was a massive platform composed largely of concrete supporting "cells." After partial construction of the supporting concrete cells, the structure was towed out to sea and anchored. Then the remaining work on the cells and the drilling platform itself were completed on site. The Beryl Field's development included a system to load crude oil to tankers from Condeep's storage cells on the ocean floor via a single-point mooring system.[3]

In the Norwegian sector the Statfjord Field developed into the single largest discovery in the North Sea. Texas Eastern's interest in this massive field was only 1.04 percent, but even this small holding yielded substantial returns. The company also had a 7.44 interest in the Tor Field, which was expected to produce seventy-five thousand barrels of oil per day and 120 mmcf/d

TABLE 10.2   Texas Eastern Interest in North Sea Fields, 1987

Field/Facility	Percent of Company Working Interest	Commencement of Production Oil	Gas
UK			
Beryl A Platform	20.00	1976	—
B Platform	20.00	1984	—
Ness	20.00	1987	—
Montrose	15.38	1976	1985
North West Hutton	10.38	1983	1983
Indefatigable	9.11	—	1971
Leman	7.29	—	1969
Hutton	3.48	1984	—
Fulmar	0.63	1982	1986
Norway			
Valhall	28.09	1982	1983
Tor	7.44	1978	1978
Statfjord A Platform	0.88	1979	1985
B Platform	0.88	1982	1985
C Platform	0.88	1985	1985
Murchison	0.23	1980	1983
Netherlands			
P/6	3.75	—	1983

Source: Texas Eastern, *Twenty-five Years in the North Sea* (company publication, 1987).

of natural gas. Production from this field was transported eight miles through a twelve-inch oil pipeline and a fourteen-inch natural gas pipeline to Phillips's Ekofisk Center.

Texas Eastern marketed its natural gas production under long-term sales contracts for use in the United Kingdom and Northern Europe. By 1983 the company held an interest in the U.K. Indefatigable and Leman Fields; the Tor, Murchison, and Valhall in the Norwegian sector; and the P/6 in the Netherlands sector. The gas from these finds were transported by subsea pipelines to onshore pipeline systems at Fergus, Scotland, Bacton, England, Emden, Germany, and Uithuizen, Holland.

Texas Eastern sold and exchanged its crude oil production through Texas Eastern North Sea, Incorporated, its London-based marketing subsidiary, and Stavanger-based Texas Eastern Norwegian, Incorporated. Production from the Beryl, Montrose, Fulmar, and Statfjord fields, which were not connected to major pipelines, was loaded offshore into tankers. Some of its North Sea crude production was exchanged for crude deliveries to its La Gloria Oil and Gas Company refinery (rated at forty-six thousand barrels per day). The refinery, which produced no-lead premium, premium no-lead, and commercial aviation jet fuel, was directly connected to Texas Eastern's Little Big Inch products pipeline, which transported the refined oil to markets in the Midwest and Northeast. Success in the North Sea allowed Texas Eastern to integrate its products pipeline, refinery, and North Sea output into a single

Mobil Oil's Beryl "A" North Sea Platform

petroleum operation, one much more profitable than the company's previous domestic operations in oil.

Profits from the North Sea grew steadily and became a spectacular source of revenues for the company as a whole (see table 10.3). In 1979 the petroleum group's operating income rose above that of domestic natural gas operations for the first time in the company's history: Operating profits increased from $58 million in 1977 to $170 million in 1979, a 200 percent increase in two years. Foreign oil and gas production operating profits peaked in 1980, when they almost doubled to $318 million.

224

Valhall Platform, Norwegian Sector of the North Sea

Such figures posed several important questions for the company's strategists. Ironically, one recurring question was "Can TE afford this sort of success?" Hostile takeovers had become a new way of life in the oil and gas industry, and the company's executives knew that the retention of valuable oil-producing properties would make their firm vulnerable to a takeover. Companies as large as the Gulf Oil Corporation ultimately fell victim to the merger-and-acquisitions mania of the 1980s, in part because their stock prices did not reflect the value of their oil reserves. Texas Eastern was aware of the danger that a "predator" might use the proceeds of the sale of the firm's North

225

TABLE 10.3   Texas Eastern Corporation: Oil and Gas Exploration
and Production Revenues (in thousands)

Year	Amount
1969	$ 3,040
1970	6,865
1971	10,955
1972	15,459
1973	15,023
1974	20,066
1975	19,324
1976	48,214
1977	125,965
1978	113,087
1979	258,079
1980	402,313
1981	330,907
1982	340,784
1983	269,935
1984	328,937
1985	530,121
1986	333,486
1987	402,163
1988	329,140

Source: Texas Eastern Financial and Statistical Summary, 1979 and 1988.

Sea reserves to finance the acquisition of the remainder of the company.

Instead of protecting against such an eventuality by divesting its lucrative North Sea holdings, Texas Eastern decided to use the revenues from oil production to build a stronger, more diversified company. Both CEO's who headed the company between 1973 and 1984 embraced the general strategy of oil-led diversification. George Kirby (1973–80) emphasized international oil production while aggressively seeking opportunities to enter the chemical industry. Some of the firm's longtime gas men felt that in the process Kirby slighted natural gas transmission. Not so with his successor, I. David Bufkin (1980–84), an experienced gas man who had grown up with Texas Eastern as a rate specialist. But even as Bufkin reassured his colleagues in gas transmission, he continued the search for other profitable ventures. He had observed first-hand the excitement of the North Sea success. Soon after becoming president he told an interviewer that "one of our principal interests is to continue to manage and balance those businesses [natural gas and oil] so that no one becomes dominant over the rest." He acknowledged that "our exploration and production activity has been somewhat dominant in the last couple of years. It continues to grow, and we expect it to have a big influence on earnings in the near term."[4] As long as oil prices remained high and the North Sea remained productive, TE's management had a pleasant dilemma: how could they best use this bonanza to build a stronger company?

One area which required attention was Texas Eastern's real estate venture

I. David Bufkin

in downtown Houston. The original design for the much ballyhooed "city of the future" did not get off the drawing board. Instead, Houston Center was shaved down from a grandiose tiered city-within-a-city to a cluster of high-quality developments connected primarily by skywalks. Now it began

227

to look as if the original plan had in part been a dramatic public relations effort to focus attention on the city's largely undeveloped east side. After it had accomplished this purpose, the visionary master plan was scaled down to fit the practical realities of a competitive market for office space. Although this kind of adaptation is a normal part of real estate development, in the case of Houston Center the original plan had been so ambitious and so highly publicized that it came back to haunt the company. No matter what the actual accomplishments in Houston Center, TE's efforts almost inevitably were judged a failure when compared to the original extravagant vision of a city of the future.

In the first flush of publicity, however, neither the proponents nor the critics had given much ink to the critical question from the developer's point of view: could the project be completed at a cost that would make it competitive with other developments in the city? If land acquisition was the tricky part and planning was the fun part, constructing and leasing the buildings in Houston Center was to become the hard part. There were indeed serious problems of cost. Who was to pay for the five-story covered parking garage–shopping mall, underneath the major buildings, and the ambitious people movers, and the pedestrian plazas? How many potential tenants would pay for such "accessories" when excellent office space was being built throughout the city at a lower cost per square foot? Texas Eastern had to learn how to market its properties — and quickly — if it was to make the project a long-term success.

As the company set out to accomplish this task, it soon encountered problems resulting from the overbuilding of prime office space in and around the city. Texas Eastern was not alone in planning ambitious developments to take advantage of the late 1960s boom in Houston. The city was alive with expansion plans. The new construction included individual office buildings as well as several multistructure projects. Dallas-based Trammell Crow and the Metropolitan Life Insurance Company launched Allen Center, a projected $1 billion, twenty-one-acre development with five large interconnected office buildings on the east side of Main Street. Shell Oil announced Plaza del Oro, another billion-dollar development south of downtown near the Astrodome. At the same time, large-scale multi-use projects outside the central business district went forward under the leadership of Gerald Hines Interests and Kenneth Schnitzer's Century Development Corporation. Houston was booming. But the massive construction of this era crowded the real estate market, fostering intense competition.[5]

Immediately after the initial publicity blitz for Houston Center, Texas Eastern was surprised to discover that "nothing happened."[6] It soon became apparent that the firm would have to march vigorously ahead without any firm commitments from major tenants. Such commitments were traditionally used to help obtain external financing, but Texas Eastern was forced back on its internal resources for construction expenses. Since its own real estate market survey suggested that in twelve to eighteen months there would be a demand for one million feet of downtown office space, the company decided to forge ahead, using its credit to finance the construction of the first Houston Center building. It is in this incremental way that "master plans" are normally transformed as they are implemented, but in this case the gap between the plan and reality was dangerously large.[7]

Amid much fanfare, the official ground-breaking of Two Houston Center (which despite its name was the first major building in the complex) took place in January of 1972. This forty-story building went up on a block of land purchased nearly ten years before, largely from the University of Texas. Before the building was completed in 1974, IBM signed a lease for a part of the office space. Later, after prolonged and difficult negotiations with Gulf Oil, that company moved its corporate engineering headquarters into Two Houston Center. Other early tenants included Ethyl Corporation, Cooper Industries, and Mitsubishi International. These major companies had numerous choices as they searched for new office space in the early 1970s. They forced Houston Center to establish competitive leasing rates — future city or not.

The difficulties in leasing space in Two Houston Center set off a warning light for some within the company. TE might have to adjust the master plan, they decided, to the harsh realities of a competitive marketplace. As the company set about the work of planning and building its next major structure, One Houston Center, a second warning signal went off. Initially, it was easy to ignore even this second warning. It would, in fact, be some years before it would be obvious that the energy crisis of the winter of 1973 and 1974 marked a clear turning point in the history of Houston. Ultimately, however, the fluctuations in oil prices that would ensue would affect all phases of life in the city. First came a boom and then a bust in the early 1980s. Real estate proved to be particularly vulnerable to this cycle, since its health mirrored that of the region's major industry. Grand plans based on the sustained expansion of the postwar era then collapsed along with the Gulf Coast's oil economy.

Complicating this situation for Texas Eastern was a change of leadership with the firm. The fall from power of Baxter Goodrich made the venture's future tenuous. Goodrich's retirement in 1974 removed the last of the long-time Brown faithfuls from the ranks of the company's top leaders. Goodrich embodied the traditional way of doing business at Texas Eastern. His engineering background, unquestioned loyalty to George Brown, and unswerving commitment to the business values of TE's formative years made him a source of unity in a company increasingly pulled in different directions. On the question of Houston Center, Goodrich had no doubts. Houston would grow to absorb this bold proposal; the market ultimately would accept the Center on a scale approximating that put forward in Pereira's master plan.

The top managers who followed Goodrich were less certain of the project's future. Although the board of directors remained confident that Houston Center ultimately would pay off, executives facing mounting short-term financial pressures from other parts of TE's diversified operations were often frustrated by the high debt required by real estate development. Texas Eastern was an industrial company with very high capital needs, and as such it was quite sensitive to the opinions of investment specialists and their clients. Long-term debt from Houston Center weakened the company's financial profile in the shortterm, and executives after Goodrich hesitated to commit the resources needed to build the original complex of buildings in an uncertain and highly competitive market for office space.

Despite the growing doubts about the original plan, the company cautiously pushed ahead. In announcing the completion of Two Houston Center, the company proclaimed, "the end that is a beginning."[8] In an ironic sense, this publicity proved correct. The realities of the market place were steadily pushing management toward a reevaluation of the entire master plan. First to go was the platform city concept, a victim of the declining markets for oil and office space. Planners within the company had to accept the fact that TE had allowed its pride to override its good judgment in designing the center. The original plan was no longer economically feasible and without fanfare, it was substantially altered.

Meanwhile, the company's real estate specialists inched ahead, planning, constructing, and leasing one project at a time. As each building went forward, TE sought to retain the primary principles of the initial plan while adapting to the new market conditions. The complex of buildings that gradually emerged on Houston's east side in the 1970s and 1980s retained the original commitment to street-spanning structures of high quality in a mixed-use development. But the futuristic and prohibitively expensive air-conditioned tiers gave way to a simpler approach using above-ground "skywalks" constructed over streets. The elaborate "people movers" of Pereira's drawings gave way to a reliance on more traditional forms of transportation — trolleys, buses, and escalators. All in all, an architect's vision of a twenty-first-century city gave way to a more practical mixed-use development seeking to pay its own way in the late twentieth century.

The second major office building, One Houston Center, was completed in 1976. This forty-six story building had a skywalk connection to Two Houston Center. TE initially hoped to attract a major tenant to this skyscraper and then to build a third for its own headquarters. But the company's managers also wanted to avoid carrying the debt on One Houston Center while waiting for such a tenant to materialize. Instead, a decision was made to take a safer, more predictable path by moving Texas Eastern's own headquarters into the new building.

Soon after making this decision in 1978, Texas Eastern took another conservative step by selling two prime blocks of the original Houston Center

Two Houston Center (left) and One Houston Center under construction

parcel. First City Bancorp purchased this property, which was nearer Main Street than any of TE's as yet undeveloped blocks. Texas Eastern and First City had strong historical ties cemented by the personal friendship of George Brown and First City's longtime chairman, Judge James A. Elkins. TE's leaders felt strongly that First City should be persuaded to construct its new office building and related facilities on the east side of Houston; the loss of a major project by a company closely allied with Texas Eastern seemed likely to

231

stop the momentum building up behind Houston Center. TE's planners decided to sell part of the Center's land to assure that this major bank building went up on the east side of Main Street.

By the end of the 1970s the company had completed two office buildings and a parking garage, representing an investment of about $120 million. Although this total represented a dramatic departure from past investment patterns on Houston's east side, it was a far cry from the massive project announced at the beginning of the decade. At this point, TE's management decided not to expand its involvement in real estate. Some within the Houston Center project argued, of course, that the company should spend additional funds to develop more expertise, becoming competitive in real estate throughout Houston. This sort of logic had earlier led Texas Eastern to purchase Pyrofax and enter the LPG business as a way of bolstering its Little Big Inch petroleum products pipeline. But this time top management was not persuaded. Instead, they gave a curt reply: "Our plate is already full."

Instead of pushing forward alone, in 1979 Texas Eastern brought in a specialist, Cadillac Fairview, to buy into the project and take the lead in managing it. This Toronto-based concern had been founded in 1959 to acquire shopping centers, and it had subsequently grown through internal expansion and merger into one of the largest publicly owned real estate development companies in North America. Through its Cadillac Fairview Urban subsidiary, with headquarters in Dallas, the company was involved in multiple-block mixed-use projects in Dallas, Fort Worth, New York City, Washington, D.C., and Atlanta.[9]

In its eagerness to bring an able new partner on board, Texas Eastern gave Cadillac Fairview an attractive deal. For a 50 percent stake in Houston Center, the new partner paid "current market value for developed properties and book value plus interest costs and taxes on the rest." If the project moved forward, Cadillac Fairview stood to profit handsomely.

For its first major joint project, the new partnership announced that it would join with Four Seasons Hotels, Limited, to build a Four Seasons Hotel on the Center's property. In this instance, the developer's established relationship with the hotel firm helped bring a well-known luxury hotel to the property. The new partnership soon began to build a twenty-nine-story luxury hotel with 428 rooms, 140 corporate suites, restaurants, and shops — a building which certainly added a sense of excitement to the east side. To keep the momentum going, the partners shortly announced plans for Three Houston Center, a new fifty-two-story office building adjacent to One Houston Center. This new building ultimately was sold to its lead tenant, Gulf Oil Corporation, and it breathed new life into the Houston Center project.

In early 1981 Texas Eastern and Cadillac Fairview announced their most dramatic addition. They proposed to construct The Park, a major retail shopping project. A two-block, 987,000-square-foot project, The Park was similar to a suburban mall but was located in the downtown business district where there had been no retail construction since the late 1950s. Some observers expressed doubts about the prospects for a large shopping mall in a downtown area, which was virtually deserted after regular business hours. The Park would be competing with numerous huge shopping centers in suburban areas of the city, but TE and its new partner thought they could reverse the drift outward to the suburbs.[10]

The Four Seasons Hotel, the new office building, the shopping mall, and, later, an athletic club pumped new life into the Houston Center project. The new partners in construction then boldly targeted a mammoth convention center for the eastern edge of the property. The partnership's interest in locating a convention center on its property stemmed from the late 1970s. During 1979 Houston Mayor Jim McConn had appointed a Civic Center Improvement Committee to study Houston's need for a new convention center. Subsequently, the committee hired consultants to analyze both the overall need for a center and the feasibility of six different sites, including one on Houston Center property. The consulting firm also considered the viability of expanding existing convention facilities before recommending a site in the central business district. After several consultants and the Civic Center Improvement Committee reaffirmed the desirability of a central business district site on the east side of downtown, the Houston City Council voted in favor of that proposition.[11]

Texas Eastern and Cadillac Fairview realized the significance of having the Convention Center built on their property, and they offered to donate 264,000 square feet of land adjacent to a major freeway. By this time, only one other location remained as a competitor, a west side site which would use city-owned land. Texas Eastern pointed to its new hotel and shopping center as evidence of the vitality of the east side. The company also noted that the city would not have to use land vital to its own expansion if it opted for Houston Center. These arguments were compelling, and the city government was interested. But the selection process was slow, and a decision had still not been reached when events suddenly took a new twist in early 1983.

On January 22, 1983, George Brown died at the age of eighty-four. Although he had resigned as chairman of the board of Texas Eastern in 1971, Brown had continued to serve as chairman of the company's executive committee. He was still very much involved with Houston Center, and following his death, the Houston City Council decided to name the new convention center in his honor. It was unlikely that the George R. Brown Convention Center would be built elsewhere than on TE's development, and as Dennis Greer, Houston Center president, observed: "Mr. Brown was noted as a leader in efforts to build Houston into one of the foremost business, cultural and educational centers in the county. The Brown Convention Center and the new downtown development it will generate are prime examples of Mr. Brown's legacy to Houston's future."[12]

Still, the matter was not entirely settled. Those favoring other sites con-

George R. Brown Convention Center

tinued to lobby against the Houston Center location. They created enough controversy to compel the city to add a proposition to the city elections (November, 1983) for or against the construction of a convention center and the use of certain hotel occupancy tax funds for the project. In a determined civic effort that would have made George Brown proud, Texas Eastern's executives spearheaded a wide-ranging campaign to build electoral support for the convention center and for their location. The company's employees volunteered time to a phone bank from which calls were made to citizens urging them to vote in favor of the center. When the votes were counted, the convention center proposal had been approved.[13]

The new facility would become a visible reminder of George Brown's influence on the city and many of its institutions. When it was finally completed, the futuristic building would in some respects be even more fanciful than the original Houston Center plan. Its exterior was red, white, and blue, and the thirty-five-thousand-person-capacity center included a hundred-thousand-square-foot exhibit hall and forty-three meeting rooms. Valuable to the city, the George R. Brown Convention Center was as well a sturdy anchor for the eastern boundary of Houston Center.

234

Despite the convention center, The Park, and the Four Seasons Hotel, Houston Center as a whole did not become highly profitable. As oil prices slid downward and the Gulf Coast economy collapsed, Houston real estate by the mid-1980s was badly depressed, with a significant glut of office space. Depression undermined the partnership between Texas Eastern and Cadillac Fairview. The two organizations had never really fit tightly together; their histories and cultures made a successful joint venture unlikely. Texas Eastern was one of numerous big oil and gas companies that had a less than ideal partnership with a real estate development specialist; there was too wide a gulf between their respective management approaches to make cooperation effective. The partners had little in common except the desire to make Houston Center highly profitable. When this did not happen quickly, Texas Eastern concluded that the tensions generated by the partnership were not worth the trouble. In June of 1986 Texas Eastern ended the "unhappy marriage" with a divorce, buying back most of the interest of Cadillac Fairview.[14]

By this juncture, Houston Center was a formidable development that had remade one side of the city's business district. Photographs of the east side of Houston in 1970 — when the company announced the city of the future — and then again in the late 1980s illustrate the dramatic change created by the Center. If the actual development paled in comparison to Pereira's master plan, it nonetheless transformed an entire side of one of the nation's largest cities. In the process it also transformed the status of Texas Eastern. In its role as a major developer and particularly in its work on the convention center, the company built a much stronger and more visible presence in Houston. The Center pulled the company into deeper involvement in community activities, greatly enhancing its status as a corporate citizen.

Such benefits came at a high price. In venturing far away from its traditional areas of expertise, Texas Eastern learned a harsh lesson; as one national business publication observed: "It's not the first time a newcomer has learned real estate lessons the hard way."[15] Houston Center never yielded the financial returns TE needed to make it a long-term success. Indeed, it served as a drag on the firm's performance in much of the 1970s and 1980s, particularly during the severe downturn in Houston real estate after the early 1980s.

Like many other diversified corporations, Texas Eastern learned how difficult it was to manage a "new industry" that called for new tactics, new strategies, and new managerial attitudes. In the case of Texas Eastern, the demands of managing in the risky world of real estate development proved quite different from those encountered in the highly regulated gas transmission business. Top managers, long highly concerned with debt and accustomed to being judged by stock analysts on the basis of short-term financial results, had a difficult time adjusting to the riskier, more fluid world of real estate. These differences caused much of the tension between the company and its real estate partner, Cadillac Fairview. They also help explain the organiza-

Houston Center development in downtown Houston

tional tensions between those in charge of the company as a whole and those in charge of Houston Center.

That said, the most important problems in the company's real estate venture were not internal. Instead, they were generated by unpredictable fluctuations in a crowded real estate market tossed and turned by an oil-led boom and bust in the regional economy. The severe downturn in oil prices in the mid-1980s had a crushing impact on Houston Center and all other major real estate developments in Houston. As had been predicted in the early years of planning for Houston Center, Texas Eastern's "deep pockets" allowed it to protect its substantial investment in real estate during these trying years. Short-term losses from the Center hurt overall financial performance, but the company's other businesses cushioned the impact of hard times in real estate. The company was able to wait for the Houston economy to rebound, but it paid a heavy price for that luxury.

Fluctuating oil prices also undermined another of Texas Eastern's diversified businesses, LPG. The company had become a retailer of propane and butane with its purchase of Pyrofax in 1962. Between then and 1984, LPG became a steady, if unspectacular, part of operations. In 1984 management moved aggressively to build LPG into a major profit center by purchasing Petrolane Incorporated, a diversified firm that included one of the largest retail propane companies in the nation.

In an earlier day Texas Eastern's management would probably not have seriously considered an acquisition of this size, but in the heady environment of the acquisitions mania of the 1980s these sorts of mergers were commonplace. During that decade a wave of mergers swept through the American economy. Flushed with growing revenues from higher energy prices and seeking greater size as protection against uncertainties, oil and gas companies took the forefront in this mergers-and-acquisitions movement. In previous decades Texas Eastern's billion-dollar purchase of Petrolane would have stood out as a giant transaction, but in the 1980s this deal was simply one substantial merger in a flurry of highly publicized larger ones. The somewhat frantic tone of the time was captured in the title of an article in a major business journal: "Asset Redeployment: Everything is for Sale Now."[16]

With its bounty from oil revenues, Texas Eastern was in an excellent position to absorb a major acquisition. This major purchase permitted the company to round out in a decisive way its existing investment in LPG. This was simply TE's traditional approach to diversification on a grander scale. But the associated risks were also on a grander scale. If a giant acquisition did not work out, the consequences for the company could be far-reaching. This was especially true in the 1980s because of the grand proportions of the merger and acquisitions movement. Antitrust was no longer a serious barrier to the takeover specialists.

Now, as never before in its history, TE also found itself vulnerable to a takeover. No longer could the company assume that its size alone ensured against its acquisition by another organization. Indeed, in these years, the firm's access to northeastern gas markets and its profitable holdings in the North Sea made it an often mentioned takeover target.[17] This new reality added a certain sense of urgency to managers, who had to go about their work with one eye warily on the lookout for hostile takeovers.

Texas Eastern responded to this uncertainty by exploring legal means to insulate its managers from the pressures of hostile advances. In August of 1983 company representatives met with well-known merger and acquisitions specialist Martin Lipton, of Wachtell, Lipton, Rosen and Katz. The committee "considered whether in view of the continuing possibility of an unsolicited tender offer or takeover bid which may be unsettling to the Corporation's executives, it would be in the best interests of the Corporation and its stockholders to take steps to help assure such executives' continuing dedication to their duties to the Corporation notwithstanding the occurrence of a tender offer or takeover bid."[18] This was to be done in part through a severance plan for senior executives, who would receive "golden parachutes" in the event of a takeover. A modification of the certificate of incorporation called for the activation of this plan after any "change in control." The board of directors later amended the program by stipulating that it would be activated only after the acquisition by a third party of 30 percent or more of Texas Eastern Corporation's voting securities. Then in February of 1984 the board further modified the company's certificate of incorporation to stipulate that 80 percent of the stockholders would have to vote in favor of certain business combinations and mergers for them to become effective. Such measures were becoming quite common in the early 1980s. They were designed to thwart hostile acquisitions and to raise the price of a takeover attempt. They would also give top managers some breathing room in the event of a bid and would give top executives incentives to place shareholders' welfare ahead of their own short-term financial considerations while debating the company's options.

As the firm braced to protect itself, I. David Bufkin neared retirement age. In February of 1984 he recommended that Executive Vice President Henry King be elected to the office of president, chief operating officer, and director. The board approved the change, while keeping Bufkin on as chairman of the board. King had been with Texas Eastern since 1958. He had held several important administrative positions in personnel and public relations, while also serving as an aid to both George Kirby and Bufkin. King's experience was in administration, not in natural gas. He had as well spent much time on the issue of diversification, especially as it applied to oil-related activities, potential acquisitions in the chemical industry, and real estate. He was the first head of the firm whose primary experiences were in diversified activities, across a range comparable to those in which TE was engaged.

King and Bufkin decided to strengthen the company through acquisition rather than to wait passively for a possible takeover. They decided to seek a $500 million revolving credit agreement from Manufacturers Hanover Trust Company, and then raised the figure twice, finally settling on a credit line of $1.5 billion, "convertible into a loan."[19] This "kitty" gave Texas Eastern considerable financial flexibility to pursue an acquisition. And the right acquisition would make TE all the more difficult for a takeover specialist to swallow.

With large credits assured, Texas Eastern began looking for a suitable partner to acquire. It wanted a nonregulated company that would provide a good financial return while fitting well with the company's existing operations. It wanted a new source of dependable revenues to supplement gas transmission earnings, which no longer seemed dependable in an industry undergoing fundamental changes. Finally, the company's planners sought an acquisition that would complement existing holdings instead of one in a completely unrelated field.

Management turned to a number of investment banks, including First Boston Corporation, for help in identifying likely companies. In these sessions Petrolane Incorporated, a Long Beach, California–based LPG retailer,

Henry H. King

kept coming up.[20] Petrolane, which also had substantial holdings in an assortment of petroleum services companies, offered several attractions. Texas
Eastern's existing LPG business was not yet large enough to make an impact
on the corporation's bottom line. There was a sense that "we either had to

239

sell Pyrofax or substantially increase the size of Pyrofax." Since Petrolane was one of the nation's largest independent propane retailers, it would make Texas Eastern a leader in this market. The combination of Petrolane's LPG business with that of Pyrofax promised to give Texas Eastern a strong "third leg"—in addition to gas transmission and oil and gas production—to stand on if Petrolane could be acquired at a reasonable price.

Calculating the price would be difficult because, in addition to LPG, Petrolane had a number of oil-related manufacturing and service subsidiaries, some of which had uncertain futures. The firm had acquired most of these companies during the oil boom of the 1970s, and by the early 1980s they represented one-third to one-half of the company's assets and revenues. Some were proven winners with excellent long-term prospects. One, Eastman Whipstock, Incorporated, was "a world leader in manufacturing and supplying directional drilling and surveying instruments and providing related services."[21] But taken as a package (see table 10.4), these companies represented a considerable risk. With the downturn in oil prices, drilling activity had declined sharply. When the price of oil "bottomed out," these oil supplies and service companies might rebound. In that case, Texas Eastern would find itself well positioned for long-term growth. Moreover, these activities meshed well with the Halcon SD Group, a chemical and energy technology research specialist that TE had purchased in 1982. If oil prices improved, Texas Eastern might even build a "fourth leg" in the oil supply field. But the crucial variable was the price of oil, and therein lay the risk. Who could predict what would happen to oil prices in the years after 1984?

In June of 1984 Texas Eastern's management decided to take this risk and acquire Petrolane. On June 4 King reported to the board on the status of his discussions with the management of Petrolane,[22] with whom Texas Eastern had been doing business for twenty years.[23] The other firm's management seemed open to a friendly purchase, making it possible to complete the deal quickly and without legal warfare. It would require Texas Eastern, a company of some $1.24 billion in assets and 7,000 employees, to absorb a company with more than $800 million in assets and approximately 7,800 employees. This was clearly a big bite for TE and a transaction of historic significance to the company.[24] It was a strategic turning point perhaps even more crucial than the decision to invest in Houston Center.

The board approved the acquisition at a maximum purchase price of twenty dollars per share (using the $1.5 billion credit agreement). This tender offer reflected the expert financial advice of First Boston, which "kept telling us that this . . . is really worth a premium price."[25] At the premium, negotiations with Petrolane went smoothly, and Texas Eastern obtained an option purchase 9,662,000 shares (18.5 percent) of Petrolane's stock. Texas Eastern also received an option on all of the stock of Eastman Whipstock Manufacturing, Incorporated, at a price of $250 million cash, in the event that the Petrolane acquisition fell through.[26]

TABLE 10.4   Holdings of Petrolane, Inc.

Business	Name	Headquarters	Activities
LP Gas	Petrolane	Long Beach, Calif.	International sale of "bottled gas"
Oil tools and services	Eastman-Whipstock	Houston	Worldwide directional drilling
	Seahorse, Inc.	Morgan City, La.	Work vessels serving offshore sites
	Grant-Norpac Geophysical	Houston	Domestic geophysical services
	GUS Mfg.	El Paso	Recording seismic equipment
	Drilling Tool, Inc.	Houston	Rental of oil field drilling tools
	Fishing Tools, Inc.	Harvey, La.	Remedial or repair services for damaged wells in U.S. Gulf Coast area
Air	Air Drilling	Denver	Supply of compression services used in drilling (international)
	Brinkerhoff-Signal, Inc.	Denver	Operation of contract drilling rigs
Automobile	Mark C. Bloom	Southern California	Auto services
	Gerard Tire Services	San Jose, Calif.	Auto services
	Sims Tire & Automotive Service Centers		Auto services

Source: Various Petrolane, Inc., and Texas Eastern Corporation publications.

On June 20 the Petrolane board discussed Texas Eastern's tender offer. Bruce Wasserstein, of First Boston Corporation, "advised the members that in the opinion of the evaluation team and First Boston the price offered, i.e. $20 per share, was a 'fair price'—even beyond fair, it was a 'full price,' 'a very good price.'" Petrolane then approved a merger agreement under which Texas Eastern would purchase all of the outstanding stock for $20 per share.[27] Two days later, on June 22, 1984, Texas Eastern began its public tender offer, and in September Petrolane's stockholders voted overwhelmingly in favor of the acquisition. The total price was more than $1 billion.

When Texas Eastern announced the completion of the merger, it placed the acquisition in the context of its long-term strategy: "The acquisition of Petrolane will enable Texas Eastern to expand the geographic diversity of existing businesses and provide new areas of growth."[28] Another spokesman for the company addressed questions about the future of Petrolane's oil services: "In the longer term, as the oil field service industry recovers, Petrolane's broad position in that area will offer substantial growth opportunities."[29] Some analysts explained the transaction as part of a "two-pronged strategy" to further diversification and "help protect it [TE] against any unwanted take-over." King discounted these reactions, stressing that the acquisition was aimed at "complementing Texas Eastern's liquified petroleum gas business and its products pipeline segment," not at warding off possible takeovers.[30] Analysts differed sharply in their reaction to the price paid for Petrolane. A specialist at Shearson/American Express noted that TE was "not paying excessively for it."[31] But his counterpart at Paine Webber argued that "Texas Eastern is paying an awfully high price."[32]

Criticisms of the merger were also voiced by a competitor, the Coastal Corporation, which filed suit against Texas Eastern to block its acquisition of Petrolane. Coastal said it owned 633,000 shares of Texas Eastern, slightly more than one percent of the total outstanding stock. As a stockholder, it contended that Texas Eastern had breached its fiduciary duty to its stockholders by agreeing to the acquisition. The state district judge who heard the case refused, however, to enter a temporary restraining order, and no other hearings were scheduled.[33] Coastal subsequently agreed to drop its suit and to sell its TE stock. The acquisition went forward without further delays.

The company now owned the largest LPG distributing system in the nation, and it quickly moved to create a unified Liquified Petroleum Gas Group. It folded its Pyrofax operations into the larger LPG system acquired from Petrolane. At the same time, plans went forward to move the petroleum services companies into TE's petroleum group, which also included oil exploration and production.[34]

Shortly after the Petrolane deal, Texas Eastern divested one of its own subsidiaries, Transwestern Pipe Line Company. Again First Boston Corporation assisted. The sale would help fund the acquisition. Besides, from the perspective of a company headquartered in the relatively probusiness regulatory environment of Texas, California state and local regulations seemed unnecessarily strict, and the attitudes of regulators appeared unnecessarily antibusiness and confrontational. After grappling with California regulations for nearly twenty years, Texas Eastern decided to liquidate its West Coast investment. This deal proved easy to complete, and on November 4, 1984, Texas Eastern officially agreed to sell Transwestern to Houston Natural Gas (HNG) for $390 million.[35] As the smoke cleared from both the largest acquisition, Petrolane, and the largest divestment, Transwestern, in Texas Eastern's history, management set out under trying conditions to consolidate its operations.

It did so during a sudden and unpredicted plunge in oil prices. The acquisition of Petrolane had been predicated on the assumption that oil prices had hit bottom after sliding from the low thirty dollar per barrel range in 1980 to the low twenty dollar per barrel range in 1984–85. This assumption proved badly mistaken. During the winter of 1985–86, the price of oil fell precipitously to the ten dollar per barrel range, shredding Texas Eastern's strategic justification for the Petrolane acquisition and knocking down profits in every phase of the company's diversified operations. During 1985 the company showed operating losses from petroleum services of $141 million. Profits from the North Sea declined sharply in the same year, while the cost of exploring for and producing oil both domestically and internationally remained relatively high. The petroleum services companies obtained with Petrolane were devastated. Oil-driven diversification had seemed natural and almost easy in the years of rising oil prices; it was to prove anything but easy in the late 1980s.

Chapter 11

REFOCUSING ON THE CORE

Hard times forced some difficult choices on Texas Eastern. One of these was the decision to look outside the company for a new leader to guide the firm through this turbulent era. The new president would face the formidable task of reversing the company's strategy of diversification. He would have to manage the short-term financial problems brought by the oil bust and position the company to survive and prosper in an industry wracked by change. To face these challenges, Texas Eastern hired Dennis Hendrix. Under his guidance, the company laid out a strategy of "refocusing on the core," of returning to the company's traditional business strengths.

Hendrix brought to Texas Eastern experiences that well suited him for his demanding task. He had served from 1978 through 1983 as the president and chief executive officer of Texas Gas Transmission Corporation, which enjoyed a long and close working relationship with Texas Eastern. He subsequently worked as a vice chairman for CSX Corporation and as an executive vice president of Halliburton, the firm which had acquired Brown & Root in the early 1960s. In 1984 he joined the board of Panhandle Eastern. Hendrix was friends with Texas Eastern Chairman David Bufkin; the two had worked together on various gas industry committees. Bufkin recommended Hendrix to the board, which named him as president, chief operating officer, and director effective November 7, 1985. Henry King became vice chairman of the board and Bufkin remained as chairman.

In Hendrix, Texas Eastern acquired a young, but experienced, natural gas pipeline executive with a background in accounting and finance. His management experience seemed well suited to Texas Eastern's particular needs in the mid-1980s. At Texas Gas, Hendrix had overseen the divestiture of an unprofitable trucking subsidiary and had placed more emphasis on the firm's gas operations. Texas Eastern seemed ready for a similar strategic reform. Hendrix's experience at Texas Gas also included a heated takeover battle in which the company avoided a hostile tender offer from the Coastal Corporation by agreeing to be purchased by CSX.[1]

Hendrix came to Texas Eastern predisposed to strengthen its natural gas operations, decentralize its existing non-pipeline ventures, and streamline

Dennis R. Hendrix

the company's holdings by liquidating investments in unprofitable areas such as petroleum services. He quickly set out to prune away some of the companies acquired through thirty years of diversification. While he would build up those parts of the enterprise that were "the core businesses that offered growth prospects for the future," he realized that "others were dead end streets that we could no longer afford."[2] "Refocusing on the core" became a rallying point for building morale in the company's major businesses and reassuring current and potential investors regarding the ultimate fate of Texas Eastern.

Of course, in the mid-1980s Texas Eastern faced more than simply problems with morale; it also was experiencing serious setbacks on its bottom line. Most segments of the company's diverse business were suffering, but the newly acquired holdings in petroleum services were particularly hard hit. One of the early signs of things to come occurred in December of 1984 when the company took a pretax write-down of approximately $80 million stemming from its Tyler, Texas, refinery and a gas processing plant in Louisiana. This write-down "was taken in light of the continuing uncertainty regarding the profitability of U.S. crude oil refineries due to depressed energy markets. . . ."[3] By 1985 and 1986 "uncertainty" no longer characterized the energy market. Conditions were definitely bad and getting worse. A precipitous drop in drilling activities (see chart 11.1) accompanied the devastating decline in all segments of the oil industry. In 1985 Texas Eastern's petroleum services companies reported losses of $141 million. The total losses could have been as high as $200 million without various restructuring efforts undertaken during the year. Drastic measures were recessitated to prevent the severe problems in petroleum services from undermining the recovery of the company as a whole.[4]

Hendrix and his key managers defined four core industries: (1) natural gas transmission, (2) North Sea oil and gas production, (3) petroleum products shipments, and (4) LPG marketing. These were the areas in which the company had built strengths, and they were to be protected by cutting losses in less promising operations. In particular, refocusing on the core would require drastic measures to remedy problems in clusters of peripheral activities, notably oil services, domestic oil exploration and production, and real estate.

The economic environment for disinvestment of the petroleum services companies was poor, but the job had to be done quickly to stem the flow of red ink. Much of the responsibility for handling this problem went to Paul Anderson, who subsequently became a senior vice president deeply involved in strategic planning. Anderson thought that the extreme drop in drilling activities in the mid-1980s reflected a harsh new fact of life that had not been evident before: the Iranian Revolution in 1979 had spawned a "false" drilling boom that could not be sustained. As the sharp downturn in oil prices in 1985 revealed, drilling and associated activities were vastly overbuilt. Anderson proceeded on the assumption that TE's newly acquired petroleum services companies would not rebound strongly and quickly, since their industries were in for a long period of readjustment to drastically lower levels of drilling.

Anderson's task was similar to a bankruptcy "work out." He first had to "stop the bleeding" by making severe cutbacks in employment and operating expenses. Then he had to "separate the wheat from the chaff." The fate of

CHART 11.1 Rotary Rig Count, 1973–1985
Texas, Southwest (Texas, Oklahoma and Louisiana) and the U.S.

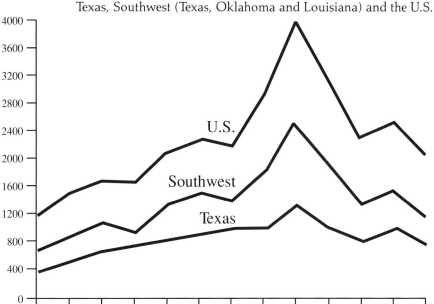

Source: Hughes Tool Company, Rotary Rigs Running- by States, Annual Averages.

the weak petroleum services companies was clear: "The company is continually pursuing the disposal of all its discontinued petroleum services operations and remains committed to their disposition at the earliest date."[5] Meanwhile, Anderson sought to "identify potential survivors" and "to salvage as many of our operations as possible through non-cash joint ventures." Since there often was literally no market for petroleum service companies and little prospect for recovery in the short term, he had to do some creative bargaining with other major companies to try to "create survivors."

The guiding idea was to match those of its petroleum service subsidiaries which seemed to have a future with other strong companies in the same business. Through joint ventures Anderson tried to build enough strength to help the consolidated company survive the severe downturn. Once combinations had been created, the plan was to nurture them gradually back to health as the petroleum industry as a whole rebounded.[6]

This enterprise was not for the faint of heart. In about a year Texas Eastern eliminated some forty-four hundred of its approximately five thousand employees in petroleum services through a combination of layoffs, sales, joint ventures, and closing facilities. The managers of the individual companies often resisted cuts, but without success. After all, the company was instituting similar cuts at the corporate level, where there were layoffs, early retirements, and wage and hiring freezes. But the pain was greatest in petroleum services, where TE's managers were forced to come up with innovative responses if they were going to avoid a complete disaster.

The difficulties of "creating survivors" during these years were well illustrated by the case of Eastman Whipstock (EW). This company was widely viewed as the jewel among the firms acquired with Petrolane, since it was an international leader in the promising new technology of directional drilling. Yet even Eastman Whipstock suffered as new drilling came to a standstill. In 1985 EW recorded losses from continuing operations of $15.2 million (on revenues of $112.6 million); in the first nine months of 1986 it had losses of $24.9 million on revenues of $64.2 million.[7] To salvage as much as possible of this valuable company, Texas Eastern agreed to merge it with Norton Christensen, another drilling specialist with short-term problems but a strong outlook for the future. To prepare for this joint venture TE made a provision of $13.8 million "for downsizing and expected consolidation costs."[8] The combination of the two companies into a newly created partnership, the Eastman Christensen Company, took place in September of 1986, with TE retaining a 50 percent share. The devastation in oil services was captured in a sobering footnote to the description of this transaction: "The Company's [TE's] investment exceeds the amount of the underlying equity of net assets by approximately $244 million and is being amortized over approximately 30 years."[9] The newly created combine would thus require considerable "nurturing," but the parent company remained confident that Eastman Christensen would rebound and become a dominant firm when oil drilling recovered.

Texas Eastern pursued a similar approach with several other petroleum services subsidiaries. First came a $54.5 million charge in December, 1985, to account for the losses associated with the restructuring of the offshore supply and transportation activities of Seahorse and the write-down of the value of the marine geophysical assets of Grant-Norpac, Incorporated. In March of 1986, after deep cutbacks in Seahorse, TE negotiated a non-cash transaction that integrated what remained of its assets into one of the largest marine service companies in the world, Zapata Gulf Marine Corporation (ZGM). The size and strength of ZGM's owners (Zapata Corporation, HNG/InterNorth, Incorporated, and Halliburton Company) made this a likely survivor in the ongoing consolidation of a business which served the crippled offshore drilling industry. Texas Eastern received 18.5 percent of ZGM's voting stock in exchange for the assets of Seahorse, giving it a strong position in another company which was a good bet to return to profitability in the long run.[10]

What could not be salvaged of course were all of the employees of these firms or their assets. Great financial and personal pains accompanied these transactions. Seahorse had been the largest employer in the Louisiana coastal town of Morgan City, and cutbacks in the company "essentially shut down the city." Paul Anderson, who managed these cutbacks, said four years later, "There are parts of the country I still don't dare show my face, like Morgan City, Louisiana."[11]

Two other petroleum services subsidiaries survived as parts of consolidated concerns. In September, 1986, TE and W. R. Grace and Company combined the domestic contract drilling operations of Brinkerhoff-Signal and Grace Drilling Company, with Texas Eastern receiving a minority stock interest through a statutory merger of the two companies. In December, 1987, TE took a different approach in its efforts to protect its investment in Grant-Norpac. To build a stronger, larger company, Texas Eastern traded 40 percent of the stock of Grant-Norpac for the assets of another geophysical company, Seiscom Delta, Incorporated, which had been in bankruptcy.[12] Management struggled in these several ways to create survivors while protecting the long-term future of the parent firm.

Where the company decided it could not create survivors, it disposed of ailing subsidiaries as quickly as possible. After several charges against net income in connection with the reorganization of Halcon SD Group, Incorporated (a research and development company originally acquired in 1982), TE shut down the group's major research lab and then sold the parts of the company which remained to Denka Chemical Corporation in February of 1987. When no buyers were forthcoming even at bargain basement prices for several of the subsidiaries, TE negotiated their sale to management groups who wanted to try nursing the companies back to health.[13]

By the end of 1987 Texas Eastern had carried through a dramatic and sweeping restructuring of its ailing petroleum services subsidiaries. By writing off millions of dollars as bad investments, selling several subsidiaries, making deep cutbacks in the operations of others, and creating joint ventures with other large companies, Texas Eastern had protected a substantial part of its investment in petroleum services. It had as well cleared the deck of problems that, if unattended, threatened to undermine the performance of the company as a whole.

One major step remained. Since 1950 Texas Eastern had been involved in domestic exploration and production. Despite considerable efforts and large investments in the search for oil and gas both onshore and offshore, TE had failed to build a strong position as a domestic producer. As it made cutbacks in its petroleum services companies, Texas Eastern also reevaluated its commitment in this risky area. In 1986 it suspended all domestic drilling operations. Then in the following year it sold most of its oil properties in the United States for about $183 million. In 1988 the company wrote off its $41 million investment in Alaska.[14] By the end of 1988 TE had moved completely out of domestic exploration and production. Thirty-eight years of experience had yielded too little production to justify further investments in this area. One of the company's long-standing efforts to diversify out of gas transmission had been abandoned.

Texas Eastern planned to continue pursuing exploration and production opportunities, principally in the North Sea, where previous efforts had been extremely successful. The firm moved its exploration and production headquarters to its London office late in 1986 and simultaneously expanded its Stavanger, Norway, office. At this time, the company had proved oil and gas reserves of 140 million barrels and 440 billion cubic feet, respectively, ranking it among the top twenty companies with North Sea reserves.[15] But even these highly prized holdings did not escape the cutbacks. In search of ready cash, Texas Eastern sold 50 percent of its interest in the Beryl and recently discovered Ness oil fields.[16] The company's North Sea revenues were thus reduced, but they were still substantial, and they still justified further investments in production.

Another source of strength amid the chaos of the late 1980s was the LPG business. The merger of Pyrofax into Petrolane made Texas Eastern a strong competitor in the LPG market. The fall in oil prices bolstered the LPG business by spurring demand and increasing the retailers' margin. Ultimately, LPG did for Texas Eastern what diversification was supposed to accomplish: create an investment with a cycle counter to that of the firm's primary business. To give the LPG undertaking greater flexibility and also to generate some much needed cash without a substantial tax penalty, in 1987 Texas Eastern reorganized Petrolane into a master limited partnership (MLP). Under the MLP form of organization, Texas Eastern was able to sell 57 percent of Petrolane's unit stock to the public while retaining a controlling interest (43 percent) in the company. By forming an MLP, Texas Eastern removed Petrolane's debt from its own books and received from the sale of stock approximately $256 million (most of which was used to retire Petrolane-related corporate debt and for assets leased to the MLP). Now the LPG company had greater autonomy and could, if necessary, borrow funds for expansion. The reorganized LPG operation continued to grow in the late 1980s. During 1988, in fact, Petrolane made a major acquisition, Tropigas, an LPG distributor serving the southeastern United States and several Caribbean countries.

Of Texas Eastern's core businesses, the petroleum products pipeline was probably least damaged by the drop in oil prices. This line had operated profitably since the mid-1960s, and it continued to do so in the 1980s. As midwestern refineries shut down, the demand for Gulf Coast refined products increased. By 1986 TE's products line was accounting for approximately 29 percent of the refined products sold in the midwestern market. Carrying LPG as well as refined products from Texas Eastern's La Gloria refinery, this pipeline made a steady contribution to the corporation's balance sheet.

Less secure was the natural gas transmission business, which was decisive to the financial health of Texas Eastern Corporation. As management restudied the needs of the gas pipelines in the 1980s, the economic and regulatory uncertainties seemed overwhelming. The financials were cause for alarm. Between 1983 and 1987 operating revenues from gas transmission had fallen more than 50 percent, from $4.2 billion to $2 billion. Revenues fell in part because the firm's role was shifting from that of a merchant to that of a transporter. The Federal Energy Regulatory Commission was encouraging this transition as one part of the transformation from a regulated to a market-oriented industry. Deregulation and consolidation were completely restructuring the industry, and management realized it would have to adapt quickly in order to survive.

Most of the regulatory uncertainty centered on two sets of issues: price, and the status of interstate gas pipelines. Prices provoked the most volatile debates. The numerous categories of gas and the convoluted timetable for deregulation were enough to confuse the best efforts of any industry planner trying to project long-term patterns of supply and demand. The transition to market-driven pricing spawned legal and regulatory disputes between buyers and sellers, and wild swings in energy prices hampered the smooth resolution of such disputes. The second ongoing source of controversy was the energy commission's determination to transform interstate pipelines from gas merchants into common carriers. As the regulatory agencies and courts struggled with these two major issues, companies like Texas Eastern found it next to impossible to frame long-term plans.

The transition to unregulated pricing was greatly complicated by the battle over "take-or-pay" contracts. When natural gas prices fell, many pipeline companies were still bound to producers with long-term contracts for high-priced natural gas. These contracts had been made in an era of shortages. Some pipeline customers, particularly the major utility companies which distributed natural gas to residential consumers, complained bitterly as they were forced to continue purchasing expensive natural gas when market prices were substantially lower.

Citing the high fuel costs to the residential consumer, utilities pleaded with the FERC and state commissions for permission to break their long-term contracts so they could purchase gas on the "spot market." The spot market had grown during the early 1980s and could now furnish substantial amounts of low-priced gas. In May, 1984, the commission issued Order 380, which released pipeline customers from their contracts with gas suppliers, freeing them to contract for the less expensive gas. But Order 380 did not give the pipelines relief from their own contracts with producers. This left the pipelines in a dire situation. Most gas purchase agreements between pipelines and producers contained take-or-pay clauses, a provision which assured that a pipeline company would pay a producer a certain "minimum" amount for its contracted gas whether or not the pipeline actually took delivery of that gas. Thus, pipeline companies were obligated to fulfill their take-or-pay contracts with the producers even after their customers had legally and often unconditionally broken their purchase agreements.[17]

FERC sought to alter substantially the way pipelines did business. In late 1985 the commission issued Order 436, which was designed to encourage pipelines to move away from their traditional role as buyers and sellers of natural gas and refocus their business on the nondiscriminatory transportation of gas. Order 436 set rules under which gas producers and consumers could deal directly with each other. In effect this policy meant that pipelines would be paid only for transportation services, which would have to be available to all shippers within the limits of a pipeline's capacity. Producers and consumers who could make better deals between themselves than through pipelines could compete with pipelines for a part of the line's business.[18]

Pipeline companies objected that Order 436 did not deal with the problems of take-or-pay; and they took the commission to court over this issue. The District of Columbia Court of Appeals heard a case brought against the FERC regarding Order 436, and during June, 1987, the court remanded it back to the commission because it did not address take-or-pay issues.[19] Two months later, in August, 1987, the FERC issued the first of several versions of Order 500, which dealt with the take-or-pay issue. Now the commission allowed a pipeline to transport a particular volume of gas for a producer in return for an equal volume of credit against the producer's take-or-pay claims against the line. In this way, the producer would essentially take over the pipeline's existing contract with both the producer and the consumer.[20]

Texas Eastern coped with those regulatory tangles quite well compared to other pipeline companies. Unlike most of its competitors, Texas Eastern avoided significant liabilities from take-or-pay claims. The company had protected itself by putting in its contracts "market-out" or "FERC out" provisions. When suppliers had not agreed to such contractual stipulations or demanded a price higher than Texas Eastern felt was justified, the company simply passed up the opportunity to make the gas purchase. This had been a risky policy in the mid-1980s, when most companies were frantically lining up long-term supply contracts. But Texas Eastern took a longer, historical view of gas prices, refusing to contract on terms which seemed "unreasonable from a business standpoint."[21] In this case, experienced leadership from David Bufkin, Jack Head, and others helped the company avoid the worst pitfalls of the take-or-pay contracts.

The company also rode out the early movement toward common carrier status without serious short-term damage. This change hurt the interstate pipelines by encouraging producers contract directly with consumers. But even in these circumstances, the pipelines could adjust their rate structures in order to continue earning the maximum allowed rate of return. If they did this successfully, they were able to avoid financial disaster and retain some traditional merchant business.[22]

Even the most skillful management could not, however, prevent the firm from taking a solid body blow from the Environmental Protection Agency (EPA). For many years now the energy industry had been under increasing scrutiny on environmental issues. Growing concerns about air, water, and soil pollution had produced a wave of new regulations and the creation of the EPA, a powerful new federal regulatory agency. A confrontation with the EPA further diverted the resources of Texas Eastern at a time when it could least afford it. The dispute, which was played out in the media, produced a substantial fine, bad publicity, and headaches for TE's top executives.

At issue was the company's disposal of polychlorinated biphenyls, or PCBs. Pipelines had commonly used PCBs as a lubricant at gas pipeline compressor stations. Texas Eastern had used the PCB–laden lubricating oil in its stations in the 1950s and had not stopped using it until 1972. Then the company began phasing out this oil. In 1977, before the manufacture of PCBs was prohibited by federal law, Texas Eastern had completely eliminated its use of the chemical. But the environmental issue in the 1980s involved not only use as a lubricant, but also disposal. Before the 1970s PCBs often had been buried in pits near the compressor stations where they had been used. When Congress passed new regulations concerning these toxic wastes, the EPA began to pay closer attention to this issue. In 1985 Texas Eastern conducted a pilot study of PCB contamination at some of its compressor stations, and the investigation revealed that a number of compressor station sites contained the dangerous chemicals.[23]

On November 9, 1987, Texas Eastern signed an agreement-in-principle with the EPA and the U.S. Department of Justice. The nonbinding agreement provided that Texas Eastern would complete its PCB cleanup program in as many as eighty-nine sites in fourteen states over a ten-year period. The original estimated cost was $400 million, which Texas Eastern said it would attempt to recover through insurance, other claims, and rate recovery mechanisms. To avoid further litigation, Texas Eastern also agreed to pay the EPA a $15 million fine for violating regulations governing the disposal of PCBs. When the agreement was completed in 1988, it was the largest ever negotiated between the EPA and a corporation.[24]

Despite these highly publicized problems, Texas Eastern's natural gas system continued to provide the corporation with profitable business. Northeastern gas markets were still growing. Despite the changing regulations regarding contract carriage, take-or-pay provisions, and rate adjustments, Texas Eastern managed to do well in this part of its business. It rebounded along with the gas industry as a whole, and consolidated its presence in the Northeast by purchasing for $117.4 million Algonquin Energy, Incorporated (parent company of Algonquin Gas Transmission Company), a firm in which it had long held a substantial stock position. This purchase symbolized the company's resolve to build its core businesses.

The oil bust of the mid-1980s had delivered a serious blow to Texas Eastern, but by the late 1980s the company had struggled back to its feet. It had cut costs and refocused on its core enterprises. Hard times had forced management to pare away activities which no longer seemed essential to the future of the organization. The company's leaders made a number of pain-

Texas Eastern's Board of Directors, 1988. *Left to right, standing:* A. Frank Smith, Jr., Charles W. Duncan, Jr., John R. Beckett, Lawrence E. Fouraker, Edward B. Walker III, Ralph S. O'Connor, Bobby R. Inman, Melvin E. Kurth, Jr., Robert E. Seymour. *Left to right, sitting:* Dennis R. Hendrix, I. David Bufkin, Henry H. King; *inset:* Robert Cizik, who replaced A. Frank Smith on the board later in the year.

ful choices in this period of adjustment, and many employees and organizations were left behind or unemployed as the firm cut back on its operations. But by the late 1980s the organization was a more streamlined version of what it had been before its ordeal, an international diversified energy company.

During the spring of 1988, however, press reports continued to mention the possibility of a takeover at Texas Eastern. Employees were concerned enough to ask Hendrix directly at the company's annual employee meeting in March about the rumors. Hendrix said he knew of no such plans, but "that's not to say that a desire or intent does not exist."[25] He reminded them that the firm had implemented several changes in its charter in recent years to help prevent an ill-advised takeover. Good management which enhanced shareholder value, Hendrix said, was the best guarantee of corporate independence. By this time, the company's stock price and earnings had begun to rebound from the low points reached in the mid-1980s. Much remained to be done, and Hendrix knew that he and Texas Eastern were in a race with time. Could the company regain a position of financial strength that would make it less vulnerable to a takeover before such an event occurred?

Epilogue

ACQUISITION ENDURED

Time caught up with Texas Eastern. On January 16, 1989, Coastal Corporation offered $42 per share in a $2.6 billion tender offer for Texas Eastern's fifty-three million shares of common stock. Coastal announced its intentions on Martin Luther King's birthday, a national holiday, so its actual tender could not begin until the next day, January 17, 1989. Such an offer had been long rumored, and it set off a flurry of activities as Texas Eastern's top managers explored their options. They closed their offices on the forty-sixth floor of One Houston Center to all but essential personnel and pulled the curtains to prevent spying. Texas Eastern was under siege.[1]

The immediate response of the stock market to Coastal's bid gave Texas Eastern some much needed breathing space. Texas Eastern's stock had been trading at $29 per share prior to Coastal's stock tender, but it climbed to $45 on Monday and soon leveled off in the $48 to $50 range. Texas Eastern's executives could confidently state that Coastal's bid was too low. Coastal could either raise its bid or wait for the stock price to go down, but the longer the stock price stayed high, the more likely it was that it would not fall. The stock traded heavily. Many investors paid prices between $47 and $50 per share, supporting speculation that Texas Eastern stock was worth something close to $50.

The bid for Texas Eastern was in keeping with the history of Coastal Corporation, which had been built by way of acquisitions. Founded in 1955 by Oscar Wyatt, Jr., Coastal started in the business of gathering gas from local producers and reselling it to large pipeline customers. In 1973 Wyatt began to expand his company through takeovers. He first acquired Colorado Interstate Corporation, a pipeline system operating from the Texas Panhandle into Colorado and Wyoming. Another successful takeover was completed in 1985, when American Natural Resources (ANR) was acquired for $2.5 billion. Coastal had been unsuccessful in acquiring Texas Gas Resources Corporation in 1983, and it failed the following year to take over Houston Natural Gas. In a particularly vicious takeover battle, HNG countered Coastal's hostile offer by tendering for Coastal's stock and then its own. As had been the case in its unsuccessful bid for Texas Gas, however, Coastal ended up with a profit when it sold its stock back to HNG.[2] By that time, Coastal had become one of the largest gas firms in the nation. It was nearly twice as big as Texas Eastern in assets, miles of pipeline, and numbers of world-wide employees.

Coastal's aggressive behavior was viewed in two ways. Critics felt that the company and its chairman were belligerent and overly aggressive. But industry analysts generally perceived Coastal as a hard-driving company attempting to build a nation-wide pipeline system through acquisitions. Just as the founders of Texas Eastern had recognized that the northeastern and New England gas markets were vital for a successful pipeline company, Coastal's managers believed that only a handful of the largest gas pipeline systems would survive the late twentieth century. Coastal recognized that despite Texas Eastern's immediate problems, its natural gas transmission system held great intrinsic value.

Coastal's plan of attack was simple. In the SEC filing of its tender offer Coastal announced that it would pay off a portion of the debt accrued in its $2.6 billion takeover by selling Texas Eastern's North Sea oil and gas properties. Although Coastal did not discuss other possible asset sales, informed observers speculated that it ultimately planned to divest most or all of the company's non-pipeline assets. Indeed, the debt accrued in acquiring Texas Eastern might be paid off largely by the sale of non-pipeline assets, leaving the pipeline system intact and purchased at an attractive price.

Texas Eastern's executives, however, became convinced that Coastal was not their most promising suitor. Indeed, Coastal's bid was not at all appealing from their perspective. Texas Eastern's stock continued to trade in the $47 to $50 per share range, reinforcing the desire to look elsewhere for a buyer. Of course, Coastal's position was that its offer adequately reflected Texas Eastern's real value. James R. Paul, Coastal's president and chief spokesman during its tender offer, wrote to Dennis Hendrix, "In the last two days, uninformed arbitrageurs and speculators have pushed the price of the Texas Eastern stock to levels which we believe, based on the public information presently available to us, are not supported by the fundamentals of your businesses."[3] Price was the key to the struggle. Once Texas Eastern had been put in play, its officers accepted their responsibility to seek the maximum return to shareholders.

Texas Eastern's public response to the Coastal offer was low keyed. Texas Eastern invited appropriate executives from Coastal to meet at Texas Eastern. On Sunday, January 22, Coastal's and Texas Eastern's executives and their legal representatives finally met. Paul and his advisors journeyed to Texas Eastern, where they were met by that firm's officers as well as "more than a dozen advisers alongside the directors in a cramped, standing-room only board room."[4] Coastal's representatives presented their company's reasons for the offer and asked questions about the company's operations. They were then asked to leave the room while Texas Eastern's board and its advisors met to discuss Paul's offer. Hendrix briefly met again with Paul and told him that "Texas Eastern didn't see any reason to continue the meeting."[5] The gathering ended without a formal response by Texas Eastern, which had under SEC regulations until January 30 to do so.

Texas Eastern's intent to look for a more promising bidder than Coastal soon became very evident. During a court hearing an attorney representing the company told the judge that Texas Eastern had acquired a list of about fifty "white knights" it would contact in regard to the possibility of making a competing bid.[6] Dennis Hendrix took pains to emphasize that his company's interest in other possible bidders did not preclude a future transaction with Coastal. Instead, "they are intended to provide adequate time to ensure that our shareholders receive a full and fair price for their investment in Texas Eastern."[7] James Paul dictated Coastal's response: "The longer Texas Eastern waits, the less likely we would increase our bid." But as Paul well knew, the longer they waited, the more likely it was that Texas Eastern would find an alternative to Coastal's offer.

Texas Eastern's official response to Coastal's bid came on Sunday, January 29, when its board "unanimously rejected as inadequate the $42 per share tender offer made by The Coastal Corporation. . . ."[8] Hendrix noted that Coastal had indicated that it might raise its bid if a higher offer came in, yet refused "to allow a reasonable time for a fair bidding process to be conducted." Citing the view of its financial advisors that given time, greater values for the company's stock could be obtained, Texas Eastern set its own deadline for a higher bid at March 15. This gave the company six weeks to find a better offer.

Perhaps sensing that time was running out, Coastal began discussing Texas Eastern's PCB liabilities as a major reason why the company would not raise its bid. Published reports by analysts continued to cite Texas Eastern's PCB problems and the potential cleanup costs of $400 million as a major reason for the lack of competing bids. Yet Texas Eastern's stock price remained well above Coastal's bid, indicating interest in the company from sources other than Coastal. The expiration of Coastal's original tender found that firm with less than 10 percent of Texas Eastern's stock, and Coastal began discussing in the press its options to sell out, extend its offer, or perhaps raise its bid.

Coastal chose to renew its bid on February 14 without raising its price. A Coastal spokesman noted to the press that "there are a lot of stockholders waiting to see if there's going to be another offer, or whether we'll raise the price. If we go on and there's not another offer, the $42 looks awfully good compared to what the stock was when we made the offer."[9] Yet the stock price held firm and even rose slightly.

Events then took a dramatic turn on Monday, February 20. Without any public hint that a deal was in the works, Texas Eastern's board of directors publicly announced that they had approved a $3.22 billion merger agreement between Texas Eastern and Panhandle Eastern Corporation, a large natural gas pipeline holding company with headquarters in Houston. Panhandle Eastern offered fifty-three dollars cash per share, or approximately $2.6 billion, for up to 80 percent of Texas Eastern's stock and an exchange of Panhandle Eastern stock for the remaining 20 percent.[10] Although Panhandle Eastern's name had surfaced along with many others as a possible "white knight," the impending deal had been kept very quiet.

The two companies had made initial contact on the day of Coastal's tender offer, when Panhandle Eastern chairman Robert Hunsucker telephoned Dennis Hendrix with an offer of assistance. Panhandle's executives were already preparing for a long-scheduled corporate strategy meeting for later the same week, and this meeting now focused on the study of a possible bid for Texas Eastern. Realizing that there was a good "fit" between their company and Texas Eastern, Panhandle's executives worked overtime to prepare a bid. "I don't think I had, or any of us had," recalled Hunsucker," a day off for the next thirty days, maybe longer, seven days a week and all night." Negotiations remained secret, since publicity might affect the price of Texas Eastern's stock and undermine the completion of the merger.[11]

Panhandle Eastern's pipeline system was concentrated in the midwestern markets. Although Panhandle Eastern Corporation was significantly smaller in terms of assets than Texas Eastern, its two major systems, (Panhandle Eastern Pipe Line Company and Trunkline Gas Company), accounted for 17,000 miles compared to Texas Eastern's 10,567 miles of line. Chartered in 1929 as the Interstate Pipe Line Company, Panhandle Eastern was one of the several new interstate pipelines constructed during the late 1920s boom. Extending from the Panhandle of Texas into Illinois and later Detroit, the company was a pioneer in transporting gas from the large southwestern fields to the large industrial centers of the Midwest. In the early 1950s Panhandle formed the Trunkline Gas Company, with lines extending from the Texas Gulf Coast into Illinois and Michigan.

Panhandle Eastern and Texas Eastern had discussed the possibility of merging before 1989. In 1986 when Panhandle Eastern was the target of a hostile takeover, officials at Texas Eastern approached Panhandle about a possible friendly merger. The Panhandle chairman recalled that "Dennis [Hendrix] did give me a call. . . . It was what can I [Texas Eastern] do to help to retain your independence?" Such discussions were facilitated by the fact that Hendrix had served briefly on Panhandle's board before becoming Texas Eastern's president.

After the hostile takeover had failed, the two companies continued discussions of a possible merger. During August, 1986, they entered a confidentiality and five-year standstill agreement "pursuant to which the two companies exchanged confidential information in connection with their mutual interest in exploring the possibility of a combination of the two companies."[12] Discussions continued off and on into 1987, but then the two companies agreed that a merger would not be feasible. These previous talks seemed to ease the way for successful merger negotiations in 1989.

The new Panhandle Eastern Corporation would have access to broader markets throughout much of the nation. It would be the second largest gas pipeline system in the nation, ranking behind only the Houston-based Enron Corporation in total miles of pipeline. Once the merger had been completed and the pipeline system had been combined, Panhandle Eastern would emerge as a much larger company, one positioned to face turbulent times in a rapidly changing industry (see map 12.1).

The process of combining the companies would involve the cutting of hundreds of overlapping jobs and the sale of most of Texas Eastern's non-pipeline assets.[13] Soon after this bid Panhandle announced its intention to sell Texas Eastern's North Sea interests, the Houston Center, Petrolane, Incorporated, and the La Gloria refinery and to use the proceeds to help pay for its $3.22 billion tender offer.

Within two weeks of Panhandle's offer, Texas Eastern announced the first of what would be many asset sales. On March 1, 1989, Texas Eastern announced the sale of its most valuable non-pipeline asset, its North Sea oil reserves. A British company, Enterprise Oil PLC, purchased these holdings for $1.4 billion. Before the deal was completed, British Gas PLC, of London, and Amerada Hess Corporation, of New York, both of which were partners with Texas Eastern in the original seismic testing and development of the North Sea in the early 1960s, indicated that they wanted to purchase Texas Eastern's North Sea properties. When the original group agreed to conduct seismic tests jointly and then develop the North Sea, they had granted each other the right of first refusal on any sale of their interest in the North Sea. Eventually, British Courts ruled that Enterprise Oil, which had been spun off by British Gas years earlier, could legally purchase the North Sea properties, and that deal was consummated.[14]

Other sales followed quickly. Texas Eastern announced that it would sell its large stake in the Petrolane Master Limited Partnership to Quantum Chemical Corporation and First Boston Corporation. For its 44 percent interest in Petrolane Partners, Texas Eastern received $300 million. It received an additional $150 million for terminals and tanks used by Petrolane but still owned by Texas Eastern.[15] The total sales of price of Petrolane amounted to more than $1 billion, indicating, perhaps, the idea that the original purchase price of Petrolane had been realistic.

Next, Crown Central Petroleum purchased La Gloria, including the refineries facilities, pipeline, and fuel inventories, for $112 million. Originally purchased in 1957 to facilitate Texas Eastern's entry into the refined products transportation business, La Gloria had been a part of the company's program to reconvert its Little Big Inch from natural gas to products. Now, thirty-two years later, with both the sale of La Gloria and the North Sea, Texas Eastern's long struggle to build strength in the petroleum business ended.

MAP 12.1 Panhandle Eastern Corporation

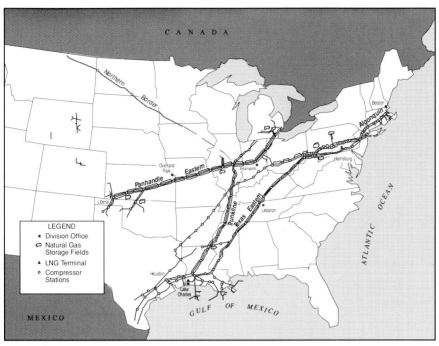

Houston Center was the next major asset to be sold. In the months just before Coastal's hostile offer, Texas Eastern had appeared to be on the verge of selling all or a portion of its real estate holdings. Now the auction began anew. Texas Eastern set up a data room, as it did for all its assets, in which financial and other information was available for review by serious bidders. Names of eight major real estate investors surfaced in press reports about the sale. These included Japanese investors, Gerald Hines, and Trammel Crow. Finally, after a considerable delay, JMB Realty Corporation, of Chicago, made a successful offer of approximately $400 million.[16] At the same time, Panhandle Eastern's chairman, Robert Hunsucker, announced that over a period of three years Texas Eastern's operations would be moved to Panhandle's offices in the Galleria area. No longer would Houston Center house its founding corporation. Texas Eastern's ambitious real estate enterprise had been passed on to another concern, one which specialized in real estate development.

One major asset not related to natural gas transportation remained — the Little Big Inch products line. In late November Panhandle announced that it would be placing 88 percent of the line into an MLP in order to raise approximately $588 million. The Big Inch and the Little Big Inch Lines would be under separate ownership for the first time since their construction during World War II.[17]

With the sale of these major assets, Panhandle had realized approximately three billion dollars, before taxes. This went a long way toward paying down the $3.22 billion debt incurred in the takeover. As an operating subsidiary of Panhandle Eastern, Texas Eastern again resembled the original 1947 corporation, an undiversified natural gas transporter. With outside intervention, Texas Eastern had "refocused on the core" with a vengeance, this time being forced back to the narrowest definition of its core, gas transmission. Panhandle Eastern now could make use of the newly acquired properties once owned by Texas Eastern, and it quickly announced plans for a new 225-million-cubic-feet-per-day expansion of its northeastern system.

Well before all of Texas Eastern's subsidiaries had been sold, the company had lost its corporate independence. On June 28, 1989, Texas Eastern's last annual meeting was immediately followed by Panhandle Eastern's annual meeting during which Panhandle's stockholders voted in favor of the merger. Panhandle then began the process of exchanging its common stock for TE's outstanding shares and removing Texas Eastern's name from the New York Stock Exchange. The company became a wholly owned subsidiary of Panhandle Eastern Corporation. Texas Eastern's history as a diversified international energy company and pipeliner of energy had become just that — history.

Of course, many longtime Texas Eastern employees felt disappointment as they watched their company disappear. Many sensed a loss of pride after the merger. How could this happen to George Brown's company? Who was to blame? There are no pleasing answers to these questions. Nor was it comforting to realize that perhaps no one was to blame. George Brown's company had been caught in a whirlwind of political and economic forces — deregulation, the bust in oil, the mania for acquisitions — which proved to be beyond the limits of the company to manage. Perhaps a George Brown and a Reginald Hargrove in the prime of life could have pulled their company through. Perhaps not. The problems of the 1980s were far more varied and complex than were those faced by Texas Eastern's leaders during the era of expansion that preceded diversification.

In contemplating Texas Eastern's demise, one should take the longer view. In the mid-1980's Texas Eastern had embarked on a new strategy, to refocus on core businesses, in general, and gas transmission in specific. From the larger industrial perspective, Panhandle Eastern carried that process forward to a new level, selling off subsidiaries more completely, more thoroughly, and much more rapidly than Texas Eastern's executives had ever contemplated. In announcing his company's payoff of the $2.6 billion bank debt of the Texas Eastern acquisition, Panhandle announced that "we have completed the divestiture program started by Texas Eastern much faster than originally anticipated and can now concentrate on being the industry leader in our primary business of natural gas transmission."[18] Divestiture of all but the gas transmission system was the strategic choice that offered Panhandle Eastern the greatest benefits from acquisition.

And what of the fate of the divested companies? The companies acquiring them in each case saw a strategic fit with their existing operations. Texas Eastern had devoted considerable resources to building its diversified businesses. They still existed, not as parts of a diversified company, but as new additions to the ongoing businesses of specialists who might be expected to put their assets to good use. In a sense, Texas Eastern had come full circle from its origins as a gas transmission company. After decades of diversification through acquisition, the longtime acquirer became the acquired. The various subsidiaries which had been pieced together gradually over forty years around the pipeline system were spun off in a quick burst of activity, leaving only the gas pipeline for Panhandle Eastern to absorb into its own system.

Did this mean that Texas Eastern's long-term strategy must be judged a failure? Over its forty-two year history the company had its share of successes and failures. It remained eager to tackle large-scale projects, taking substantial risks in search of substantial rewards — and adventure. For almost a quarter century after its winning bid for the Inch Lines, the company had the great luxury of dependable profits from its regulated gas pipelines. During the first half of its history, Texas Eastern could move into activities as varied as liquefied petroleum gas, oil production, and Houston Center, confident that its core business would generate ample capital to support such ventures. In retrospect, it seems likely that this comfortable situation encouraged an "easy" approach to diversification which discounted the prospect that acquisitions might perform poorly enough to affect the health of the entire corporation.

After the early 1970s such an assumption was no longer safe. With little chance to expand the gas system, due to gas shortages and huge sums of investment projected for supplemental gas ventures, Texas Eastern suddenly faced a new set of challenges; its past offered few clear guide posts for its new situation. As old assumptions about supply, price, and regulation all fell by the wayside, the company's strategists had to fashion new assumptions amid fundamental uncertainties.

Many institutions and individuals in the energy industries fell victim to the same chaotic events which undermined Texas Eastern's planning after the energy crisis of the early 1970s. The best laid plans — and the worst — often came apart in the confusion of the 1970s and 1980s. Tumultuous and largely unpredictable shifts in basic economic and regulatory conditions required far-reaching adjustments. The merger and acquisition mania of the 1980s added urgency to efforts to adapt since a hostile takeover was an ever-present threat.

Some of the diversified gas transmission companies which grew up with

Texas Eastern remained independent; others joined the ranks of the acquired. All were staggered by the boom and bust in energy prices and the uncertainties regarding gas supply. Texas Eastern's management faced a wide range of difficult choices in the 1970s and early 1980s. It chose what appeared at the time to be a logical strategy of exploring all available alternatives for greater gas supplies while continuing to diversify so as to become less dependent on gas for its revenues. Events of the mid-1980s made such a strategy economically infeasible, at least in the short run, and Texas Eastern paid with its corporate life.

While this is perhaps the ultimate failure from the perspective of a long-term employee or an organizational historian, it was not failure from a broader perspective. Operating under predictable economic and regulatory conditions before the early 1970s, Texas Eastern developed a variety of subsidiaries around an ever expanding gas transmission system. Despite the uncertainties of the next two decades, these subsidiaries remained strong enough to bring reasonable bids in 1989. Through it all, the gas still flowed from Texas to the East. And it still does.

Notes

PREFACE

1. From 1947 to 1973, the company name was Texas Eastern Transmission Corpora-tion. After 1973, a parent company called Texas Eastern Corporation was formed, and the natural gas system became Texas Eastern Transmission Company, or TETCO.

2. Kenneth J. Lipartito and Joseph A. Pratt, *Baker and Botts in the Development of Modern Houston* (Austin: University of Texas Press, 1991).

3. Joseph A. Pratt, *A Managerial History of Consolidated Edison, 1936–1981* (New York: Consolidated Edison Company of New York, 1988) and Walter L. Buenger and Joseph A. Pratt, *But Also Good Business: Texas Commerce Banks and the Financing of Houston and Texas, 1886–1986* (College Station: Texas A&M University Press, 1986).

4. Christopher J. Castaneda, Regulated Enterprise: Natural Gas Pipelines and North-eastern Markets (Columbus: Ohio State University Press, 1993).

INTRODUCTION

1. For an account of the rapid rise of natural gas after World War II, see Alfred M. Leeston, John A. Crichton, and John C. Jacobs, *The Dynamic Natural Gas Industry* (Nor-man: University of Oklahoma Press, 1963).

2. Christopher J. Castaneda, *Regulated Enterprise: Natural Gas Pipelines and North-eastern Markets, 1938–1954* (Columbus: Ohio State University Press, 1993).

3. See Arlon R. Tussing and Connie C. Barlow, *The Natural Gas Industry: Evolu-tion, Structure, and Economics* (Cambridge: Ballinger Publishing Company, 1984).

4. See Richard H. K. Vietor, *Energy Policy in America since 1945: A Study of Busi-ness-Government Relations* (Cambridge: Cambridge University Press, 1984).

5. See Frank Mangan, *The Pipeliners: The Story of El Paso Natural Gas* (El Paso, Tex.: Guynes Press, 1977), and L. L. Waters, *Energy to Move . . . Texas Gas Transmis-sion Corporation* (Owensboro, Ky.: Texas Gas Transmission Corporation, 1985).

6. Michael Porter, *Competitive Strategy: Techniques for Analyzing Industries and Competitors* (New York: The Free Press, 1980), p. 4.

7. The names of these two rivals have evolved with the companies. Tenneco is the current name of the conglomerate which includes the gas transmission company origi-nally called Tennessee Gas and Transmission Company; the name was later modified to Tennessee Gas Transmission Company. Transco Energy Company was originally named the Trans-Continental Gas Pipe Line Corporation, although the hyphen was later removed from "Transcontinental,"

8. For a useful collection of case studies related to this managerial problem, see Richard H. K. Vietor, *Strategic Management in the Regulatory Environment* (Englewood Cliffs, N.J.: Prentice-Hall, 1989).

9. FERC took over most of the traditional powers of the FPC over the natural gas industry after the comprehensive reorganization of the federal government's energy agen-cies in 1977.

10. For a general history of the modern American political economy, see Louis Ga-

lambos and Joseph Pratt, *The Rise of the Corporate Commonwealth* (New York: Basic Books, 1988).

11. John W. Frey and H. Chandler Ide, eds., *A History of The Petroleum Administration for War, 1941-1945* (Washington, D.C.: G.P.O., 1946).

12. Stephen Breyer and Paul MacAvoy, *Energy Regulation by the Federal Power Commission* (Washington, D.C.: The Brookings Institution, 1974).

CHAPTER 1

1. The best brief overview of the wartime economy is Harold Vatter, *The U.S. Economy in World War II* (New York: Columbia University Press, 1985).

2. The best source for these developments remains the "official" history of the Petroleum Administration for War, Frey and Ide, eds., *Petroleum Administration for War.*

3. Tussing and Barlow, *The Natural Gas Industry: Evolution, Structure and Economics*, pp. 34-37.

4. Ralph E. Davis, Deputy Petroleum Administrator, PAW, "Oil's Fighting Ally—Natural Gas," *Proceedings,* 25th Annual Meeting, American Gas Association (New York: AGA, 1943), p. 78.

5. John H. Murrell, "Science—Skill—Service, The Story of DeGolyer and MacNaughton," (New York: Newcomen Society in North America, 1964).

6. Hearings before the Special Committee Investigating Petroleum Resources and the Surplus Property Subcommittee of the Committee on Military Affairs, United States Senate, *War Emergency Pipe-Line Systems and other Petroleum Facilities,* 79th Cong., 1st sess., November 15, 16, and 17, 1945 (Washington, D.C.: G.P.O., 1945).

7. Harold L. Ickes, *Fightin' Oil* (New York: Alfred A. Knopf, 1943).

8. War Emergency Pipelines, Inc., "Fuel for the Fighting Fronts . . . 'Big Inch and Little Big Inch'" (1946), p. 4, [TE] Texas Eastern Archives, Houston, Texas.

9. J. R. Parten, interview with Christopher Castaneda and John King, Madisonville, Tex., June 27, 1988.

10. Arthur M. Johnson, *Petroleum Pipelines and Public Policy, 1906-1959* (Cambridge: Mass.: Harvard University Press, 1967), pp. 322-27.

11. The original seven companies were: Standard Oil Co. (New Jersey), Consolidated Oil Corp., The Atlantic Refining Co., Socony-Vacuum Oil Co., Inc., Sun Oil Co., Cities Service Co., and Tide Water Associated Oil Co. Later, four more companies joined: Gulf Refining Co., Pan American Petroleum & Transport Co., Shell Oil Co., Inc., and The Texas Company.

12. War Emergency Pipelines, Inc., "Fuel for the Fighting Fronts . . . 'Big Inch' and 'Little Big Inch,'" p. 4.

13. On December 2, 1942, Ickes became the Petroleum Administrator for War in charge of the federal Petroleum Administration for War (PAW) which directed all U. S. petroleum operations.

14. Gerald D. Nash, *United States Oil Policy, 1890-1964* (Pittsburgh: University of Pittsburgh Press, 1968), pp. 163-65. See also Charles Morrow Wilson, "Paul Bunyan Underground," *World Petroleum,* June, 1945; and Major A. N. Horne, "Emergency Pipelines—Their Record in Review," *World Petroleum,* June, 1945.

15. Johnson, *Petroleum Pipelines and Public Policy,* pp. 309-10.

16. Ibid.

17. Ibid. See also D. Thomas Curtin, *Men, Oil and War* (Chicago: Petroleum Industry Committee, 1946), pp. 222-24.

18. Ibid. See also Jesse Jones, *Fifty Billion Dollars* (New York: The Macmillan Company, 1951), p. 343. A prominent Houstonian, Jones was publisher of the *Houston Chronicle,* principal owner of a major Houston bank, owner of real estate including several

hotels, and financier. After the war Jones and the Brown brothers were prominent members of Houston business and civic elite.

19. Johnson, *Petroleum Pipelines and Public Policy,* p. 308.

20. The best contemporary accounts of the construction of the Inch Lines were in the major trade journals such as *Oil and Gas Journal, Oil Weekly,* and *World Petroleum.* For a collection of several of the best of these articles, see War Emergency Pipelines, Inc., "Fuel for the Fighting Fronts . . . 'Big Inch' and 'Little Big Inch,'" p. 1–4.

21. "Big-Inch Pioneers New Pipelining Methods," *Oil Weekly,* Aug. 16, 1943, pp. 18–84.

22. Ibid., p. 84.

23. These figures are taken from "Petroleum Pipe Line Projects Summary," Appendix 11, in Frey and Chandler, eds., *A History of the PAW,* p. 417. Elsewhere in the PAW history are slightly higher figures which appear to be based on projects proposed rather than projects completed.

24. Frey and Chandler, eds., *A History of the PAW,* p. 101.

25. Ibid.

26. *Pipe Line News,* Mar., 1943, p. 28. For the early background of Tennessee Gas, see Tussing and Barlow, *The Natural Gas Industry,* pp. 42–43, and "In the Matter of Tennessee Gas and Transmission Company," *Opinions and Decisions of the Federal Power Commission,* G–230, July 5, 1943 (Washington, D.C.: G.P.O., 1944), 3:442–48.

27. Tussing and Barlow, *The Natural Gas Industry,* pp. 42–43; "Lessee of Big Inch Pipe Lines is War Baby of Curious History," *The Washington Daily News,* Dec. 9, 1946.

28. In congressional hearings after the war, Secretary of the Interior Harold Ickes raised questions about the political influence of The Chicago Corporation. His suspicions are echoed in the more recent account in Tussing and Barlow, *The Natural Gas Industry,* pp. 42–43.

29. Tennessee Gas and Transmission Company, *Annual Report,* 1945.

CHAPTER 2

1. See Christopher J. Castaneda, *Regulated Enterprise.*

2. Hearings before the Special Committee Investigating Petroleum Resources, p. 3. See also Jones, *Fifty Billion Dollars,* p. 402; Harry N. Scheiber, et al., *American Economic History* (New York: Harper and Row, 1976), pp. 407–408; and Otto Scott, *The Exception: The Story of Ashland Oil & Refining Company* (New York: McGraw Hill, 1968), which discusses Ashland Oil and Refining Company's attempt to retain a gasoline plant it operated during the war.

3. Vatter, *The U.S. Economy in World War II,* p. 88.

4. Reconstruction Finance Corporation, press release, Sept. 14, 1945, Folder 6, Box 70074–01, TE Archives.

5. Ibid.; J. Ross Gamble to E. Holley Poe, Sept. 14, 1945, Folder 6, Box 70074–01, TE Archives.

6. Hearings before the Special Committee Investigating Petroleum Resources, p. 3. See also Jones, *Fifty Billion Dollars,* p. 402, and Scheiber, et al., *American Economic History* pp. 407–408.

7. Hearings before the Special Committee Investigating Petroleum Resources, p. 264–65.

8. Ibid., p. 385.

9. Ibid., p. 373.

10. Surplus Property Administration (W. Stuart Symington), *Government-Owned Pipelines: Report of the Surplus Property Administration to the Congress* (Washington, D.C.: G.P.O., 1946), p. 13.

11. Ibid., p. 2.

12. *Second Interim Report of the Select Committee to Investigate Disposition of Surplus Property*, 79th Cong., 2d sess., House of Representatives (Washington: G.P.O., Dec., 1946), pp. 3-4.

13. Charles I. Francis to Jack Clarke, Feb. 24, 1955, Charles I. Francis Correspondence File, TE Archives.

14. J. Howard Marshall, interview with Christopher Castaneda, Houston, Tex., Dec. 7, 1988.

15. Charles Francis to Jack Clarke, Feb. 24, 1955, Charles I. Francis Correspondence File, TE Archives. Robert Poe, telephone conversation with Chris Castaneda, Dec. 6, 1988. After the successful bid of Texas Eastern, Poe transferred approximately one-third of his share of the founders' stock to Ashland Oil.

16. "WAA Proceeding Cautiously Disposing of Two Big Inch Pipelines," *Oil & Gas Journal*, June 8, 1946, p. 57.

17. Ibid.

18. E. T. Robinson, interview with Christopher Castaneda, Houston, Tex., Aug. 25, 1988; August Belmont, interview with Joseph Pratt and Christopher Castaneda, Easton, Md., June 14, 1988.

19. "A Decade for Texas Eastern," *The Inch* [Texas Eastern Transmission Corporation], June, 1957, p. 3. See also Winsor H. Watson, Jr., "History of the Texas Transmission Corporation," (no date), TE Archives; James Ward Hargrove, interview with Louis Marchiafava and Christopher Castaneda, Houston, Tex., Mar. 31, 1988; S. E. Sentell, interview with Christopher Castaneda, Houston, Tex., Apr. 6, 1988; Charles Francis to Jack Clarke, Feb. 24, 1955, Charles I. Francis Correspondence File, TE Archives.

20. J. R. Parten, interview with John King and Christopher Castaneda, Madisonville, Tex., June 27, 1988.

21. Jayne Andrews, telephone interview with Christopher Castaneda, Apr. 11, 1988.

22. Charles Francis to Judge J. A. Elkins, June 14, 1946, Charles I. Francis Correspondence File, TE Archives. See also George Allen, *Presidents Who Have Known Me* (New York: Simon and Schuster), pp. 168, 216-17.

23. Charles Francis to Judge J. A. Elkins, June 14, 1946, Charles I. Francis Correspondence File, TE Archives.

24. Charles Francis to Judge J. A. Elkins, June 14, 1946, Charles I. Francis Correspondence File, TE Archives.

25. See Joe R. Feagin, *Free Enterprise City: Houston in Political-Economic Perspective* (New Brunswick, N.J.: Rutgers University Press, 1988).

26. Jayne Andrews, conversation with Christopher Castaneda, Apr. 11, 1988; John H. Murrell, interview with Christopher Castaneda, Dallas, Tex., June 6, 1988.

27. Dana Blankenhorn, "The Brown Brothers: From Mules to Millions as Houston's Contracting and Energy Giants," *Houston Business Journal*, Mar. 19, 1979, sect. 2, pp. 1-4.

28. Ibid., p. 3.; Otto J. Scott, *The Professional: A Biography of J. B. Saunders* (New York: Atheneum Press, 1976), pp. 305-306.

29. Ibid., p. 1.

30. August Belmont, interview with Christopher Castaneda and Joseph Pratt, Easton, Md., June 14, 1988.

31. J. Ross Gamble to Charles I. Francis, June 18, 1946, Folder 6, Box 70074-01, TE Archives.

32. United States Corporation Company to Ross Gamble, Esq., July 12, 1946, Folder 6, Box 70074-01, TE Archives.

33. In the proposal submitted by E. Holley Poe on July 29, 1946, the bidding group

estimated that working capital needed "during the development stages of the enterprise would not exceed $500,000." This capital would be raised by stock purchases by the promoters. George and Herman Brown would each subscribe to 25 percent of the stock, while Poe, Francis, DeGolyer, and Reginald Hargrove—who was to be hired if the bid was successful—would each get 12.5 percent interest in the company.

34. Quoted in Ronnie Dugger, *The Politician: The Life and Times of Lyndon Johnson* (New York: W. W. Norton and Co.), p. 282.

35. Ibid. Cook had worked at the SEC between 1937 and 1945 in a number of positions, including that of utilities analyst with the public utilities division, and he subsequently became executive assistant to United States Attorney General Thomas Clark.

36. "Letter of Transmittal and Proposal of E. Holley Poe for Purchase or Lease of Big Inch and Little Big Inch Pipe Lines," July 30, 1946, Folder 1, Box 70074–01, TE Archives. The proposal was accompanied by confirmation of receipt by WAA listing John H. Poe and J. Ross Gamble as the deliverers of the proposal.

37. All information from the bids is from War Assets Administration, *Transcript of Proceedings: Proposals to Buy or Lease the Big and Little Big Inch Pipe Lines* (Washington, D.C.: G.P.O., July 31, 1946).

38. War Assets Administration, press release, Aug. 2, 1946, Folder 6, Box 70074–01, TE Archives.

39. Charles Francis to General John J. O'Brien, Aug. 10, 1946, Charles I. Francis Correspondence File, TE Archives.

40. Charles Francis to Jack Clarke, Feb. 24, 1955, Charles I. Francis Correspondence File, TE Archives. See also *Platt's Oilgram News,* Nov. 14, 1946, p. 3.

41. Harold L. Ickes to Charles I. Francis, Oct. 18, 1946, Charles I. Francis Correspondence File, TE Archives. Four years after this furor, George Butler joined the board of Texas Eastern. Gus Wortham was a founding stockholder in the company.

42. War Assets Administration, press release, Oct. 3, 1946, Folder 6, Box 70074–01, TE Archives.

43. E. Holley Poe to L. Gray Marshall, Oct. 7, 1946, Folder 6, Box 70074–01, TE Archives.

44. "'Uncle Jesse's' Bid for Oil Pipelines . . . ," *The Evening Star,* Oct. 2, 1946.

45. "Former Big Names in Government Are Involved in Bids for Pipelines," *Washington Daily News,* Oct. 17, 1946.

46. See Elliot Taylor, "Thermally Thinking," *Gas,* Nov., 1946, pp. 21–22. See also Marshall McNeil, "Former Big Names in Government Are Involved in Bids for Pipelines," *Washington Daily News,* Oct. 17, 1946.

47. Ibid.

48. "Big Inch Awards for Oil Seen Near; Poe Chides WAA," *Chicago Journal of Commerce,* Oct. 23, 1946.

49. War Assets Administration, *Government-Owned Pipe Lines* (Washington, D.C.: G.P.O., Dec. 18, 1946), p. 7.

50. *Second Interim Report of the Select Committee to Investigate Disposition of Surplus Property,* 79th Cong., 2d sess., House of Representatives (Washington, D.C.: G.P.O., Dec., 1946), p. 14.

51. War Assets Administration, *Government-Owned Pipelines,* pp. 21–22.

52. R. G. Rice to the Department of the Interior, Nov. 30, 1946, Folder 6, Box 70074–01, TE Archives.

53. Charles Francis to Robert Littlejohn, Dec. 16, 1946, Charles I. Francis Correspondence File, TE Archives.

54. War Assets Administration, *Government-Owned Pipe Lines,* p. 9.

55. August Belmont, interview with Christopher Castaneda and Joseph Pratt, Easton,

Md., June 14, 1988. Also, see James Ward Hargrove interview with Louis Marchiafava and Christopher Castaneda, Houston, Tex., Mar. 31, 1988, and with Christopher Castaneda, Houston Tex., Apr. 13, 1988.

56. Memorandum written by J. Ross Gamble, Dec. 24, 1946, Folder 6, Box 70074–01, TE Archives.

57. Texas Eastern Transmission Corporation, Board of Directors Minutes, vol. 1, Jan. 30, 1947.

58. James W. Hargrove, interview with Christopher Castaneda, Houston, Tex., Mar. 31, 1988; August Belmont, interview with Christopher Castaneda and Joseph Pratt, Easton, Md., June 14, 1988.

59. August Belmont to Chris Castaneda, Feb. 6, 1989, August Belmont File, TE Archives.

60. August Belmont, interview with Christopher Castaneda and Joseph Pratt, Easton, Md., June 14, 1988. For the bid amounts see the "Original Bid Proposals" left by Charlie Francis at TE archives. Another account of this meeting, written in the late 1940s or early 1950s by Winsor H. Watson, a public relations writer for Texas Eastern, gives different figures. Watson states that the low bid was by Hargrove at $134 million and the high bid was from Francis at $148 million. Still another version has George Brown settling on the figure $133,127,000 and raising it by $10 million to $143,127,000 at Herman Brown's suggestion via long-distance phone call.

61. Watson, *"History of the Texas Eastern Transmission Corporation."* See also, James W. Hargrove, interview with Christopher Castaneda and Joseph Pratt, Houston, Tex., Mar. 31, 1988.

62. August Belmont, interview with Christopher Castaneda and Joseph Pratt, Easton, Md., June 14, 1988.

63. All information about bids is from War Assets Administration, *Transcript of Proceedings: Proposals for Purchase of War Emergency Pipe Lines Commonly Known as Big and Little Big Inch Pipe Lines* (Washington, D.C.: G.P.O., Feb. 10, 1947).

64. Ibid.

65. August Belmont, interview with Christopher Castaneda and Joseph Pratt, Easton, Md., June 14, 1988.

CHAPTER 3

1. M. Elizabeth Sanders, *The Regulation of Natural Gas: Policy and Politics, 1938–1978* (Philadelphia, Pa.: Temple University Press, 1981), p. 42.

2. Tom J. McGrath to Leon Fuquay, Secretary of the FPC, Feb. 21, 1947, Folder 6, Box 70074–01, TE Archives.

3. Department of Justice questions dated Feb. 8, 1947, Memorandum of J. Ross Gamble to Department of Justice, Feb. 20, 1947, and J. Ross Gamble to Mr. Moyer of the Department of Justice, Feb. 19, 1947, Folder 16, Box 70074–01, TE Archives.

4. Robert M. Poe, interview with Christopher Castaneda and John King, Lake Charles, La., June 20, 1988.

5. James Ward Hargrove, interview with Louis Marchiafava and Christopher Castaneda, Houston, Tex., Mar. 31, 1988; S. E. Sentell, interview with Christopher Castaneda, Apr. 6, 1988.

6. James W. Hargrove, interview with Christopher Castaneda, Houston, Tex., Mar. 31, 1988.

7. August Belmont, interview with Christopher Castaneda and Joseph Pratt, Easton, Tex., June 14, 1988.

8. Ibid.

9. The FPC required Tennessee to deliver 20 mmcf/d (million cubic feet per day)

to Panhandle Eastern, 5 mmcf/d to Equitable Gas Company, 3.5 mmcf/d to National Fuel Gas Company, and 1.5 mmcf/d to Carnegie Natural Gas Company. Tennessee's remaining gas was to be distributed to The Columbia Gas System, Incorporated, 47 percent (includes The Ohio Fuel Gas Company and the Manufacturers Light & Heat Company); Consolidated Natural Gas Company, 33 percent (The East Ohio Gas Company, New York State Natural Gas Corporation, and The Peoples Natural Gas Company); National Fuel Gas Company, 10 percent (United Natural Gas Company); and Equitable Gas Company, 10 percent. The precise allocations changed several times during the course of Tennessee's lease.

10. August Belmont, interview with Christopher Castaneda and Joseph Pratt, Easton, Md., June 14, 1988.

11. E. T. Robinson, Jr., "Economics of Internally Cleaning Gas Lines During Operation," *Oil & Gas Journal*, July 27, 1953, pp. 34–38.

12. *Pipeline Industry*, June, 1966, p. 29.

13. Federal Power Commission, *Opinions and Decisions of the Federal Power Commission* (Washington, D.C.: G.P.O., 1949), 6:148–75.

14. Federal Power Commission, *Opinions and Decisions of the Federal Power Commission* (Washington, D.C.: G.P.O., 1949), 6:150–52.

15. Charles I. Francis to E. R. Cunningham, May 24, 1957, Charles I. Francis Correspondence File, TE Archives.

16. Ibid.

17. Ibid.

18. Federal Power Commission, *Opinions and Decisions of the Federal Power Commission* (Washington, D.C.: G.P.O., 1949), 6:167.

19. August Belmont, interview with Christopher Castaneda and Joseph Pratt, Easton, Md., June 14, 1988.

20. Nelson Lee Smith to August Belmont, (telegram), Oct. 21, 1947, August Belmont File, TE Archives.

21. Watson, "History of Texas Eastern Transmission Corporation," pp. 32–34.

22. *PM Daily*, 8 (Nov. 11, 1947), pp. 1–4.

23. Watson, "History of Texas Eastern Transmission Corporation," p. 35.

24. James W. Hargrove, interview with Louis Marchiafava and Christopher Castaneda, Houston, Tex., Mar. 31, 1988.

25. Extract from Fulton Lewis, Jr., Broadcast (Mutual Broadcasting Network), Nov. 13, 1947, Folder 6, Box 70074-01, TE Archives.

26. In the *Harvard Business Review* two articles appeared, taking opposite sides in the Texas Eastern financing debate. The first one (*HBR* 26 [Mar., 1948]) discussed the transaction in terms of "excessive profits" while the second (*HBR* 26 [July, 1948]) pointed out the risks and benefits to society of such large venture capital endeavors.

27. Charles I. Francis to Judge J. A. Elkins, June 14, 1946, and marginalia signed and dated, Feb. 25, 1965, Charles I. Francis Correspondence File, TE Archives.

28. Allen, *Presidents Who Have Known Me*, pp. 168, 216–17.

29. Paul L. Howell and Ira Royal Hart, "The Promoting and Financing of Trans-Continental Gas Pipe Line Company," *The Journal of Finance*, 6 (Sept., 1951): 324.

30. Watson, "History of Texas Eastern Transmission Corporation," p. 36.

CHAPTER 4

1. See Castaneda, *Regulated Enterprise*.

2. "History of United Energy Resources, Inc., 1930–1977," a pamphlet prepared by the company (Houston: United Energy Resources, n.d.).

3. "Natural Gas," *Fortune*, Aug., 1940, p. 99.

4. Good portraits of these and other companies are presented in Leeston, Crichton, and Jacobs, *The Dynamic Natural Gas Industry*.

5. See Mangan, *The Pipeliners*.

6. Texas Eastern Transmission Corporation, *Annual Report, 1948*, p. 18.

7. John Osborne, "A Brawling, Bawling Industry," *Life*, Mar. 10, 1952, p. 101.

8. See Castaneda, *Regulated Enterprise*.

9. Waters, *Energy to Move*, pp. 43–44. In 1988 Transco acquired Texas Gas, which had been a subsidiary of CSX Corporation since 1984.

10. Nicholas B. Wainwright, *History of the Philadelphia Electric Company* (Philadelphia: Philadelphia Electric Co., 1961), p. 320.

11. Ibid.

12. See Joseph A. Pratt, *A Managerial History of Consolidated Edison of New York, 1936–1981* (New York: Consolidated Edison, 1988).

13. Howell and Hart, "The Promoting and Financing of Transcontinental Gas Pipe Line Corporation," pp. 311–24.

14. C. A. Williams, "The Story of Transcontinental Gas Pipe Line Corporation," *Oil and Gas Journal*, May 4, 1950. For the quote, see Transcontinental Gas Pipe Line, *Annual Report, 1950*, p. 2.

15. Texas Eastern Transmission Corporation, *Annual Report, 1948*, pp. 7–8.

16. "Natural Gas—Whoosh," *Fortune*, Dec., 1949, p. 199. See also Texas Eastern Transmission Corporation, *Annual Report, 1949*, pp. 6–7.

17. Robert M. Poe, interview with John King and Christopher Castaneda, Lake Charles, La., June 20, 1988.

18. Osborne, "Bawling Industry," p. 107.

19. Ibid., pp. 101–108.

20. Texas Eastern Transmission Corporation, *Annual Report, 1949*, p. 16; Texas Eastern Transmission Corporation, *Annual Report, 1951*, p. 13.

21. "Natural Gas—Whoosh," *Fortune*, p. 109; Osborne, "Bawling Industry," p. 101; "Texas in New England," *Forbes*, Dec. 15, 1952, p. 16; "Battle for New England," *Time*, Dec. 8, 1952, pp. 152–53.

22. "Texas in New England," *Forbes*, p. 14.

23. "Key Dates in Northeastern's History," Algonquin Calendar, p. 6 (pamphlet prepared by Public Relations Department, Eastern Gas and Fuel Associates), TE Archives.

24. Gardiner Symonds to Algonquin, Oct. 9, 1950, John F. Rich to Gardiner Symonds (telegram), Oct. 9, 1950, TE Archives.

25. Osborne, "Bawling Industry," p. 107.

26. Federal Power Commission, *Opinions and Decisions of the Federal Power Commission* (Washington, D.C.: G.P.O., 1958), 12:210–15. This opinion concluding the litigation in the Algonquin-Northeastern matter reviews the extensive legal maneuvering from 1950 through 1953; Algonquin Calendar, pp. 3–4, TE Archives.

27. Ibid., p. 4.

28. Algonquin Calendar, pp. 15, 20, 29.

29. R. H. Hargrove, "Natural Gas and New England," Address to the New England Council, Polar Springs, Maine, Sept. 16, 1950, p. 14, Folder R. H. Hargrove—Personal—Speeches, Box 74170-01, TE Archives.

30. Ibid.

31. "Natural Gas—Whoosh," *Fortune*, p. 204; "Battle for New England," *Time*, p. 53.

32. "Battle for New England," *Time*, p. 53.

33. Texas Eastern Transmission Corporation, *Annual Report, 1953*, p. 3.

34. Osborne, "Bawling Industry," pp. 107–108.

35. Ibid., 108.

36. Algonquin Calendar, TE Archives, pp. 30-48.

37. Ibid., p. 18.

38. Ibid., p. 45.

39. Ibid., pp. 48-49.

40. Federal Power Commission, *Opinions and Decisions of the Federal Power Commission* (Washington, D.C.: C.P.O., 1958), 12:210-15.

41. "Time Clock," *Time*, Aug. 17, 1953, p. 79.

42. "FPC Lets Natural Gas Company Ship to Canada," *Business Week*, Sept. 5, 1953, p. 30.

43. R. H. Hargrove, "Where Do We Go from Here?" Address before the Eastern Pennsylvania Group of the Investment Bankers Association of America, Philadelphia, Apr. 13, 1951, p. 6, Folder "Where Do We Go From Here," Box 74170-01, TE Archives.

CHAPTER 5

1. Texas Eastern Transmission Corporation, *Annual Report*, 1951, p. 7.

2. Charles I. Francis to Orville S. Carpenter, Jan. 30, 1957, Folder Brown & Root, Inc., Box 70045-04, TE Archives.

3. Jack Head, interview with Joseph Pratt and Christopher Castaneda, Houston, Tex., Mar. 23, 1988.

4. Texas Eastern Transmission Corporation, *Annual Report*, 1952, p. 12.

5. Texas Eastern Transmission Corporation, *Annual Report*, 1953, p. 14.

6. "Presidents of Braniff Airways and "Big and Little Inch" and 10 others die in fiery crash," *Gettysburg (Pa.) Times*, Jan. 11, 1954.

7. August Belmont, interview with Christopher Castaneda and Joseph Pratt, Easton, Md., June 14, 1988.

8. Sanders, *The Regulation of Natural Gas*, p. 103.

9. "Regulating the Gas Producer, 1954-1964: 10 Years of Turmoil," (Washington, D.C.: Independent Petroleum Association of America, 1964), pp. i-xv.

10. Vietor, *Energy Policy in America Since 1945*, pp. 84-85.

11. Tussing and Barlow, *The Natural Gas Industry*, p. 214.

12. Texas Eastern Transmission Corporation, *Annual Report*, 1958, p. 2.

13. Brief of Petitioner, *In the United States Court of Appeals for the Fifth Circuit*, *Texas Eastern Transmission Corporation v. Federal Power Commission*, Folder Rayne Field, Box 70045-08, TE Archives.

14. Orville S. Carpenter, "Memo: File–Rayne Case," May 5, 1959, Folder Rayne Field, Box 70045-08, TE Archives.

15. Ibid.

16. Texas Eastern Transmission Corporation, Docket No. G–12446, FPC Order Denying Application for Rehearing, Issued Aug. 21, 1959, TE Archives.

17. August Belmont to Orville Carpenter, June 24, 1959, Folder Rayne Field, Box 70045-08, TE Archives.

18. See "Regulating the Gas Producer, 1954-1964: 10 Years of Turmoil," p. xv. for a summary of the Rayne Field case through 1964.

19. Federal Power Commission, *Opinions and Decisions of the Federal Power Commission* (Washington, D.C.: G.P.O., 1965), 29:249-70.

20. Ibid., p. 257.

21. "Continental Oil Attacks FPC Rulings," *Journal of Commerce & Commercial*, New York, Jan. 6, 1964.

22. Federal Power Commission, *Opinions and Decisions of the Federal Power Commission* (Washington, D.C.: G.P.O., 1976) 42:367-467.

23. Ibid.

24. Ibid.

25. John F. Lynch, Memorandum to Files, Nov. 17, 1960, Folder "South Louisiana Gas—Block 24, Box 70045-08, TE Archives.

26. Orville S. Carpenter, "Gulf Eastern Project," Dec. 13, 1961, Folder South Louisiana Gas—Block 24, Box 70045-08, TE Archives.

27. Ibid.

28. Charles I. Francis to Herman Brown, July 3, 1961, Folder South Louisiana Gas—Block 24, Box 70045-08, TE Archives.

29. Texas Eastern Transmission Corporation, *Annual Report, 1963*, p. 7.

30. "Texas Eastern, Gulf Oil in Billion-Dollar Project," *Houston Post*, Dec. 20, 1963.

31. Jack Head, interview with Joseph Pratt and Christopher Castaneda, Houston, Tex., July 18, 1988.

32. See Mangan, *The Pipeliners*.

33. American Gas Association, *Historical Statistics of the Gas Industry* (New York: AGA, 1961), p. 231-B.

34. J. Fred Ebdon, "Transwestern Builds an 'Advanced Inch,'" *GAS*, May, 1960, p. 6–7.

35. Richard Austin Smith, "T. G. T. *vs.* El Paso: They Play Rough in the Gas Business," *Fortune*, Jan., 1966, p. 135.

36. David Rulison Palmer, "American Politics and Policies in the Regulation of Mexican Natural Gas Imports" (Ph.D. diss., University of California, Berkeley, 1982).

37. "Smith, "T. G. T. vs. El Paso," p. 135.

38. Ibid., p. 230.

39. Ibid., p. 231.

40. Ibid., p. 233.

41. Jack Head, interview with Christopher Castaneda and Joseph Pratt, Houston, Tex., Feb. 22, 1989.

42. "Notice of Offer to Purchase Common Stock of Transwestern Pipeline Company," *Los Angeles Times*, Mar. 27, 1967.

CHAPTER 6

1. Millard Neptune, interview with Joseph Pratt, Austin, Tex., Oct. 31, 1988, p. 10.

2. John Jacobs, interview with Joseph Pratt and Christopher Castaneda, Dec. 14, 1988.

3. "The Gas Pipelines: A New Set of Rules?," *Forbes*, Sept. 1, 1963, p. 22.

4. Ibid., p. 23.

5. Texas Eastern Transmission Corporation, "Notes for Historical Review," Management Conference, July 18–20, 1967, Galveston, Texas, pp. 8–9, TE Archives.

6. Ibid., pp. 20–21.

7. R. H. Hargrove, "Where Do We Go from Here?" Address before Eastern Pennsylvania Group of the Investment Bankers Association of America, Philadelphia, Apr. 13, 1951, pp. 7–8, Folder "Where Do We Go from Here," Box 74170-01, TE Archives.

8. Texas Eastern Transmission Corporation, *Annual Report, 1952*, p. 21.

9. Texas Eastern Transmission Corporation, *Annual Report, 1957*, pp. 14–15.

10. Texas Eastern Transmission Corporation, "Notes for Historical Review," Management Conference, July 18–20, 1967, Galveston, Texas, pp. 8–9.

11. Ibid., p. 23.

12. Millard Neptune, Texas Eastern Transmission Corporation—Little Big Inch Division, "Grand Design for the Future," June 25, 1962 (a planning report to the company's officers from the head of the Little Big Inch Division), Pyrofax Box, TE Archives. See also "Notes for Historical Review," Management Conference, July 18–20, 1967, Galveston, Tex., p. 17.

13. Scott, *The Professional: A Biography of J. B. Saunders*, pp. 358–59, 363–65, 367.

14. Texas Eastern Transmission Corporation, *Annual Report, 1956*, p. 10.

15. Charlie Francis to Orville Carpenter, Nov. 23, 1957, Folder Lawsuits, Box 70045–06, TE Archives.

16. Millard Neptune, interview with Joseph Pratt, Austin, Tex., Oct. 31, 1988.

17. Ibid., pp. 5–6.

18. Texas Eastern Transmission Corporation, *Annual Report, 1956*, p. 2.

19. John Jacobs, interview with Joseph Pratt and Christopher Castaneda, Houston, Tex., Dec. 14, 1988.

20. Millard Neptune, interview with Joseph Pratt, Austin, Tex., Oct. 31, 1988.

21. Ibid.

22. LPG is used to designate a variety of closely related products, including propane and butane.

23. Texas Eastern Transmission Corporation, "Little Big Inch LPGas Storage and Transportation System," n.d., LPG Box, TE Archives; Neptune, "Grand Design for the Future," June 25, 1962, Appendix A, Pyrofax Box, TE Archives.

24. Millard Neptune to Orville Carpenter, "Propane Retailing," May 18, 1961, Pyrofax Box, TE Archives.

25. W. A. Naumer to Millard Neptune, "Pyrofax Gas Corporation and Subsidiaries," July 12, 1963, Pyrofax Box, TE Archives.

26. Millard Neptune, interview with Joseph Pratt, Austin, Tex., Oct. 31, 1988, pp. 21–22.

27. Texas Eastern Transmission Corporation, *Annual Report, 1964*, pp. 10–11; *Annual Report, 1965*, pp. 5, 11.

28. George Kelcec, et al., "Coal Slurry-Firing at the Werneer Station," ASME Conference, July 31, 1962, TE Archives.

29. Texas Eastern Transmission Corporation, "Consolidation Coal Pipeline Project," Mar. 28, 1960, Coal Slurry Pipeline Box, TE Archives.

30. W. T. Thagard, "Coal Pipelining," Paper Number SPE 515, American Institute of Mining, Metallurgical, and Petroleum Engineers, 1963 Annual Meeting, TE Archives.

31. Robert L. Keatley, "Big New Projects Pose Stiff Competition for Rails, Other Carriers," *Wall Street Journal*, July 5, 1962.

32. "Portrait of an Underdeveloped Country," *LOOK*, Dec. 4, 1962, pp. 25–33.

33. Ibid.

34. Lyndon B. Johnson to Daniel Mich, Nov. 23, 1962, Folder Coal Pipeline – General #2, Box 77045–04, TE Archives.

35. Ibid.

36. Orville S. Carpenter to Officers and Directors of Texas Eastern, Mar. 1, 1962. Quoted in Texas Eastern Transmission Corporation, press release, no date, TE Archives.

37. Charles Francis to Orville Carpenter, Mar. 9, 1962, Coal Slurry Pipeline Box, TE Archives.

38. Jack Head to Orville Carpenter, May 24, 1962, Coal Slurry Pipeline Box, TE Archives.

39. Texas Eastern Transmission Corporation, *Annual Report, 1962*, p. 5.

40. Consolidation Coal Company, press release, May 7, 1963, Coal Slurry Pipeline Box, TE Archives.

CHAPTER 7

1. For an overview of the history of the Mexican oil industry, see Lorenzo Meyer, *Mexico and the United States in the Oil Controversy, 1917–1942*, 2nd ed. (Austin: University of Texas Press, 1977); Jonathan C. Brown, "Why Foreign Oil Companies Shifted Their Production from Mexico to Venezuela During the 1920s," *American Historical Review* 90 (Apr., 1985): 362–85; and George Grayson, *The Politics of Mexican Oil* (Pittsburgh: University of Pittsburgh Press, 1980).

2. "Mexico Planning Gas Sales to U.S.," (author unknown, A.P. story), Jan. 3, 1952, Folder Petroleos Mexicanos, Box 70042–13, TE Archives.

3. E. DeGolyer to Antonio J. Bermudez, Jan. 7, 1952, Folder Petroleos Mexicanos, Box 70042–13, TE Archives.

4. R. H. Hargrove to E. DeGolyer, Jan. 13, 1953, Folder Petroleos Mexicanos, Box 70042–13, TE Archives.

5. R. H. Hargrove to Senator Antonio J. Bermudez, Mar. 13, 1953, Folder Petroleos Mexicanos, Box 70042–13, TE Archives.

6. Fredda Jean Bullard, *Mexico's Natural Gas: The Beginning of an Industry* (Austin: University of Texas Bureau of Business Research, 1968), p. 87. See also "Mexican Gas to Be Piped Into New England," *The New York Times,* Oct. 10, 1956, financial section, p. 57.

7. Proposal for Argentine gas pipeline from John B. O'Connor, President Dresser Industries, Inc. and John Lynch, Senior Vice President, Texas Eastern Transmission Corporation to Ing. Esteban R. Perez, Administrator, Gas del Estado, June 4, 1959, Folder Argentine Pipeline, Box 70045–01, TE Archives.

8. Mario Barrera, *Information and Ideology: A Case Study of Arturo Frondizi* (Beverly Hills, Calif.: Sage Publications, 1973).

9. H. N. Mallon to John Lynch, et al., Feb. 3, 1960, Folder Argentine Pipeline, Box 70045–01, TE Archives.

10. Ibid.

11. McKenna to Carpenter (telegram), Nov. 27, 1960, Folder Argentine Pipeline, Box 70045–01, TE Archives.

12. McKenna to Carpenter, Mar. 14, 1961, Folder Argentine Pipeline, Box 70045–01, TE Archives.

13. McKenna to Goodrich, et al., and O'Connor, et al., dictated in Buenos Aires on Apr. 6 and transcribed in New York on Apr. 7, 1961, Folder Argentine Pipeline, Box 70045–01, TE Archives.

14. Jack Head to Dick Carpenter, n.d., Folder Argentine Pipeline, Box 70045–01, TE Archives.

15. Hargrove to Officers of Texas Eastern, Dresser, and McKenna, Aug. 17, 1961, Folder Argentine Pipeline, Box 70045–01, TE Archives.

16. Millard Neptune, interview with Joseph Pratt, Austin, Tex., Oct. 31, 1988.

17. Millard Neptune to Orville S. Carpenter, Feb. 15, 1960, Folder LeRiche Concession, Box 70045–06, TE Archives.

18. Ibid.

19. Southwest Africa is now known as Namibia.

20. Proposal by Joe Hargrove, p. 4., Folder LeRiche Concession, Box 70045–06, TE Archives.

21. Ibid.

22. Millard Neptune to H. Steele Bennett, Jr., July 25, 1957, Folder V. Algeria – Bennett Accounting Matters, Box 70042–04, TE Archives.

23. Memo from Millard K. Neptune to Orville S. Carpenter, Jan. 22, 1960, p. 4, Folder Algerian–European Pipeline, Box 70042–04, TE Archives.

24. Leeston, Chrichton, and Jacobs, *The Dynamic Natural Gas Industry,* p. 378.

25. Amoco's strategy was to form ventures with government-owned oil companies. Most oil companies in these years feared that a government-owned partner might be able to learn all about the private company's operations and adjust its tax policies to exploit the company's earnings. See John C. Jacobs, interview with Joseph Pratt and Christopher Castaneda, Houston, Tex., Dec. 14, 1988.

26. Inter-office correspondence from J. W. Hargrove and John C. Jacobs to the Management Committee, Aug. 30, 1963, Folder North Sea, Box North Sea, TE Archives.

27. Ibid.

28. J. W. Hargrove to H. Steele Bennett, Dec. 23, 1963, Folder North Sea, Box North Sea, TE Archives.

29. Jim Hargrove to Texas Eastern Management Committee, June 28, 1963, Folder North Sea, Box North Sea, TE Archives.

30. Memorandum from Jim Hargrove to Members of the Management Committee, July 10, 1963, Folder North Sea, Box North Sea, TE Archives.

31. Derek Redwood, "Venture into the Unknown: North Sea Search Intensifies," *Public Utilities Fortnightly,* Oct. 8, 1964, pp. 82–83.

32. Clive Callow, *Power from the Sea: The Search for North Sea Oil and Gas* (London: Gollancz, 1974), p. 164. Also see Christopher J. Castaneda, "An American Offshore Entrepreneur in the North Sea: The Case of Brown & Root." Paper presented at the Society for the History of Technology Conference, Uppsala, Sweden, Aug. 19, 1992.

CHAPTER 8

1. William L. Pereira Associates and Brown & Root, Inc., *Houston Center, Volume 1: A Master Development Program for Texas Eastern Transmission Company* (Houston, Mar. 1971), p. 3.

2. Much of this chapter is based on interviews with individuals deeply involved in the Houston Center project, including I. David Bufkin, Jan. 8, 1990; Henry H. King, Dec. 11, 1989; Charles Staffa, Aug. 10, 1989; Gordon Jennings, Aug. 8, 1989; Dennis Greer, Sept. 4, 1990; John Bixby, Apr. 12, 1988; William Kendall, Sept. 27, 1989; and George R. Bolin, Aug. 4, 1989.

3. Robert A. Sigafoos, *Corporate Real Estate Development* (Lexington, Mass.: Lexington Books, 1976), pp. 122–23, 157, 185.

4. Gordon Jennings and George Bolin, interview with Joseph Pratt and Christopher Castaneda, Houston, Tex., Aug. 4, 1989; John Edmund Bixby interview with Christopher Castaneda and Joseph Pratt, Houston, Tex., Apr. 12, 1988.

5. Orville Carpenter to W. W. Heath, Oct. 24, 1960, Folder Houston Center, Box Houston Center, TE Archives.

6. Memorandum to Orville S. Carpenter from Mr. Kearns, n.d., Folder Houston Center, Box Houston Center, TE Archives.

7. For an overview of construction in Houston in the post–World War II years, see Walter Buenger and Joseph Pratt, *But Also Good Business: Texas Commerce Banks and the Financing of Houston and Texas* (Texas A&M University Press, 1986).

8. Ibid., pp. 224–26.

9. John Bixby, interviews with Joseph Pratt and Christopher Castaneda, Houston, Tex., Apr. 12, 1988, pp. 40–44.

10. "Huge Development Seen Out a Window," *Houston Chronicle,* Apr. 26, 1970, p. 18.

11. George R. Bolin and Gordon Jennings, interview with Joseph Pratt and Christopher Castaneda, Houston, Tex., Aug. 4, 1989.

12. Charlie Evans, "Key Factors in Project Were Speed, Secrecy," *Houston Chronicle,* Sept. 20, 1970, sec. 3, p. 13.

13. Charlie Evans, "Operation Command Post: Project Like Military Attack, *Houston Chronicle,* Sept. 21, 1970; Charlie Evans, "Canning and Cooking Was Just A Day's Work for Bolin's Brigade," *Houston Chronicle,* Sept. 22, 1970.

14. Texas Eastern Transmission Corporation, news release, "Texas Eastern Announces Major Real Estate Acquisition in Downtown Houston," Apr. 26, 1970, Box Houston Center, TE Archives.

15. Charlie Evans, "Big Downtown Area to be Rebuilt," *Houston Chronicle,* Apr. 26, 1970, p. 1; Gerald Egger, "Growing Houston: Up, Up, Up," *Houston Post,* Apr. 26, 1970,

p. 1; "Gas Firm Buys Downtown Houston," *Cincinnati Enquirer,* Apr. 26, 1970; "Texas Eastern Buys a Substantial Chunk of Central Houston," *Wall Street Journal,* Apr. 27, 1970.

16. *Los Angeles Times,* Sept. 14, 1969.

17. Houston Center, Master Plan, p. 8, Folder Houston Center, Box Houston Center, TE Archives.

18. *Houston Magazine,* Nov., 1970, pp. 20–21.

19. Houston Center, Master Plan, Box Houston Center, TE Archives, "Houston Center," *Texas Builders Journal,* June, 1974, pp. 10–12, 26.

20. Texas Eastern Transmission Corporation, news release, "Texas Eastern Unveils Master Plan for Houston Center" Oct. 11, 1970, Box Houston Center, TE Archives.

21. Transcript of interview of Louie Welch for radio program, Box Houston Center, TE Archives.

22. Transcript of interview of Lee McLemore for radio program, Box Houston Center, TE Archives.

23. Lynn Ashby, "Not Pie-in-Smog," *Houston Post,* Sept. 19, 1973.

24. Alf Collins, "Houston's Monster Not for Us," *Seattle Times,* Jan. 24, 1971.

25. Joe R. Feagin, *Free Enterprise City* (New Brunswick, N.J.: Rutgers University Press, 1988).

26. William Kendall, interview with Joseph Pratt and Christopher Castaneda, Sept. 27, 1989; "Overstreet Bridges Called Air Pollution, *Houston Post,* Sept. 12, 1973.

CHAPTER 9

1. The best overview of energy policy in the United States since World War II is Richard H. K. Vietor, *Energy Policy in America Since 1945.*

2. Texas Eastern Transmission Corporation, *Annual Report, 1972,* p. 2.

3. For a general discussion of the Natural Gas Policy Act of 1978, see Sanders, *The Regulation of Natural Gas: Policy and Politics.*

4. Tussing and Barlow, *The Natural Gas Industry,* pp. 63–64, 72.

5. Joseph C. Robert, *Ethyl: A History of the Corporation and the People Who Made It* (Charlottesville: University Press of Virginia, 1983), p. 259–60.

6. Texas Eastern Transmission Corporation, *Annual Report, 1965,* p. 8.

7. Joseph C. Swidler, "The Public Interest in Effective Natural Gas Regulation," Address before Independent Natural Gas Association Meeting, New York, New York, Sept. 22, 1964, p. 11, Folder Swidler, Box Regulation, TE Archives.

8. Jack Head, interview with Joseph Pratt and Chris Castaneda, Houston, Tex., Feb. 22, 1990, p. 7.

9. Numerous economists began to point out this problem by the early 1970s. See Breyer and MacAvoy, *Energy Regulation by the Federal Power Commission.*

10. The rise of the intrastate market was widely noted in both popular and technical journals. See, for example, "Interstate Firms Hustle for Texas Gas," *Oil and Gas Journal,* Sept. 11, 1967, p. 47; John A. Carver, Jr., "Interstate and Intrastate Sales of Natural Gas: Two Markets or One?" *Public Utilities Fortnightly,* June 20, 1968, pp. 15–21; "Study Shows Nearly All Texas Coast Gas Sold Intrastate," *Oil Daily,* Dec. 5, 1969, pp. 1, 8.

11. Clyde LaMotta, "6 Louisiana Gas Purchasers Seek Higher Prices," *Houston Post,* Dec. 1, 1968, sec. 3, p. 7.

12. Texas Eastern Transmission Corporation, *Annual Report, 1970,* p. 2.

13. Vietor, *Energy Policy in America,* pp. 275–77.

14. For a description of this political bargaining, see Sanders, *The Regulation of Natural Gas,* pp. 165–92.

15. Texas Eastern Transmission Corporation, *Annual Report, 1973,* pp. 2–3.

16. Tussing and Barlow, *The Natural Gas Industry*, pp. 114–17.

17. Ibid., p. 63.

18. Vietor, *Energy Policy in America*, p. 295.

19. "Texas Eastern Unveils LNG Tank Plan," *Oil and Gas Journal*, Sept. 13, 1965, pp. 64–65; Robert E. Stiles, "World's Largest Above-Ground Storage Tank in Operation," *Pipe Line Industry*, May, 1970, p. 41.

20. "Chronology of Texas Eastern's Development of an LNG Facility on Staten Island, Borough of Richmond, New York City," Folder LNG–Staten Island Facility, Box LNG, TE Archives.

21. "Opposition Growing to Many Applications for Import of LNG," *Oil Daily*, Mar. 24, 1970.

22. Texas Eastern's Statement Before Special Subcommittee on Investigation of House of Representatives Committee on Interstate and Foreign Commerce, July 10, 1973, TE Archives.

23. "Talks for Soviet Gas Heat Up," *Oil and Gas Journal*, Mar. 27, 1967, pp. 66, 67.

24. "2 U.S. Firms Agree to Import Gas from Russia," *Houston Chronicle*, July 8, 1973. See also "Jack H. Ray, Oral Testimony—June 17, 1974, draft copy dated June 12, 1974, Folder North Star, TE Archives.

25. Nick Kotz and Nick Mintz, "Houston Gas Exec's Gifts to Nixon's Drive Probed," *Houston Chronicle*, July 1, 1973, p. 1.

26. "U.S. Companies Sign Agreement with Soviets," Texas Eastern Transmission Company, news release, July 2, 1973, Folder North Star, TE Archives.

27. Nevil M. E. Proes [President, Texas Eastern LNG, Inc.], "LNG Can Play Important Role in U.S.–U.S.S.R. Trade," *Pipeline and Gas Journal*, June, 1975, pp. 79, 83.

28. Texas Eastern Transmission Corporation, *Annual Report, 1973*, pp. 21–22.

29. W. T. Kendall, interview with Joseph Pratt and Christopher Castaneda, Houston, Tex., Sept. 27, 1989.

30. R. J. Fitzpatrick to George Kirby, Oct. 9, 1972, Folder North Star, TE Archives; George H. Ewing to JFE, Aug. 10, 1972, Folder North Star, TE Archives.

31. Kotz and Mintz, "Houston Gas Execs' Gifts to Nixon's Drive Probed," p. 1.

32. W. T. Kendall, interview with Joseph Pratt and Christopher Castaneda, Houston, Tex., Sept. 27, 1989.

33. William Beecher, "Politics Derail U.S.–Soviet Deal," *Boston Globe*, Nov. 3, 1978.

34. Tussing and Barlow, *The Natural Gas Industry*, p. 84. For a lively account of the development of Alaskan oil, see James P. Roscow, *800 Miles to Valdez: The Building of the Alaska Pipeline* (Englewood Cliffs, N.J.: Prentice-Hall, Inc., 1977).

35. Tussing and Barlow, *The Natural Gas Industry*, p. 79.

36. Edward R. Leach, "Arctic Energy: In Search of a Route," *Pipeline and Gas Journal*, July, 1971, p. 52.

37. Nicholas P. Biederman, "Arctic Gas: Potential Looks Good, Many are Studying How to Move It," *Pipeline and Gas Journal*, July, 1972, pp. 21–23.

38. Texas Eastern Transmission Corporation, *Annual Report, 1968*, pp. 4–5.

39. Vietor, *Energy Policy in America*, p. 294.

40. Paul Anderson, interview with Joseph Pratt and Christopher Castaneda, Houston, Tex., Aug. 7, 1989.

41. Vietor, *Energy Policy in America*, p. 324.

42. *Oil Daily*, July 17, 1980, p. 3, Folder Tri-State Joint Venture Agreement, Box Synfuels, TE Archives.

43. William F. Nicholson, "SASOL: From South Africa to Kentucky," *Owenboro (Kentucky) Messenger-Inquirer*, Oct. 5, 1980.

44. Paul Anderson, interview with Joseph Pratt and Christopher Castaneda, Houston, Tex., Aug. 7, 1989.

45. Deborah Duffy, "Political Changes Threaten Synfuels Plants," *Owensboro (Kentucky) Messenger-Inquirer,* Jan. 6, 1982.

46. Quoted in "Synfuels: Once a Flame, Now a Flicker," *Courier & Press* [Evansville, Indiana], May 23, 1982.

47. "SFC Aid Needed for N.M. Gas Plant," *Synfuels Week,* Dec. 20, 1982, p. 3.

48. The only two coal slurry pipeline companies to operate in the United States, the Ohio Pipeline (which went out of business in 1963), and the Black Mesa Pipeline (which transported slurry from Arizona to Nevada), used this same method in order to acquire subsurface rights to construct their pipelines.

CHAPTER 10

1. Irvin L. White, Don E. Kash, et al., *North Sea Oil and Gas* (Norman: University of Oklahoma Press, 1973), p. 3. For a brief overview of Texas Eastern's involvement in the North Sea, see *Texas Eastern News* [Texas Eastern Corporation], May, 1983.

2. For a historical view of the development of energy policies in the United States, see Craufurd D. Goodwin, ed., *Energy Policy in Perspective* (Washington, D.C.: The Brookings Institution, 1981). For an excellent overview of the international repercussions of the rise of OPEC, see Peter Odell, *Oil and World Power,* 8th ed. (New York: Penquin Books, 1986).

3. Texas Eastern Corporation, *Annual Report, 1974,* pp. 12–13.

4. *Texas Eastern News* [Texas Eastern Corporation], July–August 1980, p. 3.

5. For an overview of this period in Houston real estate, see Buenger and Pratt, *But Also Good Business,* pp. 262–335.

6. Jack Bixby, interview with Joseph Pratt and Chris Castaneda, Houston, Tex., Apr. 12, 1988.

7. The following section on Houston Center draws from a variety of company records and interviews with I. David Bufkin, Jan. 8, 1990; Henry H. King, Dec. 11, 1989; Charles Staffa, Aug. 10, 1989; Gordon Jennings, Aug. 8, 1989; Dennis Greer, Sept. 4, 1990; John Bixby, Apr. 12, 1988; and William Kendall, Sept. 27, 1989.

8. Houston Center brochure, Box Houston Center, TE Archives.

9. "Developer for Big Business," *Real Estate Forum,* May, 1985, pp. 74–80.

10. *Texas Eastern News* [Texas Eastern Corporation], March, 1981, pp. 1–2. See also *Texas Eastern News* [Texas Eastern Corporation], June–July 1983, pp. 14–15.

11. Leslie Loddeke, "2 Sites Urged for New Convention Facility," *Houston Chronicle,* July 18, 1980, p. 16; Fred Harper, "City Facing Hard Decision on Where to Build Convention Center," *Houston Chronicle,* Sept. 28, 1980; Elizabeth Ashton, "Convention Center Site in Limbo as Five-Way Debate Flares," *Houston Business Journal,* Oct. 6, 1980, pp. 16–17; Ann Holmes, "East Side, West Side," *Houston Chronicle, Zest Magazine,* Jan. 4, 1981, p. 13; Tom Kennedy, "Council Lobbied from 2 Sides on Convention Center," *Houston Post,* Apr. 5, 1981, p. 1–A; and Fred Harper "Convention Center Going to East Side," *Houston Chronicle,* Apr. 30, 1981, p. 1.

12. *Texas Eastern News,* [Texas Eastern Corporation], Mar. 1983, p. 1.

13. Patricial Cronkright, "East Side, West Side: Which Way to the Convention Center?," *Houston Business Journal,* May 30, 1983, p. 1; Jim Barlow, "The Proposed Convention Center: Some Questions and Answers," *Houston Chronicle,* Nov. 5, 1983, sec. 1, p. 1; and Mark Carreau, "Convention Center Wins by Landslide," *Houston Post,* Nov. 9, 1983, p. 1–A; *Texas Eastern News,* [Texas Eastern Corporation], Nov. 1983, pp. 1, 3.

14. Texas Eastern Corporation, *Annual Report, 1986,* p. 20.

15. Toni Mack, "Learning Real Estate – the Hard Way," *Forbes,* May 7, 1984, p. 128.

16. "Asset Redeployment: Everything Is For Sale Now," *Business Week,* Aug. 24, 1981, p. 74.

17. Laurel Bruebaker, "Is Coastal Laying Legal Groundwork for Texas Eastern Takeover Try?" *Houston Business Journal,* Aug. 13, 1984.

18. Texas Eastern Corporation, Board of Directors Minutes, Aug. 3, 1983.

19. Texas Eastern Corporation, Board of Directors Minutes, Mar. 9, 1984.

20. R. J. Munzer, *Petrolane Incorporated* (New York: The Newcomen Society in North America, 1979).

21. Texas Eastern Corporation, "A Strategic Fit: Petrolane" (pamphlet dated 1984), Folder Petrolane, TE Archives. Directional drilling uses specialized drilling tools to guide the underground path of a well in an outward curve away from the drilling site to a predetermined bottomhole location. It is particularly valuable in drilling wells offshore.

22. Texas Eastern Corporation, Board of Directors Minutes, June 4, 1984.

23. "Petrolane Will Merge with Texas Eastern in Deal Worth $1 Billion," *Los Angeles Times,* June 22, 1984.

24. Mark Zieman, "Texas Eastern Sets Tender Bid for Petrolane," *Wall Street Journal,* June 22, 1984, p. 2.

25. Background for this section came from interviews with David Bufkin, Henry King, and Paul Anderson.

26. Petrolane, Inc., Board of Directors Minutes, June 20, 1984, TE Archives.

27. Ibid.

28. Texas Eastern Corporation, news release, "Texas Eastern Makes Cash Tender Offer for Petrolane," news release, June 21, 1984, TE Archives.

29. Barbara Shook, "Texas Eastern Offers $1.1 Billion for Petrolane," *Houston Chronicle,* June 22, 1984, sec. 3, p. 1.

30. Mark Zieman, "Texas Eastern Sets Tender Bid for Petrolane," *Wall Street Journal,* June 22, 1984, p. 2.

31. Ibid. See also Daniel F. Cuff, "Takeover of Petrolane Set by Texas Eastern," *New York Times,* June 22, 1984, p. 27.

32. Sam Fletcher, "Energy Firm Eyes Takeover," *Houston Post,* June 22, 1984, p. 1–C.

33. Texas Eastern, news release, August 2, 1984, TE Archives. See also Gene Willouin, "Coastal Seen Failing to Halt Texas Eastern Purchase," *Oil Daily,* August 6, 1984, p. 1; and "Coastal Corp. Sues to Block Texas Eastern Purchase of Petrolane," *Wall Street Journal,* August 3, 1984, p. 24.

34. "Texas Eastern Realigns Operations into Four Groups," Management Newsletter, May 23, 1985, vol. 8, no. 20, TE Archives.

35. Houston Natural Gas was later renamed as Enron Corporation.

CHAPTER 11

1. Waters, *Energy to Move,* pp. 204–11.

2. Dennis R. Hendrix, interview with Joseph Pratt and Christopher Castaneda, Houston, Tex., Dec. 13, 1989.

3. Texas Eastern Corporation, *Annual Report, 1984,* p. 34.

4. Texas Eastern Corporation, *Annual Report, 1985,* p. 17; Paul Anderson, interview with Joseph Pratt and Christopher Castaneda, Houston, Tex., August 10, 1989.

5. Texas Eastern Corporation, *Annual Report, 1987,* p. 36.

6. Paul Anderson, interview with Joseph Pratt and Christopher Castaneda, Houston, Tex., August 10, 1989.

7. Texas Eastern Corporation, *Annual Report, 1987,* p. 37.

8. Texas Eastern Corporation, *Annual Report, 1986,* p. 38.

9. Ibid.

10. Texas Eastern Corporation, *Annual Report, 1987,* p. 36.

11. Paul Anderson, interview with Joseph Pratt and Christopher Castaneda, Houston, Tex., August 10, 1989.

12. Texas Eastern Corporation, *Annual Report, 1987,* p. 36.

13. Such was the case with Fishing Tools, Inc., and Air Drilling Services, Inc., which were sold to management groups in early 1987.

14. Texas Eastern Corporation, *Annual Report, 1986,* p. 5, *Annual Report, 1987,* p. 2; and *Annual Report, 1988,* p. 2.

15. *Texas Eastern Today,* [Texas Eastern Corporation], Fall, 1987, p. 7.

16. Texas Eastern Corporation, *Annual Report, 1988,* p. 2. It also sold its interests in Australia at that time.

17. "U.S. Natural Gas Industry Ends Another Year Full of Change," *Oil & Gas Journal,* Dec., 1985, pp. 33–38.

18. "Court Rejects Key Provisions of FERC Order 436," *Oil & Gas Journal,* June 29, 1987, p. 18.

19. Ibid.

20. "FERC Trying to Solve Problems in Order 500," *Oil & Gas Journal,* Oct. 26, 1987, p. 30.

21. "No Promises to Keep," *Forbes,* June 17, 1985, pp. 58, 59.

22. "FERC Order 500 Draws More Fire from Industry," *Oil & Gas Journal,* Nov. 2, 1987, p. 21.

23. *Texas Eastern Today,* [Texas Eastern Corporation], Summer, 1987, pp. 14, 15.

24. Dennis R. Hendrix to All Employees (interoffice correspondence), Nov. 9, 1987. See also *New York Times,* Nov. 10, 1978, p. 1. The agreement did not, however, guarantee an end to either further litigation or further fines at the state level.

25. *Texas Eastern Today,* [Texas Eastern Corporation], Spring, 1988, p. 8.

EPILOGUE

1. The Coastal Corporation, Offer to Purchase for Cash All Outstanding Shares of Common Stock of Texas Eastern Corporation, Jan. 17, 1989.

2. Barbara Shook, "Takeovers Shape Coastal's History," *Houston Chronicle,* Jan. 17, 1989, p. 4–c.

3. Barbara Shook, "Coastal, Texas Eastern Execs to Meet," *Houston Chronicle,* Jan. 19, 1989, p. B–1.

4. Caleb Solomon and Dianna Solis, "Texas Eastern to Seek Bidders Against Coastal," *The Wall Street Journal,* Jan. 23, 1989.

5. Ibid.

6. Barbara Shook, "Houston Firm Picks 50 Possible Suitors," *Houston Chronicle,* Jan. 25, 1989, p. 1–B.

7. Statement read by Dennis R. Hendrix, TE Archives.

8. Texas Eastern Corporation, news release, Jan. 29, 1989, TE Archives.

9. Barbara Shook, "Texas Eastern Stock Climbs," *Houston Chronicle,* Feb. 15, 1989, p. 3–B. See also Barbara Shook, "Coastal Expected to Renew Bid for Firm," *Houston Chronicle,* Feb. 14, 1989, pp. 1–C.

10. The precise exchange formula was each Texas Eastern share would be exchanged for not less than 2.038, nor more than 2.304 shares of Panhandle Eastern common stock, and the exact exchange ratio would be determined by dividing $53 by the average trading price per share of Panhandle Eastern common stock on the ten trading days immediately preceding the effective date of merger.

11. Robert Hunsucker, interview with Joseph Pratt and Chris Castaneda, Houston, Tex., Jan. 23, 1990.

12. Ibid. See also Brian Levinson, "Panhandle Bidders Revealed," *Houston Chronicle*, July 1, 1986, sec. 3, p. 1.

13. Barbara Shook, "Panhandle Eastern to Cut Jobs," *Houston Chronicle*, Apr. 27, 1989, pp. 1–B.

14. "Enterprise Leaps into North Sea Big League," *Financial Times*, Mar. 2, 1989, p. 17; Barbara Shook, "Texas Eastern Plans $1.4 Billion Sale," *Houston Chronicle*, p. B-1.

15. Anne Pearson, "Texas Eastern Agrees to Sell Petrolane Inc.," *Houston Chronicle*, May 31, 1989, p. B-1; Randall Smith, "Panhandle Unit Is Set for Sale at $1.18 Billion," *Wall Street Journal*, May 30, 1989, p. 5.

16. Ralph Bivins, "Houston Center Sold for Whopping Price Tag," *Houston Chronicle*, Sept. 16, 1989, p. 1.

17. Anne Pearson, "Panhandle Plans Pipeline Sale," *Houston Chronicle*, Nov. 23, 1989, p. D-1.

18. Panhandle Eastern Corporation, press release, Mar. 7, 1990, TE Archives.

Index

Gaz de France, 168

General Crude Oil Company, 112

Geneva Convention on the Continental Shelf, 169

Georesearch, Inc. (acquired by Texas Eastern), 134

George R. Brown Convention Center, 234

Gerald Hines, Interests, 178, 228

Gerard Tire Services, 241

Germany, 167–69, 215, 223

Gibraltar, Straits of, 166

Gibson, Harvey, 52, 74, 75

Gillette, Wyo., 217

Goodrich, Baxter, 103, 229–30; as chief engineer, 61, 64, 67–68, 83, 96, 102, 119, 142; and expansion of Texas Eastern, 83, 102, 113–14; as president of Texas Eastern, 126, 149, 179–81, 183, 193

Governor's Committee of the State of Texas, 38

Grace and Company, W. R., 249

Grace Drilling Company, 249

Grant-Norpac, Inc., 248, 249

Grant-Norpac Geophysical, 241

Great Britain. *See* United Kingdom

Great Depression, 13, 14, 33, 56, 62, 78

Great Plains coal gasification plant, 216–17

Green, A. D., 49

Greenburg, Pa., 147

Green's Bayou, 42, 43

Greer, Dennis, 233, 277

Groningen (Holland) Field, 166, 168, 169, 206

Gulf Oil Corporation, 118–23, 125, 126, 128, 225, 229, 232

Gulf Pacific (subsidiary of Tennessee Gas), 125

Gulf Refining Co., 266

Gulf South, 35, 77

Gulf Warranty contract, 119–21, 125, 127

GUS Mfg., 241

Halcon SD Group (subsidiary of Texas Eastern), 216, 217, 240, 249

Halliburton Company, 244, 248

Hargrove, James W. (Jim), 59, 68, 72, 152, 163, 167, 168, 169

Hargrove, Joseph L., 72, 164, 165

Hargrove, Reginald H., 77, 96, 262; death of, 108, 176; and formation of Texas Eastern, 40–42, 44, 51–53, 58–64, 73–75; and operation of Texas Eastern, 84, 91–95, 132, 137, 157–59; sons of, 163–64; stockholder of Texas Eastern, 51, 71–72, 269

Hargrove, Robert, 72

Harris-Fulbright Gas Bill, 110

Harvard Business Review, 73

Hassi R'Mel Field, 165

Head, Jack, 87, 112, 113, 163, 195, 252; and Gulf Warranty Contract, 119, 120; and lobbying, 153, 154, 200

Heath, W. W., 177

Hemphill, Herbert "Bert," 133, 134

Hendrix, Dennis R., 244–46, 254, 255, 257, 258, 259

Herter, Christian, 92

Hillman, J. H., Jr., 84

Hines, Gerald, 178, 179, 261

HNG. *See* Houston Natural Gas

HNG/InterNorth, Inc., 248

Hodges, Luther, 151

Holland, 166–69, 223

Hope Natural Gas Company (subsidiary of Standard Oil of New Jersey), 30, 31, 78

hostile takeovers, 191, 225, 226, 237, 238, 244, 255–60

House Committee on Interstate and Foreign Commerce, 21

House of Representatives, 218

House Surplus Property Committee, 46, 48, 73

Houston: and businessmen, 41, 42, 46, 61, 177; companies in, 3, 47, 50, 59, 95, 132, 173, 205, 256, 260; and real estate, 129, 173–87, 220, 226, 236

Houston Center, 260; building of, 229–34; financing of, 229, 230, 263; marketing of, 228, 229, 230, 232; plans for, 9, 173, 174, 181–87, 240, 277; revised plans for, 227, 228–36; sale of, 260–61

Houston Chronicle, 180, 181, 183, 266

Houston City Council, 233

Houston Lighting and Power, 219

Houston Natural Gas (HNG), 242, 256, 281

Houston Post, 181

Hugoton, Okla., 30

Hugoton oil fields, 78

Hull, Burt, 22

Humble Building (Houston), 177

Humble Oil and Refining Co. (Exxon), 118, 119, 208

Hunsucker, Robert, 259, 261

Hunt, H. L., 62

hydrostatic testing, 66, 67, 83, 102

IBM, 229

Ickes, Harold, 17, 18, 19, 20, 21, 29, 46, 47, 266, 267

Inch Lines, 41, 44, 73, 76, 85, 97; bid for,

Panhandle Eastern Pipe Line Company, 49, 112, 259
Paris, 166, 168
Park, The (Houston Center), 232, 233, 235
Parten, J. R., 40
Patterson, N.J., 77
Paul, James R., 257, 258
Pauley, Edwin, 159
PAW. *See* Petroleum Administration for War
PCBs. *See* polychlorinated biphenyls
Pemex plan, 103, 124. *See also* Petróleos Mexicanos
Peoples Natural Gas Company, 271
Pereira, William L., 182, 183, 229, 230, 235
Pereira Associates, William L., 181, 182
Permian Basin (west Texas), 78, 121, 123, 133
Perón, Juan, 161
Persons, General, 153
Petrolane, Inc. (subsidiary of Texas Eastern), 237–43, 248, 250, 260
Petrolane Partners, 260
Petróleos Mexicanos (Pemex), 157, 158, 159, 160
petroleum, 15–19, 36, 153; products of, 14, 15, 131; shortages of, 19–21, 31, 45–49, 192
Petroleum Administration for Defense, 141
Petroleum Administration for War (PAW), 16, 18, 21, 28, 35, 38, 141, 266
Petroleum Coordinator for National Defense, 18
Petroleum Industry War Council (PIWC), 18, 20–21
PG & E. *See* Pacific Gas and Electric Company
Philadelphia: coal shipments to, 37, 150, 153; Electric Company of, 68, 85, 86; gas shipments to, 68, 70, 83, 85, 119, 206; Gas Works Company of, 68–70, 85; market in, 78, 80, 82, 87; oil shipments to, 21, 23
Phillips Petroleum Company, 109, 110, 141, 143, 221, 223
Phillips Petroleum Co. v. Wisconsin et al., 5, 8, 101, 110, 111
Phoenix, 78
Phoenixville Junction, Pa., 23
Pidot, George, 53
Pittsburgh, 68, 77, 78, 94, 106, 138
Pittsburgh Coke and Chemical, 84
PIWC. *See* Petroleum Industry War Council

Plantation Pipe Line, 19
PM (newspaper), 71
Poe, E. Holley, 15–16, 35–47, 50–53, 58–59, 72, 74, 77, 89–90, 268–69
Poe, John H., 269
Poe and Associates, E. Holley, 36, 38, 44
Poe group, 38–41, 43, 50; financial backing for, 41, 43, 51, 52; opposition to, 46, 56, 57; and preparation of bid, 44, 49, 52, 53
polychlorinated biphenyls (PCBs), 253, 258
Port Arthur, Tex., 138
Power Plant and Industrial Fuel Use Act (1978), 202
Prince William Sound, Alaska, 209
Proes, Nevil M. E., 205
Providence Gas Company, 89
Provident City, Tex., 108
Prudhoe Bay, Alaska, 208, 209
P/6 (North Sea field), 223
Public Service of New Jersey, 88
Public Utility Holding Company Act (1935), 40, 79
Pure Oil Company, 131
Putnam, H. I., 61
Pyburn, Keith, 113
Pyrofax (subsidiary of Texas Eastern), 146–49, 155, 232, 236, 240, 242, 250

Quantum Chemical Corporation, 260
Querbes, Justin R., 51, 72, 108
Querbes, Randolph A., 51, 72, 108

railroads, 5, 19, 33, 36, 37, 57, 68, 70; and opposition to coal slurry pipelines, 149, 150, 152, 218, 219; regulation of, 54; and transportation of coal, 81, 149, 151, 152, 154, 218
Rather, Charles Pratt, 40
Rayne field, 112–16, 118, 128
Reagan, Ronald, 216
Reconstruction Finance Corporation (RFC), 22, 33–74 passim
Red River, 26
Reynosa, Tex., 158
Reynosa Fields, 157–59
RFC. *See* Reconstruction Finance Corporation
Rice Institute, 41, 59
right of way, 19, 68–70, 150–54, 209–11, 218
Roberts, Owen, 47
Rockefeller Center, 184
Rock Springs project, 124
Roeger, Tony, 216
Roosevelt, Franklin D., 17–19, 30, 44, 47

Tenneco, Inc. (holding company for Tennessee Gas Transmission Company),
131, 205, 207, 265
Tennessee Gas Transmission Company
(subsidiary of Chicago Corporation),
28–32, 48–95 passim, 112, 123–25, 130,
158–59, 177, 265, 270–71
Texane Gas Company (subsidiary of
Texas Eastern), 145
Texas Company, 22, 266
Texas Eastern, 3; annual reports of, 80,
93, 133, 134, 142, 154, 175, 192, 196,
199; and board of directors, 50, 52, 77,
152, 176, 254, 257, 258; headquarters of,
59, 173, 176, 177, 230, 261; management
of, 61, 62, 108–109, 192–93, 229, 238,
244; and "pipelines of energy," 9, 135,
145, 149, 154, 220; real estate development of, 129, 173–87, 220, 226, 236;
stockholders of, 51, 108, 255–58; stocks
of, 51, 71–73, 133, 255–58, 262
Texas Eastern diversification: and acquisitions, 236–38, 253, 256, 263; attitudes
toward, 131, 132, 242, 244, 245; financing of, 161–63, 173–81, 186, 201; impetus for, 129, 226, 262; and internal tensions, 141, 142, 146, 148, 149, 236;
strategy for, 131–91 passim, 220, 226,
250, 263
Texas Eastern Engineering, Ltd. (subsidiary of Texas Eastern), 171
Texas Eastern expansion program: 83–108,
118–21, 126–29; and "508 Program," 83,
84; and "433 Program" (New England
Plan), 83, 88; and "740 Program," 84;
strategy and goals of, 79, 112, 121, 129,
175, 238
Texas Eastern Management Committee,
167, 169
Texas Eastern North Sea, 223
Texas Eastern Norwegian, Inc., 223
Texas Eastern Penn-Jersey Transmission
Company (subsidiary of Texas Eastern),
108
Texas Eastern Production Company (sub-
sidiary of Texas Eastern), 132
Texas Eastern (U.K.), Ltd. (subsidiary of
Texas Eastern), 170
Texas Gas Resources Corporation, 256,
272
Texas Gas Transmission Corporation, 84,
85, 215, 244
Texas Old-Age Assistance Commission,
134
Texas Panhandle field, 123
Texas Railroad Commission, 46
Texas Selective Service System, 134

Texas Unemployment Compensation
Commission, 134
Thagard, W. Tom, 149, 168
Thompson, Charles I., 77
Thompson, Ernest O., 45–46
Three Houston Center, 232
Tide Water Associated Oil Co., 266
Time, 71, 94, 182
Tipsa, 162
Tobin, Maurice, 94
Todhunter, Ohio, 144, 145
Topock, Ariz., 123
Torfelt (North Sea field), 222
Tor Field, 171, 222, 223
Trade Act (1974), 207
Trammell Crow, 228, 261
Trans-Alaska Pipeline System (TAPS)
(joint venture of Arco, Humble Oil and
Refining Company, Standard Oil of
Ohio, and British Petroleum), 208–10
Transamerica Tower (San Francisco), 182
Transco Energy Company, 265, 272
Transcontinental Gas Pipe Line Corpora-
tion, 5, 39, 45, 48, 53, 74, 79–88 passim,
95, 131, 265
Transit Pipeline Agreement, 210
Trans-Mediterranean Pipeline, 156, 160,
165, 168
Transwestern Coal Gasification Company
(subsidiary of Texas Eastern), 213
Transwestern Pipeline Company (subsidi-
ary of Texas Eastern), 8, 102, 121–23,
125–28, 242
Triangle Pipeline (subsidiary of Texas
Eastern), 137–41
Triangle Refineries, 137, 138, 140
Tri-State Synfuels Company (Tri-State)
(joint venture of Texas Eastern and
Texas Gas Transmission Corporation),
215, 216
Tropigas (acquisition of Petrolane), 250
Trunkline Gas Company, 259
Tulsa, Okla., 20
Tulsa Plan, 20–21, 28
Two Houston Center, 186, 229, 230
Tyler, Tex., 134, 135, 246

Udall, Morris, 218
Uithuizen, Holland, 223
UMW. *See* United Mine Workers
Union Carbide, 146, 149
United Energy Resources Corporation,
217
United Gas Corporation, 35, 51–77 pas-
sim, 105, 108, 109, 118
United Gas Pipe Line Company, 40, 44,
49, 52, 61, 84, 132